Oxford AQA History

A LEVEL AND AS

Component 2

Democracy and Nazism: Germany 1918–1945

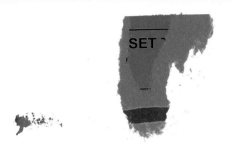

SET

Robert Whitfield

SERIES EDITOR
Sally Waller

OXFORD
UNIVERSITY PRESS

OXFORD
UNIVERSITY PRESS

Great Clarendon Street, Oxford, OX2 6DP, United Kingdom

Oxford University Press is a department of the University of Oxford.
It furthers the University's objective of excellence in research, scholarship, and education by publishing worldwide. Oxford is a registered trade mark of Oxford University Press in the UK and in certain other countries

British Library Cataloguing in Publication Data
Data available

978-0-19-835457-4

10

Paper used in the production of this book is a natural, recyclable product made from wood grown in sustainable forests.
The manufacturing process conforms to the environmental regulations of the country of origin.

Printed in Great Britain by Bell and Bain Ltd. Glasgow.

Acknowledgements

The publisher would like to thank the following for permissions to use their photographs:

Cover image: Mary Evans/Sueddeutsche Zeitung Photo; **p1:** akg-images/Alamy; **p3:** (r) Everett Collection Historical/Alamy; (l) dpa picture alliance/Alamy; **p7:** INTERFOTO/Alamy; **p12:** GL Archive/Alamy; **p14:** Three Lions/Stringer/Getty Images; **p16:** SZ Photo/Scherl/Mary Evans Picture Library; **p19:** World History Archive/Alamy; **p22:** World History Archive/Alamy; **p24:** Hulton Archive/Stringer/Getty Images; **p28:** World History Archive/Alamy; **p32:** INTERFOTO/Alamy; **p33:** (r) Heritage Image Partnership Ltd /Alamy; (l) World History Archive/Alamy; **p36:** Pictorial Press Ltd/Alamy; **p38:** E. O. Hoppe/Contributor/Getty Images; **p41:** INTERFOTO/Alamy; **p43:** AKG-images/Alamy; **p45:** ITAR-TASS Photo Agency/Alamy; **p47:** (t) ullstein bild/AKG-images; (b) Keystone Pictures USA/Alamy; **p49:** Peter Horree/Alamy; **p54:** INTERFOTO/Alamy; **p56:** INTERFOTO/Alamy; **p57:** RIA Novosti/Alamy; **p61:** AFP/Stringer/Getty Images; **p62:** Central Press/Stringer/Getty Images; **p64:** Popperfoto/Contributor/Getty Images; **p67:** INTERFOTO/Alamy; **p68:** Bettmann/Corbis UK Ltd.; **p71:** (t) John Frost Newspapers/Alamy; (b) picture-alliance/dpa/Mary Evans Picture Library; **p73:** AKG-images; **p75:** (t) dpa picture alliance/Alamy; (b) Archivart/Alamy; **p76:** CBW/Alamy; **p79:** Photo 12/Contributor/Getty Images; (b) AF archive/Alamy; **p80:** PHAS/Contributor/Getty Images; **p82:** Pictorial Press Ltd/Alamy; **p86:** AKG-images; **p87:** Hulton Archive/Stringer/Getty Images; **p90:** (t) dpa picture alliance/Alamy; (b) Imagno/Getty Images; **p92:** (l) Everett Collection Historical/Alamy; (r) The Print Collector /Alamy; **p93:** Hulton-Deutsch Collection/Corbis UK Ltd.; **p94:** INTERFOTO/Alamy; **p96:** dpa picture alliance/Alamy; **p100:** John Frost Newspapers/Alamy; **p103:** Hulton Archive/Staff/Getty Images; **p105:** John Frost Newspapers/Mary Evans Picture Library; **p108:** Popperfoto/Contributor/Getty Images; **p109:** (t) dpa picture alliance/Alamy; (b) AKG-images; **p114:** Larry Burrows/The LIFE Picture Collection/Getty Images; **p119:** Pictorial Press Ltd/Alamy; **p121:** dpa picture alliance/Alamy; **p125:** war posters/Alamy; **p126:** Topical Press Agency/Stringer/Getty Images; **p129:** World History Archive/Alamy; **p131:** Mary Evans Picture Library/Alamy; **p133:** Sueddeutsche Zeitung Photo/Mary Evans Picture Library; **p139:** AKG-images; **p140:** Mary Evans Picture Library/Alamy; **p144:** Sueddeutsche Zeitung Photo/Mary Evans Picture Library; **p149:** INTERFOTO/Alamy; **p152:** Mary Evans Picture Library/Alamy; **p153:** INTERFOTO/Alamy; **p156:** Everett Collection Historical/Alamy; **p157:** Heritage Image Partnership Ltd /Alamy; **p167:** akg-images/Alamy; **p169:** World History Archive/Alamy; **p176:** Adrian Muttitt/Alamy; **p183:** (t) dpa picture alliance/Alamy; (b) akg-images/Alamy; **p185:** AKG-images; **p188:** Bettmann/Corbis UK Ltd.; **p189:** dpa picture alliance archive/Alamy; **p191:** Alessandro0770/Alamy; **p192:** Sovfoto/Contributor/Getty Images; **p195:** unbekannt/Stadt Koeln NS-Dokumentationszentrum; **p197:** George (Jürgen) Wittenstein/AKG-images; **p198:** Everett Collection Historical/Alamy; **p201:** World History Archive/Alamy

We are grateful for permission to reprint from the following copyright texts:

Wibke Bruhns: *My Father's Country: The story of a German family* translated by Shaun Whiteside (Wm Heinemann, 2004), reproduced by permission of The Random House Group Ltd; Richard J Evans: 'Song of the Storm Columns' in *The Coming of the Third Reich* (Penguin, 2004), copyright © Richard J Evans, 2003, reproduced by permission of Penguin Books Ltd; **Ian Hislop: Commentary on Not Forgotten: Soldiers of Empire**, Channel 4, November 2009, reproduced by permission of Casarotto Ramsay and Associates Ltd on behalf of Ian Hislop; **Adolf Hitler: Mein Kampf** translated by Ralph Manheim (Hutchinson, 1974/Pimlico, 1992), reproduced by permission of The Random House Group Ltd; **Anton Kaes, Martin Jay, and Edward Dimendberg:** *The Weimar Republic Sourcebook* (University of California Press, 1995), copyright © 1994 by the Regents of the University of California, reproduced by permission of the University of California Press; **J. Noakes and G. Pridham:** *Nazism 1919–1945*, in 4 volumes (Exeter University Press, 2001), reproduced by permission of Liverpool University Press; **Rudolf Reder: 'Belzec'**, translated into English by M. M. Rubel, from *Polin: Studies in Polish Jewry, Volume 13: Focusing on the Holocaust and its Aftermath* edited by Antony Polonsky, published on behalf of the Institute for Polish-Jewish Studies and the America Association for Polish-Jewish Studies by the Littman Library of Jewish Civilization (Oxford and Portland, Oregon, 2000), reproduced by permission of the Littman Library, Oxford; **William L. Shirer: Berlin Diary: the Journal of a Foreign Correspondent** (Hamish Hamilton, 1941) copyright © renewed 1998 by William L. Shirer, reproduced by permission of Don Congdon Associates; Lyn Smith: *Forgotten Voices of the Holocaust* (Ebury Press, in association with the Imperial War Museum, 2005), reproduced by permission of The Random House Group Ltd; **Albert Speer: Inside the Third Reich** translated by Richard and Clara Winston (Simon & Schuster, 1997), copyright © 1969 by Verlag Ullstein GmbH, English translation copyright © 1970 by Macmillan Company, reproduced by permission of Scribner, a Division of Simon & Schuster, Inc. All rights reserved; **Jill Stephenson: Women in Nazi Germany** (Taylor & Francis, 2014), copyright © Taylor & Francis 2014, reproduced by permission of Taylor & Francis Books UK; **Ernst Toller: I Was a German: The autobiography of a revolutionary**, translated by Edward Crankshaw (John Lane, Bodley Head 1934), reproduced by permission of The Random House Group Ltd.

We have made every effort to trace and contact all copyright holders before publication, but if notified of any errors or omissions, the publisher will be happy to rectify these at the earliest opportunity.

The publisher would like to thank the following people for offering their contribution in the development of this book:

Allan Gillingham, Chris Rowe, Sally Waller, Roy Whittle

Links to third party websites are provided by Oxford in good faith and for information only. Oxford disclaims any responsibility for the materials contained in any third party website referenced in this work.

Approval message from AQA

This textbook has been approved by AQA for use with our qualification. This means that we have checked that it broadly covers the specification and we are satisfied with the overall quality. Full details of our approval process can be found on our website.

We approve textbooks because we know how important it is for teachers and students to have the right resources to support their teaching and learning. However, the publisher is ultimately responsible for the editorial control and quality of this book.

Please note that when teaching the AQA A Level History course, you must refer to AQA's specification as your definitive source of information. While this book has been written to match the specification, it does not provide complete coverage of every aspect of the course.

A wide range of other useful resources can be found on the relevant subject pages of our website: www.aqa.org.uk.

Please note that the Practice Questions in this book allow students a genuine attempt at practising exam skills, but they are not intended to replicate exam questions in every respect.

FSC
MIX
Paper from responsible sources
www.fsc.org   FSC® C007785

Contents

Contents (continued)

Introduction to features

The **Oxford AQA History** series has been developed by a team of expert history teachers and authors with examining experience. Written to match the new AQA specification, these new editions cover AS and A Level content together in each book.

How to use this book

The features in this book include:

TIMELINE

Key events are outlined at the beginning of the book to give you an overview of the chronology of this topic. Events are colour-coded so you can clearly see the categories of change.

LEARNING OBJECTIVES

At the beginning of each chapter, you will find a list of learning objectives linked to the requirements of the specification.

SOURCE   EXTRACT

Sources introduce you to material that is primary or contemporary to the period, and **Extracts** provide you with historical interpretations and the debate among historians on particular issues and developments. The accompanying activity questions support you in evaluating sources and extracts, analysing and assessing their value, and making judgements.

PRACTICE QUESTION

Focused questions to help you practise your history skills for both AS and A Level, including evaluating sources and extracts, and essay writing.

STUDY TIP

Hints to highlight key parts of **Practice Questions** or **Activities**, and to help prepare you for success.

ACTIVITY

Various activity types to provide you with opportunities to demonstrate both the content and skills you are learning. Some activities are designed to aid revision or to prompt further discussion; others are to stretch and challenge both your AS and A Level studies.

CROSS-REFERENCE

Links to related content within the book to offer you more detail on the subject in question.

A CLOSER LOOK

An in-depth look at a theme, event or development to deepen your understanding, or information to put further context around the subject under discussion.

KEY CHRONOLOGY

A short list of dates identifying key events to help you understand underlying developments.

KEY PROFILE

Details of a key person to extend your understanding and awareness of the individuals that have helped shape the period in question.

KEY TERM

A term that you will need to understand. The terms appear in bold, and they are also defined in the glossary.

AQA History specification overview

Part One content

The Weimar Republic 1918–1933

1 The establishment and early years of the Weimar Republic 1918–24
2 The 'Golden Age' of the Weimar Republic 1924–28
3 The collapse of democracy 1928–33

Part Two content

Nazi Germany 1933–1945

4 The Nazi dictatorship 1933–39
5 The racial state 1933–41
6 The impact of war 1939–45

AS examination papers will cover content from Part One only (you will only need to know the content in the blue box). A Level examination papers will cover content from both Part One and Part Two.

The examination papers

The grade you receive at the end of your AQA AS History course is based entirely on your performance in two examination papers, covering Breadth (Paper 1) and Depth (Paper 2). For your AQA A Level History course, you will also have to complete an Historical Investigation (Non-examined assessment).

Paper 2 Depth Study

This book covers the content of a Depth Study (Paper 2). You are assessed on the study in depth of a period of major historical change or development, and associated primary sources or sources contemporary to the period.

Exam paper	Questions and marks	Assessment Objective (AO)*	Timing	Marks
AS Paper 2: Depth Study	**Section A: Evaluating primary sources** One compulsory question linked to two primary sources or sources contemporary to the period (25 marks) • The compulsory question will ask you: *'with reference to these sources and your understanding of the historical context, which of these sources is more valuable in explaining why…'*	AO2	Written exam: 1 hour 30 minutes	50 marks (50% of AS)
	Section B: Essay writing One from a choice of two essay questions (25 marks) • The essay questions will contain a quotation advancing a judgement and will be followed by: *'explain why you agree or disagree with this view'*.	AO1		
A Level Paper 2: Depth Study	**Section A: Evaluating primary sources** One compulsory question linked to three primary sources or sources contemporary to the period. The sources will be of different types and views (30 marks) • The compulsory question will ask you: *'with reference to these sources and your understanding of the historical context, assess the value of these three sources to an historian studying…'*	AO2	Written exam: 2 hours 30 minutes	80 marks (40% of A Level)
	Section B: Essay writing Two from a choice of three essay questions (2 x 25 marks) • The essay questions require analysis and judgement, and <u>could</u> include: *'How successful…'* or *'To what extent…'* or *'How far…'* or a quotation offering a judgement followed by *'Assess the validity of this view'*.	AO1		

*AQA History examinations will test your ability to:

AO1: Demonstrate, organise and communicate **knowledge and understanding** to analyse and evaluate the key features related to the periods studied, **making substantiated judgements and exploring concepts**, as relevant, of cause, consequence, change, continuity, similarity, difference and significance.

AO2: **Analyse and evaluate** appropriate source material, primary and/or contemporary to the period, within the historical context.

AO3: **Analyse and evaluate**, in relation to the historical context, different ways in which aspects of the past have been interpreted.

Visit **www.aqa.org.uk** to help you prepare for your examinations. The website includes specimen examination papers and mark schemes.

Introduction to the *Oxford AQA History* series

Depth studies

The exploration of a short but significant historical period provides an opportunity to develop an 'in-depth' historical awareness. This book will help you to acquire a detailed knowledge of an exciting period of historical change, enabling you to become familiar with the personalities and ideas which shaped and dominated the time. In-depth study, as presented here, allows you to develop the enthusiasm that comes from knowing something really well.

However, 'depth' is not just about knowledge. Understanding history requires the piecing together of many different strands or themes, and depth studies demand an awareness of the interrelationship of a variety of perspectives, such as the political, economic, social and religious – as well as the influence of individuals and ideas within a relatively short period of time. Through an 'in-depth' study, a strong awareness of complex historical processes is developed, permitting deeper analysis, greater perception and well-informed judgement.

Whilst this book is therefore designed to impart a full and lively awareness of a significant period in history, far more is on offer from the pages that follow. With the help of the text and activities in this book, you will be encouraged to think historically, question developments in the past and undertake 'in-depth' analysis. You will develop your conceptual understanding and build up key historical skills that will increase your curiosity and prepare you, not only for A Level History examinations, but for any future studies.

> **Key Term**, **Key Chronology** and **Key Profile** help you to consolidate historical knowledge about dates, events, people and places

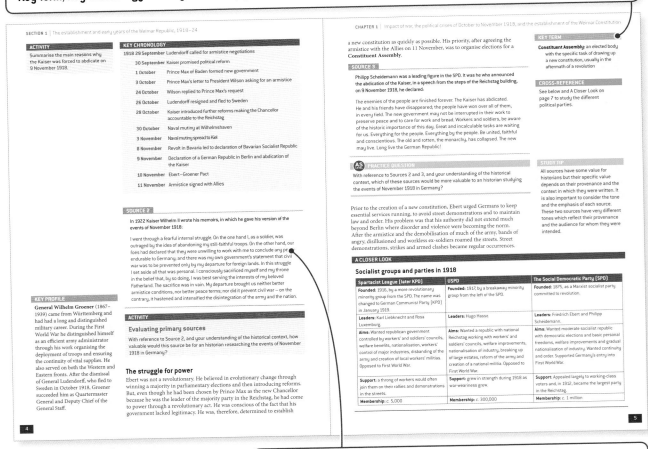

▲ Democracy and Nazism: Germany 1918–1945

> **Source** features support you with assessing the value of primary materials

This book also incorporates primary source material in the **Source** features. Primary sources are the building blocks of history, and you will be encouraged to reflect on their value to historians in trying to recreate the past. The accompanying questions are designed to develop your own historical skills, whilst suggestions for **Activities** will help you to engage with the past in a lively and stimulating manner. Throughout the book, you are encouraged to think about the material you are studying and to research further, in order to appreciate the ways in which historians seek to understand and interpret past events.

The chapters which follow are laid out according to the content of the AQA specification in six sections. Obviously, a secure chronological awareness and understanding of each section of content will be the first step in appreciating the historical period covered in this book. However, you are also encouraged to make links and comparisons between aspects of the period studied, and the activities will help you to relate to the key focus of your study and the key concepts that apply to it. Through intelligent use of this book, a deep and rewarding appreciation of an important period of history and the many influences within it will emerge.

Developing your study skills

You will need to be equipped with a paper file or electronic means of storing notes. Organised notes help to produce organised essays and sensible filing provides for efficient use of time. This book uses **Cross-References** to indicate where material in one chapter has relevance to that in another. By employing the same technique, you should find it easier to make the final leap towards piecing together your material to produce a holistic historical picture. The individual, group and research activities in this book are intended to guide you towards making selective and relevant notes with a specific purpose. Copying out sections of the book is to be discouraged, but recording material with a particular theme or question in mind will considerably aid your understanding.

There are plenty of examples of examination-style 'depth' **Practice Questions** for both AS Level, in Part One, and A Level in Parts One and Two of this book. There are also **Study Tips** to encourage you to think about historical perspectives, individuals, groups, ideas and ideology. You should also create your own timelines, charts and diagrams, for example to illustrate causation and consequence, analyse the interrelationship of the differing perspectives, consider concepts and identify historical processes.

It is particularly important for you to have your own opinions and to be able to make informed judgements about the material you have studied. Some of the activities in this book encourage pair discussion or class debate, and you should make the most of such opportunities to voice and refine your own ideas. The beauty of history is that there is rarely a right or wrong answer, so this supplementary oral work should enable you to share your own opinions.

Writing and planning your essays

At both AS and A Level, you will be required to write essays and, although A Level questions are likely to be more complex, the basic qualities of good essay writing remain the same:

- **read the question carefully** to identify the key words and dates
- **plan out a logical and organised answer** with a clear judgement or view (several views if there are a number of issues to consider). Your essay should advance this judgement in the introduction, while also acknowledging alternative views and clarifying terms of reference, including the time span
- use the opening sentences of your paragraphs as stepping stones to take an argument forward, which allows you to **develop an evolving and balanced argument** throughout the essay and also makes for good style
- **support your comment or analysis** with precise detail; using dates, where appropriate, helps logical organisation
- **write a conclusion** which matches the view of the introduction and flows naturally from what has gone before.

Whilst these suggestions will help you develop a good style, essays should never be too rigid or mechanical. This book will have fulfilled its purposes if it produces, as intended, students who think for themselves!

Sally Waller

Series Editor

Timeline

The colours represent different types of event as follows:

- Blue: Economic
- Yellow: Social
- Red: Political
- Black: International (including foreign policy)
- Green: Religious

1914
- Germany enters First World War in alliance with Austria-Hungary, fighting against Great Britain, France and Russia

1918
- Germany defeats Russia but defeated on Western Front
- Kaiser Wilhelm II abdicates and a new republic established
- **November** New German government signs armistice to end the war on Western Front

1919
- **January** Communist (Spartacist) uprising in Berlin, suppressed by army and Freikorps
- **June** Germany forced to accept Treaty of Versailles
- **July** Constitution of the new German Republic approved by Reichstag

1920
- Kapp Putsch in Berlin attempts to overthrow government
- NSDAP established

1925
- Field Marshal Hindenburg elected president of German Republic
- *Mein Kampf* published

1926
- SS established
- Germany accepted into League of Nations

1929
- **June** Young Plan introduced to reorganise reparations payments
- **October** Wall Street Crash leads to collapse of German economy and mass unemployment

1930
- **March** Collapse of coalition government led by Müller. Replaced by Brüning who needs to rule by presidential decree
- **September** NSDAP gain support in Reichstag election

1934
- Protestant Confessional Church established as breakaway group from official Evangelical Church
- **June** SA purged in Night of Long Knives
- **August** Death of Hindenburg allows Hitler to become president and chancellor with title of Führer

1935
- **March** Hitler announces start of rearmament programme
- **September** The Nuremberg Laws

1936
- **March** German troops enter the demilitarised Rhineland
- Law for the Incorporation of German Youth makes the Hitler Youth an official education movement
- Olympic Games held in Berlin
- Four Year Plan introduced with Goering in charge
- Himmler placed in charge of SS, SD and Gestapo

1937
- Encyclical letter from the Pope criticises repression of Catholic Church in Germany

1940
- **January** First gassing of mentally ill
- **April** Germany invades Denmark and Norway
- **May** Germany invades Holland, Belgium and France
- **June** France defeated
- Start of Madagascar Plan
- **October** Warsaw ghetto sealed

1941
- **June** German forces invade the USSR
- *Einsatzgruppen* deployed behind Eastern Front
- **August** Euthanasia programme halted
- **December** German declaration of war on USA

1942
- **January** Wannsee Conference
- 'Total war' measures implemented in Germany
- April Opening of Sobibor death camp
- Mass deportations of Jews from Western Europe to Auschwitz
- **December** German Gypsies deported to Auschwitz

1943
- **January** Defeat of German army at Stalingrad marks the decisive turning point in the war
- Start of sustained bombing campaign against German cities by British and Americans
- Warsaw ghetto uprising

1921
- Adolf Hitler becomes leader of NSDAP
- SA established

1922
- Murder of Walther Rathenau
- Treaty of Rapallo with USSR

1923
- German economy hit by hyperinflation
- **January** French and Belgian troops occupy the Ruhr industrial area to force Germany to pay reparations
- **November** Hitler and Nazis attempt to seize power in Beer Hall Putsch in Munich

1924
- **February** Hitler sentenced to five years' imprisonment for leading the Beer Hall Putsch
- **April** Dawes Plan introduced to ease reparations payments
- **December** Hitler released from prison
- Start of economic recovery

1932
- **April** Hitler challenges Hindenburg in presidential election and achieves second place
- **July** NSDAP becomes largest party in Reichstag after election
- **November** NSDAP loses votes in Reichstag election

1933
- **January** Hindenburg appoints Hitler chancellor, in coalition with other parties
- **February** Reichstag fire leads to Decree for Protection of the People and the State, which suspends basic freedoms
- **March** NSDAP gain 44% of vote in Reichstag election

1933
- **March** Enabling Act gives Hitler dictatorial power
- **April** Law for the Re-establishment of a Professional Civil Service leads to purge of Jews from public employment
- **April** Boycott of Jewish shops and businesses

1933
- **May** Trade unions banned and replaced with German Labour Front
- **July** All non-Nazi parties either banned or voluntarily disbanded
- Nazi regime and Catholic Church sign a concordat

1938
- **February** Hitler purges army leadership to increase his control over military
- **March** Germany annexes Austria in the Anschluss

1938
- **September** Germany gains control over Sudeten area of Czechoslovakia after negotiations with Britain, France and Italy at Munich
- **October** Jewish passports stamped with letter 'J'
- **November** Jewish property and synagogues attacked on Reichkristallnacht

1939
- **March** Germany occupies the rest of Czechoslovakia
- RSHA established to bring all police forces under SS control
- Membership of Hitler Youth becomes compulsory
- **August** Nazi-Soviet Pact agreed to divide Poland between the two powers

1939
- **August** Rationing of some key foodstuffs begins
- **September** German forces invade Poland, leading to start of Second World War
- Start of ghettoisation in Poland
- October Euthanasia programme approved

1944
- **June** Allied forces open 'second front' in west with D-Day landings
- Mass deportation of Hungarian Jews to Auschwitz
- **July** Attempt to assassinate Hitler by army officers in Bomb Plot fails
- Start of the death marches

1945
- **January** Soviet forces enter Germany from east
- Liberation of Auschwitz and other camps
- **March** British and American forces enter Germany from west
- **April** Hitler commits suicide
- **May** Germany concedes defeat with unconditional surrender

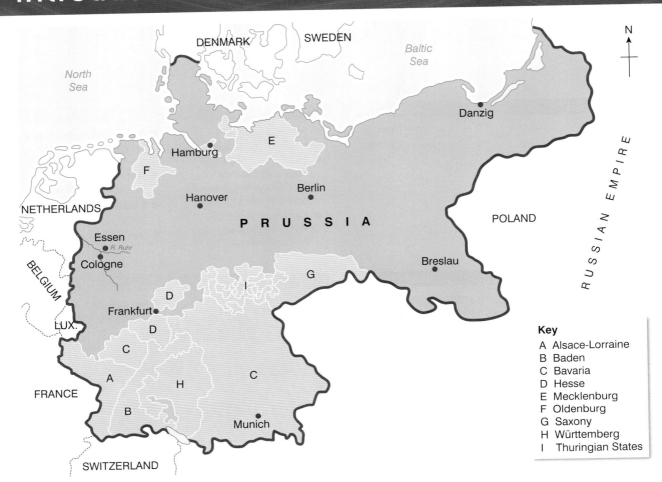

Fig. 1   *The German Reich, 1871–1918*

The German Reich

The German Reich, which was established in 1871, was referred to as the Second Reich. The First Reich, the Holy Roman Empire which lasted from 962 until 1806, was a loose confederation of mainly German states ruled over by the Holy Roman Emperor. For much of the history of the Holy Roman Empire, the emperor was also the ruler of Austria.

During the Second Reich (or Second Empire), there were three Kaisers:

- Kaiser Wilhelm I, 1871–88
- Kaiser Frederick, 1888
- Kaiser Wilhelm II, 1888–1918.

This book will cover in depth a period of German history following the First World War, during which a newly developed democratic form of government gave way to a dictatorial Nazi regime. To put this development in context: before 1871, Germany consisted of a number of separate states of varying sizes. In 1871, the largest German state, Prussia, brought most of the German states together into a new German **Reich** (Empire) dominated by Prussia.

For some time before this, many German-speaking people had wanted the separate states to unite together to form a strong, united and independent German nation-state which would include all Germans; in other words, they were German nationalists. Most nationalists were also liberal in their political allegiances: they envisaged the unification of Germany being achieved by the German people themselves, through democratic elections and popular consent. In the event, unification was achieved by the military victories of the Prussian army in a series of wars against Denmark, Austria and France. This posed a dilemma for many German nationalists. The new German Reich was not exactly the one they had wanted: Austria was excluded, and it was ruled over by the Prussian Kaiser (Emperor), not by a government elected by the people. But the Reich did include most Germans and it gave them a sense of national pride. There was also a democratic element in the new government, with a **Reichstag** elected by **universal male suffrage**, although this had little real power. This led to growing political tension within the German Reich in the years 1871 to 1914, as the Reichstag increasingly became the focus for opposition parties to challenge the rule of the Kaiser.

German economy grew rapidly after 1871 and Germany became one of the most powerful states within Europe, and was a leading industrial nation by 1900. Industrialisation transformed German society in many ways, leading to the emergence of a wealthy middle class and an increasingly discontented working class. Many of Germany's leading industrialists saw political stability as the best guarantee of their future prosperity, and formed an alliance with the aristocratic landowners (known as Junkers) to support the Kaiser's rule. Workers, on the other hand, formed trade unions to campaign for higher wages and better conditions. They also increasingly voted in Reichstag elections for the Social Democratic Party (Sozialdemokratische Partei Deutschlands or SPD), a party which campaigned for greater democracy and social change. By 1912, the SPD had become the largest single party in the Reichstag and Germany had become an increasingly divided nation, both socially and politically. No political party was genuinely national or broadly based, and politics became fragmented, with many different parties representing different interest groups. The result was a growing sense of crisis in the German political system, and paralysis in the Reichstag.

The outbreak of the First World War in August 1914 transformed the political situation in Germany, albeit temporarily. There was a wave of popular support for the Kaiser's declaration of war, as most Germans regarded their country as being the victim of 'encirclement' by the Allied powers of Great Britain, France and Russia. The result was a political truce between the parties in the Reichstag, with even the normally anti-war party SPD voting in favour of the war budget. As long as German forces were perceived to be successful in the war, and German civilians did not experience undue hardship, support for the Kaiser and the war effort remained high. By the winter of 1916–17, however, severe food shortages, together with rapidly rising food prices, damaged civilian morale.

The mounting crisis in Germany led Kaiser Wilhelm II to give more political power to his top military leaders, particularly **General Erich Ludendorff** and **Field Marshal Paul von Hindenburg**. The entry of the USA into the war on the Allied side in 1917 added to the pressure on Germany. On the other hand, the defeat of Russia by German forces in 1918 freed many of the German soldiers on the **Eastern Front** for a major offensive on the **Western Front**. However, with the arrival of large numbers of American troops in France in the spring of 1918, the balance was tipped decisively in favour of the Allies. By November 1918, German forces were in retreat along the whole length of the Western Front. At the same time Germany's main ally, the Austro-Hungarian Empire, was being defeated on other fronts. Facing certain defeat, Germany's military leaders advised the government to start peace talks with the Allied powers. Military defeat was a profound shock for Germany's leaders and its people, and led in a very short time to the end of the Kaiser's rule and the establishment of a democratic system of government.

The first half of this book tells the story of the Weimar Republic, which was established in Germany in the wake of military defeat and political revolution. This democratic system of government lasted less than fifteen years. It was plagued from the beginning by economic crises and political divisions.

On the right wing of the political spectrum, German nationalists blamed the democratic politicians for Germany's defeat in 1918 and the humiliation of the peace treaty which followed, and they were prepared to go to extreme lengths to overthrow the Weimar Republic. They were appalled by the ways in which the new political freedoms were allowing diverse groups – men and women,

KEY PROFILE

Field Marshal Paul von Hindenburg (1847–1934) was an aristocratic landowner and professional soldier, who became a hero after defeating a large Russian army at the battle of Tannenberg in 1915. In 1916, he became chief of the general staff. After Germany's defeat in 1918, Hindenburg shifted the blame for this humiliation onto the politicians who took power after the abdication of the Kaiser.

General Erich Ludendorff (1865–1937) was a key figure, alongside Hindenburg, in the German victories against the Russian army. In 1916, he joined Hindenburg in engineering the overthrow of the Chancellor (German Prime Minister), Theobald von Bethmann-Hollweg, and became a member of the military committee which effectively ruled Germany until the end of the war. He was reactionary in his politics and an implacable opponent of the New Republic which was established after the abdication of the Kaiser in November 1918.

A CLOSER LOOK

Western and Eastern Fronts

The Western Front refers to the battlegrounds of Belgium and northern France, where British and French troops fought the German army. The Eastern Front refers to the conflict between Russia and the forces of Germany and Austria-Hungary.

artists and writers, young people, and others – to challenge social conventions and experiment with radical, new ideas. They blamed the Jews and other racial minorities for Germany's problems. Above all, they wanted an end to democracy and its replacement by a more authoritarian form of government. For some, this meant the return of the Kaiser; for others, a new form of dictatorship in which one person rules over a nation with total power.

On the left wing of the political spectrum, there were divisions between those who wanted to make the democratic system work (such as the SPD) and those who wanted another revolution to establish a communist form of government. The Weimar Republic faced many challenges during the years 1918 to 1933 but it survived most of them. What it could not survive was the steady erosion of support after 1929 as a result of an economic crisis, as well as its undermining from within by powerful political and military figures who had no commitment to democracy.

The Nazi regime, which took power in January 1933, quickly established a political dictatorship which lasted for a little over twelve years. The second half of this book tells the story of how this dictatorship was established, how that had an impact on the lives of ordinary Germans, and how that dictatorship was sustained. Of particular importance in establishing and sustaining the dictatorship was the creation of a police state and the use of propaganda. This book also looks at the racial policies of the Nazi regime and how these led to involvement in another world war, the implementation of a policy of racial extermination, and eventually to another military defeat in 1945.

This book will encourage you to reflect on how governments work, and the problems that democratic states face. In the course of your journey through these years of German history, you will come to appreciate how difficult it can be to establish true 'democracy' – a form of government held in high regard by most western nations today – and how the line between democracy and dictatorship is narrower than might at first be thought.

1 The establishment and early years of the Weimar Republic, 1918–24

1 Impact of war, the political crises of October to November 1918, and the establishment of the Weimar Constitution

The abdication of the Kaiser

At 1:30pm on 9 November 1918, in a house adjacent to the German army headquarters in Spa, Belgium, Kaiser Wilhelm II of Germany was brought the news that his abdication had been announced in Berlin. His reign was at an end. He might well cry 'treason' but, by 5:00pm in the afternoon, he had been forced to accept what had happened. His companions advised him that his only hope of safety was to travel northwards into Holland, which had remained neutral during the war which Germany had been waging on the Western Front for the last four years against the British and French. Wilhelm, however, was uncertain what to do. His wife, the Empress Dona, was still in Berlin and it was not until just before dawn on 10 November, that a convoy of 10 cars, including the Kaiser's, with its royal insignia removed, set off to the Dutch border at Eysen. Here, the royal party was kept waiting for six hours while the Dutch authorities decided what should happen to such an important visitor, but eventually they were allowed to continue by special train. When Wilhelm met the German ambassador the next day he complained, 'I am a broken man. How can I begin life again? My prospects are hopeless. I have nothing left to believe in.' However, as Europe celebrated the **armistice** on 11 November 1918, Wilhelm sat down to 'a good cup of English tea' at his new residence.

By the end of September 1918 it had been clear to General Ludendorff and the German High Command that Germany was on the brink of defeat. Although the Allied armies had not yet entered German territory, German forces were in retreat along the Western Front. Elsewhere in Europe, Germany's Allies were trying to negotiate peace terms. Ludendorff concluded that Germany's only hope of avoiding a humiliating surrender was to ask the Allies for an armistice. US **President Wilson's Fourteen Points** offered a possible basis for a negotiated peace settlement but Ludendorff understood that Germany's autocratic political system was an obstacle to this. He, therefore, advocated a partial democratisation of the political system in Germany as a way of getting better peace terms from the Allies.

A CLOSER LOOK

President Wilson's Fourteen Points

Woodrow Wilson was an idealist and his Fourteen Points were devised as a means of dealing fairly with the aftermath of war. Some points, such as the return of Alsace-Lorraine to France, were quite specific and punitive towards Germany. However, there were also some general principles, such as the establishment of a League of Nations to monitor future disputes and self-determination, whereby different nations should rule themselves, together with general disarmament and Wilson's determination to create a peace that would last and prevent another war.

KEY TERMS

Republic: a system of government in which the Head of State, or President, is elected into office

Armistice: an agreement to suspend fighting in order to allow a peace treaty to be negotiated

Fig. 1 *Kaiser Wilhelm II (left) celebrated 30 years of government in 1918, but he was forced to resign in November of that year*

CROSS-REFERENCE

A key profile of information on General Erich Ludendorff is in the introduction, page XII.

KEY PROFILE

Prince Max of Baden (1867–1929) was a member of the royal house of the Grand Duchy of Baden and a former army officer. In 1914 he became President of the Baden section of the German Red Cross, working to improve conditions for prisoners of war. This humanitarian work earned him widespread respect.

KEY TERM

Constitutional: an established set of principles governing a state

ACTIVITY

Evaluating primary sources

In what ways would Source 1 be of value to an historian investigating the feelings of the German people at the end of the war?

The October Reforms

In October, following the recommendations of Ludendorff, the Kaiser began a series of reforms that effectively ended his autocratic rule:

- He appointed **Prince Max of Baden** as his new Chancellor
- The Chancellor was to be responsible to the Reichstag and he established a new government based on the majority parties in the Reichstag, including the German Social Democratic Party (SPD)
- The armed forces were put under the control of the civil government.

These reforms were a major **constitutional** transformation in Germany but they did not come about as a result of popular pressure, nor because of pressure from the main democratic parties in the Reichstag. They amounted to a 'revolution from above' which was not only designed to save Germany from humiliation, but also to save the Kaiser's rule.

The Peace Note

On 3 October, Prince Max wrote to President Wilson asking for an armistice. It took nearly three weeks for Wilson to reply, largely because he was suspicious that the German High Command was using the request for an armistice as a means of buying time to regroup and prepare for a new offensive. When Wilson replied, he demanded that Germany must evacuate all occupied territory, call an end to submarine warfare and fully democratise its political system. These terms, which effectively demanded a German surrender and the Kaiser's abdication, were too much for Ludendorff to accept. He tried but failed to gather support for a last ditch military effort to resist, whereupon he resigned and fled to Sweden. The reforms had failed to achieve his objectives.

The impact on the German people

SOURCE 1

Ernst Toller, a Jewish writer and member of the Independent Socialist Party, recalled the events of 1918 in his autobiography which was published in 1933:

Germany's needs became ever more desperate. The bread got ever worse, the milk got thinner, the farmers would have nothing to do with the towns. The men at the front were incensed. For four years they had fought, on the Eastern Front, on the Western Front, in Asia, in Africa; for four years they had stood their ground in the rain and mud of Flanders. During the night of 3rd October the Peace Note was dispatched to President Wilson. This unexpected bid for peace opened the eyes of the German people at last; they had no idea of the impending catastrophe. So it was all for nothing – the millions of dead, the millions of wounded, the starvation at home. All for nothing. The people thought only of peace. They had been thinking of war too long, believing in victory too long. Why hadn't they been told the truth?

The news that Prince Max's government was asking for an armistice was a shattering blow to the morale of the German people and to their armed forces. The Peace Note was an admission that Germany had lost the war. This was the first occasion on which the German people had learned the truth about their country's hopeless military situation. It undermined their respect for the Kaiser and his military and political leaders. Civilians who had borne the hardships of food shortages with fortitude were no longer prepared to show restraint. Many soldiers and sailors lost respect for their officers. The Kaiser was increasingly seen as an obstacle to peace but he resolutely refused to abdicate. During a strike in Friedrichshafen on 22 October, workers shouted 'The Kaiser is a scoundrel' and 'Up with the German Republic'. On 28 October, when the German navy's high command, in one last futile act of resistance to a humiliating peace, ordered ships from Wilhelmshaven to attack British ships in the English Channel, the crews of two cruisers refused to obey orders. This naval **mutiny** was the beginning of a much broader revolutionary movement.

The November Revolution of 1918

Unrest in the navy spread to the main German naval base at Kiel. On 3 November 1918, sailors there mutinied against their officers and took control of the base. On the following day the revolt spread to the city, and workers' and soldiers' councils were established, similar to the **Soviets** in Russia during the Revolution of 1917. Despite attempts by the government to meet the mutineers' demands, the revolt spread to many other German ports and cities. By 6 November there were workers and soldiers councils springing up spontaneously all over Germany. Radical socialists did not lead these revolts, although it might seem to outsiders as though Germany was on the verge of a communist revolution like Russia's. In fact, most members of the councils were patriotic Germans who wanted the Kaiser to abdicate and a democratic republic to be established.

Once the authority of military officers, government officials and police had been successfully challenged, the collapse of the regime happened with extraordinary speed. On 8 November a republic was proclaimed in Bavaria and the Bavarian monarchy was deposed. This, according to the historian William Carr, was the 'decisive moment in the German Revolution'. It was certainly a key stage in the establishment of an all-German republic, as it brought home to Prince Max that he had lost control of the situation, but the most important developments were happening in Berlin.

On 9 November 1918, the SPD called on workers in Berlin to join a general strike to force the Kaiser to abdicate. They also threatened to withdraw support from Prince Max's government unless the Kaiser abdicated within 24 hours. Max knew he could not continue to govern without the SPD, so when the Kaiser still refused, Max took matters into his own hands and, on 9 November, he released a press statement claiming the Emperor had abdicated! This was a desperate move by Prince Max to keep some control over the situation, even though he had no constitutional authority to act in this way. On the same day, Prince Max resigned as Chancellor and handed the position to **Friedrich Ebert**, the leader of the

SPD. At about the same time, Phillip Scheidemann, another leading figure in the SPD, stood on the Reichstag balcony and declared that the German Republic was now in in existence. All of these events happened before the Kaiser had, in fact, abdicated. Later in the day, **General Groener** told the Kaiser that the army would no longer fight for him. At this point the Kaiser had lost control of the situation and had no choice but to abdicate, although he did not actually *sign* his abdication until after it had been announced.

Fig. 2 *Revolutionary sailors and civilians demonstrate in Berlin, led by a sailor from Kiel*

Fig. 3 *Friedrich Ebert was a saddle-maker by trade*

Friedrich Ebert (1871–1925) became active in the SPD and was elected to the Reichstag in 1912. A year later he rose to become President of the party. He led the party into supporting German entry into World War I and expelled the anti-war faction from the party in 1917. He became the first Chancellor in the new German Republic in November 1918 and its first President in 1919.

ACTIVITY

Summarise the main reasons why the Kaiser was forced to abdicate on 9 November 1918.

KEY CHRONOLOGY

1918 29 September	Ludendorff called for armistice negotiations
30 September	Kaiser promised political reform
1 October	Prince Max of Baden formed new government
3 October	Prince Max's letter to President Wilson asking for an armistice
24 October	Wilson replied to Prince Max's request
26 October	Ludendorff resigned and fled to Sweden
28 October	Kaiser introduced further reforms making the Chancellor accountable to the Reichstag
30 October	Naval mutiny at Wilhelmshaven
3 November	Naval mutiny spread to Kiel
8 November	Revolt in Bavaria led to declaration of Bavarian Socialist Republic
9 November	Declaration of a German Republic in Berlin and abdication of the Kaiser
10 November	Ebert–Groener Pact
11 November	Armistice signed with Allies

SOURCE 2

In 1922 Kaiser Wilhelm II wrote his memoirs, in which he gave his version of the events of November 1918:

I went through a fearful internal struggle. On the one hand I, as a soldier, was outraged by the idea of abandoning my still-faithful troops. On the other hand, our foes had declared that they were unwilling to work with me to conclude any peace endurable to Germany; and there was my own government's statement that civil war was to be prevented only by my departure for foreign lands. In this struggle I set aside all that was personal. I consciously sacrificed myself and my throne in the belief that, by so doing, I was best serving the interests of my beloved Fatherland. The sacrifice was in vain. My departure brought us neither better armistice conditions, nor better peace terms; nor did it prevent civil war – on the contrary, it hastened and intensified the disintegration of the army and the nation.

KEY PROFILE

General Wilhelm Groener (1867–1939) came from Württemberg and had had a long and distinguished military career. During the First World War he distinguished himself as an efficient army administrator through his work organising the deployment of troops and ensuring the continuity of vital supplies. He also served on both the Western and Eastern fronts. After the dismissal of General Ludendorff, who fled to Sweden in October 1918, Groener succeeded him as Quartermaster General and Deputy Chief of the General Staff.

ACTIVITY

Evaluating primary sources

With reference to Source 2, and your understanding of the historical context, how valuable would this source be for an historian researching the events of November 1918 in Germany?

The struggle for power

Ebert was not a revolutionary. He believed in evolutionary change through winning a majority in parliamentary elections and then introducing reforms. But, even though he had been chosen by Prince Max as the new Chancellor because he was the leader of the majority party in the Reichstag, he had come to power through a revolutionary act. He was conscious of the fact that his government lacked legitimacy. He was, therefore, determined to establish a new constitution as quickly as possible. His priority, after agreeing the armistice with the Allies on 11 November, was to organise elections for a **Constituent Assembly**.

KEY TERM

Constituent Assembly: an elected body with the specific task of drawing up a new constitution, usually in the aftermath of a revolution

SOURCE 3

Philipp Scheidemann was a leading figure in the SPD. It was he who announced the abdication of the Kaiser, in a speech from the steps of the Reichstag building, on 9 November 1918, he declared:

The enemies of the people are finished forever. The Kaiser has abdicated. He and his friends have disappeared; the people have won over all of them, in every field. The new government may not be interrupted in their work to preserve peace and to care for work and bread. Workers and soldiers, be aware of the historic importance of this day. Great and incalculable tasks are waiting for us. Everything for the people. Everything by the people. Be united, faithful and conscientious. The old and rotten, the monarchy, has collapsed. The new may live. Long live the German Republic!

CROSS-REFERENCE

See below and A Closer Look on page 7 to study the different political parties.

AS LEVEL | PRACTICE QUESTION

With reference to Sources 2 and 3, and your understanding of the historical context, which of these sources would be more valuable to an historian studying the events of November 1918 in Germany?

STUDY TIP

All sources have some value for historians but their specific value depends on their provenance and the context in which they were written. It is also important to consider the tone and the emphasis of each source. These two sources have very different tones which reflect their provenance and the audience for whom they were intended.

Prior to the creation of a new constitution, Ebert urged Germans to keep essential services running, to avoid street demonstrations and to maintain law and order. His problem was that his authority did not extend much beyond Berlin where disorder and violence were becoming the norm. After the armistice and the demobilisation of much of the army, bands of angry, disillusioned and workless ex-soldiers roamed the streets. Street demonstrations, strikes and armed clashes became regular occurrences.

A CLOSER LOOK

Socialist groups and parties in 1918

Spartacist League (later KPD)	USPD	The Social Democratic Party (SPD)
Founded: 1916, by a more revolutionary minority group from the SPD. The name was changed to German Communist Party (KPD) in January 1919.	**Founded:** 1917, by a breakaway minority group from the left of the SPD.	**Founded:** 1875, as a Marxist socialist party committed to revolution.
Leaders: Karl Liebknecht and Rosa Luxemburg.	**Leaders:** Hugo Hasse.	**Leaders:** Friedrich Ebert and Philipp Scheidemann.
Aims: Wanted republican government controlled by workers' and soldiers' councils, welfare benefits, nationalisation, workers' control of major industries, disbanding of the army and creation of local workers' militias. Opposed to First World War.	**Aims:** Wanted a republic with national Reichstag working with workers' and soldiers' councils, welfare improvements, nationalisation of industry, breaking up of large estates, reform of the army and creation of a national militia. Opposed to First World War.	**Aims:** Wanted moderate socialist republic with democratic elections and basic personal freedoms, welfare improvements and gradual nationalisation of industry. Wanted continuity and order. Supported Germany's entry into First World War.
Support: a throng of workers would often join them on their rallies and demonstrations in the streets.	**Support:** grew in strength during 1918 as war-weariness grew.	**Support:** Appealed largely to working-class voters and, in 1912, became the largest party in the Reichstag.
Membership: c. 5,000	**Membership:** c. 300,000	**Membership:** c. 1 million

Pressure from the left

Ebert's efforts to contain the revolution were further threatened by pressure for more radical change from the left. He could not ignore the fact that the workers' and soldiers' councils, in which the USPD and the Spartacists had established a foothold, had made the running in the early stages of the revolution. They were not about to allow Ebert's government to take the key decisions without any reference to them. On 22 November an agreement was reached between the new government and the Berlin workers' and soldiers' councils whereby the government accepted that it only exercised power in the name of these councils. This was merely a temporary compromise. Many in the USPD, whose leaders were part of Ebert's government, saw the councils as the true expression of the revolutionary will of the people and the means by which the revolution could be extended. They believed that the autocratic system of government would not finally be abolished unless the **aristocratic** estates were broken up, the army, civil service and judiciary were democratised, and the key industries were nationalised under workers' control.

Pressure from the army and the Ebert–Groener Pact

In this situation, the survival of Ebert's government depended on the support of the army. Most army officers came from aristocratic backgrounds, had been loyal to the Kaiser and were vigorously opposed to democracy. They had no wish to see Germany become a republic. In late 1918, however, the political situation in Germany was highly unstable and many officers believed that Germany faced the danger of a Bolshevik revolution (like Russia's in October 1917), which would lead to civil war and possible occupation by Allied forces. Their first concern, therefore, was to prevent the revolution going any further. On 10 November, General Groener telephoned Ebert to assure him that the army leadership would support the government. In return, Groener demanded that Ebert should resist the demands of the soldiers' councils to democratise the army and defend Germany against communist revolution. Ebert assured Groener that the government was determined to resist further revolution and to uphold the existing command structure in the army. This agreement became known as the Ebert–Groener Pact.

For Ebert the Pact was a necessary and unavoidable device to ensure an orderly transition to the New Republic. For his critics on the left, however, it was an abject betrayal of the revolution. Whilst Ebert and his cabinet made preparations for elections to a Constituent Assembly, to be held in January 1919, the struggle for power continued:

- On 6 December a Spartacist demonstration in Berlin was fired on by soldiers, killing sixteen
- On 23–24 December, a sailors' revolt against the government in Berlin was put down by the army. In protest, the three USPD ministers in the government resigned
- On 6 January, the Spartacists launched an armed revolt against the government in what became known as the January Revolution, or the Spartacist Uprising. After a week of heavy fighting in Berlin, the revolt was crushed.

The establishment of the Weimar Constitution in 1919

Elections to the Constituent Assembly

Amidst the political and social tensions, the elections for the Constituent Assembly were held on 19 January 1919. Women were allowed to vote for the first time. The SPD secured the largest share of the vote and the largest number of seats in the Assembly but they did not have an overall majority and

KEY TERM

Aristocracy: the highest class in certain societies, typically comprising people of noble birth holding hereditary titles and offices

CROSS-REFERENCE

Read page 27 in Chapter 4 to find out more about the left-wing Spartacist Party and their attempt to bring about a Bolshevik revolution in January 1919.

CROSS-REFERENCE

The precise terms of the constitution are set out in Fig. 5 of this chapter.

The Versailles Treaty will be discussed later in Chapter 2, page 12.

Fig. 4 *SPD propaganda team campaigns on the streets before the January election*

Philipp Scheidemann (1865–1939) was a popular, long-standing member of the SPD, having first joined in 1883. He became a Reichstag deputy in 1903. Although he supported Germany's entry to the war, he was in favour of a negotiated peace. On 9 November 1918, it was Scheidemann who announced the birth of the New Republic even before the Kaiser had officially abdicated. He was Chancellor of the first coalition government in the New Republic from February to June 1919, when he resigned in protest against the harsh terms of the Versailles Treaty.

would, therefore, have to compromise with other parties in order to establish a new constitution and govern the country. The Assembly met in the small town of Weimar rather than Berlin, as the political situation in the capital was still unstable in the aftermath of the January Revolution. This was how the new political order came to receive its name – the Weimar Republic. Ebert was elected by the Assembly as the first President of the Republic and a new government, led by **Philipp Scheidemann**, was formed by the SPD in coalition with the Centre and German Democratic parties. The workers' and soldiers' councils handed over their powers to the Constituent Assembly, which could then concentrate on the business of drawing up a new constitution. Although the representatives did not agree on all issues concerning the new constitution, there was general agreement that it should represent a clear break with the autocratic constitution drawn up by **Otto von Bismarck** for the German Empire in 1871. It, therefore, began with the clear declaration that 'Political authority derives from the people', and the constitution was designed to enshrine and guarantee the rights and powers of the people.

Otto von Bismarck (1815–98) was the Minister-President of Prussia from 1862 to 1871 who led his state through three wars (against Denmark, Austria, and France) which resulted in the unification of Germany under Prussian domination. He continued to serve as Chancellor in the new German Empire from 1871 to 1890.

A CLOSER LOOK

The main non-socialist political parties in the new republic:

Centre Party	**German Democratic Party (DDP)**
• Formed in 1870 to protect Catholic interests in the mainly protestant German Reich • Had strong support in the main Catholic areas of Bavaria and the Rhineland • Supported a democratic constitution	• A left-leaning liberal party, based on the old Progressive Party • Most support came from intellectuals and middle class • Supported a democratic constitution
German National People's Party (DNVP)	**German People's Party (DVP)**
• A nationalist party, based on the old Conservative Party • Most support came from landowners and some small business owners • Rejected the democratic constitution	• A right-leaning liberal party, based on the old National Liberal Party • Most support came from upper-middle class and business interests • Opposed to new republic but willing to participate in its governments

Table 1 *The election results of January 1919*

Party	Number of seats gained
SPD	163
USPD	22
Centre	91
DDP	75
DNVP	44
DVP	19

The Weimar Constitution, 1919
Strengths of the constitution

The Constitution of the Weimar Republic was, in many ways, more democratic than the systems of government in force at the time in other democratic countries. It also marked a clear break with Germany's autocratic past.

KEY TERM

Proportional representation: a system of elections in which parties are allocated seats in parliament according to the proportion of votes they receive

- The new German constitution provided a wider right to vote than in countries such as Great Britain and France. Women were able to vote on the same terms as men and they were allowed to become deputies in the Reichstag and state parliaments.
- The system of **proportional representation** enabled even the smaller parties to win seats in the Reichstag and influence government decisions. The country was divided into 35 electoral districts, each with about one million voters.
- There was full democracy in local government as well as central government. Unlike in the Second Empire, the largest state, Prussia, was not in a position to dominate the rest of Germany.
- The constitution also set out clearly the rights of the individual. The 'Fundamental Rights and Duties of German citizens' were guaranteed in the second part of the constitution. Statements included: 'all Germans are equal before the law'; 'personal liberty is inviolable'; 'censorship is forbidden'; 'the right of property is guaranteed'; and 'all inhabitants enjoy full religious freedom'. It gave illegitimate children the same rights as legitimate ones and promised 'economic freedom for the individual'.
- Referendums could be called for by the president, the Reichsrat, or by 'people's request' if a tenth of the electorate applied for one.

Weaknesses of the constitution
Proportional representation

Proportional representation was designed to ensure that all shades of political opinion were represented in the Reichstag, since parties were allocated seats in proportion to the percentage of votes that they received in an election. This was a very fair system but it had two clear consequences:

- **The proliferation of small parties:** Smaller parties could gain representation in the Reichstag – something that does not usually happen in a system of elections based on the first-past-the-post principle (Britain uses this election process). This enabled smaller parties – many of which were anti-republican – to exploit the parliamentary system to gain publicity. Proportional representation did not, in itself, create the fragmented party system. This was due to the deep divisions in German society and the lack of a national consensus.
- **Coalition governments:** Because of the proliferation of small parties, none of the larger parties could gain an overall majority in the Reichstag. Since governments had to command majority support in the Reichstag, all governments in the Weimar Republic were coalitions, many of which were very short-lived.

CROSS-REFERENCE

See tables on pages 5 and 7 in this chapter for a summary of the socialist and non-socialist parties in Germany at the time.

More details on the problems of coalition governments are in Chapter 4, pages 26–27

ACTIVITY

Divide the class into pairs. Each pair should consider their answers to the following questions and then report their conclusions to the rest of the class:
1. Which were the **most** democratic features of the Weimar Constitution?
2. Which were the **least** democratic features of the constitution?

President – Head of State

- Elected every seven years by men and women over the age of 20
- Appointed and dismissed ministers and could dissolve the Reichstag and call new elections
- Supreme commander of the armed forces
- Had reserve powers (Article 48) to rule by decree in an emergency without the Reichstag's consent (see page 10)

Appoints

Chancellor

- Had to have the support of at least half the Reichstag
- Proposed new laws to the Reichstag

Provides advice

Needs 50% majority before appointed

Drafts laws for the Reichstag to debate

The Reichsrat

- The second chamber of the German parliament, made up of 67 representatives from the separate 17 states (**Länder**)
- Each state represented in proportion to its population, but no state to have more than 40 per cent of the seats (to prevent domination by the largest state, Prussia)
- Could provide advice on laws but could be overridden by the Reichstag

Individual voter's rights

- Vote for local state assembly every four years and for the President every seven years
- Vote occasionally on important issues
- 'All Germans are equal before the law'
- Guaranteed the freedoms of speech, of conscience and of travel
- Guaranteed the right to belong to trade unions, political parties and other forms of organisation
- Guaranteed the right to work and employees were given equal rights with employers to determine working conditions and wages
- Had the responsibility to use their intellectual and physical powers in the interests of the community

The Reichstag

- Elected every four years by all Germans over 20 using proportional representation
- The Chancellor and ministers were responsible to the Reichstag
- Voted on the budget; new laws had to originate in the Reichstag and required the approval of a majority of Reichstag deputies

Other features

- There was a supreme court, independent of the Reichstag and the President
- The Republic had a federal system whereby there were separate state governments in the 17 Länder which kept control over their own internal affairs

Fig. 5 *The constitution of the German Republic*

Länder: the 17 local states of Germany

Before unification in 1871, Germany consisted of separate states of varying sizes. After unification, these were incorporated into the German Reich but local traditions and loyalties remained strong. Each state (Land) retained control over some functions of government. In the Weimar Constitution, the states retained their powers over the police, education, religion and social welfare.

Autocracy: a system of government in which power is concentrated in the hands of one person

Hans von Seeckt (1886–1936) was a career soldier who had been placed in charge of the German forces in East Prussia at the end of the war. He was a member of the German delegation to Versailles and was appointed head of the Truppenamt ('troop office'), which replaced the forbidden army general staff. He became Commander of the Reichswehr (army) from 1920. He was instrumental in disbanding the Freikorps units. Under his command from 1920 to 1926, the army became a privileged elite beyond accountability.

See page 28 in Chapter 4 for more on the volunteer Freikorps units.

Rule by presidential decree

Article 48 of the constitution gave the President the power to rule by decree in exceptional circumstances. The granting of such powers was not remarkable in itself – indeed, all democratic constitutions allow for an executive authority to use exceptional powers in a time of national emergency. It was not anticipated by those who wrote the constitution, however, that these powers might be used on a regular basis. Ebert, the first President, used Article 48 powers on 136 occasions. Some of these occasions could be deemed to be genuine emergencies but Ebert also used his power in non-emergency situations when he simply wanted to override opposition in the Reichstag. There were no effective safeguards since a president could threaten to dissolve the Reichstag and call new elections if it refused to agree to a presidential decree. It is ironic that Ebert, who had been a leading voice for the cause of parliamentary democracy in the 1918–19 revolutionary upheavals, should, as President, undermine democracy through his overuse of Article 48.

The survival of undemocratic institutions

In the Second Empire, the army, the civil service and the judiciary were key pillars of the regime. Army officers, senior civil servants and judges were recruited from the aristocracy, supported the **autocracy** and looked with disdain on democratic politicians. They would not, therefore, fit easily into the new democratic republic. An opportunity existed for the architects of the new constitution to reform these institutions but, because they placed the need for stability above the desire for a thoroughly democratic system of government, they did not do so.

- **The army:** It had been largely free from political control in the Second Empire and its leaders were determined to preserve as much independence as they could in the Weimar Republic. The officer corps of the army in the Second Empire was allowed to continue intact into the new republic with the result that the army was far from being politically neutral. The full force of military power would be used against left-wing revolts whilst conspirators from the Right were often supported by elements within the army. General **Hans von Seeckt**, who was appointed Commander-in-Chief of the army in 1920, believed that the army owed loyalty not to the Republic, which he regarded as merely temporary, but to a timeless Reich that was the true expression of German nationhood. Although he would not allow his officers to meddle in politics on their own initiative, he nevertheless believed that the army as a whole, and under his command, could intervene in politics whenever he saw fit.

- **The civil service:** Under the Weimar Constitution, civil servants were given a guarantee of their 'well-earned rights' and of their freedom of political opinion and expression as long as this did not conflict with their duty of loyalty to the state. This meant that government administration in the new republic was left in the hands of those who were anti-democratic in their outlook. Senior civil servants, especially in the German Foreign Office, were still recruited overwhelmingly from the aristocracy. Top civil servants could wield enormous power, especially when ministers in coalition governments were frequently changing.

- **The judiciary:** Article 102 of the constitution guaranteed the independence of the judges. This would be a basic requirement in any democratic constitution but in Weimar Germany the judges who had served the Second Empire remained in their posts. These men were staunchly monarchist and anti-democratic and showed their bias in their legal judgements. The penal code of the Republic stipulated that anyone attempting to overthrow the constitution by force should be sentenced to life imprisonment. Members of left-wing groups who were brought before the courts were punished with great severity. Right-wing conspirators, on the other hand, were treated very leniently.

ACTIVITY

Review the terms of, and comments on, the constitution in this chapter. Copy and complete the table below.

Aspects of the constitution	Strengths	Weaknesses
The powers of the President		
The voters and the system of elections		
Other aspects		

Summary

The defeat of Germany in the First World War brought about the abdication of the Kaiser and the emergence, after a period of conflict and instability, of a new democratic republic. Henceforth, Germany was to be governed by a President and Reichstag, both of which were elected under one of the most democratic electoral systems in Europe at the time. But the circumstances under which the new republic was created left a legacy of bitterness and distrust that was to cause problems for Germany's new rulers for years to come. On the one hand, those on the left who had fought for a more radical change to Germany's political, social and economic structures were disappointed and felt betrayed. Key centres of power in Germany – the landowners, the officer corps, the civil service and judiciary, and the owners of big businesses – were largely untouched and unreformed. On the other hand, these supporters of the Kaiser blamed the leaders of the November revolution for the humiliation of military defeat and for the illegal overthrow of the monarchy. In the eyes of the right, the German army had not been defeated on the battlefield in 1918 but had been 'stabbed in the back' by the revolution in Berlin. For them the Republic, which owed its existence to that revolution, was illegitimate and deserved to be overthrown. As the historian William Carr has written, 'The Republic was accepted by many Germans not as a superior form of government but as a convenient means of filling the void left by the collapse of the monarchy'.

 PRACTICE QUESTION

'The Weimar constitution was not democratic nor did it provide the basis for stable government.'
Assess the validity of this view.

STUDY TIP

When faced with this type of question, you should challenge the quotation, but you should also look for points of agreement. You will need to examine the strengths and weaknesses of the constitution, identifying both the democratic and the non-democratic elements in it. You will also need to assess whether the constitution was designed to enable stable governments to be formed. Both elements are important, and try to link them if you can.

2 The Impact of the Versailles Settlement on Germany

LEARNING OBJECTIVES

In this chapter you will learn about:

- Germany's expectations of the terms of the Peace Treaty of Versailles, and the reality
- the terms and problems of the Treaty
- attitudes to the Treaty within Germany and abroad.

Fig. 1 *German delegates signed the Treaty of Versailles in the Hall of Mirrors in 1919*

KEY TERM

Diktat: an order or decree imposed by someone in power without popular consent

KEY CHRONOLOGY

1918	**11 November** Armistice agreement to end the fighting on the Western Front
1919	**18 January** Peace Conference convened at Palace of Versailles
7 May	German delegates given document containing first draft terms of the treaty
16 June	Germans given seven days to sign the treaty
20 June	Coalition cabinet collapsed because of divisions over signing treaty
22 June	Reichstag voted to accept the treaty
28 June	German delegates signed the Treaty of Versailles

The Peace Settlement of Versailles, 1919

SOURCE 1

The German delegates to the Versailles Peace Conference expressed their opposition in May 1919 to the terms of the treaty in a letter to the Allies:

We came to Versailles in the expectation of receiving a peace proposal based on the agreed principles. We were firmly resolved to do everything in our power with a view of fulfilling the grave obligations which we had undertaken. We hoped for the peace of justice which had been promised to us. We were aghast when we read the demands made upon us, the victorious violence of our enemies. The more deeply we penetrate into the spirit of this treaty, the more convinced we become of the impossibility of carrying it out. The exactions of this treaty are more than the German people can bear.

ACTIVITY

With reference to Source 1, summarise the main German objections to the Treaty of Versailles.

The war had ended with the armistice agreement on 11 November 1918. Although Germany was on the brink of defeat, the armistice was not a surrender. It was an agreement to stop fighting and withdraw German forces from occupied territory, pending a full peace settlement. A conference to settle the peace terms between the Allied powers and Germany met at the Palace of Versailles, outside Paris, in January 1919. The Germans were not invited to attend or allowed to see the terms of the treaty until 7 May. The German government suggested changes to the treaty but the **Allies** agreed to very few and, on 16 June, gave the German government seven days to accept the treaty. This provoked a political crisis in Berlin and led to the formation of a new coalition government. Finally, on 28 June, the Versailles Treaty was signed by all the powers. It imposed much harsher conditions on Germany than most Germans had expected or were prepared to accept. Moreover, because Germany had not been allowed to participate in the conference or to negotiate over the terms, the treaty was regarded by Germans of all political viewpoints as a *Diktat* or dictated peace. Hatred of the treaty, and of the politicians who had signed it, would continue to cause political divisions throughout the life of the Weimar Republic.

A CLOSER LOOK

The Allies at Versailles

The Paris Peace Conference opened on 12 January 1919 and meetings were held at various locations in and around Paris. Leaders representing about 75 per cent of the world's population attended but the defeated powers were excluded and all the major decisions were taken by the four most influential leaders: US President Woodrow Wilson, British Prime Minister David Lloyd George, French Prime Minister and conference chairman Georges Clemenceau and Italian Prime Minister Vittorio Orlando.

The terms of the treaty

Territorial losses: The treaty removed over 70,000 km^2 (13 per cent) of German territory and all Germany's overseas colonies: Alsace-Lorraine was returned to France; Eupen and Malmedy were given to Belgium; Northern Schleswig-Holstein was given to Denmark; Most of Posen, West Prussia and part of Pomerania (the Polish Corridor) were given to Poland; Danzig, a city with a majority German population, became a free state under League of Nations protection; Memel was taken by Lithuania; Eastern Silesia was given to Poland, although Western Silesia voted to remain part of Germany. This all meant that Germany lost 75 per cent of its iron ore, 68 per cent of its zinc ore, 26 per cent of its coal and 15 per cent of its arable land. All of Germany's overseas colonies in Africa and the Far East were placed under League of Nation's control (in practice, divided between the Allies).

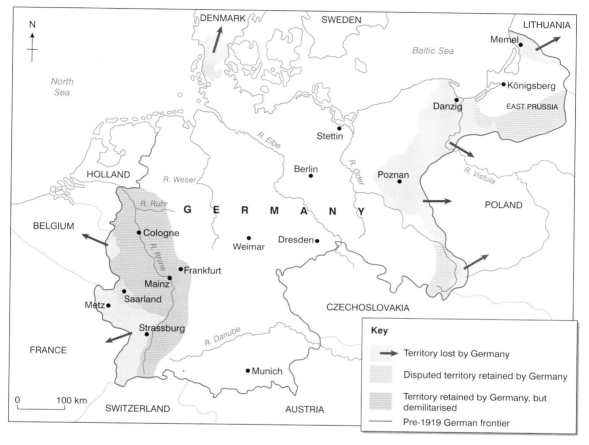

Disarmament of Germany: Germany had to surrender all heavy weapons and dismantle fortifications in the Rhineland and on the island of Heligoland. Conscription to the German armed forces was forbidden and the German army was limited to a maximum of 100,000 men. The German army was forbidden to use tanks or gas. The German navy was limited to 15,000 men. The navy was allowed a maximum of six battleships but no submarines and a small number of coastal defence vessels. Germany was forbidden from having an air force.

War guilt: Under Article 231 of the treaty, Germany had to accept responsibility for starting the war. This 'war guilt clause' made Germany liable to pay reparations to the Allies to cover the costs of damage suffered in the war. The final amount of reparations was fixed by a commission in 1921 at £6.6 billion; Germany also had to hand over to the Allies most of its merchant shipping fleet, railway locomotives and rolling stock, patents and overseas investments.

The Rhineland: The left bank of the Rhine (western side) and a 50 km strip on the right bank (eastern side) was permanently demilitarised. An Allied army of occupation was based in the Rhineland to ensure Germany fulfilled its treaty obligations.

The Saarland: This area of south-western Germany, which contained rich reserves of coal, was separated from Germany and placed under League of Nation's control for 15 years, so Germany would supply France, Belgium and Italy with free coal as part of the reparations agreement. France was allowed to exploit coal mines in the area.

Other terms of the treaty: Austria was forbidden from uniting with Germany; Germany was not allowed to join the new League of Nations; The Kaiser and other Germans were to be put on trial for war crimes.

Fig. 2   *The terms of the Treaty of Versailles*

Fig. 3 *German military aircraft being dismantled and scrapped; the German air force was destroyed in 1919 according to the Versailles Treaty terms*

German reactions to the treaty

The terms of the treaty, and the decision by the government to sign it, was greeted with horror and disbelief by the majority of Germans. Until 1914, Germany had been one of the greatest military powers in Europe. For much of the war, and especially in the early months of 1918, victory in the war seemed to be only a matter of time. This, at least, was the way Germany's war effort was portrayed in official propaganda, even after the Allies began to force the German army to retreat, after halting its advance in France in the spring of 1918. Neither ordinary soldiers nor the civilian population were told how desperate Germany's military situation on the Western Front had become by the autumn of 1918. Despite the hardship caused by the Allied blockade, support for the war effort was still very strong. The abdication of the Kaiser and subsequent signing of the armistice, therefore, came as a profound shock to millions of Germans. When followed by the signing of a humiliating and 'dictated' peace treaty, there was almost universal resentment at the harsh terms and few Germans would accept moral responsibility for fulfilling the terms of the treaty.

German objections to the treaty focused, in particular, on a number of its provisions:

- Whilst Wilson's Fourteen Points stressed the importance of the right of **national self-determination** as a basis for a just peace, this right was denied to the Germans themselves. Millions of people who spoke German and considered themselves to be German were now living in non-German states such as Czechoslovakia and Poland. The separation of East Prussia from the rest of Germany by the so-called Polish Corridor was a major source of resentment.
- The 'war guilt clause' was seen as an unjust national humiliation since Germans believed they had been forced into a just war against the Allies, who had attempted to encircle Germany.
- **Reparations** were a major cause of anger, partly because Germans felt that the level was too high and would cripple the German economy, and they did not accept the 'war guilt clause', which justified the reparations.
- Allied occupation of parts of western Germany, and French control of the Saarland coal mines, led to continuing friction. German nationalists were outraged by the outlawing of nationalist groups and banning of German patriotic songs and festivals in areas under French control.
- The disarming of Germany and its exclusion from the League of Nations were seen as unjust discrimination against a proud and once-powerful nation.

CROSS-REFERENCE

See Chapter 1, page 1 for the potential obstacles to Wilson's Fourteen Points.

KEY TERM

National self-determination: nations being able to decide whether they govern themselves, independent of larger empires or groupings of nations

STUDY TIP

This type of question requires a balanced response. There is plenty to agree with in the quotation, as the new German government entered into peace negotiations from a position of weakness but expected the Treaty to reflect Wilson's Fourteen Points, forgetting that France and Britain would demand a much harsher peace settlement. Much of Germany's reaction to the treaty was motivated by the belief that Germany had not been defeated and therefore did not anticipate that Germany would be severely punished. The key points of the treaty which were resented by all Germans were the war guilt clause, the scale of reparations, and the loss of territory, especially that lost to Poland in the east – which left millions of Germans living in Poland.

 AS LEVEL PRACTICE QUESTION

'German horror at the terms of the Treaty of Versailles was the result of unrealistic expectations'.
Explain why you agree or disagree with this view.

How justified were German complaints about the Treaty of Versailles?

It is possible to sympathise with the German reaction, but in some ways it was based on unrealistic expectations:

- Wilson's Fourteen Points and the armistice agreement had made it clear that Alsace-Lorraine would have to be returned to France, that a new state of Poland with access to the sea would be created, that Germany would be expected to hand over some of her assets and that considerable German disarmament would be expected.
- The treaty was not as severe as it might have been. Had Clemenceau had his way, he would have extended the French border to the Rhine, or annexed the Saar coalfields and created an independent Rhineland. The French wanted to ensure that Germany could not threaten them again, but the other Allies resisted this as they wanted Germany to remain strong enough to withstand the spread of communism from Russia.
- The treaty did not punish Germany as severely as the Germans had punished Russia in the Treaty of Brest-Litovsk in March 1918. Then, Germany had broken up the western part of the Russian Empire and annexed large swathes of territory. In the Reichstag debate on that treaty, only the USPD had voted against this action.
- Germany's war aims of 1914 had included the annexation of territory from its enemies, the expansion of Germany's colonial empire and a very severe reparations bill to be paid by the defeated Allies. In other words, if Germany had won the war, the peace settlement would have been very harsh on the defeated Allies.
- The reparations bill was much lower than demanded by the French. Although reparations were a continuing source of friction between Germany and the Allies during the life of the Weimar Republic, it was not beyond Germany's capacity to pay.

Reparations: the compensation for war damage paid by a defeated state

Class debate

Work in four groups, representing Britain, France, the USA and Germany. Each group should research what their country wanted from the Treaty of Versailles and how far it would have been satisfied by the final terms. Each group should then present its findings to the class.

The political impact of the Versailles Treaty in Germany

The political crisis of June 1919

A conservative DNVP deputy, speaking in the Reichstag debate on the treaty, expressed his party's opposition to the Versailles Treaty:

Our Fatherland finds itself in the most difficult hour of its history. We in our party are aware of the results for our people which a rejection of the peace treaty will entail. The resulting harm, however, will only be temporary, but if we accept this treaty we will abandon countless generations of our people to misery. For us, the acceptance of the treaty is impossible for many reasons. In addition to making Germany defenceless, there is also the matter of the theft of our territory.

With reference to Source 2, explain the main reasons why this deputy was opposed to the Versailles Treaty.

When the harsh terms of the treaty were revealed to the German government in May 1919, ministers from all parties shared Chancellor Scheidemann's view that accepting it would be incompatible with German honour. At that stage, however, it seemed possible to negotiate some amendments to the treaty. In the event, the rejection of German requests for extensive changes and the

Fig. 4   *Gustav Bauer*

Gustav Bauer (1870–1944) had been a trade union official before he entered the Reichstag as an SPD deputy in 1912. In the political upheaval of 1918–19 he was appointed as Minister of Labour in the cabinets of Prince Max, Ebert and Scheidemann. After Scheidemann resigned in June 1920, Bauer became Chancellor, but he was forced to resign in March 1920 after the Kapp Putsch. He continued to serve as a minister and a Reichstag deputy for several more years.

CROSS-REFERENCES

To remember who Hindenburg was, you can return to his profile in the introduction of this book, page XIII.

The policy of fulfillment is discussed further in chapter 8, page 60.

The Kapp Putsch was a coup attempt in March 1920 aimed at overthrowing the Weimar Republic. Turn to Chapter 4, page 29, to find out what happened.

demand for acceptance of the treaty within seven days caused a political crisis in Germany. Scheidemann and some of his ministers wanted to reject the treaty, whereas the majority of the cabinet and of the SPD members of the Reichstag believed that Germany had no other choice but to sign the treaty. Scheidemann resigned and a new coalition cabinet, led by **Gustav Bauer**, was formed. Meanwhile, some high-ranking officers in the German army, with the tacit support of Field Marshal Paul von Hindenburg, were discussing the possibility of resisting the signing of the treaty through renewed military action. President Ebert told General Groener that he would support rejection of the treaty if there was any chance that military action could be successful. Groener was a realist. He informed Ebert that military resistance would be futile and Germany had no alternative but to accept the treaty. The Bauer cabinet bowed to the inevitable and signed the treaty.

The reaction of pro-republican parties

The divisions over the signing of the Versailles Treaty continued to dominate German political life throughout the years of the Weimar Republic. The SPD and its allies in government in 1919 were well aware that signing it would rebound upon them. Indeed, they were so concerned that they asked their main opponents in the DNVP, DVP and DDP to state that those who had voted for the treaty were not being unpatriotic. They also took the view that the most sensible course of action in the coming years was to outwardly comply with the terms of the treaty whilst negotiating modifications to it. This became known as the policy of fulfilment.

Even more importantly, however, the treaty turned some (even former supporters) against the Weimar Republic. Its real damage was in alienating moderates who had been happy to accept the new constitution and its promises of a 'better' Germany, but who could not stomach politicians who appeared to have betrayed an unbeaten country. The treaty caused political demoralisation at the very centre of government, associating the Republic once again with weakness and failure. The politicians who agreed to it were forced to become defensive. To the public at large, the gains of the revolution seemed unimpressive.

Reaction on the Right

Right-wing resentment of the Republic was intensified by the signing of the Versailles Treaty. German nationalists could not accept the fact of Germany's military defeat, nor the establishment of the new republic. The signing of the peace settlement was the final straw and led many to join groups committed to overthrowing the Republic. In the eyes of extreme nationalists, the politicians who now governed Germany lacked any legitimacy because they had betrayed the 'Fatherland' several times – in the dethroning of the Kaiser, the signing of the armistice and the acceptance of the Versailles Treaty. These politicians became labelled the 'November Criminals' and their actions of 'betrayal' were referred to as 'the stab in the back'. The German army bore no responsibility for the defeat of 1918. The fact that Ludendorff had advised the Kaiser in late-September 1918 that the army was on the verge of defeat was conveniently forgotten. Indeed, Ludendorff had advised the Kaiser to appoint a new civilian-led government in the hope that better peace terms would be secured and that the high command would avoid responsibility for the defeat and signing of the armistice. It was Ludendorff, and his superior von Hindenburg, who actively promoted the 'stab in the back' myth. This myth was the justification for continued nationalist attacks on the Republic, its political supporters and on the treaty. It was particularly appealing to ex-soldiers who had suffered in fighting for what they regarded as a noble cause and had then experienced insults and humiliation when they returned to a Germany in the throes of revolution.

SOURCE 3

Field-Marshal Hindenburg gave his view of who was responsible for the defeat and humiliation of Germany, at a commission into defeat in November 1919:

Our repeated requests to the government for strict discipline were never met. Thus our operations were bound to fail. The revolution was only the last straw. An English general said with justice: 'The German army was stabbed in the back.' No guilt applies to the good core of the army. Its achievements are just as admirable as those of the officer corps. Where the guilt lies has clearly been demonstrated. If it needed more proof, then it would be found in the quoted statement of the English general and in the boundless astonishment of our enemies at their victory.

Not all the soldiers who returned to Germany in the wake of the defeat were hostile to the new republic. Many working-class soldiers, who had previously been members of trade unions and supported the SPD, supported the new democratic system. Others gravitated towards the communists. Many, however, could not adjust to civilian life, especially as they had great difficulty in finding employment and yearned for the comradeship and sense of purpose that the war years had given them. These men gravitated towards the **Freikorps** and right-wing nationalist groups. As a result, in the early years of the Weimar Republic, democratic politics was under continuous threat from violent nationalist groups.

SOURCE 4

One German soldier recalled his experiences on returning to Germany in November 1918:

On 15 November 1918 I was on my way from the hospital at Bad Neuheim to my garrison at Brandenburg. As I was limping along with the aid of my cane at the Potsdam station in Berlin, a group of uniformed men, sporting red armbands, stopped me, and demanded that I surrender my epaulettes and insignia [i.e. military badges of rank]. I raised my stick in reply, but my rebellion was soon overcome. I was thrown down and only the intervention of a railway official saved me from my humiliating position. Hate flamed in me against the November Criminals from that moment. As soon as my health improved somewhat, I joined forces with the groups devoted to the overthrow of the rebellion.

 PRACTICE QUESTION

Evaluating primary sources

Look back at Sources 2, 3 and 4. In what ways would these sources be of value to an historian studying right-wing political views in the Weimar Republic?

Reactions from abroad

The Allies who drew up and imposed the treaty on Germany had varying reactions to the treaty.

Britain

When Prime Minster Lloyd George returned to London after the signing of the treaty, he was given a rapturous reception from a large crowd. On the

---

ACTIVITY

Evaluating primary sources

1. What is the value of Source 3 for understanding Hindenburg's motives for claiming that the German army was 'stabbed in the back'?

2. Read Source 4 in this chapter, followed by Source 1 in Chapter 1. Which source do you think is of most value for studying the experiences of soldiers returning to Germany at the end of the war?

CROSS-REFERENCE

The instability and violence of the early years of the Weimar Republic are explored in more detail in Chapter 4.

Read A Closer Look on page 28 of Chapter 4 for more detail on the Freikorps.

STUDY TIP

The three sources come from different social perspectives among the right wing. Source 2 gives an insight into the views of conservative politicians in the Reichstag, Source 3 is a statement from Hindenburg and Source 4 comes from an ordinary soldier. Sources 3 and 4 reflect the feelings on the right about the politicians who took power in November 1918, that they stabbed the army in the back and were the so-called 'November Criminals'. Taken together, the three sources are valuable for building up an understanding of why the nationalist right hated the Republic, but be aware that the narrowness of these perspectives may limit their value.

whole, British public opinion was satisfied that Germany had lost its overseas empire, along with its large fleet, and would be unable to threaten European peace for a generation. Privately, however, Lloyd George believed that Germany should not be so weak that it would be unable to resist the expansion of the USSR westwards, and he wanted Germany to become a strong trading partner with Britain again. Many in Britain saw the French as being greedy and vindictive and there was a growing feeling in Britain that Germany had been unfairly treated at Versailles. One influential view was put forward by the economist, John Maynard Keynes, who argued that the level of reparations was too high. He believed that the level of reparations 'was one of the most serious acts of political unwisdom for which our statesmen have ever been responsible.'

France

The French felt they had suffered the most out of all the combatant nations and they were determined to seek revenge at Versailles. The recovery of Alsace-Lorraine, the demilitarisation of the Rhineland and the payment of reparations were key French demands which had been met. Despite this, there were many in France who regarded the treaty as being too lenient on Germany, and Prime Minister Clemenceau, who was blamed for making too many concessions, was defeated at the next election in 1920. Marshal Foch, the wartime military commander, expressed a widely held view in France when he said, 'This is not peace. It is an armistice for twenty years.'

The United States

Reactions to the Treaty in America were generally negative. There was a widespread opinion that the treaty had been unfair on Germany and that Britain and France had used the treaty to enrich themselves at Germany's expense. The Republicans in the American Congress opposed the treaty and Wilson failed to win the Congressional vote to ratify the treaty, leaving the USA to make a separate peace with Germany in 1921. The USA refused to join the League of Nations and, in the 1920s, retreated from involvement in European affairs.

Summary

The Treaty of Versailles stripped Germany of land, people, resources and military power. Although Germany might have suffered even greater losses if the demands of the French Prime Minister Clemenceau had been accepted by the other Allies, the German people viewed the treaty in wholly negative terms. Its signing by Bauer's socialist-led government in June 1919 was viewed by many as an act of national betrayal. The circumstances in which the new republic had been founded in November 1918 prompted many Germans to reject its legitimacy, despite the democratic process that later led to the drawing up of the Weimar Constitution. For German nationalists the new republic – and, in particular, the socialist politicians who had taken the lead in its foundation – was permanently tainted by its association with betrayal and the humiliation of an unjust and dictated peace.

3 Economic and social problems in Germany, 1919–24

SOURCE 1

The left-wing German artist **George Grosz** recalled his experience of shopping during the hyperinflation crisis of 1923:

Lingering at shop windows was a luxury because shopping had to be done immediately. Even an additional minute could mean an increase in price. One had to buy quickly. A rabbit, for example, might cost two million marks more by the time it took you to walk into the store. A few million marks meant nothing, really. It was just that it meant more lugging. The packages of money needed to buy the smallest item had long since become too heavy for trouser pockets. They weighed many pounds. People had to start carting their money around in wagons and knapsacks. I used a knapsack.

LEARNING OBJECTIVES

In this chapter you will learn about:

- the impact of the war on Germany's finances
- how reparations affected the German economy
- inflation and the hyperinflation crisis of 1923
- the invasion of the Ruhr and its economic impact
- social welfare and the social impact of hyperinflation.

In the aftermath of defeat, revolution and the imposed peace settlement of Versailles, Germany experienced severe economic difficulties. These problems culminated in a hyperinflation crisis, which gripped the country for much of 1923. The origins of this crisis and its effects are explored in this chapter.

Financial problems in the aftermath of the war

Germany's defeat plunged the finances of the state into crisis. For all the countries involved, the war effort required unprecedented levels of government spending. In Britain, this was financed through a combination of higher taxes and government borrowing. In Germany, however, wartime governments chose to finance the war through increased borrowing and by printing more money. This meant that government debt grew and the value of the currency fell. This highly risky strategy was based on a simple but flawed calculation – that Germany would win the war and would be able to recoup its losses by annexing the industrial areas of its defeated enemies and forcing them to pay heavy financial reparations. Defeat for Germany not only deprived the country of this repayment method, but also imposed a heavy burden of reparations and the loss of some industrial areas.

In 1919, the new government of the Weimar Republic was faced with a debt of 1.44 billion marks. In situations where the national debt needs to be reduced, governments can either raise taxes or reduce spending, or they can do both. In the context of the political instability of the early years of the Weimar Republic, both of these policies carried serious risks. A rise in taxation would risk alienating support for the new republic as anti-republican parties would be able to claim that taxes were being raised to pay reparations to the Allies. It was also very difficult for governments to reduce spending. Although military expenditure was dramatically reduced, there were civil servants to be paid. Support for the new republic was considered to be so fragile that successive governments avoided making civil servants redundant and even extended welfare benefits.

Given the severe political difficulties Germany faced in the immediate aftermath of war, it is hardly surprising that the governments of the Weimar Republic did not try to address economic issues with unpopular measures such as raising taxes or cutting spending. Although national debt was high, unemployment had virtually disappeared by 1921 and there was a rapid

Fig. 1 *During the hyperinflation crisis German currency became so worthless that children played with the stacks of money*

KEY PROFILE

Konstantin Fehrenbach (1852–1926) was a leading member of the Centre Party and was President (speaker) of the Reichstag in 1919–20. He became Chancellor in 1920, leading the first cabinet in the new republic that did not include the SPD (German Social Democratic Party).

CROSS-REFERENCES

Read Chapter 4 to find out more about the SPD.

The hyperinflation of 1923 is explained later in this chapter on page 21.

KEY PROFILE

Joseph Wirth (1879–1956) was a schoolteacher by profession but entered politics as a member of the Centre Party. He became Minister of Finance in 1920 before becoming Chancellor in 1921.

recovery in economic activity. In many ways, the German economy coped with the transition from war to peace much more successfully than other European economies. However, allowing inflation to continue unchecked was a policy fraught with danger. Prices, which had doubled between 1918 and 1919, had quadrupled again between 1919 and 1920, reaching a point 14 times higher than in 1913. The reason why governments allowed this to happen was partly political. The 1920 coalition, led by **Konstantin Fehrenbach**, was dominated by the Centre Party which was supported by many powerful German industrialists. They were benefiting from inflation by taking short-term loans from Germany's central bank to expand their businesses. By the time the loans were due for repayment, their real value had been significantly reduced by inflation. Furthermore, inflation had the effect of lessening the government's burden of debt (although the reparations themselves were not affected because these were paid in gold marks or goods) and it is often suggested that German politicians had a vested interest in allowing it to continue unchecked.

In some ways, therefore, inflation was beneficial. By 1921, unemployment in Germany was only 1.8 per cent compared with nearly 17 per cent in Great Britain. This in turn encouraged investment, especially from the USA. However, left unchecked, inflation eventually became uncontrollable and, by 1923, Germany's high inflation became hyperinflation.

 PRACTICE QUESTION

'The economic policies of German governments in the years 1919–22 successfully managed the transition from wartime to peacetime conditions'. Explain why you agree and disagree with this view.

The impact of reparations

The political impact of reparations

The Treaty of Versailles included the requirement that Germany would have to pay reparations, in both cash and goods, but it had not fixed the actual amount. A Reparations Commission was set up to determine the scale of the damage caused by the German armed forces in Allied countries. The Reparations Commission's report concluded that Germany should pay 132 billion gold marks, or £6.6 billion, to be paid in annual instalments. When the report was presented to the German government in 1921, with the ultimatum to accept the terms within six days, it caused a political crisis in Germany. The cabinet of Fehrenbach resigned in protest at what it considered to be excessively harsh terms and was replaced by another led by **Chancellor Joseph Wirth**. Just as in 1919, with the Allied ultimatum to Germany to sign the Versailles Treaty, there was no alternative to acceptance and the new government signed unwillingly. Germany made its first payment soon after. This was the start of the German policy of fulfilment of the Treaty of Versailles under which successive German governments calculated that cooperation would win sympathy from the Allies and a revision in the terms once it became clear that full payment of the reparations was beyond Germany's capacity.

This, however, was far from being a final settlement of the reparations issue. By January 1922 Germany was in such economic difficulties that the Reparations Commission granted a postponement of the January and February instalments. In July, the German government asked for a further suspension of the payments due that year. In November 1922, it asked for a loan of 500 million gold marks and to be released from its obligations for three to four years in order to stabilise its currency. The French were deeply suspicious that this was simply an excuse and refused to agree to Germany's requests. This dispute set the scene for a major clash over reparations in 1923, during which French and Belgian forces occupied the Ruhr industrial area of western Germany in an attempt to extract payment by force.

The economic impact of reparations

The burden of reparations undoubtedly made a bad situation much worse. Reparations payments made repayment of the huge government debt resulting from the war even more difficult. In addition, Germany's gold reserves were inadequate for the scale of the reparations payments that had to be made in gold. Another part of the reparations payments had to be made in coal, but Germany had lost a large part of its coal reserves in the Versailles Treaty. A further possible method of payment was in manufactured goods, but workers and manufacturers in the Allied countries would not agree to this as they regarded it as a threat to their jobs and businesses. Germany might have been able to increase its reserves of foreign currency, in order to make the payments, by increasing its exports to other nations. However, the Allies hampered Germany's export trade by confiscating its entire merchant fleet and, later, by imposing high tariffs on imports of German goods. The Allies were forcing Germany to pay reparations, but making it difficult for Germany to find the money to do so. The response of the German government was to print more money, thereby making inflation even worse and making the value of the mark fall even further.

A CLOSER LOOK

The reparations issue

The English economist John Maynard Keynes was highly critical of the Allied demand for £6.6 billion in reparations. He calculated that £2 billion was a 'safe maximum figure of Germany's capacity to pay' and he predicted that the burden of reparations would not only damage the German economy but also the economies of Allied countries, since it would hamper economic recovery across the continent. However, the modern historian Peukert (1991) has argued that the final figure for reparations was actually quite manageable for Germany since it amounted to only 2 per cent of its gross national product. His view is that the effects of reparations have been exaggerated. It is certainly the case that German governments in the immediate post-war years allowed inflation to spiral since it suited their foreign policy objectives. They could use the rapid decline in the value of the German currency to support their case that reparations should either be abolished altogether or, at least, reduced and rescheduled to give Germany more time to pay.

The hyperinflation crisis of 1923

The Franco-Belgian occupation of the Ruhr

By the end of 1922 Germany had fallen seriously behind in its payment of reparations to France in the form of coal. This prompted the French, together with the Belgians, to send a military force of 60,000 men to occupy **the Ruhr** industrial area in January 1923 in order to force the Germans to comply with the Treaty of Versailles. Their aim was to seize the area's coal, steel and manufactured goods as reparations. These troops occupied the whole Ruhr area and, in the course of 1923, the numbers of occupying forces grew to 100,000. They took control of all the mines, factories, steelworks and railways, demanded food from the shops and set up machine-gun posts in the streets.

CROSS-REFERENCES

The instability of German governments is dealt with in Chapter 4.

The policy of fulfilment is explained in Chapter 2, page 16. Its impact is discussed in more detail in Chapter 8, page 60.

ACTIVITY

Thinking point

'The Germans had a strong case to support their view that the scale of reparations was too high.' To what extent do you agree with this statement?

CROSS-REFERENCE

Germany had coalfields in the Saarland which had been placed under the League of Nation's control as part of the Treaty of Versailles. See Fig. 2 in Chapter 2, page 13, where this is discussed.

KEY TERM

The Ruhr: the heavily industrialised area of western Germany that includes the towns of Dusseldorf, Essen and Dortmund; at that time, it generated 85 per cent of German coal and also had many large iron and steel works and engineering factories

A British journalist, working for *The Times*, described the scene in Essen on 11 January 1923:

Essen was occupied this afternoon by two divisions of French troops headed by cavalry and armoured cars. Despite the machine-guns, the swords, and slung rifles of the cavalry, who came cantering down the street behind the armoured cars, there were angry murmurs from the crowd – many took no trouble to hide the hatred in their hearts. Near the station I saw a man of some 30 years suddenly turn aside with a sob and muttering 'The swine. My God, the pack of swine. May God pay them for this cruel outrage.' At the head of one cavalry squadron rode a French officer, a fine figure, with snow-white moustache, perfect seat in his saddle, and erect as a lance. The French looked straight before them, sparing no glance for the serried ranks of angry men. The French troops behaved with absolute correctness. As on a ceremonial parade these men in pale blue passed silently through the equally silent lanes of human beings. But the French rode as conquerors.

ACTIVITY

Evaluating primary sources

How valuable would Source 2 be to an historian studying the German reaction to the occupation of the Ruhr?

KEY TERM

Paramilitary: a group of civilians organised into a military style group with uniforms and ranks; such groups take on military functions

KEY PROFILE

Wilhelm Cuno (1876–1933) was a lawyer and businessman who had no party allegiance. Germany went through many changes of coalition cabinets during this period and Cuno was chosen as Chancellor because it was thought that his business experience would help him to steer Germany through these difficult economic times.

The government of **Chancellor Wilhelm Cuno** knew the Germans could not fight back. The Versailles Treaty had reduced the size of the German army and the Rhineland, of which the Ruhr was a part, was demilitarised. Instead, he responded by stopping all reparations payments and ordering a policy of 'passive resistance' whereby no one living in the area, from businessmen and postal workers to railwaymen and miners, would cooperate with the French authorities. German workers were promised by their government that their wages would continue if they went on strike while **paramilitary** troops working with the German army secretly organised acts of sabotage against the French. They crossed the customs barrier secretly at night and blew up railways, sank barges and destroyed bridges in order to disrupt the French effort.

The scale of the French operation grew in response. The French set up military courts and punished mine owners, miners and civil servants who would not comply with their authority. Around 150,000 Germans were expelled from the area. Worse still, some miners were shot after clashes with police. Altogether, 132 Germans were shot in the eight months of the occupation, including a seven-year-old boy. The French also brought in their own workers to operate the railways and get coal out of the Ruhr, but this did not prove particularly effective. In May 1923, deliveries were only a third of the average monthly deliveries in 1922 and output in the Ruhr had fallen to around a fifth of its pre-occupation output.

Fig. 2   *The French army occupied the Ruhr in Germany 1923 and used violence against Germans*

The economic effects of the occupation

The economic results of the occupation, and the policy of passive resistance, were catastrophic for the German economy for a number of reasons:

- Paying the wages or providing goods for striking workers was a further drain on government finances
- Tax revenue was lost from those whose businesses were closed and workers who became unemployed
- Germany had to import coal and pay for it from the limited foreign currency reserves within the country
- Shortage of goods pushed prices up further.

The combined cost of all of this amounted to twice the annual reparations payments. Since the government still refused to increase taxes, its only option was to print more money. This was the trigger for the hyperinflation that gripped Germany during the course of 1923.

The hyperinflation crisis

During the hyperinflation crisis, money lost its meaning as prices soared to unimaginable levels. Printing presses worked continuously to keep banks supplied with worthless paper money. Workers collected their wages and salaries in wheelbarrows and shopping baskets, and tried to spend their money immediately before prices rose even further. The rising prices for food had the most serious effects. Food began to run short as speculators hoarded supplies in anticipation of higher prices in the future. In many areas, this led to a breakdown in law and order. There were food riots when crowds looted shops. Gangs of city dwellers travelled to the countryside to take food from farms, but were confronted by angry farmers determined to protect their livelihoods. There was a large increase in the number of convictions for theft. People bartered their possessions in exchange for vital supplies.

Table 1 *Number of American dollars to one German mark*

July 1914	4.2
January 1919	8.9
January 1920	64.8
January 1923	17,972.0
July 1923	353,412.0
August 1923	4,620,455.0
September 1923	98,860,000.0
October 1923	25,260,208,000.0
15 November 1923	4,200,000,000,000.0

SOURCE 3

The historian Konrad Heiden, then a German student, described the situation during the hyperinflation crisis:

The printing presses of the government could no longer keep pace. You could see mail carriers on the streets with sacks on their backs or pushing prams before them, loaded with paper money that would be devalued the next day. Life was madness, nightmare, desperation, chaos. Communities printed their own money, based on goods, on a certain amount of potatoes, of rye, for instance. Shoe factories paid their workers in bonds which they could exchange at the bakery for bread or at the meat market for meat.

A CLOSER LOOK

The price of bread

Rye bread is one of the staples of the German diet. In January 1923, a kilo loaf cost 163 marks. By October, the price had soared to 9 million marks and, by 19 November, it had risen again to 233 billion marks.

Social welfare

Those involved in the revolution of November 1918 – the sailors, soldiers and workers who had helped to bring down the Kaiser – were motivated by a desire for a better and freer life. There were also very large numbers of people who needed support as a result of death or injury during the war. The challenge for those politicians who wrote the Weimar Constitution in 1919, and for those who served in later coalition governments, was to enshrine those aspirations into new legal rights. One of the key rights set out in the constitution was that every German citizen should have the right to work or to welfare. This led to a series of reforms to the welfare system and to employment rights.

1919	A law was passed limiting the working day to a maximum of eight hours
1919	The state health insurance system, introduced by Bismarck but limited to workers in employment, was extended to include wives, daughters and the disabled
1919	Aid for war veterans incapable of working because of injury became the responsibility of national government; aid for war widows and orphans was also increased
1922	National Youth Welfare Act required all local authorities to set up youth offices with responsibility for child protection and decreed that all children had the right to an education

However, the social welfare budget put a huge demand on the government. The printing of money was largely to pay out to welfare benefits that the Weimar Republic was committed to providing, which exacerbated the hyperinflation crisis.

The social impact of hyperinflation

Hyperinflation was not a disaster for everyone – there were winners as well as losers within the increasingly divided German Society.

Winners

The winners included people who had the means and the guile to speculate and manipulate the situation to their advantage.

- There were black-marketeers who bought up food stocks and sold them at vastly inflated prices.
- Those who had debts, mortgages and loans did well since they could pay off the money they owed in worthless currency.
- Hyperinflation also helped enterprising business people who took out new loans and repaid them once the currency had devalued further.
- Those leasing property on long-term fixed rents gained because the real value of the rents they were paying decreased.
- Owners of foreign exchange and foreigners living in Germany could also benefit.
- In the countryside, most farmers coped well since food was in demand and money was less important in rural communities.

Losers

Those relying on savings, investments, fixed income or welfare support lost out. Among these were students, the retired and the sick.

- Pensioners were particularly badly hit, including war widows living on state pensions.
- Those who had patriotically lent money to the government in wartime by purchasing fixed interest rate 'war bonds' also lost out because the interest payments decreased in value.
- Landlords reliant on fixed rents were hit badly.
- Of the workers, the unskilled and those who did not belong to trade unions fared the worst. Although workers were given wage increases, these did not keep up with rising prices, so standards of living declined. By 1923, there was also an increase in unemployment and short-time working; at the end of the year, only 29.3 per cent of the workforce was fully employed.
- Artisans and small business owners – the **Mittelstand** – were badly hit. Their costs rose and the prices they charged could not keep pace with inflation. They also paid a disproportionate share of taxes.
- The sick were very badly hit. The costs of medical care increased whilst the rapid rise in food prices led to widespread malnutrition. Death rates in large cities increased. The suicide rate also went up.

Fig. 3 *Hugo Stinnes became known as the 'king of the Ruhr'*

Hugo Stinnes – one of the winners

Hugo Stinnes was the owner of substantial businesses before 1923, owning the German-Luxemburg Mining Company and the Rhine-Westphalian Electric Company. He was also a deputy of the DVP (German People's Party) in the Reichstag. With his businesses providing security, and using his political contacts, he was able to raise large bank loans in 1923 and purchase whole forests to supply lumber to his mines. He went on to build an empire that included 150 newspapers and magazines, plus interests in railways, banks and more.

Mittelstand: 'middle rank'; a large but diverse social group including small farmers, small shopkeepers and artisans; without steady sources of income, they felt themselves to be vulnerable to inflation and tended to look to governments to protect their position

- Amongst children suffering from malnutrition, the incidence of diseases such as tuberculosis and rickets – both of which are associated with dietary deficiency – increased.

The effects of hyperinflation varied between different classes and geographic regions. Nevertheless it was an 'unreal' time, which left many people uncertain about what the future might hold. Many, but not all, middle-class people became impoverished as a result of hyperinflation and were left with a sense that they had lost the most. These people had grown up believing in hard work, thrift and saving for the future, only to find their savings wiped out and their comfortable lifestyles destroyed.

SOURCE 4

Phyllis Knight recollects her views on the German government and its handling of the 1923 hyperinflation in a 1973 memoir of her life:

Of course all the little people who had small savings were wiped out. But the big factories and banking houses and multimillionaires didn't seem to be affected at all. They went right on piling up their millions. Those big holdings were protected somehow from loss. But the mass of the people were completely broke. And we asked ourselves, 'How can that happen? How is it that the government can't control an inflation which wipes out the life savings of the mass of people – yet the big capitalists can come through the whole thing unscathed?' We who lived through it never got an answer that meant anything. But after that, even those people who used to save didn't trust money any more – or the government. We decided to have a high-ho time whenever we had any spare money, which wasn't often.

 PRACTICE QUESTION

Evaluating primary sources

How valuable would Sources 1, 3 and 4 be to an historian studying the impact of hyperinflation on the German people?

 PRACTICE QUESTION

'The Franco-Belgian invasion of the Ruhr was the main cause of the hyperinflation crisis in Germany in 1923.' Assess the validity of this view.

Summary

In the immediate post-war years, the German economy, in common with the economies of all the countries involved in the war, had to adjust from wartime to peacetime conditions. After such a long and damaging conflict, the transition was bound to be difficult. In some ways, German governments coped well with the change as unemployment was kept low in 1921–22 when other countries (in particular Great Britain) were experiencing a severe post-war depression. Nevertheless, the legacy of the war and defeat left Germany with a serious debt. On top of this, the large reparations payments demanded by the Allies added to Germany's economic difficulties. Price inflation, largely due to governments printing more and more money to close the gap between revenue and spending, was a constant feature of these post-war years. By 1923, however, inflation spiraled out of control and brought chaos to millions of Germans.

ACTIVITY

Draw up a balance sheet of winners and losers from hyperinflation. Discuss with a partner: In what ways did hyperinflation increase tensions in German society?

CROSS-REFERENCE

The political consequences of hyperinflation in 1923 are explored in more detail in Chapter 4.

STUDY TIP

All three sources give an insight into the impact of hyperinflation on the German people but in different ways. It is important that you show what an historian could learn from each of the three sources, and also their limitations, before coming to a judgement about their overall value by using knowledge and context.

STUDY TIP

This is a view that can be challenged but it is also possible to find points of agreement. There were many factors which contributed to the hyperinflation crisis, of which the invasion of the Ruhr was one. It would be useful to distinguish between long- and short-term factors. A good answer would identify the range of factors and support the analysis with carefully selected evidence, and it would also have a clear view which was made clear in the introduction, sustained through the essay and rounded off in the conclusion.

Political instability and extremism, 1919–24

LEARNING OBJECTIVES

In this chapter you will learn about:

- the problems of coalition government
- political instability and extremism; risings on the left and right, including the Kapp Putsch
- the political impact of the invasion of the Ruhr and the Munich Putsch
- the state of the Republic by 1924.

ACTIVITY

Evaluating primary sources

As an historian, what can we learn from Source 1 about the use of political violence in Germany in 1923?

Table 1 *The 1919 and 1920 Reichstag elections*

Party	Seats in January 1919	Seats in June 1920
USPD	22	83
SPD	163	103
DDP	75	39
Centre	91	64
DVP	19	65
DNVP	44	71
KPD	0	4

ACTIVITY

Study Table 1. Compare the results of the two elections:

1. What happened to the combined strength of the pro-republic – SPD, DDP, Centre – parties in the Reichstag?
2. What happened to the combined strength of the extreme left parties – USPD and KPD?
3. What happened to the combined strength of the extreme right parties – DVP and DNVP?
4. Overall, how had the political balance in the Reichstag changed between 1919 and 1920?

SOURCE 1

Agnes Smedley was an American journalist living in Bavaria in 1923. In this letter to a friend she reflected on political violence in Germany:

Here in Bavaria, I am in the stronghold of reaction. At night I am often awakened by the military commands and the march of men (monarchists) who are training at night in the forests. It is a gruesome feeling – this secret training of men to kill other men. And these men being trained are peasants and working-men – not the class we usually think of.

In Saxony the same thing occurs; there at night the men who are under training are also workingmen, but the leaders are communists. And they are preparing to kill their kind also. Sometimes I see no difference between the two. What is this business everywhere – men preparing to murder their own kind for the sake of an idea?

Not their own idea either, but that of men who use them as tools to set themselves in power. We only wait for the day when the two groups will start massacring each other. Both groups are bitterly opposed to passive resistance as a method; it isn't bloody or sadistic enough.

As we saw in Chapter 1, German society, in the aftermath of war, defeat and revolution, was deeply divided. Even after the new Weimar Republic was established in 1919, political violence continued and coalition governments were unstable.

The problems of coalition government

Before 1914 there were a wide array of political parties representing different religions, classes, regions and special interest groups. Since political parties in the Reichstag had no say in the choice of governments, this was not a major problem. In the Weimar Republic, however, the fragmentation of political parties was a matter of great importance since governments needed to command majority support in the Reichstag. With an electoral system based on proportional representation, no one party was ever in a position to form a government by itself and all governments, therefore, were coalitions.

The fragmentation of political parties became even more pronounced as German society became more divided. Moreover, many parties, both large and small, were dedicated to the overthrow of the Republic. This placed an even greater burden of responsibility on the moderate centre parties, such as the SPD, the Centre Party and the DDP, to work together to form stable coalitions. Although the party leaders understood the need for compromise, the country faced unprecedented problems which called for tough and unpalatable decisions, which placed severe strains on coalition governments. In June 1919, for example, the Scheidemann cabinet resigned because it could not agree on signing the Treaty of Versailles. Similarly disagreements in the Fehrenbach cabinet, over whether to accept the Allied ultimatum on reparations, brought it down in May 1921.

Another reason why it was difficult to form stable coalitions was that, in times of social, economic and political crisis, society became more polarised and support for the moderate parties ebbed away. The more extreme parties on the left and the right gained support. Since these parties would not join coalition governments, the task of forming a government with a Reichstag majority became even harder. This was evident after the1920 Reichstag election, as can be seen in Table 1.

The story of the first four years of the Weimar Republic was one of unstable governments and shifting coalitions. It is also a story of the changing fortunes of the SPD. Whereas in 1918–19 it was the SPD that had taken the lead in establishing the Republic and trying to form stable governments, after June 1920 the SPD ceased to take a leading role in any coalition government due to internal divisions and sometimes did not participate in the ruling coalition at all. This is summarised in Table 2 below.

CROSS-REFERENCE

Refer back to Chapter 1, page 8 to refresh yourself on proportional representation.

Table 2 *Government instability in the Weimar Republic, 1919–23*

Appointment	Chancellor	Party	Members of governing coalition	Fall
February 1919	Philipp Scheidemann	SPD	SPD, Centre, DDP (moderate socialist–centre)	Treaty of Versailles
June 1919	Gustav Bauer	SPD	SPD, Centre, DDP (from October) (moderate socialist–centre)	Kapp Putsch
March 1920	Hermann Müller	SPD	SPD, Centre, DDP (moderate socialist–centre)	Election result
June 1920	Konstantin Fehrenbach	Centre	DDP, Centre, DVP (centre–right)	Reparations ultimatum
May 1921	Joseph Wirth	Centre	SPD, Centre, DDP (moderate socialist–centre)	Cabinet resigned over partition of Upper Silesia
October 1921	Joseph Wirth	Centre	SPD, Centre, DDP (moderate socialist–centre)	
November 1922	Wilhelm Cuno	None	DDP, Centre, DVP, BVP (centre–right)	Economic crisis
August 1923	Gustav Stresemann	DVP	SPD, Centre, DDP, DVP (centre–right with socialists – the 'Great Coalition')	
October 1923	Gustav Stresemann	DVP	SPD, Centre, DDP, DVP ('Great Coalition')	SDP left the coalition
November 1923	Wilhelm Marx	Centre	(centre–right)	

In the period between February 1919 and November 1923 there were no less than ten coalition governments. Although many of the changes in cabinets involved little more than a reshuffling of the political pack of cards, these frequent changes meant that continuity of policy was impossible to achieve and confidence in the whole democratic process was undermined. Overall, it was the extreme anti-democratic parties of the left and right which benefitted most from this undermining of confidence in the democratic system.

The growth of political extremism

There was continuing political violence as parties of the left and right set up armed and uniformed paramilitary squads to guard their meetings, march through the streets and beat up their opponents. Violence on the streets became the norm in many cities as political differences became more polarised.

Challenge from the left

On 5 January 1919, the Spartacus League, known as the Sparticists, led by **Karl Liebknecht** and **Rosa Luxemburg**, staged an armed uprising in Berlin to overthrow Ebert's government and set up a revolutionary communist regime. Newspaper offices and some public buildings were occupied. The revolt was poorly prepared. It was also poorly supported, as the Spartacists had not secured the support of the majority of the working class in Berlin, in whose name they claimed to be acting. Ebert's government relied upon the army to put down the revolt, but General Groener had few reliable military units at his command. He therefore had to use the irregular forces of the new **Freikorps**. By 13 January, the Spartacist rising had been crushed after brutal street fighting in which many prisoners, including Liebknecht and

KEY CHRONOLOGY

Political extremism 1919–23

1919	January	Spartacist rising in Berlin
	March	Second Spartacist rising in Berlin
	April	Strikes in Halle and the Ruhr
	October	Assassination of Hugo Haase
1920	February	Kapp Putsch
	April	Workers' revolts in Saxony and Thuringia
1921	March	Communist-led revolt in Saxony, spread to Hamburg and the Ruhr
	August	Assassination of Erzberger
1922	June	Assassination of Rathenau
1923	October	Communist-led revolt in Saxony
	November	Beer Hall Putsch in Munich

Karl Liebknecht (1871–1919), a lawyer by profession, was the son of Wilhelm Liebknecht, one of the founding members of the SPD in 1875. He thus had a thorough grounding in socialist politics in his youth. As a committed Marxist, he adopted a strong anti-war position in 1914 and continued to agitate against the war, for which he was imprisoned in 1916. Released in November 1918 in an amnesty for political prisoners, he resumed his political activities as one of the leading figures in the revolutionary Spartacus League. During the Spartacist rising in January 1919, he was captured by the Freikorps, tortured and then shot in the back on the pretext that he was trying to escape.

Rosa Luxemburg (1871–1919) was born in Russian Poland but became a German citizen after marrying Gustav Lubeck. She had a long career in revolutionary politics in both Russia and Germany, having been involved in the 1905 Russian Revolution. In Germany, she was imprisoned in 1916 for her involvement in anti-war agitation but was released in November 1918 under an amnesty for political prisoners. She resumed her revolutionary activities and was a leading figure in the Spartacus League. During the Spartacist rising in January 1919, she was captured by the Freikorps, beaten and then shot. Her body was thrown into a canal.

Comintern: the Communist International, set up in 1919 to oversee the actions of Marxist parties across the world; Socialist groups from other countries were invited to join and receive support, but leadership was in the hands of the Russian Communist Party

Luxemburg, were executed. The defeat of the uprising cleared the way for the government to hold elections to the Constituent Assembly later in January, but the brutality with which the revolt had been suppressed, and Ebert's reliance on the army and the Freikorps, deepened the divisions on the Left for many years to come.

Summarise the main reasons why the revolution of January 1919 failed to overthrow the government.

The Freikorps

Faced with the disintegration of much of the regular army in the chaos of defeat and revolution at the end of 1918, Field Marshal Hindenburg and General Groener encouraged former officers to recruit volunteer forces into new Freikorps units. The majority of the recruits came from demobilised junior army officers

Fig. 1 *Freikorps operation takes to the streets of Berlin against revolutionaries*

and NCOs (e.g. corporals and sergeants), but the Freikorps also attracted students, adventurers and drifters. Placed under the overall command of General Walter Luttwitz, the Freikorps were supplied with uniforms and weapons from army stores but were not officially part of the army. In action, therefore, the Freikorps were less disciplined and were able to give full expression to their 'rabid spirit of aggression and revenge' (as historian Richard Evans says in *The Coming of the Third Reich*).

The defeat of the Spartacists did not end left-wing rebellion. The workers, who had played a key role in the overthrow of the Kaiser in November 1918, had been disillusioned by the 'revolution' that followed and frustrated that the Weimar Republic seemed too ready to compromise with the Right. Economic conditions also bred disorder, while demobilised soldiers found it hard to adjust to civilian life. Although the new German Communist Party (KPD) had only minority support in Germany, it was nevertheless a committed, radical minority with strong support in the industrial centres in the Ruhr and Saxony. Inspired by the example of the successful Russian Bolshevik revolution in 1917, and heavily influenced by the **Comintern**, the KPD was keen to lead a communist revolution in Germany. However, ultimately it did not have the support or the determination to do so.

Left-wing risings

March 1919	There was another Spartacist rising in Berlin. In Bavaria, a communist government based on workers' councils, was established. These were both suppressed.
April 1919	There was a wave of strikes in Germany's industrial heartlands of Halle and the Ruhr valley. As well as asking for shorter hours, the strikers demanded more control over their own industries and a government based on workers' councils.

1920	The troubles continued, and after the workers had shown their power in defeating the right-wing Kapp Putsch (see below) with a general strike in Berlin, communists formed a 'Red Army' of 50,000 workers and seized control of the Ruhr. A virtual civil war followed as the regular army and Freikorps struggled to crush the rising. Troubles also broke out in Halle and Dresden, and over 1000 workers and 250 soldiers and police were killed. More disturbances in Saxony and Thuringia, where the workers organised self-defence units, were also put down in April.
March 1921	The KPD tried to force a revolution, beginning with a rising in Saxony. The strike disruption spread to Hamburg and the Ruhr, but the risings were crushed by the police and 145 people were killed.
1923	There was a further bout of strike activity at the time of Germany's economic collapse. This was again centred in Saxony and Hamburg, but it too was suppressed.

The government was never seriously threatened by these left-wing revolts, but continued working-class rebellions did damage the Republic as fear of a 'red revolution' frightened the law-abiding middle classes into supporting right-wing parties.

The challenge from the right

The powerful right wing posed a major threat to the Weimar government. The Right had been hostile to the Republic from the outset since it did not believe in democracy and it accused the politicians who now led Germany of having betrayed the Fatherland. This, however, was the limit of what they agreed upon. There were many competing right-wing groups with different objectives. Some wished to see the restoration of the monarchy, whilst others advocated a dictatorship in one form or another. In areas such as Bavaria there were groups that fought for separation from the rest of Germany, whilst others wanted a united Germany so that it could become a great power again. These divisions weakened the ability of right-wing groups to overthrow the Republic. Nevertheless, right-wing ideas were strong amongst members of the Freikorps and in the army, whilst the large landowners, industrialists, civil servants, police and judges on whom the Republic relied were also traditional conservative anti-republicans.

The Kapp Putsch, 1920

The government was obliged to put into effect the terms of the Treaty of Versailles in January 1920, and consequently needed to reduce the size of the army and to disband some Freikorps units. In February 1920, the defence minister, **Gustav Noske**, ordered two Freikorps units, comprising 12,000 men, to disband. These units were stationed 12 miles from Berlin. When **General Walther von Lüttwitz**, the commanding general, refused to disband one of them, the government ordered his arrest. Lüttwitz decided to march his troops to Berlin in protest and other sympathetic officers offered their support. Lüttwitz was also supported by the right-wing civil servant and politician **Wolfgang Kapp**, who was intent on organising a **putsch**. Crucially, however, Generals Hans von Seeckt and Ludendorff remained non-committal. They sympathised but were aware of the dangers of voicing open support.

On 12 March, the 12,000 Freikorps troops marched into Berlin unopposed, and 13 March 1920 Reich Chancellor Wolfgang Kapp issued a proclamation:

The Reich and nation are in grave danger. With terrible speed we are approaching the complete collapse of the state and of law and order. Prices are rising unchecked. Hardship is growing. The government, lacking in authority

Gustav Noske (1868–1946) was a journalist by profession and a leading member of the SPD. He played a key role in 1918 in persuading the mutinying Kiel sailors to end their revolt and was appointed Minister of Defence in the new republican government. As such, he was responsible for using the army and Freikorps to suppress the Spartacist revolt and later left-wing revolts. After the failure of the Kapp Putsch, he was forced to resign as Minister of Defence because of pressure from trade unions.

General Walther von Lüttwitz (1859–1942) was an army general who had commanded forces on the Western Front in the war. In 1919, he was appointed Commander-in-Chief of the army in Berlin and was also in charge of the Freikorps. As an outspoken opponent of the Treaty of Versailles, he became the driving force behind the Kapp Putsch. After the failure of the putsch, he escaped to Hungary but returned to Germany in 1924 after being granted an amnesty.

Wolfgang Kapp (1868–1922) had trained in law and worked as a civil servant. He was attracted to right-wing politics and co-founded the Fatherland Party in 1917. He was a monarchist and in 1919 was elected to the Reichstag for the nationalist DNVP. He attempted a putsch in 1920 and tried to set himself up as Chancellor but, after its failure, he fled to Sweden. He returned to Germany in 1922 but died in Leipzig whilst awaiting trial.

Putsch: a coup or violent attempt to overthrow a government

Reichswehr: the German army

Hugo Haase (1863–1919) was a Jewish lawyer who had become a leading figure in the SPD before 1914. His anti-war stance alienated him from the majority of the party and in 1917 he took a leading role in forming the breakaway USPD. During the revolution of November 1918, he joined with the Majority SPD in setting up a new government but resigned in December in protest at the armed suppression of a sailors' revolt in Berlin.

Matthias Erzberger (1875–1921) had entered the Reichstag as a deputy for the Centre Party in 1903. He had supported the Peace Resolution of 1917 and became a member of Prince Max's government in 1918. He led the German delegation to sign the armistice and had signed the Versailles Treaty on behalf of the German government in 1919. He was Reich finance minister from June 1919 to March 1920 and had carried out a major reform of the German taxation system. He had been subject to frequent attacks in the Conservative press and was a prime target for assassination.

Organisation Consul: an ultra-nationalist paramilitary group formed from ex-Freikorps members after their units were disbanded following the failed Kapp Putsch

and in league with corruption, is incapable of overcoming the danger. From the East we are threatened by war-like Bolshevism. Is this government capable of resisting it? How are we to escape internal and external collapse? Only by re-erecting a strong state. There is no other way but a government of action. In the best German tradition, the state must stand above the conflict of classes and parties. We recognise only German citizens. Everyone must do his duty!

Ebert's government was forced to withdraw to Dresden, and when Ebert and his chancellor, Gustav Bauer, called on the regular army to crush the rising, Seeckt famously told Ebert: 'Troops do not fire on troops; when **Reichswehr** fires on Reichswehr, all comradeship within the officer corps has vanished'.

The situation appeared dangerous, but there was actually considerable tension between the military and civilian elements of the putsch and it failed to gain widespread support, even from the right wing. Civil servants and bankers remained at best lukewarm and often hostile, whilst trade unions, encouraged by the socialist members of Ebert's government, called a general strike. Berlin was brought to a standstill and, within four days, the putsch collapsed. Kapp and Lüttwitz were forced to flee. Ebert's government returned, but not quite with the air of triumph that might have been expected.

The putsch had taught a number of lessons. The army was not to be trusted, civil servants could be disloyal, the workers as a group could show their power (a realisation that gave renewed vigour to the communist movement) and, without the army's support, the Weimar government was weak. The leniency shown by right-wing judges towards those brought to trial in the aftermath of the putsch contrasted strongly with the harsh treatment suffered by the left wing, and their behaviour sent a message that the government was not really in control.

Political assassinations

The violence continued as right-wing nationalists organised themselves into leagues, committed to the elimination of prominent politicians and those associated with the 'betrayal' of Germany. These Vaterländische Verbände (Patriotic Leagues), often formed out of the old Freikorps units, acted as fiercely anti-republican paramilitaries. They were potentially very powerful and some were actively supported by members of the regular German army. One early victim of the assassins' bullets was **Hugo Haase**, a USPD member who had been a member of the Council of People's Commissars. He was shot in front of the Reichstag in October 1919 and died of his wounds a month later.

The assassination of Erzberger

In August 1921, the former finance minister, **Matthias Erzberger**, was assassinated in the Black Forest by two members of the terrorist league **Organisation Consul**. He had already been shot in January and left wounded, but the assassins were determined to complete the job. Erzberger had led the German delegation for the signing of the armistice and had signed the Treaty of Versailles. He was also Germany's representative on the reparations committee. Even after he was buried, his widow continued to receive abusive letters, including threats to defile his grave.

The assassination of Rathenau

On 24 June 1922, it was the turn of the foreign minister, **Walther Rathenau**. He was driving to work in an open-top car when four assassins from Organisation Consul shot at him and hurled a hand grenade for good measure. Rathenau's 'crimes' were to be a Jew and a leading minister in the republican government. He had participated in the signing of the armistice and had negotiated with the Allies to try to improve the Treaty of Versailles. Nevertheless, Rathenau had been a popular figure and the following day over 700,000 protestors lined the streets of Berlin. The assassination had an impact abroad too; the value of the mark fell as other countries feared the repercussions.

Altogether, between 1919 and 1923, there were 376 political assassinations, 22 carried out by the left, 354 by the right. In an attempt to halt this rising tide of lawlessness, in July 1922 the Reichstag passed a law 'for the protection of the Republic', which imposed severe penalties on those involved in conspiracy to murder and banned extremist organisations. Organisation Consul was forced to disband, but the law was not effective because the judges who had to enforce it were often right-wing sympathisers. In Bavaria, the staunchly conservative government even refused to implement it (and so unwittingly allowed the Nazi movement to establish itself). Rathenau's killers and their accomplices received an average of only four years each in prison. Whilst 326 right-wing murderers went unpunished and only one was convicted and sentenced to severe punishment until 1923, 10 left-wing murderers were sentenced to death.

Although right-wing activity failed to destroy the Republic, the developments of the 1919–23 period bolstered the arrogance of anti-republican nationalists, who showed they could get away with murder. Since the Weimar politicians seemed constantly to exaggerate the threat from the left and to underestimate that from the right, the anti-republican right wing was able to establish itself very firmly in the new German state.

Political impact of the Ruhr Invasion

Germans of all classes and political allegiances had been outraged by the French occupation of the Ruhr. The trauma of hyperinflation had profound psychological effects. Germany was swept by a wave of anti-French feeling and the country was more united than at any time since the end of the war. As the historian Richard Evans has written, hyperinflation 'added to the feeling in the more conservative sections of the population of a world turned upside down, first by defeat, then by revolution, and now by economics'. However, many blamed the government for what happened and middle-class support for the Republic was severely damaged. Organisations representing the Mittelstand accused the government of failing in its responsibility to protect independent small traders and artisans. On the left, the communists tried to use the crisis to stage uprisings in some areas. Moreover, after the ending of passive resistance, the nationalist right accused the government of betrayal. The occupation of the Ruhr, and the subsequent hyperinflation crisis, were the backdrop to the last attempt to overthrow the Republic by force in 1923 by a small Bavarian-based party known as the National Socialist German Workers Party (NSDAP or Nazi Party).

The establishment of the Nazi Party and the Beer Hall Putsch

KEY PROFILE

Walther Rathenau (1867–1922) was a physicist and chemist by training and head of AEG Electricals. He entered politics as a Liberal. In 1919, he joined the DDP and became Minister of Reconstruction in 1921, then foreign minister in 1922. He recommended the fulfilment of the Treaty of Versailles.

CROSS-REFERENCE

Read more about the economic impact of the occupation of the Ruhr on page 23 of Chapter 3.

SOURCE 3

Morgan Phillips Price, a British journalist working in Munich in 1923, wrote this report on Hitler and Nazi Party:

Adolf Hitler, a native Austrian, has pushed his way to the leadership of the Bavarian counter-revolutionary movement. A skilful demagogue, who wins converts to Fascism by drinking beer with the common people, he has

ACTIVITY

Evaluating primary sources

What can we learn from Source 3 about the ways Hitler was able to gain support?

mastered the routine of whipping up popular passions. 'How can we help the Fatherland?' I heard Hitler ask his audience. 'I'll tell you how. By hanging the criminals of November 1918!' (These criminals are, of course, the republican workers of Germany.) 'By punishing the worthies of the Republic we shall gain the respect of foreign nations', cried Hitler. 'If we had resorted to arms two years ago, we would never have lost Silesia and there would have been no Ruhr problem.' At this point in his harangue a company of Hitler's 'shock troops' paraded across the platform beneath the banner of monarchist Germany. Such scenes are daily occurrences in Munich.

CROSS-REFERENCES

Read more about the 'November Criminals', politicians who signed the armistice and Treaty of Versailles, on page 16 of Chapter 2.

Read more about the Ruhr passive resistance, on page 22 of Chapter 3.

The Nazi party was almost alone in arguing that German patriots should first remove the 'November Criminals' from government before dealing with the French. When the government of **Gustav Stresemann** called off the passive resistance in September without winning any concessions from the French, there was an outcry from the Right. This was seen as yet another act of betrayal. In Bavaria, the right-wing government declared a state of emergency and appointed **Gustav von Kahr** as state commissioner. Amongst right-wing nationalists in the Bavarian capital, Munich, there was growing agitation for a 'march on Berlin' to overthrow the government and establish a national dictatorship. At the forefront of the agitation for a 'march on Berlin' was the leader of the NSDAP, then little known, **Adolf Hitler**.

KEY PROFILE

Gustav Ritter von Kahr (1862–1934) was a right-wing Conservative politician who was Minister-President (1920–21) of the right-wing government in Bavaria. He stepped down after disagreements with the Reich government but, in 1923, he was appointed State-Commissioner General and given wide powers by the Munich government. He favoured a strong Bavarian state with its own monarchy and he had hoped to use the Nazi Party to this end. However, although sympathetic to Hitler, he was an unwilling participant in the Beer Hall Putsch of November 1923. He spent the rest of his career as president of the Bavarian administrative court, but was murdered in 1934 during Hitler's 'Night of the Long Knives'.

A CLOSER LOOK

Adolf Hitler

Hitler was born in Austria in April 1889. Although not German by birth, he grew up believing that all Germans should be united in a greater German Reich. In his youth, however, he wanted to become an artist, not a politician. After failing to get into the Academy of Art in Vienna, he became a drifter living on the margins of society. In 1913 he moved to Munich, the capital of Bavaria, and continued to live as he had in Vienna. It was the outbreak of World War I that gave him a new purpose in life. He enthusiastically supported Germany's declaration of war on Russia and France, and volunteered for the German army. His war was spent on the Western Front in France where he gained promotion to corporal and was decorated for bravery. Like many thousands of fellow soldiers, he was outraged by the signing of the armistice in November 1918 and embraced the 'stab in the back' myth as the only possible explanation for Germany's defeat. After the armistice he returned to Munich, which was rapidly becoming a centre of ultra-nationalist, anti-Semitic and anti-Weimar political agitation. He worked as a political agent for the army and, in this capacity, was sent to investigate a small, right-wing political

KEY PROFILE

Fig. 2 *Gustav Stresemann*

Gustav Stresemann (1879–1929) was the leader of the DVP party. Although a monarchist at heart, he came round to working with republican parties in the Weimar Republic and became Chancellor in the Grand Coalition of 1923. He was responsible for the introduction of a new currency and the ending of hyperinflation but was forced to step down as Chancellor in November. Nevertheless, he continued to serve as foreign minister from 1923 until his death in 1929.

group – the German Workers' Party. This had been set up in 1919 by Anton Drexler as a party that combined socialist ideas with nationalism. Hitler joined the party and rapidly became its most effective orator. In 1920 the party changed its name to the National Socialist German Workers' Party (NSDAP), issued a 25-point programme setting out its beliefs, and in 1921 Hitler became its undisputed leader. Under his leadership, the Nazi Party became dedicated to the violent overthrow of the Weimar Republic and its replacement with a Nazi dictatorship. At this stage, however, the NSDAP was just one of many ultra-nationalist groups in Munich and was completely unknown in the rest of Germany.

Beer Hall Putsch in Munich

In November 1923, Hitler made a bid to seize power. He knew that a putsch could only succeed if he had the support of powerful figures so, having secured the support of Ludendorff, he set out to win over Gustav Ritter von Kahr and **Otto von Lossow**, the local army commander. On 8 November, he burst into a Munich Beer Hall, where the two were addressing a meeting of 2000, surrounding it with his **Stormtroopers (SA)** and announcing that the revolution had begun. At gunpoint, in a side room, Kahr and von Lossow were persuaded to agree to his plan to march on Berlin and to install Ludendorff as the new Commander-in-Chief. However, their support evaporated overnight and so too did Hitler's chances of persuading others to support him. Crucially, the

Fig. 3 *Hitler and his Stormtroopers carry the Swastika flag as they prepare for the Munich Beer Hall Putsch of 9 November 1923*

Stormtroopers were unable to gain control of the Munich army barracks and by the next day, 9 November, it was clear that Hitler's original plan had failed. Nevertheless, he went ahead with a march through Munich. The ensuing gun battle with the police later became part of the folklore of the 'courageous' Nazis who marched fearlessly through the streets into the arms of a police cordon. Hitler fell and dislocated his shoulder, possibly in response to the shooting of his companion with whom he had linked arms. He fled, only to be captured the next day, whilst Ludendorff walked straight up to the police and allowed himself to be arrested.

The incident showed again the importance of the army to the political survival of the regime. General Seeckt sent in troops to deal with the aftermath of the abortive putsch, and central control over Bavaria was soon re-imposed. The Nazis were banned and Hitler imprisoned (although he served just nine months of his five-year sentence). Once again, the Republic survived.

CROSS-REFERENCE

Nazi beliefs will be examined in detail in Chapter 10.

KEY TERM

Fig. 4 *Stormtroopers, also known as the SA (Storm Section)*

Stormtroopers (SA): the para-military wing of the Nazi Party, led by Ernst Röhm; wearing their distinctive brown shirts, they were given the job of beating up the Nazis' opponents – many members had formerly belonged to the Freikorps

KEY PROFILE

Otto von Lossow (1868–1938) was the commander of the Reichswehr in Bavaria. He was a staunch Conservative and favoured a strong national state. He refused to obey orders from the Reichswehr Ministry in Berlin and only obeyed instructions from von Kahr, with whom he was plotting to establish a new regime in Berlin. However, he was ready to be patient (unlike Hitler) and how convinced he really was by Hitler's attempted putsch is not known.

CROSS-REFERENCE

Ernst Röhm and the Stormtroopers were a formidable force in the early years of the Nazi government in Germany. This is discussed further in Chapter 12, page 92 and Chapter 13, page 103.

Group debate

Divide into two groups. One group should prepare a presentation arguing that the Communists posed the biggest threat to the survival of the Weimar Republic. The other group should prepare a presentation arguing that the right was the biggest threat. Hold a debate between the two groups.

The key phrase in this quotation is 'never seriously threatened'. With this type of question you need to assess the extent of the challenges to the Republic's survival and which threats, if any, came close to overthrowing the Republic. The quotation offers a strong, one-sided view so there will be scope to challenge its assumptions, although ultimately you will need to offer a balanced analysis.

 PRACTICE QUESTION

'The Weimar Republic was never seriously threatened in the years 1919–23.' Explain why you agree or disagree with this view.

Summary: The state of the Republic by 1924

The early years of the Weimar Republic were characterised by instability and political conflict. This was partly due to weaknesses in the constitution of the Republic but the underlying problem for Germany was a lack of national consensus on how the country should be governed. There were challenges to the Republic's very existence from the left, disappointed by what they regarded as the betrayal of the revolution of November 1918, and from the right, which accused the democratic politicians now ruling Germany of betrayal of the country's national interests. The army and the judges, whose role it was to uphold the rule of law and defend the state, could not be relied upon to use their power in an even-handed way, since the majority of military officers and civil judges did not support democracy. Yet somehow the Republic survived all of the threats to its existence in these years. By 1924, as we shall see in the next chapter, Germany's economy and its political system witnessed the start of a period of growing prosperity and greater stability. The conflicts of the early years, however, left a legacy of bitterness and distrust in the democratic process, which would leave the Republic vulnerable to further challenges in the more difficult economic and political climate after 1929.

The 'Golden Age' of the Weimar Republic, 1924–28

5 Economic developments

The stabilisation of the currency

In August 1923, at the height of the hyperinflation crisis, the government of Cuno collapsed and was replaced by a new coalition led by Gustav Stresemann. Stresemann's coalition – the so-called 'great coalition' – was the first in the short history of the Weimar Republic to include parties from both the left and the right. Stresemann's own party, the DVP, shared power with the Centre Party, the Socialists and the DDP. Stresemann, who was Chancellor for a mere 103 days, took office at a time when the Weimar Republic was in serious political and economic difficulty. By the time he left office in November, the currency had been stabilised, inflation had been brought under control and attempts to overthrow the republic from both the left and the right had ended in failure.

Stresemann's priority was to bring inflation under control. This involved three key steps.

The end of passive resistance

Passive resistance against the occupation of the Ruhr was called off in September. This was a highly unpopular and risky move, which led to serious unrest and the attempted Beer Hall Putsch in Munich. Stresemann calculated, however, that he had no alternative. Germany's economy was beginning to grind to a halt and inflation was completely out of control. Ending passive resistance, which meant that the government stopped paying workers who refused to work for the French, was an essential first step towards reducing government expenditure.

The issuing of a new currency

In November, a new currency called the Rentenmark was introduced to replace the old and worthless Reichsmark. The new currency was exchanged for the old on the basis of one Rentenmark for one trillion old marks. Since Germany did not have sufficient gold reserves to back the new currency, it was supported by a mortgage on all industrial and agricultural land. Once the new currency was successfully launched, the government kept tight control over the amount of money in circulation in order to prevent inflation reappearing. The old inflated marks were gradually cashed in and, in August 1924, the Rentenmark became the Reichsmark, backed by the German gold reserve, which had to be maintained at 30 per cent of the value of the Reichsmarks in circulation. Inflation ceased to be a problem and the value of the new currency was established at home and abroad. All this happened under the direction of **Hjalmar Schacht**.

Balancing the budget

Stresemann's government cut expenditure and raised taxes. The salaries of government employees were cut, some 300,000 civil servants lost their jobs and taxes were raised for both individuals and companies. As government debt began to fall, confidence was restored.

LEARNING OBJECTIVES

In this chapter you will learn about:

- Stresemann's government: the ending of hyperinflation and the stabilisation of the German currency
- the reparations issue and the Dawes Plan of 1924
- the extent of the economic recovery in industry and agriculture
- the issue of reparations and the Young Plan.

CROSS-REFERENCES

To find out about Chancellor Cuno and what his government did, see page 22 in Chapter 3.

Refer to Table 2 in Chapter 4, which details the various changes in government from February 1919 to November 1923.

For more information on Gustav Stresemann, see Chapter 4, page 32.

For more information on the main political parties refer to Chapter 1, pages 5 and 7.

For more information on the Beer Hall Putsch of 1923, see Chapter 4, page 31.

Fig. 1   *Hjalmar Schacht*

Hjalmar Schacht (1877–1970) had been director of the National Bank from 1916 and was a co-founder of the DDP party in November 1918. He has been described as a financial genius for his role in the stabilisation of the German currency. In 1923, he became Reich Currency Commissioner and head of the Reichsbank, and introduced the Rentenmark. He then went on to help negotiate the Dawes and Young Plans, which modified Germany's reparations payments. He later became Economics Minister under the Nazis (1934–37) but lost favour and was removed from the Reichsbank in 1939.

CROSS-REFERENCES

For more detail on the economic impact of reparations, see Chapter 3, page 21.

For detail on the different parties, see A Closer Look features on pages 5 and 7.

For more on the Treaty of Versailles, see Chapter 2, page 13.

These changes made a considerable difference to the way that the German economy operated. Well-managed companies that were run prudently and were careful not to build up excessive debt continued to prosper. Weaker companies that were heavily reliant on credit crumbled. The number of companies that went bankrupt in Germany rose from 233 in 1923 to over 6000 in 1924. Moreover, those who had lost their savings in the collapse of the old currency did not gain anything from the introduction of a new currency.

The reparations issue and the Dawes Plan

The stabilisation of Germany's economy was as much dependent on settling the reparations dispute as it was on domestic issues. In November 1923, Stresemann asked the Allies' Reparations Committee to set up a committee of financial experts to address Germany's repayment concerns. The USA had a vested interest in getting Germany back to a position where reparations could be made to France, because much of this money was then passed on to the USA to repay loans. Therefore, the American banker **Charles Dawes** acted as the new committee's chairman. By the time the Dawes Plan was finalised in April 1924, Stresemann's government had fallen, but he remained as foreign secretary and took credit for much of what was achieved. Although the Dawes Plan confirmed the original figure of a total reparations payment of £6.6 billion (132,000 million gold marks), it made the payments more manageable. It recommended that:

- The amount paid each year by Germany should be reduced until 1929, when the situation would be reappraised. It proposed that Germany should re-start reparations by paying 1000 million marks (a fraction of what had been expected before) and that this sum should be raised by annual increments over five years by 2500 million marks per year. After this, the sum paid should be related to German industrial performance.
- Germany should receive a large loan of 800 million marks from the USA to help get the plan started and to allow for heavy investment in German infrastructure.

Charles Dawes (1865–1951) was an American banker and politician. He became the US Vice-President in 1924. For his work with Stresemann to resolve the reparations issue, the two men were jointly awarded the Nobel Peace Prize in 1925.

There was a heated debate in the Reichstag over the Dawes Plan. Stresemann himself did not actually believe in the plan, privately referring to it as 'no more than an **economic armistice**', but he agreed to it as a way of securing foreign loans. The so-called 'national opposition' (mainly the DNVP, but also smaller right-wing groups like the Nazi movement) bitterly attacked this policy of compromise, since they believed Germany should defy the unjust Versailles Treaty and refuse to pay reparations altogether. However, the Dawes Plan was eventually agreed and accepted by both Germany and the Allies in July 1924. It brought several benefits to Germany:

- The Allies accepted that Germany's problems with the payment of reparations were real.
- Loans were granted, with which new machinery, factories, houses and jobs could be provided and the German economy rebuilt.

The French gradually left the Ruhr during 1924–25, once it became clear that Germany was going to restart paying reparations and the occupation could no longer be justified. Such measures contributed to German optimism that their country was once again its own master.

The extent of economic recovery

Industry

By 1925, Germany appeared more stable and prosperous. The combination of the new currency, the Dawes Plan and Schacht's work at the Reichsbank (where interest rates were kept high to attract foreign investment), helped improve Germany's situation enormously. American loans helped stimulate the economy. Industrial output grew after 1924 but did not reach 1913 levels until 1929. The extent of this boom should not be exaggerated. Growth rates were unsteady. The years 1924–25 and 1927 were good years, but the economy shrank in 1928 and 1929. Investment in new machinery and factories was falling by 1929.

A CLOSER LOOK

German industry underwent extensive 'rationalisation' as new management and production techniques were introduced and antiquated equipment was replaced with new machinery. The fact that Germany had to hand over many of its materials as reparations at the end of the war opened the way for this new start and, with American finance, the big industrialists began to buy out or make cooperative agreements with smaller firms to form **cartels**. By 1925, there were around 3000 such cartel arrangements in operation, including 90 per cent of Germany's coal and steel production. After 1925, Germany was allowed, under the terms of the Versailles Treaty, to protect its industries by introducing **tariffs** on imported foreign goods. Many firms also received state subsidies to enable them to survive. All of these practices reduced competition and propped up inefficient enterprises.

Key

...... Industrial production

- -- Coal production

—— Steel production

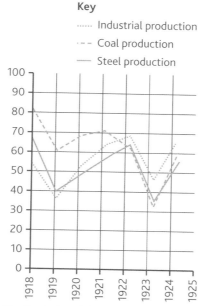

Fig. 2 *Industrial production in Germany*

Advances were made in the chemical industry, such as the large-scale production of artificial fertilisers. The car and aeroplane industries also developed, although cars were still too expensive for the average German. The inflation rate was close to zero and living standards rose as wages began to increase from 1924. Loans helped to finance the building of housing, schools, municipal buildings, road and public works. Massive population growth had created an acute housing shortage in Germany by the early twentieth century, and the overcrowding and insanitary conditions of working-class city accommodation had been linked to political instability. Consequently, state initiatives to provide affordable homes were of great importance for future stability. In 1925, 178,930 dwellings were built – over 70,000 more than in the previous year – and, in 1926, there were to be 205,793 more new homes. Money was spent on welfare payments and health improvements and, in 1924, new schemes of relief were launched.

Table 1 *Number of strikes in Germany 1924–1928*

Year	Strikes
1924	1973
1925	1708
1926	351
1927	844
1928	739
1929	429
1930	353

Compulsory arbitration: industrial disputes are often settled by arbitration, in which both sides agree to allow an independent figure, known as the arbitrator, decide on a solution; in Weimar Germany, arbitration was made compulsory by law

Lock out: an action by an employer to stop workers doing their jobs until they agree to the employer's terms and conditions

ACTIVITY

With reference to Fig. 2 and your understanding of the historical context:

1. Explain why the number of strikes fell during the years 1924–29.
2. Explain to what extent employers *and* workers were satisfied with this development.

Fig. 3 *German aircraft construction*

The number of strikes in German industry declined in these years, partly because a new system of **compulsory arbitration** for settling industrial disputes was issued. However, employers felt that this system was biased in favour of the unions and resented the state's interference in their affairs. The Weimar Republic had already set a maximum of eight hours for a working day and had given trade unions the right to be part of work councils in factories and mines.

In 1928, a dispute over wages in the iron and steel industry in the Ruhr resulted in the arbitrator granting a small wage increase to the workers. The employers then refused to pay the increase and **locked out** the workers for four weeks. In this dispute the workers were backed by the government and paid by the state. There were undoubtedly improvements in living standards for ordinary German workers, especially those who were backed by powerful trade unions. They benefited from increases in the real value of wages in each year after 1924. In 1927, real wages increased by 9 per cent and, in 1928, they rose by a further 12 per cent.

SOURCE 1

Hans Klamroth was a German businessman who recorded the changing fortunes of his company in his diary. In 1924, he welcomed the introduction of the Rentenmark by Stresemann:

'Business is suddenly extraordinarily lively', father notes in his diary. 'The balance sheet for I.G. Klamroth is healthy. It is nothing like pre-war figures, of course it isn't, ten years of war and post-war have left their scars. But the company is alive, it has managed its economy satisfactorily throughout that disastrous year, and nobody's come out with anything worse than a black eye. Business is picking up at I.G. Klamroth, the orders are accumulating and soon we won't know how to cope with them.'

SOURCE 2

A little over a year later, in January 1926, Hans Klamroth's diary has a very different tone:

Lack of credit and a shortage of money everywhere, bankruptcy, business investigations and so on. We're ending our financial year with a loss for the first time; how will it look over the whole year? Pretty poor; to start with the customers aren't paying their bills. Father has to borrow major sums from the bank just to cover company salaries. A few days later the bank cancels the credit, and I.G. Klamroth is 75,000 marks short.

Limits to the economic recovery

In a speech given shortly before his death in 1929, Gustav Stresemann warned, 'The economic position is only flourishing on the surface. Germany is dancing on a volcano. If the short-term loans are called in, a large section of our economy would collapse.' Unemployment was a continuing problem in these years. By the end of 1925, unemployment had reached one million; by March 1926, it was over three million, although it did fall after that. This was due partly to there being more people seeking work, partly to public spending cuts, but also to companies reducing their workforces in order to make efficiency savings. The mining companies reduced their workforces by 136,000 between 1922 and 1925, and reduced them by another 56,000 between 1925 and 1929.

SOURCE 3

An extract from the report of the Commissioner of the Reichsbank, 1928. This report was written to inform government ministers and business leaders about the state of the economy:

If we compare the present position with that of four years ago, we see a very great advance in regard to the economic development of the country as a whole.

There has been a far-reaching reorganisation and rationalisation of the industrial system of Germany; the standard of living of the masses of the people has appreciably risen, and in the case of a great part of the working-class has again reached or surpassed the pre-war level. The marked fluctuations of the first few years have made way for a more steady line of development. Those who foretold a rapid and serious depression under-estimated the country's economic power.

At the same time there are still considerable branches of the national economy which have had an inadequate share in the general recovery. The position of agriculture, though here and there improvement is apparent, remains on the whole less favourable than that of the rest of the national economy.

Whatever turn the future may take, it is certain that there is a serious temporary shortage of capital. The difficulties encountered in securing long-term loans have led to a growing reliance on short-term borrowing.

The Weimar 'economic miracle' did not benefit everyone. The Mittelstand, the professional middle classes, gained very little in this so-called 'golden age'. Bankrupted by the hyperinflation of 1923, middle-class managers, clerks and bureaucrats did not benefit fully from the improved economic climate. White-collar workers did not enjoy the wage rises of the industrial sector. By the late 1920s, industrial sector wages had drawn level with those of the middle class – and in some cases exceeded them.

SOURCE 4

In 1929, the German writer and former social worker Hilde Walter, wrote about the 'misery' of the new Mittelstand in the weekly news magazine *Die Weltbühne*.

Before the war the most important characteristic of the lower-middle class was a fundamentally secure existence, based on a combination of capital owned and income from work. How differently the living conditions of the new middle class appear today! The needs of the white-collar employees who have lost their jobs far exceed the capacities of unemployment provisions. In April 1928 official publications counted a total of 183,371 white-collar workers seeking employment; of those approximately 62,000 received insurance payments and approximately 31,500 received emergency provisions; therefore 90,000 unemployed white-collar workers were without unemployment support and, in the best of cases, received small payments from social welfare for the poor. Those receiving emergency support, that is, one third of all those supported, had already been unemployed for over six months, and therefore in many cases drew only about one third of their salaries for over half a year.

PRACTICE QUESTION

Evaluating primary sources

With reference to Sources 1, 3 and 4 and your understanding of the historical context, which of these sources is more valuable in explaining the extent of the economic recovery in Germany by 1928?

ACTIVITY

Statistical analysis

With reference to Fig. 4 and your understanding of the historical context, explain why unemployment remained relatively high during the years 1924–29.

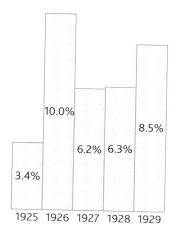

Fig. 4 *Unemployment in Germany, 1925–29*

CROSS-REFERENCE

For more information on who the Mittelstand were, see Chapter 3, page 24.

STUDY TIP

You should consider the value of different types of sources: a diary, an official report and magazine article. Make sure you understand the value and limitations of sources with different provenances.

Agriculture

Farmers gained very little benefit from the economic recovery of these years. A worldwide agricultural depression kept food prices low and few farmers were able to make a profit on their land. During the inflation of the early 1920s, large landowners and farmers borrowed money to buy new machinery and improve their farms. Smaller peasant farmers, however, tended to hoard money and their savings were wiped out by inflation.

After 1923, the government made it easier for farmers to borrow money, but this made matters worse. Farmers became saddled with debt at a time when prices were falling and they could not, therefore, keep up the repayments. The increased taxes introduced to pay for the welfare benefits of the unemployed and sick were regarded as an unfair burden on farmers and landowners. The governments of these years tried to relieve the farmers' plight by introducing high import tariffs on food products, import controls and subsidies to farmers, but these measures did not go far enough.

The plight of German farmers worsened due to a global grain surplus and price slump in 1925 and 1926. By the late 1920s, there was an increase in bankruptcies amongst farmers and many of them lost their land as the banks demanded repayment of loans. In 1928, farmers initiated a series of small-scale riots – known as the 'farmers' revenge' – in protest against **foreclosures** and low market prices. By 1929, German agricultural production was at less than three-quarters of its pre-war levels.

KEY TERM

Foreclosure: taking possession of mortgaged property when someone fails to keep up their repayments

A CLOSER LOOK

The farmers and the banks

When farmers borrowed from banks, they had to use their farms as security for the loans. When those farmers were unable to repay the loans, the banks 'foreclosed' on the contract – the banks took over the farms and evicted the farmers.

ACTIVITY

Copy and complete the table below. Use the information in this chapter to identify those who benefited from the economic recovery and those who did not benefit.

Winners	Losers
Eg. People in debt	*Eg. People living on fixed incomes*

The reparations issue and the Young Plan

The Dawes Plan of 1924 was only ever intended to be a temporary settlement of the reparations issue. Although the French and Belgians left the Ruhr by 1925, Allied forces remained in occupation of the Rhineland and the French would not agree to withdraw these forces unless and until a final settlement of the reparations issue had been agreed. Therefore Stresemann, who had continued to serve as Foreign Minister after his own coalition government collapsed, agreed that the issue should be considered by an international committee headed by the American businessman **Owen Young**. This committee met in Paris in 1929, with Schacht as one of Germany's representatives, and produced a report on the final settlement of the reparations issue.

The Young Plan obliged Germany to continue paying reparations until 1988. The total reparations bill was considerably reduced, with Germany being required to pay £1.8 billion instead of the original sum of £6.5 billion, but the annual payment Germany was required to make increased. All foreign control over reparations was ended and the responsibility for paying reparations was placed solely on the German government. In return, Britain and France agreed to withdraw all their troops from the Rhineland by June 1930.

KEY PROFILE

Owen D. Young (1874–1962) was a lawyer by profession but became a leading businessman. He was President of General Electric and founded RCA – the Radio Corporation of America. He helped in the writing of the Dawes Plan in 1924.

Despite containing a number of concessions to Germany, the Young Plan nevertheless inflamed nationalist opinion in Germany. The new leader of the right-wing DNVP, **Alfred Hugenberg**, launched a nationwide campaign against the plan, which involved other conservative groups, including Adolf Hitler and the Nazis. This campaign group drew up the draft of a law – the so-called 'freedom law'– which they demanded should be submitted to a national **referendum**. This law required the government to repudiate the war-guilt clause of the Treaty of Versailles, to demand immediate evacuation of the occupied areas and declared that any minister who signed a treaty that involved acceptance of war guilt would be tried for treason. Hugenberg's group launched a petition in support of their 'freedom law' and attracted 4,135,000 signatures. This was enough to ensure that it would have to be debated by the Reichstag and put to a referendum. In the Reichstag debate, the 'freedom law' was decisively defeated and it was also rejected in the referendum. On the other hand, the fact that 5,825,000, or 13.8 per cent of the electorate, voted for the 'freedom Law' was an indication of the depth of support for right-wing nationalism. Moreover, Adolf Hitler's leading role in the campaign, which was financed by Hugenberg, enabled him to make a decisive breakthrough as a national political figure.

ACTIVITY

Discussion point

Considering the political and economic situation at the time, to what extent did German reactions to the Young Plan show that the reparations issue could never be settled to the satisfaction of the German public?

KEY TERM

Referendum: a popular vote on a single issue in which people are asked to say yes or no to a proposal

KEY PROFILE

Alfred Hugenberg (1865–1951) had been a civil servant and then a banker before the war. He owned newspapers and film companies as well as being a deputy in the Reichstag, representing the conservative DNVP. After he became leader of the DNVP in 1928, the party became more extreme in its hostility to democratic government, and his money and media influence provided crucial support for the campaign against the Young Plan. In 1933, Hugenberg was appointed Minister for Economics and Food in the Nazi government.

Fig. 5   *Alfred Hugenberg*

 PRACTICE QUESTION

'The "golden age" of Weimar was a myth.' Assess the validity of this view.

Summary

After the trauma of hyperinflation in 1923, the German economy became more stable in the years 1924–29. Inflation was brought under control with the issue of a new currency, and diplomatic efforts to resolve the reparations issue helped Germany to attract foreign loans to help rebuild the economy. Parts of German industry boomed during these years and many Germans experienced growing prosperity. This was not, however, the experience of all Germans. Farmers faced very difficult trading conditions and many of them lost their livelihoods. The Mittelstand, particularly white-collar workers, found that their living standards did not improve and they did not have access to the range of welfare benefits available to industrial workers. Moreover, reliance on short-term foreign loans to finance industrial investment left Germany highly vulnerable to changes in the world economic climate.

STUDY TIP

The 'golden age' is a phrase that has often been used to describe the Weimar Republic during the years 1924–29. There is much evidence on which to agree with this description but, equally, there is evidence on which it is possible to disagree. A balanced answer is needed, but you should be clear, either agreeing or disagreeing with the view.

6 Social and cultural developments in Germany, 1924–28

SOURCE 1

George Grosz, the left-wing German artist, recalled life in the Weimar years in his 1946 autobiography:

Berlin was like a bubbling cauldron. You could not see who was heating the cauldron; but you could merely see it merrily bubbling, and you could feel the heat increasing. There were speakers on every street corner and songs of hatred everywhere. Everybody was hated: the Jews, the capitalists, the gentry, the communists, the military, the landlords, the workers, the unemployed, the Freikorps, the Allied control commissions, the politicians, the department stores, and again the Jews. It was a real orgy of incitement, and the Republic was so weak that you hardly took notice of it.

The war and its aftermath brought extensive social and cultural changes to Germany as well as the political and economic changes outlined in earlier chapters. The Weimar Constitution gave German citizens more rights, freedom, opportunities and greater equality than they had ever been allowed before. Many embraced these opportunities with enthusiasm and innovation. Others lamented the passing of a way of life in which roles, responsibilities and authority had been clearly defined and society was rooted in traditional values. The Weimar years, therefore, witnessed a conflict between those who challenged traditional values in the name of 'modernity' and those who resisted these changes in an attempt to preserve social stability and an older, specifically German way of life.

CROSS-REFERENCE

For details of Weimar Republic's long-term committment to social welfare, refer to Chapter 3, page 23.

Social welfare reform

Social welfare reforms between 1924–27 included:

1924	The Public Assistance system, which provided help to the poor and destitute, was modernised
1925	The state accident insurance system, introduced by Bismarck to help those injured at work, was extended to cover those suffering from occupational diseases
1927	A national unemployment insurance system was introduced to provide benefits for the unemployed, financed by contributions from workers and employers

This was an impressive list of reforms but, for many Germans, the welfare system promised more than it delivered. It was also very expensive. In 1926, the state was supporting about 800,000 disabled war veterans, 360,000 war widows and over 900,000 war orphans. This was in addition to old age pensions and, after 1927, the cost of unemployment benefits. The welfare system also needed a large and expensive bureaucracy to administer it. Taxes were increased after 1924, but there was a limit to how much the better-off were prepared to shoulder the burden of welfare expenditure. The result was that those administering benefits at a local level used many devices to keep expenditure down. **Means tests** were tightened up, snoopers were used to check that claimants were not cheating the system and there were increasing delays in paying benefits. Those in need of support, including large numbers of war veterans and their families, felt they were being humiliated and insulted by the welfare system, undermining their support for the Weimar Republic.

Living standards and lifestyles

The living standards of millions of Germans undoubtedly improved during the years 1924–28. Those in work, particularly those represented by powerful trade unions, were able to maintain their living standards by negotiating wage increases. Those dependent on welfare benefits were less well off, and undoubtedly suffered some hardships, but they were prevented from falling into abject poverty by the welfare system. Business owners and their salaried employees benefited from the improved trading position for German companies at this time. There were, however, many exceptions to this rule. Those who had lost their savings during the hyperinflation of 1923 were unable to regain the comfortable lifestyles they had once enjoyed. Farmers suffered from poor trading conditions and low prices, and their incomes were falling. The air of confidence that was exuded in cities such as Berlin was not apparent across the whole country.

Social and cultural changes in Weimar Germany affected different groups in different ways. In this section, we consider the experiences of women, young people and the Jews.

ACTIVITY

1. Which groups benefited from the welfare reforms?
2. Why did the welfare system undermine support for the Weimar Republic?

CROSS-REFERENCE

More information about living standards can be found in Chapter 5.

Position of women

In 1929, a female journalist, Elsa Hermann, wrote that 'the modern woman refuses to lead the life of a lady and a housewife, preferring to depart from the ordained path and go her own way'. There was much talk in Weimar Germany about the 'new woman', who symbolised the way women's lives had changed since the end of the war. She was portrayed as being free, independent, sexually liberated and increasingly visible in public life. The Weimar Constitution had given women equality with men in voting rights and in access to education. It had also given women equal opportunities in civil service appointments and the right to equal pay. This coincided with a major change in the gender balance of the population as a result of the war. Over two million Germans, mostly young males, had been killed in the war, so there were fewer opportunities for young women to follow the conventional path of marriage and child-rearing to economic security. The war had also brought many more women into paid employment to replace the men who had fought. It is hardly surprising, therefore, that many young German women in the 1920s had expectations about their lives which were very different from those of their mothers and that there were greater opportunities to fulfil those expectations.

The extent of change, however, should not be exaggerated. Moreover, not all German citizens approved of the changes – not even all women. Although the constitution gave women new legal and civil rights, the much more traditional **Civil Code of 1896** remained in force. Among other things, this code laid down that, in a marriage, the husband had the right to decide on all matters concerning family life, including whether his wife should undertake paid employment. The most popular women's group in the 1920s was the League of German Women (BDF), which had 900,000 members. Far from supporting the 'new woman', the BDF promoted traditional family values and maternal

Fig. 1 *A model poses in a fashionable evening dress in Berlin, 1925*

KEY TERM

Civil Code of 1896: since the unification of Germany in 1871 there had been a need to bring the separate laws of each of the German states into a uniform national framework; the Civil Code of 1896, which concerned all aspects of personal and civil rights and responsibilities, provided that common framework

responsibilities. This was echoed by the more conservative political parties and by the churches, which were alarmed by changes they considered to be a threat to the family. In many ways, therefore, the concept of the 'new woman' was more of a cultivated myth than a social reality for the majority of German women.

ACTIVITY

Make a list of the main reasons why women's lives were changing in the Weimar period. Rank your reasons in order of priority and explain your reasoning.

Table 1 *The myth of the 'new woman', versus reality*

	The myth of the 'new woman'	The reality
Employment	• The constitution gave women greater equality in employment rights • By 1925, 36 per cent of the German workforce were women • By 1933, there were 100,000 women teachers and 3000 women doctors.	• The 'demobilisation' laws after the war required women to leave their jobs so that ex-soldiers could find employment • In many occupations, women were required to give up their employment when they married • Women were paid much less than men doing equivalent work • Married women who continued to have paid jobs were attacked as 'double-earners' and blamed for male unemployment. There were campaigns in the press and by conservative parties for the dismissal of married women workers.
Sexual freedom	• Birth control became more widely available and the birth rate declined • Divorce rates increased • There was a rise in the number of abortions; by 1930, there was an estimated 1 million abortions a year.	• Abortion was a criminal offence and would often be performed by unqualified people. In 1930, there were an estimated 10–12,000 deaths each year from abortions • The decline in the birth rate was attacked by the conservative press and politicians as a 'birth strike' that threatened the health of the nation and the continued existence of the race • Catholic and Protestant churches were vigorously opposed to birth control, divorce and abortion. Many German women were committed members of church congregations.
Politics and public life	• Women gained equal voting rights and the right to be Reichstag deputies in the Weimar Constitution • In 1919, 41 women were elected to the Reichstag; the number of women deputies fell in subsequent elections (see Table 2 below) but the German Reichstag had a higher proportion of female deputies than the British House of Commons • Women were also very active in local government at state and city level.	• There were no female representatives in the Reichsrat • No woman became a cabinet member during the Weimar Republic • No political party had a female leader in the Weimar years • Only the communists (KPD) made gender equality a key element in its programme but it was the least appealing party to the new female electorate • The party that gained the most from female suffrage was the Catholic Centre Party. In Protestant areas, the conservative DNVP and the DVP appealed most to women voters. None of these parties gave any support to feminist issues.

Four women politicians in Weimar Germany

Clara Zetkin (1857–1933) was a KPD member of the Reichstag from 1920 to 1933. She had been active in the SPD before 1914 and was a leading campaigner for women's rights, having organised the first International Women's Day in 1911. She was also a close friend of Rosa Luxemburg. Clara blamed capitalism for reducing women to the status of breeders and homebuilders, and believed women would only be truly liberated by a socialist revolution.

Fig. 2 *Clara Zetkin*

Marie Juchacz (1879–1956) was a long-standing member of the SPD and elected to the National Assembly in 1919. She was the first woman to make a speech in any legislative body in Germany. She served as a Reichstag deputy for the SPD until 1933. Marie came from a poor, rural background and left school at 14 to earn money for her family. She had been introduced to politics by her older brother, Otto Gohlke, and joined the SPD in 1908, when she became one of the first female party members.

Marianne Weber (1870–1954) was an intellectual and academic, and the wife of Max Weber, a leading sociologist. She wrote several books on feminist issues and was active in the German women's suffrage movement before 1914. In 1919, she joined the DDP and was the first woman elected to state legislature in Baden. She wrote that 'It is our responsibility to infuse all life with our special mix of feminine and humane influence.'

Paula Müller-Otfried (1865–1946) was a devout Protestant and co-founder of the German Protestant Women's League. She was very active in her church and in social work, and was opposed to women's suffrage, warning that voting rights would not improve women's lives. Nevertheless, as a member of the DNVP, she became a Reichstag deputy in 1920 and continued in this role until 1932.

The achievement of women's suffrage in 1919 did not usher in a new era of female equality, but it did bring the debate on women's rights to the heart of political debate. The Weimar Republic witnessed a continuing struggle between those who wanted Germany to become a more modern, free and equal society and those who fought to retain traditional values. The clash over women's rights was on the front line in this struggle, with the so-called 'new women' increasingly being used as scapegoats for Germany's social and economic ills.

Table 2 *Female deputies in the Reichstag*

1919	41
1920	37
1924 (May)	27
1924 (December)	33
1928	33
1930	42

 PRACTICE QUESTION

'The concept of the "new woman" in the Weimar Republic was no more than a myth'. Explain why you agree or disagree with this view.

Young people

SOURCE 2

A court report on a young offender in Hamburg in 1928 stated that:

Wilhelm P. belongs to a club known as 'The Wild Boys', where he sees and hears nothing but bad things. What goes on in the club is nothing but thefts and pranks. The club consists of groups of youths which have been forming recently in all the districts; they adorn themselves with coloured school caps and with trousers and waistcoats covered with pearl buttons.

The struggle for control over the behaviour and development of German youth was another key battleground in the Weimar Republic's 'culture wars'. Source 2 reflects a more widespread concern that young people in

STUDY TIP

The term 'myth' is the key term in this question, which is asking whether women in the Weimar Republic really did experience new freedoms and opportunities, or was the concept of the 'new woman' nothing more than a figment of the imagination. There is plenty of evidence to put forward on both sides of this argument and scope for differentiation – were there some groups of women who did experience greater freedom than ever before, and were their experiences typical of women as a whole?

CROSS-REFERENCE

To recap on the acronyms of different German political parties, see Chapter 1, pages 5 and 7.

CROSS-REFERENCE

Rosa Luxemburg was introduced in Chapter 4 on page 27.

KEY TERM

Gymnasium school: a selective school that provided a classical education, children would remain at a Gymnasium for nine years before taking a university entrance examination; teaching methods were very authoritarian, discipline was maintained through corporal punishment and the curriculum was very rigid

ACTIVITY

Discussion point

To what extent does the evidence in this section support the view that young people in the Weimar Republic were becoming more rebellious?

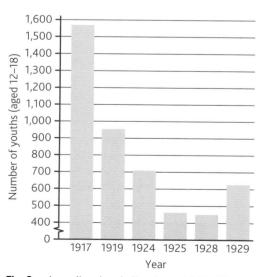

Fig. 3 *Juvenile crime in Hamburg, 1917–29*

Weimar Germany were breaking free of the constraints of family, school and religion, and turning increasingly to a life of crime and anti-social behaviour. Those children, mostly from working-class families, who did not attend the highly selective **Gymnasium schools**, were supposed to leave school at the age of 14 and begin an apprenticeship or employment. In the Weimar years, however, there were fewer apprenticeships and more youth unemployment. Young people suffered disproportionately from the rise in unemployment after 1924. In 1925–26, 17 per cent of the unemployed were in the 14–21 age group. This was partly because there had been a baby boom between 1900 and 1910, so many more young people were seeking employment at a time when employers were reducing their workforces. The benefits system provided some help for young people and day centres were established to help youths acquire the skills needed to find work, but neither could compensate for the lack of employment opportunity. The result was that many young, working-class Germans living in big cities joined gangs to find the comradeship, mutual support and sense of adventure that was otherwise lacking in their lives.

A CLOSER LOOK

Youth 'cliques' in Hamburg

Youth 'cliques' (another name for gangs) were prevalent in the working-class districts of large German cities. In Hamburg, there were cliques with such names as the Farmers' Fear, Red Apaches, Death Defiers, Tartar's Blood and Eagle's Claw. The names reflected the importance of projecting an image of physical toughness, aggressive masculinity and anti-social attitudes. Each group was associated with a particular district of the city. The cliques often used taverns as their meeting places because alcohol played an important part in their sub-culture. Prospective recruits were required to undertake an initiation test, such as stealing or vandalism, to demonstrate their willingness to break the law. Each group had their own uniform and flag.

Education

Germany prided itself on having one of the best state education systems in Europe. It had been developed in Prussia and then extended to the rest of Germany after 1871. Alongside the Gymnasiums for those aiming at university, there were Realschule, which provided six years of schooling for children who would go on to apprenticeships. Although there were very few elite private schools in Germany, the state education system was nevertheless divided along class lines, since the majority of those at Gymnasiums were drawn from the middle and upper classes. The system was also divided along religious lines, since the Protestant and Catholic churches had a powerful influence over religious education.

Education reformers in the Weimar Republic aimed to break down these divides and provide a comprehensive, non-sectarian education that would be free to all pupils. They were only partially successful in their efforts. The main educational reform of the Weimar period was the introduction of elementary schools, which all children would attend for the first four years of education. Those who did not then pass the entrance examination for a Gymnasium would be able to continue at elementary school for a further four years. The reformers did not, however, succeed in their aim of removing the influence of the churches from schools. Both the Catholic and Protestant churches vigorously and successfully defended their right to promote religious teachings through the state education system, supported by their respective political parties.

Youth groups

In Germany, the establishment of organisations catering for young people began in the 1890s and continued through the Weimar period. There were three main types of youth groups:

Wandervogel

The first Wandervogel group, or 'wandering birds', was set up in 1896 by a Berlin schoolteacher. The movement quickly spread and groups consisted of mainly middle-class boys. Although the Wandervogel were non-political, they were nevertheless highly nationalistic, with a very romanticised view of Germany's past. They hated industrialisation and big cities, and much of their time was spent hiking in the forests, swimming in lakes and rivers, and sleeping under canvas. In many ways, therefore, they rejected middle-class social conventions and sought the freedom of wild spaces. Some adopted a more unconventional lifestyle by practising nudism and vegetarianism.

Fig. 4 *The Wandervogel on a walk in the woods with their guitars*

Church youth groups

Both the Catholic and Protestant churches had youth groups. The Catholics had many different groups aimed at different sections of young people, e.g. New Germany, which was founded in 1919, and aimed at middle-class youths. The Protestants did not give youth work as high a priority and their groups had far fewer members. In both religions, the tasks of the youth groups were to promote religious observance and instil respect for the church, family and school.

Political youth groups

All of the main political parties had their youth sections, e.g.
- The Social Democratic Youth movement (SPD) was founded in 1925. It had the most members of any political youth groups in the Weimar period.
- The Young Communist League was founded in 1925 for the children of KPD members.
- The Bismarck Youth, linked to the DNVP, was founded in 1922 and reached a membership of 42,000 by 1928. Its strongest appeal was among middle and upper class youths in Protestant areas, but it also had a strong working-class following in Berlin.
- The Hitler Youth was linked to the Nazi Party. Its growth was slow in the 1920s, reaching a membership of only about 13,000 in 1929.

The Jews

There were more than half a million Jews living in Germany under the Weimar Republic. Eighty per cent of Jews in Germany (400,000) lived in cities and were well educated. Many of them felt much more German than Jewish and were intensely patriotic. Many believed in assimilation – keeping their ethnic and cultural identity but becoming fully integrated and accepted in mainstream German society.

The achievements of German Jews under the Weimar Republic were remarkable. Jews represented only one per cent of the total population, but they achieved a degree of influence out of all proportion to their numbers. German Jews achieved prominence in politics and the press, in

Fig. 5 *The Hitler Youth on a camping trip near Berlin*

Theodor Wolff (1868–1943) was a liberal journalist from a wealthy Jewish family. From 1887, he worked for the Mosse publishing house; in 1906, Mosse appointed him editor of the liberal newspaper *Berliner Tageblatt*. From 1916, Wolff and his paper came under attack for urging a negotiated peace. In 1918, he was one of the founders of the DDP. He remained active and influential until 1933, when he went into exile after his books were burned by the Nazis. In 1943, he was arrested in Italy and sent to Sachsenhausen concentration camp, where he died.

Kurt Eisner (1867–1919) was a journalist and leading member of the SPD in Bavaria. In 1917, he joined the breakaway USPD party and was also imprisoned for treason. After his release from prison in November 1918, he led the revolt in Bavaria that resulted in the establishment of the short-lived Bavarian Socialist Republic. He was assassinated in Munich in 1919 by a right-wing nationalist.

Discussion point

'The influence of Jews on the political, economic and cultural life of the Weimar Republic was out of all proportion to their numbers.'

Discuss this viewpoint in small groups and report your conclusions to the rest of the class.

business and banking, in the universities and in almost all aspects of Weimar culture. Jews had huge influence in the publishing of books and newspapers. Jewish musicians were at the forefront of musical life. Jewish producers and directors dominated theatre and the new medium of cinema.

Politics and the press

German Jews were already well established in the world of politics before 1914. Jewish publishing firms had a powerful influence in the media, with two Jewish-run newspapers in particular, the *Berliner Tageblatt* and the *Frankfurter Zeitung*, promoting liberal political views. **Theodor Wolff**, editor of *Berliner Tageblatt*, was the driving force behind the moderate Liberal DDP and Walter Rathenau, who became Foreign Minister in 1922, was also a leading member of the DDP. Jews were also prominent in the SPD and the KPD. Rosa Luxemburg, Hugo Haase and **Kurt Eisner**, the leader of the revolution in Bavaria in November 1918, all came from Jewish backgrounds.

Industry, commerce, and professions

German Jews achieved considerable wealth and influence in industry and commerce, although the extent of this influence was massively exaggerated by anti-Jewish propaganda, both at the time and afterwards. For example, the Rathenau family controlled the huge electrical engineering firm AEG until 1927. Jewish firms dominated coal-mining, steelworks and the chemical industry in Silesia, but had very little importance in the western industrial areas of the Rhineland or the Ruhr.

Jewish banking families, such as the Rothschilds, Mendelssohns and Bleichröders, owned about 50 per cent of private banks. Jewish directors also managed several major public banks. To make such a list of Jewish banking interests can be misleading, however; in the 1920s, the role of Jews in banking was actually declining. Banks owned by Jews made up about 18 per cent of the banking sector in Germany, a considerably smaller proportion than in the years before 1914.

Jews were particularly active and successful in retailing. They owned almost half of the firms involved in the cloth trade.

Jews were immensely successful in the professions, especially law and medicine, making up 16 per cent of the lawyers and 11 per cent of doctors in Germany. There were especially high numbers in Berlin; more than half of the doctors there in 1930 were Jewish and of 3400 lawyers, 1835 were Jews.

Jews also had a significant impact on the academic life of Germany. Of the 38 Nobel Prizes awarded to people working in Germany up to 1938, nine (24 per cent) were awarded to Jews. Germany was a world leader in the physical sciences, not least because of Albert Einstein, who revolutionised theoretical physics with his work on the theory of relativity and quantum mechanics.

The extent of assimilation and anti-Semitism

The vast majority of German Jews wished to assimilate. In language, dress and lifestyle, thousands of Jews looked and acted like other Germans. Many had married non-Jewish spouses, given up religious observance or converted to Christianity. By the late 1920s, the process of assimilation was far advanced. The chief factor limiting the degree of Jewish integration into German society, however, was the reluctance of many Germans to stop identifying Jews as somehow alien. There was still a significant gap between wanting to be completely assimilated and feeling the security of being completely accepted.

'German society during the years of the Weimar Republic, 1919 to 1933, experienced far-reaching social change.' Assess the validity of this view.

In the difficult early years of the Weimar Republic from 1918 to 1924, there was a backlash against the perceived threat of **Jewish Bolshevism**, as seen in events such as the Spartacus uprising in Berlin and in the breakaway regime of Kurt Eisner in Munich. Anti-Semitism was part of the violent nationalism behind right-wing movements such as the Freikorps and the NSDAP formed in 1920. There was also a surge of hostility against Jewish financiers at the time of the hyperinflation crisis in 1923. Between 1924 and 1930, however, as Weimar Germany entered its 'Golden Age' of economic recovery and political stability, anti-Semitism was pushed to the fringes of public and political life. There was still fierce opposition to perceived Jewish influence, however, with frequent accusations of corruption and exploitation by **Jewish bankers and businessmen**.

A CLOSER LOOK

Barmat scandal of 1925

Some scandals in the later 1920s provided ammunition for anti-Semitic attacks. The most sensational was the Barmat scandal of 1925. The Barmat brothers, Julius, Salomon and Henri, were Jewish businessmen who had emigrated from Galicia in Poland just after the war. After a high-profile court case, they were convicted of having bribed public officials to obtain loans from the Prussian State Bank and the National Post Office. Julius and Salomon were eventually sentenced to 11 months in jail.

'By 1930, the Jews had become fully assimilated into German society.' Explain why you agree or disagree with this view.

The development of arts and culture in the Weimar Republic

In 1919, the German writer Paul Ernst wrote, 'Our age is over! Thank God it is over! A new age dawns that will be different!' The new political and social freedom in Weimar Germany gave rise to an era of experimentation and innovation in the arts. Germany in the 1920s witnessed such an explosion of creativity in art, architecture, music, literature, theatre, film and music that it has been described as a 'cradle of modernity'. Yet, as with social and political change, not all Germans welcomed the new developments in culture and there was ongoing tension between modernists and conservatives.

Berlin's nightclubs

The greater cultural and personal freedom that was a feature of the Weimar Republic was epitomised in the vibrant nightlife of Berlin in the 1920s, especially in the more prosperous years after 1924. Berlin nightclubs became renowned for their cabarets in which nudity featured strongly. One such club, the Eldorado, was described by a German composer, Friedrich Hollaender, as a 'supermarket of eroticism'. Gay men, lesbians and transvestites, who before 1918 were forced to conceal their sexuality, now felt free to display it openly.

STUDY TIP

This question is about change and continuity in German society in the Weimar years. It requires a balanced assessment of the extent of social change as it affected different groups, at different times and in different areas. Make sure you offer a clear view and sustain your argument throughout the answer.

KEY TERM

Jewish Bolshevism: a term used by anti-Semites in the Weimar period to imply that Jews and communists were closely associated and represented a danger to German values

CROSS-REFERENCE

To find out more about Bolshevism and Spartacus/Eisner, see Chapter 4, pages 27–28 and Chapter 6, page 48.

STUDY TIP

This quote invites you to challenge it, but it is also possible to agree with the view to a certain extent. The answer should therefore be balanced between challenge and agreement, with each side of the argument being well supported with carefully selected evidence. The key to a good answer with this type of question is the extent to which you focus on the key word 'assimilation'.

American jazz music, much of it played by black American musicians, became popular. Many of the comedians performing in the clubs attacked politicians and authoritarian attitudes.

Many older, more traditionally minded Germans regarded the Berlin nightclub scene with horror and contempt. They hated the influence of the USA on German cultural life and attacked the Weimar Republic for relaxing censorship. They felt that order and discipline had been destroyed by the revolution of 1918 and that German society was becoming morally degenerate.

ACTIVITY

Group research exercise

Divide into six groups. Each group should research one of the six branches of the Weimar arts below. Focus in particular on the key people, their principal works and the influence they had on others. Present your findings to the rest of the class.

Fig. 6 *Kampfende Formen (Fighting Forms), 1914, by Franz Marc*

Art

The predominant movement in German art at this time was Expressionism. It originated in Germany in the early twentieth century and was associated with artists such as Kandinsky, George Grosz, Franz Marc and Ernst Ludwig Kirchner. Expressionist painters believed that their works should express meaning or emotion rather than physical reality, hence their paintings were abstract in style and vivid in colour.

Music

Expressionism also influenced German classical composers in this period. Among the most innovative were Hindemith and Arnold Schoenberg. Schoenberg attempted to convey powerful emotions in his music but avoided traditional forms of beauty. He was very much associated with 'atonal' music, which lacks a key, and sounds harsh and lacking in harmony to traditionalists

Literature

Expressionism was also a key influence on German literature of the period. Novelists and poets adopted a free form of writing in which they focused on a character's internal mental state rather than on the external social reality. A common theme in German expressionist literature was revolt against parental authority. The leading German writer of the period was Thomas Mann. He was awarded the Nobel Prize for Literature in 1929. Unlike many German intellectuals, he was a staunch supporter of the Weimar Republic and decided to live in Switzerland after the Nazis came to power in 1933.

Architecture

The founding of the Bauhaus at Dessau by William Gropius in 1919 was a key event in the development of modernist art in Germany. Although primarily an architectural school, the Bauhaus was also a school of art, design and photography. Its students were encouraged to break down the barriers between art and technology by incorporating new materials such as steel, concrete and glass into their designs. Students were taught to make the function of an object or building into the key element of their designs, stripping away superfluous ornamentation.

Theatre

Many German dramatists incorporated expressionist ideas into their productions. Sets were stark and plays relied on abstraction and symbolism to convey their message. Much of experimental theatre in Weimar Germany was explicitly political, attacking capitalism, nationalism and war. Bertolt Brecht and Kurt Weill developed a new form of music theatre that came to symbolise Weimar Berlin, above all *The Threepenny Opera*, a savage left-wing satire that treated respectable middle classes as villains, while making heroes out of criminals and prostitutes. They were attacked by the right as 'cultural Bolsheviks'.

Film

Berlin became an important centre for world cinema, developing modern techniques that would later be exploited by Nazi propaganda. Important figures of Jewish descent in the German film industry included Fritz Lang, Billy Wilder (later famous in post-war Hollywood) and Josef von Sternberg. It was Sternberg who directed the best-known film of the Weimar era, *The Blue Angel*, starring Marlene Dietrich as Lola, the sexy singer in a sleazy nightclub cabaret who seduces an innocent old professor played by Emil Jannings.

EXTRACT 1

To most Germans, the energy, the experimentation, the chaotic creativity which made Weimar culture the envy of so many foreigners, represented 'cultural communism', the overturning of forms and values in a world in which too much had been overturned already. The predominant cry was in favour of a 'conservative revolution'.

Peter Pulzer, *Germany, 1870–1945: Politics, State Formation, and War*, 1997

ACTIVITY

With reference to Extract 1 and your understanding of the historical context, make a list of the aspects of Weimar culture which conservatives would have labelled 'cultural communism'.

Summary

Cultural innovation divided Germans in the Weimar era, just as they were also divided by class, religion and politics. In rural areas and small towns, cultural change was no more than a rumour, something that was happening in faraway cities such as Berlin and Hamburg. In these areas, the influence of the churches was still strong: traditional family values held sway and people placed great store by traditional German culture. Yet even in the more remote areas of the country, the spread of cinema and increasing popularity of radio brought new cultural influences to the wider population. There was a fear on the right that cultural change brought in unwelcome foreign influences, whether in the form of 'cultural communism' or American influences such as jazz music and Hollywood films. Modern culture was regarded by conservatives as decadent, immoral and un-German.

The Weimar Republic gave its citizens greater freedom than would have seemed possible in the pre-war era. This freedom was welcomed by many but feared by others. It allowed experimentation in the arts and the opportunity for women and young people to break through many of the barriers that had constrained them in the past. These changes, however, provoked a fierce conservative reaction as the enemies of the Weimar Republic fought to resist cultural change.

7 Political developments and the working of democracy, 1924–28

LEARNING OBJECTIVES

In this chapter you will learn about:

- Reichstag elections and coalition governments in the years 1924–28
- the development of political parties
- the election of Hindenburg as President in 1925
- attitudes to the republic from the elites and other social groups
- the position of extremists including Nazis and Communists
- the extent of political stability in Germany by 1928.

CROSS-REFERENCE

To find out about Hindenburg's role in the war and in the years before the Weimar Republic, see page XIII in the Introduction.

ACTIVITY

Evaluating primary sources

In what ways would Source 1 be of value to an historian studying the appointment of President Hindenburg in 1925?

Wibke Bruhns came from an upper-middle class family. She wrote in her memoir in 2004, based on her father's diaries, about her family's reaction to the election of Hindenberg as President of the Weimar Republic in 1925. She describes how they hear of the death of President Ebert. His successor is Paul von Hindenburg, a convinced monarchist. He's seventy-seven years old and, before standing for the highest office in the republic, he requests the consent of his former Kaiser. The old Field Marshal wins the election.

SOURCE 1

Bruhns' diary entry from the day of Hindenburg's succession reads:

The result is greeted with jubilation by the radio audience in our living room. They applaud the victory of the past and recall earlier times when 'everything was better' and they were still unshaken by the miseries of democratic chaos. The fact that Hindenburg has stood for war gives him legendary status, and the fact that the war was lost is not a matter for reproach. Everyone knows the reason: the 'stab in the back' on the home front.

The years 1924 to 1928 were much calmer than the immediate post-war years. Political violence receded, extremist parties attracted less support in elections and the trauma of hyper-inflation had been successfully treated. In 1925, Hindenburg, a staunch opponent of the republic, was elected as its President. The extent to which these developments can be interpreted as a period of political stability is the theme of this chapter.

Reichstag elections and coalition governments

Elections

There were two elections in 1924. These elections indicated a return of greater support for the parties that supported the Weimar Republic – the SPD, DDP, DVP and Centre:

- Over 61 per cent voted for pro-republican parties in May 1924, and 67 per cent in December.
- The May 1924 election was the first contested by the Nazis, when they won 6.5 per cent of the vote. By December the Nazis' vote share was down to 3 per cent.
- On the left, the Communist Party also saw its fortunes fall after May 1924.
- Whilst the nationalist political parties of the right began to accept the republic and work within it, rather than against it, they found their electoral position weakening from December 1924. The conservative right-wing DNVP joined a Reich coalition government for the first time in January 1925.

Even so, the political developments of 1924 showed that the democratic parties were struggling to provide stable governments that commanded widespread support, as can be seen in Table 1, which illustrates the number of deputies elected from each party at the various elections during this time. As you can see from Table 1, right-wing anti-republican parties were still in a position to do political damage to the Republic.

In the 1928 election, support for extremist and anti-republican parties declined even further. The Nazis (NSDAP) made little impression on the national political scene in 1928. Their share of the vote went down even lower than in 1924. With 2.6 per cent of the vote and winning only 12 seats, the NSDAP trailed behind obscure minor parties such as the Bavarian People's Party and the Reich Party of the German Middle Class. The previously unheard-of Christian National Peasants' and Farmers' Party did almost as well as the Nazis, winning nine seats. The communist KPD, however, saw a revival of its electoral support in 1928.

Table 1 *Number of deputies elected in Reichstag elections, 1919–28*

Year	Left wing			Centre		Right wing		
	Communist (KPD)	Independent Social Democratic Party (USPD)	Social Democrat Party (SPD)	Democratic Party (DDP)	Centre (Catholic Zentrum)	Conservative (DVP)	Nationalist (DNVP)	Nazi (NSDAP)
1919	0	22	165	75	91	19	44	0
1920	4	84	102	39	85	65	71	0
May 1924	62	—	100	28	81	45	95	32
December 1924	45	—	131	32	88	51	103	14
1928	54	—	153	25	78	45	73	12

Coalition governments

There were seven coalition cabinets between November 1923 and March 1930 (see Table 2). Governments in the Weimar Republic's so-called 'golden age', therefore, were scarcely more stable than those in the years 1919–23, despite the fact that support for the anti-democratic parties of the extreme left and extreme right was falling. Coalition governments throughout the short history of the Weimar Republic were inherently unstable. Only six of the twenty-three cabinets between 1919 and 1932 had majority support in the Reichstag and many minority governments only survived as long as there was some semblance of unity between the parties that made up the coalitions.

Table 2 *Coalition governments, 1923–28*

Appointment	Chancellor	Party	Members of governing coalition
August 1923	Gustav Stresemann	DVP	DVP, SPD, DDP
November 1923	Wilhelm Marx	Centre	Centre, DVP, DDP, BVP
June 1924	Wilhelm Marx	Centre	Centre, DVP, DDP
January 1925	Hans Luther	No party	DDP, Centre, BVP, DVP, DNVP (centre-right)
January 1926	Hans Luther	No party	DDP, Centre, DVP, DNVP, BVP (centre-right)
May 1926	Wilhelm Marx	Centre	Centre, DDP, DVP, BVP (centre-right)
January 1927	Wilhelm Marx	Centre	Centre, DVP, DNVP, BVP (centre-right)
June 1928	Hermann Müller	SPD	SPD, Centre, DDP, DVP,BVP (Grand Coalition)

ACTIVITY

With reference to Table 1, answer the following questions:
1. Which party/parties commanded the most support in the years 1924–28?
2. Which party/parties suffered the biggest loss of seats?
3. At which point were the pro-Weimar parties (SPD, DDP, DVP, Centre) strongest?
4. What can you conclude after studying the statistics?

CROSS-REFERENCE

For more on the problems of coalition governments, go to Chapter 4, page 26.

In this situation, governments could not plan for the long term. Instead, they tended to muddle along from issue to issue. The historian Gordon Craig has written that government in the Weimar Republic 'resembled an endless cabinet crisis, with more time and energy expended on the task of filling ministerial chairs than in governing the country'. Sometimes, seemingly trivial issues could wreck a coalition cabinet. In 1926, for example, the government of Luther collapsed after a dispute over flags. When President Hindenburg ordered that the old imperial flag, with its black, white and red colours should be flown alongside the new republican tricolour (black, red and gold) at all German consulates in other countries, the resulting dispute led to the collapse of the government.

A CLOSER LOOK

The German flag

The Weimar Republic adopted a new flag when it was established in 1919. This was a tricolour flag of black, red and gold. It replaced the old imperial flag of black, white and red. Flags became a symbol of political allegiance in the Weimar years, with anti-Weimar, nationalist groups continuing to use the old imperial flag.

Fig. 3   *Hermann Müller*

Hermann Müller (1876–1931) was an SPD politician who had been Foreign Minister from 1919 to 1920 and Chancellor in 1928. As Foreign Minister, he was one of the German signatories of the Treaty of Versailles. He had a reputation for being a calm, hard-working politician but he lacked charisma.

Fig. 1   *The flag of the Weimar Republic (closely resembles the modern German flag)*

Fig. 2   *Old imperial flag of the German Empire*

The problems of establishing and sustaining a stable coalition government arose because the number of workable combinations of parties was limited. The SPD and the DNVP would not serve in the same cabinet and the more moderate parties did not have enough seats to command a Reichstag majority. The formation of the broadly based Grand Coalition in 1928, led by **Hermann Müller** of the SPD, appeared to offer the potential for a more stable government. It was, indeed, one of the longest-lived coalitions of the Weimar era, remaining in office until March 1930. Even this coalition, however, was fraught with divisions. Although the government was established in June 1928, it was not until the spring of 1929 that the parties involved finally agreed on the government's policies. There were ongoing disputes over the budget and over foreign policy, and the government only survived because of the strong working relationship between Müller and Stresemann, the Foreign Minister.

CROSS-REFERENCE

To read more about Stresemann's period as Chancellor of the so-called 'great coalition in 1923, see page 35 in Chapter 5.

The development of political parties

The quieter and more prosperous conditions of the years 1924–28 provided the pro-democracy parties with an opportunity to try to establish a stable democratic system that could be supported by the majority of Germans.

That they largely failed to do so was due to a number of factors. Firstly, deputies in the Reichstag did not represent a particular constituency; instead, under proportional representation, deputies were chosen from party lists to collectively represent a large area. There was thus no direct connection between a deputy and his or her constituents. Secondly, the party list system gave party committees control over Reichstag deputies. Deputies were not allowed to display any individuality but had to behave according to the dictates of their party bureaucracies. The result was that the Reichstag became a rather sterile debating chamber remote from the concerns of ordinary voters.

The leaderships of the main pro-democracy parties were also at fault. Factional rivalries weakened many parties. When leading party members became ministers in coalition cabinets, party committees would not allow them any flexibility to operate on their own initiative. Party leaders often gave higher priority to protecting the interests of their own party, and the interest groups they represented, than to the wider national interest. This brought the parliamentary system into disrepute and support for democratic institutions suffered as a result.

The SPD

Through the years 1924–28, the left-wing SPD remained the largest single party in the Reichstag. It was the party that had taken the leading role in the revolution of 1918 and the establishment of the Weimar Republic. It therefore had a vital interest in the success of democratic government. Yet the SPD participated in only one of the six coalition cabinets that were established in these years. Although it had been in the process of becoming a thoroughly reformist, moderate party since the 1890s, it could not let go of the revolutionary Marxist rhetoric that had been its trademark since its foundation in the 1860s. This hangover from the past tended to make the SPD rather inflexible on important issues and unwilling to make the kind of compromises that participation in coalition governments involved. It therefore tended to be a party that was more comfortable in opposition than in government. The SPD had close links with the trade unions and appealed mainly to industrial workers. It had limited appeal to young people and to women, and had no support among farmers, agricultural workers or the Mittelstand.

The Centre Party

The Centre Party had been established to defend the interests of the Roman Catholic Church in the German Empire and this remained its priority in the Weimar Republic. As a party based on religious affiliation, however, its appeal crossed class and occupational boundaries. It was supported by industrial workers and industrialists, farmers and their landlords, together with professional groups such as teachers. This broad-based appeal made the party more flexible and pragmatic than the SPD, but also tended to cause divisions over social and economic issues. The Centre Party was vital to the success of Weimar democracy and no coalition government was formed without its participation. There was an important leadership change in 1928, however, which reflected a growing drift to the right. The new leader, Heinrich Brüning, was less committed to parliamentary democracy than Marx, his predecessor.

The DDP

The liberal DDP was in decline by the mid-1920s. Its appeal was mainly to academics and professional groups, and it gave an impression of being composed of worthy intellectuals who had limited political experience. It was also increasingly riven by internal disputes and had great difficulty in conveying clearly and unequivocally what it stood for. It was, nevertheless, a party committed to the success of parliamentary democracy and participated in all of the coalition governments of this period.

CROSS-REFERENCE

Find out more about Brüning's role in government in the early 1930s and his controversial policies, which contributed to the demise of the Republic, on page 71 in Chapter 9.

The DVP

The conservative DVP, like the DDP, was committed to parliamentary democracy and also participated in all the coalition cabinets of the period. It had support amongst academics but its main support came from industrialists. The DVP provided the leading politician from 1924 to 1929, Gustav Stresemann, but after his death in 1929 the party drifted to the right and increasingly became a narrow pressure group promoting the interests of big business.

The DNVP

The conservative, nationalist DNVP broadened its appeal in the 1920s beyond its traditional base amongst landowners in the east of Germany. By the mid-1920s, it had attracted support from industrialists, professional groups and even some industrial workers. It was anti-democratic and nationalist, with its main aims being restoration of the monarchy and dismantling of the Treaty of Versailles. As an anti-Weimar party, the DNVP refused to join coalitions most of the time. However, growing diversity in the party led to increased divisions over policy and tactics, with many of its newer and younger members being willing to compromise with democratic parties. The decisions to join the Luther cabinet in 1926 and the Marx cabinet in 1927 were, therefore, a significant change in the party's tactics.

In the 1928 Reichstag election, however, the DNVP suffered a significant loss of support, which encouraged the right in the party to return to their anti-democratic ways. When Hugenberg was chosen as party leader in 1928, the shift to the right was confirmed. It was Hugenberg who, in 1929, led the DNVP into an alliance with the Nazis and paramilitary groups in the campaign against the Young Plan. Henceforth, the DNVP returned to its blind opposition to the Weimar Republic.

The NSDAP (Nazi Party)

After the failure of the Munich Putsch in 1923, the Nazi Party entered a period of decline, but also of reflection and reorganisation. While Hitler was in prison he wrote **Mein Kampf** and also took the opportunity to think about Nazi Party tactics. He came to the conclusion that the route to power was not through an armed overthrow of the Weimar Republic – even though paramilitary violence was still to be an essential component of the Nazis' tactics – but through winning mass support. The Nazis could not hope to win power if they did not have the support, or at least the acquiescence, of the army and other key groups among the elite.

Hitler was released from prison early and set about rebuilding the party, although he was severely hampered by the fact that the party and its Stormtroopers were banned organisations. Until 1927 he was not allowed to speak in public. He used the time to assert his undisputed control over the Nazi Party, to reorganise it and to re-orientate its campaigning.

At the end of 1927, the Nazi Party had only 75,000 members and seven deputies in the Reichstag. A key decision was taken in 1928, however, to broaden the Nazi Party's appeal. In a bid to capitalise on the discontent of farmers, the Nazis began to concentrate their efforts in rural areas, especially in the mainly Protestant north of Germany. Across the country, the Nazis did badly in the 1928 Reichstag election, losing 100,000 votes. In some rural areas in the north, however, the Nazis' share of the vote was as high as 18 per cent. The party's membership grew to 150,000 by October 1929 and, in that same year, the party took control of its first town council. Even before the campaign against the Young Plan, which gave Hitler the chance to make a name for himself as a national politician, the party was showing clear signs of revival.

CROSS-REFERENCE

See page 40 in Chapter 5 for more on the Young Plan and its final settlement of the reparations issue. See also page 33 of Chapter 4 for Hitler's role in the Beer Hall Putsch.

Fig. 4 *The original cover of* Mein Kampf

KEY TERM

Mein Kampf: (meaning 'My Struggle') Hitler's autobiography and a statement of his beliefs; it became required reading for all members of the Nazi Party

The KPD (Communist Party)

The German Communist Party was the largest communist party outside Russia, but it never became a genuinely mass party. It had support in important industrial and port areas such as the Ruhr, Saxony and Hamburg, and also in Berlin, and it had a significant presence in the Reichstag throughout the period. As an avowedly revolutionary party, however, it was dedicated to the overthrow of the Weimar Republic. As a member of the Comintern, the policies and tactics of the KPD were dictated by the Communist Party of the Soviet Union. In 1923, for example, at the height of the political and economic crisis caused by hyperinflation and the occupation of the Ruhr, the KPD leadership was summoned to Moscow to be instructed to launch a communist revolution in Germany. This led to communist uprisings in Saxony and Hamburg, which were ruthlessly suppressed by the army. After 1924, the Soviet leadership instructed the KPD that the opportunity for revolution had receded and that their main priority was to attack the SPD as a party that had betrayed the working class. The KPD labelled the SPD as 'social-fascists' and concentrated on attacking them rather than on countering the influence of the Nazi Party. This division in the working-class movement in Germany weakened the anti-Nazi forces in Weimar Germany.

The election of Hindenburg as President in 1925

Ebert, the first President of the Weimar Republic, died on 28 February 1925. He had been indirectly elected by the National Assembly, but his successor had to be elected according to the terms of the Weimar Constitution, which meant that a full national election would have to be held. Under the terms of the constitution, unless a candidate received more than 50 per cent of the vote in the first round of voting, there had to be a second ballot and it was possible to nominate alternative candidates in this second ballot.

In the first round, there were seven candidates including Karl Jarres for the right (DVP and DNVP), Otto Braun for the SPD, Wilhelm Marx for the Centre, **Ernst Thälmann** for the Communist Party and Erich Ludendorff, who stood as a Nazi Party candidate. Jarres won the most votes, with the SPD in second place, but there was no outright winner.

In the second round, Jarres withdrew in favour of Paul von Hindenburg, who allegedly consulted the exiled ex-Kaiser before he reluctantly agreed to stand. The SPD calculated that Marx had a better chance of winning against Hindenburg than Braun, so withdrew its candidate and advised SPD supporters to vote for Marx. The number of candidates was reduced to just three – Hindenburg, Marx and Thälmann. However, because of Thälmann's candidacy, the left vote was split and, in the election on 26 April, Hindenburg won with 48.3 per cent to Marx's 45.3 per cent. Thälmann trailed with 6.4 per cent.

Hindenburg was a symbol of the past. With his military uniform, his war medals and his authoritarian views, he was revered by the right, who regarded his election as the beginning of the restoration of the old order. For many, Hindenburg was the Ersatzkaiser (substitute emperor), and his election was seen as a major step away from parliamentary democracy. In the short term, this proved not to be true. When he took his presidential oath, Hindenburg appealed to the parties in the Reichstag to work with him in restoring national unity. He stuck closely to the letter of the Weimar constitution and did not abuse his powers. Moreover, his election was important in reconciling, at least temporarily, some anti-democratic political parties, such as the DNVP, to the existence of the Republic and to playing a more constructive role in making parliamentary democracy work.

CROSS-REFERENCE

To find out about the Comintern and the communist uprising, see page 28 in Chapter 4.

ACTIVITY

1. Make a list of the main reasons why it was difficult for the political parties to establish stable coalition governments. Try to identify at least five reasons.
2. Arrange your list in order of priority and explain to a partner the reasons for your rank order.

CROSS-REFERENCE

There is a key profile of Hindenberg in the Introduction on page XIII.

KEY PROFILE

Fig. 5   Ernst Thälmann

Ernst Thälmann (1886–1944) became the Chairman of the Communist KPD in 1925. He had been a member of the SPD before 1914 but split with the party in 1917 over its support for the war. Having survived an assassination attempt by a right-wing paramilitary group in 1922, he was one of the leaders of the Hamburg communist uprising in 1923. He was very much guided by Stalin after 1925 and followed unquestioningly the line that the SPD were the communists' main enemies. He was the communist candidate in the presidential elections of 1925 and 1932. In 1933, he was arrested by the Nazis and imprisoned in Buchenwald concentration camp, where he was executed on Hitler's orders in 1944.

Discussion point

'The election of Hindenburg as President was a sign that the Weimar Republic had finally won the support of the old elites.'

However, for party politicians it was generally business as usual. They continued to place party political advantage above national interest, and cooperation between the parties was merely a means to secure tactical advantage. By the early 1930s, Hindenburg was becoming increasingly impatient with this party political manoeuvring at a time of serious economic crisis and he used his powers to rule by decree on a routine basis. Therefore, after 1925, presidential power was in the hands of a man who did not believe in democracy and was not prepared to defend it against its enemies.

SOURCE 2

Arnold Brecht, a government legal officer in the Weimar years, wrote this in his 1976 autobiography:

The real surprise was not Hindenburg's victory. The real surprise came later. It was the unexpected fact that Hindenburg subjected himself quite loyally to the Weimar Constitution and maintained this attitude unhesitatingly during his first term in office. Both sides had expected his support for right-wing attempts to restore the monarchy, to abolish the colours of the democratic republic in favour of the former black-white-red, to reduce the rights of the working classes, to reintroduce more patriarchal conditions. The great surprise – disappointment on the one side, relief on the other – was that he did not do any of this. During the election campaign he said that now he had read the Constitution for the first time and had found it quite good. 'If duty requires that I act as President on the basis of the Constitution, without regard to party, person, or origin, I shall not fail.'

 PRACTICE QUESTION

Evaluating primary sources

With reference to Sources 1 and 2 and your understanding of the historical context, which of these two sources is more valuable in explaining the reactions to Hindenburg's election as President of the Weimar Republic in 1925?

Both Sources 1 and 2 give an insight into the views of Germans who supported Hindenburg. However, Source 1 reflects the hopes of Hindenburg's supporters when he was elected. Source 2 offers a more long-term perspective and talks of how, in many ways, Hindenburg disappointed many of those supporters. Each is therefore valuable but in different ways. You might conclude that Source 2 is more valuable because it has a more long-term perspective, but it is equally possible to argue that Source 1 is valuable in giving an insight into the attitudes of conservative, middle-class Germans who looked to Hindenburg to bring back the good times.

CROSS-REFERENCE

Turn to page 13 in Chapter 2 for information on the Treaty of Versailles.

Attitudes to the Republic from the elites and other social groups

The Weimar Republic could only be truly stable if it succeeded in winning the support and loyalty of the majority of its citizens. We saw in Chapter 1 how the circumstances in which the Republic was born predisposed large and important sections of German society to oppose it. The old elites, who were firmly entrenched in the army, the civil service and the judiciary, were hostile to parliamentary democracy and held firm to the view that the Republic was born out of betrayal of the Fatherland. This hostility was strengthened by the signing of the humiliating Versailles Treaty and by the political and economic crises of the early years of the Republic. The election of Hindenburg went some way towards reconciling the elites to the existence of the Republic, but only because they believed that Hindenburg would steer Germany back towards a more authoritarian form of government.

At the other end of the social spectrum, there were many industrial workers who felt that the Republic had not delivered on its promises of greater equality and social justice and that the crushing of revolts by the army and the police, at the behest of democratically elected politicians, was clear evidence that parliamentary democracy was failing.

Middle-class support for moderate political parties was therefore vital if the Weimar Republic was to succeed in establishing solid foundations. It is difficult to generalise about the middle class in Germany since it was very diverse, with many variations in wealth, in religion and in political affiliations. There were many among the middle class who continued to prosper and were broadly supportive of the Republic. There were many more, however, especially among the lower-middle class Mittelstand, who had suffered a catastrophic decline in their incomes as a result of hyperinflation and who had no organised way to defend their interests. People in this group welcomed the return of economic stability under Stresemann and political stability under Hindenburg, but their resentment of the Republic continued to fester.

CROSS-REFERENCE

To read about the impact of economic change on the Mittlestand, see page 39 in Chapter 5.

Summary: The extent of political stability by 1928

When viewed in comparison with the early years of the Weimar Republic, or with the years 1929–32, the period 1924–28 can be interpreted as a time of political stability. Political violence receded and there were no attempts by extremist groups to overthrow the republic by force. Indeed, the parties of the extreme left and the extreme right suffered a loss of support in the elections of these years. The election of Hindenburg as President in 1925 can also be seen as a sign that traditional conservatives were beginning to adapt and accommodate to the new reality of a democratic republic.

On the other hand, the fundamental weaknesses in the Weimar political system remained and stable cabinets were as elusive as they had been in the post-war years. Parties represented narrow sectional interests, making it difficult for politicians with a national appeal and national programme to emerge. The circumstances under which the Weimar Republic was created deepened these political divides. Of course, many of the Weimar Republic's democratic politicians understood the need to compromise in order to establish coalition governments but their parties, and the interests of the people they represented, placed severe constraints on their freedom of action.

Coalition governments, therefore, were fragile and temporary alliances. Even in the favourable circumstances of the years 1924–28, stable government proved impossible to achieve and respect for democratic institutions was further eroded.

ACTIVITY

Revision

Create a strengths and weaknesses chart on the Weimar political system by 1928.

PRACTICE QUESTION

'The Weimar Republic enjoyed a "golden age" of political stability in the years 1924 to 1928'. Assess the validity of this view.

STUDY TIP

This requires a balanced response, but you should also form a clear view and argue consistently in favour of it. There is a lot of evidence which can be offered in support of the view; equally, there is a lot of evidence which can be used in an argument against it. Select your evidence carefully and state your argument clearly in the introduction and the conclusion.

8 Germany's international position, 1924–28

LEARNING OBJECTIVES

In this chapter you will learn about:

- Gustav Stresemann and the foreign policy of fulfilment
- the Locarno Pact of 1925 and the League of Nations
- relations between Germany and Russia/USSR, including the Treaty of Berlin
- the extent of disarmament by Germany
- the end of allied occupation in Germany.

CROSS-REFERENCE

To help you recall the terms of the Versailles Treaty and what Germans thought of it, revisit pages 13–14 in Chapter 2.

Gustav Stresemann's Key Profile is on page 32.

KEY CHRONOLOGY

Key events in foreign policy, 1924–30

1924	Dawes Plan
1925	Locarno Pact
1926	Germany admitted to the League of Nations
	Treaty of Berlin with the USSR
	Allied forces withdraw from Zone 1 of the Rhineland
1929	Young Plan
	Allied withdrawal from Zone 2 of the Rhineland
1930	Allied withdrawal from Zone 3 of the Rhineland

SOURCE 1

In 1926, an officer in the Reichswehr, Colonel Joachim von Stulpnagel, set out his views on the aims of German foreign policy:

The immediate aim of German policy must be the regaining of full sovereignty over the area retained by Germany, the firm acquisition of those areas at present separated from her and the reacquisition of those areas essential to the German economy. That is to say:
1 the liberation of the Rhineland and the Saar area
2 the abolition of the [Danzig] Corridor and the regaining of Polish Upper Silesia
3 the Anschluss [union] of German Austria
4 the abolition of the Demilitarised Zone.
   The above exposition of Germany's political aims clearly shows the problem for Germany in the next stages of her political development can only be the re-establishment of her position in Europe, and that the regaining of her world position will be a task for the distant future.

ACTIVITY

Evaluating primary sources

To what extent do the views presented in Source 1 reflect the views of the majority of Germans about the Versailles Treaty?

Gustav Stresemann and the policy of fulfilment

Germans of all classes and political allegiances agreed on one thing after 1919 – that the Treaty of Versailles was an unjust and dictated peace treaty, which denied Germany its rightful place among the great powers of Europe. It also placed millions of Germans outside the territory of the Republic. Whichever government was in power during the years 1919–33, the foreign policy of the Weimar Republic was always based on one clear and simple aim – to revise the terms of the Treaty of Versailles. There were, however, deep divisions between the parties on how this should best be achieved. The nationalist right consistently argued that Germany should reject the treaty and rebuild its military strength in preparation for a time when the country could regain lost territory and become a fully independent great power once again. A more pragmatic approach, which came to be associated with Gustav Stresemann, was the policy of fulfilment. This involved Germany cooperating with France, Great Britain, the USA and Italy on issues such as reparations payments and removing allied occupation forces from German territory. Such cooperation, it was believed, would lead to more revision of the treaty than a confrontational approach.

Gustav Stresemann was Foreign Minister from 1923 to 1929. As seen in Chapter 5, he was responsible for bringing hyperinflation under control, ending the policy of passive resistance to the French occupation of the Ruhr and cooperating with the Allies over the Dawes Plan. As a result, French and Belgian forces left the Ruhr in 1925. Stresemann understood that French suspicion of Germany was the biggest obstacle in the way of securing revisions in the Treaty of Versailles and, therefore, he concentrated on finding ways to reassure France of Germany's peaceful intentions. This policy bore fruit in the Locarno Pact of 1925.

SOURCE 2

Stresemann set out his thoughts on German foreign policy in this letter to Kaiser Wilhelm II's son, the ex-Crown Prince, in 1925:

In my opinion there are three great tasks that confront German foreign policy in the immediate future:

In the first place, the solution of the Reparations question in a way tolerable for Germany.

Secondly, the protection of Germans abroad, those 10 to 12 million of our kindred who now live under a foreign yoke in foreign lands.

The third great task is the readjustment of our eastern frontiers; the recovery of Danzig, the Polish Corridor, and a correction of the frontier in Upper Silesia.

In the background stands the union with German Austria, although I am quite clear that this not merely brings no advantages to Germany but seriously complicates the problem of the German Reich.

The Locarno Pact, 1925

In October 1925, the western European powers met, at Germany's suggestion, at a conference in the Swiss city of Locarno. Stresemann was anxious to restore Germany's position internationally and avoid any hostile alliance between Britain and France, particularly as the latter began to feel threatened by Germany's industrial recovery. France was suspicious of the move, but eventually agreed to attend, along with the USA, Britain and Italy, but not Russia. The discussions led to the Rhineland Pact and Arbitration Treaties, usually known collectively as the Locarno Pact, although they were finally signed in London on 1 December 1925.

Under the Rhineland Pact:

- Germany, France and Belgium promised to respect the western frontier, as drawn up at Versailles in 1919. This frontier was to be regarded as fixed and internationally guaranteed.

Fig. 1 *Stresemann with other leaders at the Locarno Conference*

- Germany agreed to keep its troops out of the Rhineland, as demanded at Versailles.
- Britain and Italy promised to aid Germany, France or Belgium if any of these countries were attacked by its neighbours.

Under the Arbitration Treaties:

- Germany agreed with France, Belgium, Poland and Czechoslovakia that any dispute between them should be settled by a conciliation committee to mediate discussions.
- France signed treaties of 'mutual guarantee' with Poland and Czechoslovakia. These said that France would make sure Germany did not break the agreement above.

It was also agreed that any conflicts regarding the western borders should be referred to the **League of Nations**. In addition, France would not be permitted to cross into Germany should there be any dispute between Germany and Poland or Czechoslovakia.

The Locarno Pact was hailed as a major triumph in many quarters. It was the first time that Germany had recognised the western border imposed at Versailles and accepted the loss of Alsace-Lorraine to France and Eupen-Malmédy to

CROSS-REFERENCE

More information about the Dawes Plan of 1924 can be found on page 36 of Chapter 5.

A CLOSER LOOK

The union with German Austria

The Treaty of Versailles specifically ruled out any union between Germany and Austria, as this would make Germany an even larger state. This clause was resented by German nationalists who believed that all Germans should be part of one state.

KEY TERM

League of Nations: a permanent forum of states established after the First World War to meet and resolve disputes without resorting to war; most states joined the League but USA declined and Germany and Russia were initially excluded

Belgium. For the French, there was a guarantee of support from the British should there ever be another German attack, while for the Germans, it meant the 1923 occupation of the Ruhr could never be repeated. The French agreed to withdraw the forces occupying the Rhineland and, although this was initially postponed in January 1925 because of Germany's refusal to comply with the disarmament obligations imposed at Versailles, it was achieved over the next five years and without Stresemann giving any assurances that Germany would disarm. The city of Cologne, for example, was evacuated by the French in 1926.

However, although the Arbitration Treaties with Poland and Czechoslovakia offered some guarantees, the eastern borders were not recognised in the same way. For Germany, this left open the possibility of further revision of the eastern borders at some stage in the future. Stresemann regarded Locarno as his greatest achievement – and he was rewarded by Germany's acceptance into the League of Nations as a permanent member of the council and the Nobel Peace Prize in 1926.

SOURCE 3

In his speech to the League of Nations in 1926, Stresemann had this to say:

In many respects the League is the heir and executor of the treaties of 1919. Out of these treaties there have arisen in the past, I may say frankly, many differences between the League and Germany. I hope that our cooperation within the League will make it easier in future to discuss these questions. In this respect mutual confidence will, from a political point of view, be found a greater creative force than anything else. Germany desires to cooperate on the basis of mutual confidence with all nations represented in the League.

ACTIVITY

Analysing primary sources

Stresemann is closely associated with the policy of fulfilment towards the Treaty of Versailles. Identify the phrases he uses in the speech in Source 3 that reflect his commitment to the policy of fulfilment.

Stresemann could take pride in the fact that he had established Germany's position as an equal partner in diplomatic negotiations with the three major western powers – France, Britain and the USA. Strategically, he had achieved a good deal with very little loss to Germany. The German nationalist right, however, attacked Stresemann for appeasing the Allies and giving too much away.

Relations with the USSR

After the revolutions of 1917 in Russia and 1918 in Germany, the two former enemies took very different political paths. Russia, later (1922) the USSR, became the world's first communist state, in which the rights of the individual were subordinated to those of the state. Germany adopted a democratic system of government, which guaranteed individual freedom. Although there was a large Communist Party, which campaigned for close links with the USSR, most Germans were opposed to the communist political system. There were, however, some similarities in the post-war situation of each country:

- Both countries had been defeated in the war and had suffered from punitive peace treaties.
- Both countries felt that the existence of an independent Poland, supported by French guarantees, was a threat to their security. Poland also contained large German and Russian minorities.
- Both Germany and Russia/USSR were treated as 'outcast' nations by the victorious powers and were not allowed to join the League of Nations.

These similarities led some in Germany to see advantages in a closer working relationship with Russia/USSR. Among these was Walther Rathenau who, in April 1922, had negotiated the Treaty of Rapallo with Russia under the following terms:

- Germany and Russia resumed trade and economic cooperation
- diplomatic relations between the two countries were restored

Fig. 2 *Stresemann addressed the League of Nations on numerous occasions*

CROSS-REFERENCE

More information about Rathenau can be found on page 31 of Chapter 4.

Fig. 3 *Map of the Polish borders, 1924*

- all outstanding claims for compensation for war damage were dropped
- Germany was allowed to develop new weapons and train pilots in Russia, away from the scrutiny of the Allied powers.

Although the treaty did not specify cooperation between Germany and Russia against Poland, this was clearly implied in the existence of the treaty. For Germany, therefore, the Treaty of Rapallo was an important but symbolic step away from its post-war isolation. However the Allies, particularly France, were angered by this treaty, which showed Germany's intention to get around the disarmament terms of the Treaty of Versailles and its refusal to accept its eastern frontier with Poland.

The Treaty of Berlin

In April 1926, Germany and the USSR renewed their earlier treaty in the Treaty of Berlin. This added very little to the original treaty, except for the agreement that Germany would remain neutral if the USSR were to be involved in a war, as long as the USSR was not the aggressor. This treaty was signed a year after the Locarno Pact and showed that, despite his agreement to guarantee Germany's western frontiers, Stresemann had not abandoned his desire to secure a revision of Germany's eastern frontiers. In order to achieve this, a close relationship with the USSR was vital because the USSR would resist any border changes it did not agree with.

The extent of disarmament

Under the disarmament clauses of the Treaty of Versailles, Germany's army was limited to 100,000 men, it was not allowed to have an air force and its navy was prevented from having submarines and large battleships. In addition, the Rhineland area was to be demilitarised, meaning that German fortifications had to be dismantled and no German troops were allowed to be based in the area. In order to ensure compliance with the treaty, allied forces occupied the Rhineland and an **Inter-Allied Control Commission (IMCC)** was established

A CLOSER LOOK

Inter-Allied Control Commission (IMCC)

The IMCC was a commission established under the Treaty of Versailles to ensure that Germany complied with the disarmament clauses. It was staffed largely by French and British army officers. Its task was primarily to check that existing weapons were destroyed and that no new weapons outside the terms of the treaty were being produced.

KEY TERM

Krupps: a large German company, based in Essen in the Ruhr, which had produced much of the weaponry for the German army since the nineteenth century

Fig. 4 *The **Krupps** works in Essen*

CROSS-REFERENCE

More information on von Seeckt can be found on page 10 of Chapter 1.

More information on the Kapp Putsch, and Freikorps' involvement in it, can be found on page 29 in Chapter 4.

To remind yourself about the Young Plan, turn to page 40 in Chapter 5.

ACTIVITY

Talking point

Write a speech to support or oppose the view that 'Gustav Stresemann deserved the Nobel Peace Prize'. Give your speech to the rest of the class and try to come to a class decision as to whether or not this statement is true.

in Germany to monitor Germany's disarmament. These disarmament clauses were a cause of burning resentment in Germany, especially as the Allies were free to maintain their own formidable armed forces.

As the Treaty of Rapallo with Russia showed, Germany sought and found ways to get around the disarmament clauses. Similar arrangements with other countries allowed Germany to build submarines in Spain and tanks and artillery in Sweden.

This secret rearmament did not provide Germany with a fully operational air force, or the army with unlimited supplies of modern weapons, but it did ensure that Germany did not fall behind other powers in technological developments. German fortifications along the Rhine were dismantled in accordance with the Treaty of Versailles, but new fortifications were built along the Polish frontier.

Under the Chief of the Army **General von Seeckt's** command, the Reichswehr found other ways of getting round the limit on the size of the army. Most recruits to the army were enlisted for short periods, during which they would receive intensive military training. This ensured that there was a reserve of highly trained men who could be recalled to the army at short notice. The army sponsored a number of paramilitary groups, which also formed a potential military reserve force. Even when the Freikorps was disbanded after the failed Kapp Putsch, there were many unofficial paramilitary groups that had a close relationship with the army.

General von Seeckt aimed to restore Germany's military might and he worked towards a military alliance with Russia/USSR, which aimed to destroy the newly independent Poland. Many of the details of his agreements with the Red Army were kept secret from the politicians to whom he was supposed to be accountable. However, politicians such as Rathenau and Stresemann were involved in negotiating the Treaties of Rapallo (1922) and Berlin (1926), which formalised the relationship with Russia/USSR, and chose to turn a blind eye to the extent of military cooperation. Secret rearmament was a policy driven by army commanders such as von Seeckt, but was tacitly approved by the politicians.

Kellogg-Briand Pact

In 1928, Germany also signed the Kellogg-Briand Pact with France and the USA. Frank Kellogg, the American Secretary of State, and Aristide Briand, the Foreign Minister of France, drew up an international agreement under which states would agree voluntarily to renounce the use of offensive wars to resolve disputes. Germany was one of the first states to sign, and was followed by many other countries. The Pact had symbolic importance as an international agreement to avoid war, but its lack of any enforcement mechanism limited its effectiveness.

The end of allied occupation

The removal of foreign forces from German soil was an aim shared by Germans of all parties. Stresemann's policy of fulfilment secured this objective by 1930. The French, concerned for their own security and suspicious of Germany's willingness to comply with the Treaty of Versailles, were the most reluctant of all the allied powers to withdraw occupying forces. The withdrawal of forces was, therefore, a step-by-step process, which involved compromise and concession on both sides. After the Dawes Plan of 1924 and the Locarno Pact of 1925 provided evidence of German willingness to cooperate with the Allies, occupation forces were withdrawn from Zone 1 of the Rhineland in 1926. The Allies also withdrew the IMCC from Germany in the same year. Further progress, however, was dependent on a final settlement of the reparations issue. Once the Young Plan had been agreed by Germany in 1929, the way was clear for the withdrawal of the remaining allied forces. They were withdrawn from Zone 2 in 1929 and from Zone 3 in 1930, five years ahead of the schedule laid down in the Treaty of Versailles. Although Stresemann had died in 1929 before this process was completed, this success was largely due to his policies.

 PRACTICE QUESTION

Evaluating primary sources

With reference to Sources 1 and 2 and your understanding of the historical context, which of these two sources is more valuable for an historian studying of German foreign policy in the years from 1924 to 1928?

Summary

Stresemann was both an able politician and a skilful and influential diplomat. While he liked to appear as the champion of European cooperation, his long-term aim was a revision of the Versailles Treaty. He had, after all, been an outspoken nationalist during the First World War and he desperately wanted to make Germany a great, and perhaps dominant, power once more. It could be argued that his commitment to 'fulfilment' was no more than a devious policy to cover up his nationalist agenda. It must be remembered that Stresemann's policies provided Germany with far more than the country gave up – American money and protection from a French invasion together with hopes of revisions to the eastern borders. What is more, he maintained secret military arrangements with the USSR and so laid the basis for Hitler's later foreign policy.

However, this judgement may be too harsh. Stresemann certainly chose to follow the route of negotiation and compromise, and was fully aware that Germany's recovery depended on moderation and on maintaining good relations with the West. He never regarded the Russian alliance as any substitute for that and in his actions he showed courage in the face of opposition, intelligence in the way he set about his tasks and determination in the way he saw them through. In the view of the historian William Carr, Stresemann was one of the 'few really outstanding political figures of the Weimar period'.

 PRACTICE QUESTION

'By 1928, Germany had accepted the terms of the Treaty of Versailles.' Assess the validity of this view.

STUDY TIP

Both of these sources refer to the aims of German foreign policy, but from different perspectives. The fact that Source 2 comes from Stresemann himself, and that it is a private communication, may be used as evidence that it gives a highly valuable insight into his thinking. Source 1 comes from a high-ranking army officer and may be said to reflect the thinking of the army at this time. There are clear similarities between the sources, which may indicate that the views are shared across the government and the army, but there are also differences of emphasis, which indicate that the priorities of the army and politicians were not entirely the same. You could use this type of approach when asked to compare sources.

STUDY TIPS

This quotation invites challenge but can also be agreed with to a certain extent. The key to a good answer with this type of question is to present both sides of the argument. In the end, you must come to a clear judgement on one side or the other.

It is possible to argue that Germany voluntarily signed the Locarno Pact, which guaranteed its western frontiers, joined the League of Nations and joined in disarmament negotiations. On the other hand, the Locarno Pact did not settle the issue of Germany's eastern frontiers, there was secret rearmament going on through the alliance with Russia and the reparations issue was still far from settled.

9 The impact of the Depression of 1929

- the collapse of the German economy in 1929 and the growth of mass unemployment during the Depression
- the social impact of the Depression on Germans
- the political consequences of the Depression, including elections, governments and policies.

KEY TERM

Wall Street Crash: the sudden collapse of the stock market in New York in October 1929 after a long period of rising prosperity and overconfidence by investors

ACTIVITY

1. Draw a diagram to show how the Wall Street Crash affected European countries, including Germany.
2. Draw a diagram to show how the economic collapse affected Germany in particular.

The economic impact

On 24 October 1929, the New York Stock Exchange experienced its worst ever fall in share prices in an event that became known as 'Black Thursday'. This was followed by another collapse the following Tuesday, on 29 October. On that one day alone, the value of the largest American companies fell by ten billion dollars. Overnight, millionaires lost their fortunes and many smaller investors lost all their savings. Many companies went bankrupt, workers lost their jobs, and banks stopped lending and called in their existing loans. This was the start of a prolonged depression, which spread from the USA around the world. For Germany, the **Wall Street Crash** had a profound impact on its economy, its society and its political system.

The German economy had been stagnating since 1928 as investment decreased. Germany's economic recovery in the years 1924–28 had been largely financed by American loans but, in the aftermath of the Wall Street Crash, those loans dried up. To make matters worse, the American banks that had lent money to Germany on short-term loans demanded immediate repayment. Thus, at a time when the German economy needed more investment to stimulate the economy, money was being withdrawn. The USA had also been the largest overseas market for German manufactured goods, but the Depression drastically reduced demand for imported goods in the USA and Germany's export trade declined rapidly. Between 1929 and 1932, Germany's export trade declined by 61 per cent and its industrial production fell by 58 per cent of its 1928 level. The result was that the German economy entered a deep depression.

The Depression affected other countries as well, but Germany suffered a greater fall in industrial production than other European countries. In Britain, for example, the decline in industrial production between 1929 and 1932 was 11 per cent. As Germany's foreign trade collapsed and prices fell, many companies had no alternative but to declare themselves bankrupt and make their workers redundant. Even those companies that survived had to reduce their workforces and cut the hours and wages of those workers who continued working. Banks also began to get into difficulties as customers withdrew their money and outstanding loans were not repaid. Following the collapse of an Austrian bank in May 1931, the German banking system was plunged into crisis. In July 1931, the government closed the banks and the stock exchange for two days to provide the financial system with some breathing space, but these measures gave mere temporary respite. The Depression deepened, became more prolonged and economic conditions for millions of Germans became more desperate.

Unemployment increased. By 1932, about one third of all German workers was registered as unemployed. These official figures did not, however, reflect the true scale of unemployment since they only recorded those who registered as unemployed. Many redundant workers, especially women, did not register and so were not counted. It has been estimated that in January 1933, the true number of unemployed was about eight million. The impact of the Depression fell very heavily on the main industrial areas, such as the Ruhr, Silesia and the main port cities such as Hamburg. White-collar workers were also badly hit. In the civil service, there were severe cuts in the workforce and reductions in the salaries of those who remained.

Farming was also very badly hit by the Depression. Farmers had struggled even during the so-called 'golden age' between 1924 and 1928, but the Depression pushed many of them into serious difficulty. Prices collapsed, exports of agricultural produce declined and sales of food fell as Germans had less money to spend. Many more farmers were forced to give up their farms as the banks demanded repayment of loans. Unemployment spread to the countryside as farm labourers lost their jobs.

The social impact

Increasing poverty

The German artist Lea Grundig recalled the Depression in her 1964 autobiography:

The unemployed had to do a lot to get their benefits. They stood in endless lines in every kind of weather at the unemployment offices. There we stood and waited until it was our turn. Unemployment became a tragedy for many. Not only because of the poverty that mutely sat at their table at all times. Not working, doing nothing, producing nothing – work that not only provided food, but also, despite all the harassment and drudgery, was satisfying, developed skills, and stimulated thinking; work, a human need – it was not available; and wherever it was lacking, decay, malaise, and despair set in.

Fig. 1 *Unemployed Germans at a job centre during the Depression*

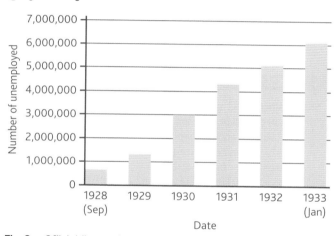

Fig. 2 *Official figures for unemployment in Germany, 1928–33*

Mass unemployment had a highly corrosive effect on German society. Although the Weimar Republic had a well-developed system of unemployment and welfare benefits, the costs very quickly overwhelmed the welfare budget and, from 1930, there were moves to limit the amount of benefits being paid. The unemployed were only entitled to state benefits for a fixed period, after which they had to apply to local authorities for relief, and local benefits were less generous and strictly means-tested. Women received less benefit than men and young people less than adults. Some areas were hit harder than others by the Depression. In towns that depended on a single industry, the impact was far worse than in towns with a more diverse economy.

Effects of the Depression on Brand-Erbisdorff

For example, the small town of Brand-Erbisdorff near Dresden was a centre for glass-making. By April 1931, after the local glassworks had closed, nearly half of the population was receiving welfare payments. However, since most of the unemployed had been out of work for at least two years, they no longer qualified for state unemployment benefits. Instead, they had to rely on the much less generous relief provided by the local authority. A visitor to the area in 1930 reported that: 'Everywhere, I came to: increasing poverty, increasing bitterness, increasing doubt; a world of impoverishment and hunger and exploitation. I got to know Germany from below'.

CROSS-REFERENCE

For more on how farmers gained very little from the economic boom during the 'golden age', see Chapter 5, page 40.

ACTIVITY

Evaluating primary sources

Read Source 1. In what ways does the author justify her claim that 'Unemployment became a tragedy for many'?

Fig. 3 *Shanty housing in Berlin during the Depression; an unemployed family constructed a rough shelter*

Shanty town: rough shelters built without official permission in areas with no access to running water or gas and electricity supplies; they were inhabited by the poor, especially those who no longer qualified for benefits

There were many indications that poverty was rising as a result of the Depression. Diseases linked to poor nutrition and living conditions – such as tuberculosis and rickets – began to show an increase after a period of decline. Doctors reported numerous cases of malnutrition among children. The suicide rate increased as hope for the future disappeared. Meanwhile, as unemployed tenants were unable to pay their rents and were evicted, tent cities and **shanty towns** began to appear on the edges of large cities such as Berlin.

A CLOSER LOOK

Poverty diets

An American journalist, Hubert Knickerbocker, who travelled through Germany during the Depression, reported on the average family's diet. He said that the daily meal for an average family consisted of six small potatoes, five slices of bread, a small cabbage and a knob of margarine. Each adult could expect to eat a herring on about three Sundays in every month. Meat rarely figured in the diet. He expressed the view that this diet was 'too little to live on but too much to die from'.

A CLOSER LOOK

Male and female unemployment rates

The difference between the unemployment rates of males and females was partly because women were less likely to register as unemployed and partly because some traditional female occupations in service industries were less affected by the Depression than traditional male occupations in manufacturing and transport.

The impact on young people

The Depression led to a high rate of unemployment among young people. In Hamburg in June 1933, for example, the unemployment rate among males in the 14–25 age group was 39 per cent, whilst among females it was 25.2 per cent. Such high rates of youth unemployment had a number of consequences. With no jobs, and little prospect in the foreseeable future, gangs of young men congregated in public spaces in German towns and cities, their very presence causing alarm among older, middle-class citizens. There were fears that youth involvement in crime was increasing and that young men were being drawn into extremist political organisations.

Juvenile crime

Although the overall rate of juvenile convictions did not increase during the Depression, the number of 14–25-year olds accused of crime did increase. The number of young men charged with theft grew during the Depression years but there was also a significant increase in youths charged with offences against the state and with assault and threatening behaviour. Offences against the state included participating in violent disorder during political demonstrations and the rise in these offences undoubtedly reflected the deteriorating political situation.

Political extremism

The involvement of young men in extremist political organisations increased during the Depression. The KPD, for example, had some success in recruiting working-class youths from the 'wild cliques' to join political demonstrations and engage in street battles with their opponents. The paramilitary organisations of the nationalist right also set out to recruit unemployed youths. Organisations such as the Hitler Youth and the SA (Nazi Stormtroopers) offered unemployed boys and young men food, uniforms, shelter and the excitement of fighting street battles, all of which could relieve the insecurity and boredom of unemployment. Youth membership of these organisations, however, was not stable and the majority of young unemployed males still had little or no contact with the political extremes. Girls and young women were even less involved.

Schemes to help the young unemployed

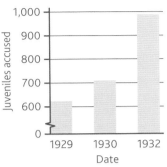

Fig. 4 *Juveniles accused of crimes in Hamburg*

CROSS-REFERENCE

To recall the KPD's (German Communist Party) role in Weimar politics leading up to the 1930s, see page 57 in Chapter 7. Read Chapter 6, page 46 for more on youth 'cliques'.

SOURCE 2

In March 1931, the Minister of Labour, Adam Stegerwald, set out in his instructions to Labour Exchanges (places where the unemployed could find jobs) his priorities in establishing courses for the young unemployed:

Our task must lie not in giving a relatively small number of young people the most thorough vocational knowledge possible, but rather in getting as many youngsters on the courses as possible, getting them off the streets, maintaining their will to work and protecting them from the physical, intellectual and moral dangers of unemployment.

This letter reflected the policies of Brüning's government towards the unemployed. Placing their faith in market forces to revive the economy at some time in the future, the government's priorities were to keep control over expenditure on unemployment benefit and to lessen the damaging effects of unemployment on the young. To this end, they established day centres for young people where they could participate in work-related activities and socialise. There were also emergency labour schemes in which unemployed youths were required to undertake unskilled manual labour, receiving wages that were below the legal minimum. Needless to say, these schemes were unpopular with young people, resulting in two waves of strikes for higher wages in October 1930 and June 1932. In addition to the compulsory schemes, there were voluntary labour schemes, which involved young unemployed people being sent away from the cities to residential work camps for periods of six months. Few of these schemes offered any prospect of vocational training, still less of finding permanent employment. As the Minister of Labour's letter said, the priority was to get the young unemployed 'off the streets'.

CROSS-REFERENCE

To find out more about the government in power during the Depression, read about Chancellor Brüning and his Central Party on page 71.

ACTIVITY

Read Source 2. What were the government's priorities in its policy towards youth unemployment?

The impact on women

SOURCE 3

In her magazine article 'Twilight for Women', written in 1931, the journalist Hilde Walter wrote this about the effect of the depression on women:

Women have become unpopular. An uncomfortable atmosphere is gathering around all working women. Along the entire spectrum from left to right, the meaning of women's employment and their right to it are suddenly being questioned. At the moment it is not even the old discussion over so-called 'equal rights' or 'equal pay for equal work' that occupies the foreground. Suddenly we are obliged to counter the most primitive arguments against the gainful employment of women.

A LEVEL PRACTICE QUESTION

Evaluating primary sources

With reference to Sources 1, 2 and 3 and your understanding of the historical context, assess the value of these three sources to an historian studying the impact of the Depression on German society.

STUDY TIP

These three sources were all contemporary but from different perspectives. Their value can be assessed in relation to their provenance but also in relation to the extent and quality of the information they provide. Each source needs to be evaluated and placed in context, and the limitations of a source should be considered.

In some ways, women workers weathered the effects of the Depression better than their male counterparts. The female proportion of the total workforce increased during the Depression years. Nevertheless, the onset of depression and the dismissal of many millions of workers from their jobs reignited the debate about whether married women should continue to be employed when males were out of work. The campaign waged by right-wing parties against the employment of so-called 'double-earners' achieved some success in May 1932 when a law was passed allowing married women civil servants to be dismissed. Although the extent of the law was limited to central government employees and women could only be dismissed if it could be proved that their economic circumstances were secure, this was nevertheless an important symbolic victory for those who believed that a married woman should not be employed outside the home. After the law was passed, the Reich Postal Service dismissed about 1000 married women from its employment. The cause of equal rights for women, therefore, suffered a serious setback during the Depression.

ACTIVITY

In what ways did the Depression have an impact on the employment of women? You should refer to Source 3 and to the contextual information. You should also refer back to Chapter 6 for information on women's employment before the Depression.

The political impact

KEY CHRONOLOGY

1929	October	Wall Street Crash
1930	March	Collapse of Müller's Grand Coalition government
		Brüning appointed as Chancellor
	September	Reichstag election – major gains by Nazis and communists
1931	May	Collapse of an Austrian bank
	July	Financial crisis in Germany
1932	April	Ban on Nazi SA
		Hindenburg re-elected as President
	May	Brüning resigns and is replaced by Papen as Chancellor
	July	Reichstag election – Nazis become the largest party

CROSS-REFERENCE

To read about the formation of the Grand Coalition in 1928, see page 54 in Chapter 7.

The strains on the political system caused by the Depression had far-reaching consequences:

- It caused the collapse of the Grand Coalition, led by Hermann Müller, in March 1930.
- It provided an opportunity for the parties of the extreme left and extreme right to gain support and, in so doing, fatally undermine the democratic system.
- It led to an intensification of political violence.

The collapse of the Grand Coalition

The Grand Coalition was one of the most broadly based coalition governments in the Weimar period, representing five political parties from the SPD on the left to the moderate right wing in the form of the DVP. Therein lay both its strength and its weakness. After the Wall Street Crash, in October 1929, unemployment soared and the rising cost of unemployment benefit placed a severe strain on state finances. With falling tax revenues adding to the problem, the state budget was in serious deficit by the end of 1929. This split the coalition. On the right, the DVP wanted to reduce unemployment benefit whilst, on the left, the SPD wanted to protect the level of benefits and raise taxes. The government was deadlocked on the issue and, in March 1930, Müller resigned.

His successor, appointed by Hindenburg, was **Heinrich Brüning**, leader of the Centre Party. Hindenburg's decision to appoint Brüning was heavily influenced by two key military figures – General Groener, who since 1928 had been the Defence Minister, and **General Kurt von Schleicher**, Groener's political adviser. Their role in the appointment was an indication that the army had begun to play a key role in politics. Both men were opposed to parliamentary democracy and saw the political crisis of March 1930 as an opportunity to begin to impose a more authoritarian style of government. In President Hindenburg, they had a leader who shared their contempt for democracy (but respected the constitution) and in Brüning they had a Chancellor who also had authoritarian leanings.

Table 1 *Number of laws passed, 1930–32*

Year	Laws passed by Reichstag	Laws passed by decree
1930	98	5
1931	34	44
1932	5	66

Brüning's coalition excluded the SPD, the largest party in the Reichstag, which meant that his government did not have enough support in the Reichstag to pass laws. After March 1930, no government had majority support in the Reichstag and governments had to rely on ruling by presidential decree. Even before Hitler was appointed Chancellor in January 1933 and began to establish a Nazi dictatorship, Weimar democracy was effectively dead in the water.

Fig. 5 *Heinrich Brüning*

Heinrich Brüning (1885–1970) was a financial expert and leading member of the Centre Party in the Reichstag. He had not held any ministerial office before becoming Chancellor in 1930, but became the longest continuously serving Chancellor of the Weimar Republic. He was a controversial figure.

CROSS-REFERENCE

To familiarise yourself with the Weimar Constitution and the allowance of presidential decrees, return to Chapter 1, page 9.

KEY PROFILE

Kurt von Schleicher (1882–1934) was an aristocratic army officer. During the early years of the Weimar Republic, he played a crucial role in the political activities of the army, helping to negotiate the Ebert–Groener Pact and handling negotiations with the USSR on the building of German arms factories in Russia. After 1926, he was effectively the political head of the army. Together with General Groener, he was part of Hindenburg's inner circle of advisers and helped steer Hindenburg towards imposing a more authoritarian style of government. Although not a Nazi himself, he saw the Nazis' mass support as the most effective counterweight to the popular support for the SPD and KPD, and looked for ways to work with Hitler. He was a master of political intrigue and was largely responsible for later bringing down Brüning's government in May 1932. Despite his attempts to work with Hitler, he was murdered by the Nazis in 1934.

Fig. 6 *Kurt von Schleicher*

CROSS-REFERENCE

More on Schleicher's growing influence in German politics is discussed in Chapter 11, page 83.

The September 1930 Reichstag election and growth in support for extremist parties

Brüning's response to the Depression was to cut expenditure and raise taxes, in order to balance the budget. Since he did not have majority support in the Reichstag, he persuaded Hindenburg to issue a presidential decree passing the budget into law. This provoked another political crisis, since Article 48 of the constitution was only supposed to be used in an emergency, not for the conduct of normal political business. The SPD won Reichstag support for a motion demanding that the decree be withdrawn. Brüning dissolved the Reichstag and called an election in September 1930. The result of this election (see Table 2) completely changed the political landscape in Germany.

Table 2   *Number of deputies elected in the 1930 election*

Party	Left		Centre		Right		
	KPD	SPD	DDP (renamed the State Party)	Centre	DVP	DNVP	NSDAP (Nazi)
Number of deputies elected	77	143	20	68	30	41	107

The extremist parties of the left and right gained the most in the 1930 election. The communists gained over a million votes, mostly from the SPD, and 77 seats in the Reichstag. Far more significant, however, was the growth in support for the Nazi Party. In 1928, the Nazis had received a mere 810,000 votes, whereas in September 1930, they gained nearly 6.5 million votes and their representation in the Reichstag increased from 12 to 107 seats, making them the second largest party. In the election as a whole, two out of five voters gave their support to anti-democratic parties. From this breakthrough in September 1930, support for the Nazis continued to grow. Moreover, with 107 deputies in the Reichstag, the Nazis now had the opportunity to disrupt its proceedings through chanting, shouting and interrupting.

As the Reichstag became unmanageable, its proceedings became increasingly irrelevant. It did not meet at all between February and October 1931 and, even after that, its sessions became shorter and more infrequent. Political power in Weimar Germany had shifted from the Reichstag to the President and his circle of advisers, but also to the streets.

CROSS-REFERENCES

To remind you of the names of the different parties, return to Chapter 1.

To read about how the Nazis appealed to the public in 1930, go to Chapter 10.

The intensification of political violence

SOURCE 4

The Nazi Stormtroopers (SA) chanted many songs on their marches. The 'Song of the Storm Columns' was one of their most popular:

We are the Storm Columns, we put ourselves about,
We are the foremost ranks, courageous in a fight.
With sweating brows from work, our stomachs without food!
Our calloused, sooty hands, our rifles firmly hold.
So stand the Storm Columns, for racial fight prepared.
Only when Jews bleed, are we liberated.
No more negotiation; it's not help, not even slight:
Beside our Adolf Hitler, we're courageous in a fight.
Long live our Adolf Hitler! We're already marching on.
We're storming in the name of German revolution.
Leap onto the barricades! Defeat us only death can.
We're Storm Columns of Hitler's dictatorship of one man.

ACTIVITY

Read Source 4. Identify three key ideas that the Stormtroopers were articulating in this song.

CROSS-REFERENCE

More on the Stormtroopers can be found in Chapter 4, page 33.

The early years of the Weimar Republic, between 1919 and 1923, had seen frequent riots, political assassinations and political uprisings. During the years 1924–29, the violence had subsided but not completely disappeared: the Nazis claimed that 29 of their men had been killed in clashes with communists, whilst the communists said that

Fig. 7   *A Red-Front Fighters' League march*

KEY TERM

Red-Front Fighters' League: the paramilitary arm of the KPD Party; it had been established in 1924, under the leadership of Ernst Thälmann, and engaged in street battles with the SA, the police and other right-wing paramilitary groups

92 of their supporters had been killed. In the years 1930–33, however, the level of political violence increased dramatically. Nazis and communists, the latter with their **Red-Front Fighters' League**, took their political struggle onto the streets. Each side attempted to break up the political meetings of their opponents and rival marches often degenerated into full-scale riots. The violence was particularly severe at election times.

By the end of 1931, the violence had become so intense that Brüning decided to act. He issued a decree in December 1931 banning the wearing of political uniforms, but this had little effect since the Nazi Stormtroopers (SA) continued to march wearing white shirts. In April 1932, therefore, Hindenburg was persuaded to sign a decree outlawing the SA. Even this ban, however, failed to curb the activities of the Stormtroopers. Their membership continued to grow and political violence was not brought under control. By the end of 1932, the SA was estimated to have 400,000 members.

Table 3   *Reported deaths from political violence*

Year	Nazis	Communists
1930	17	44
1931	42	52
1932*	84	75

*Figures are for the first six months only. Figures for the second half of 1932 are not available, but as the level of political violence increased during this period, there would have been many more KPD members killed.

ACTIVITY

Group or pair discussion

The Depression had a number of political consequences:

- the end of parliamentary government and an increasing use of presidential decrees
- the growth in support for extremist, anti-democratic parties
- an intensification of political violence.

Discuss the relative importance of each of these factors in undermining Weimar democracy and rank them in order of importance.

Summary

The Depression, which began with the Wall Street Crash in 1929, had a devastating effect on German society and political life. Although the worst economic and social effects of the Depression did not appear until 1931 and 1932, the rise in unemployment placed an intolerable strain on the fragile consensus in the Grand Coalition and it collapsed in March 1930. The election of September 1930 showed a major increase in support for the extremist parties of the right and left, which rendered the Reichstag unmanageable and increasingly irrelevant. Long before Hitler came to power in January 1933, authoritarian government had been reinstated in Germany and Weimar democracy was effectively dead.

STUDY TIP

This type of question needs to be considered in a wider context. In addition to this chapter you will need to read earlier chapters to provide a long-term perspective on the issue. A balanced assessment is needed and it might be helpful to consider long-term as well as short-term factors, and differentiate between those factors which had their origins in Germany (political and economic weaknesses) and those factors which were due to external events.

 PRACTICE QUESTION

'The collapse of the Grand Coalition in March 1930 was caused by the economic depression, an event which was outside Germany's control'.
Assess the validity of this view.

10 The appeal of Nazism and communism

ACTIVITY

Evaluating primary sources

1. In what ways does the author of Source 1 convey the attitudes of her class towards the Nazis?
2. Why does she believe that 'it would have been worth listening to them'?
3. How valuable is this source in giving an insight into German attitudes towards the Nazis?

Electoral support for Nazism and communism up to July 1932

SOURCE 1

In her book, *My Father's Country*, Wibke Bruhns recalls the reaction of her upper-middle class family to the electoral success of the Nazis in 1932:

The Nazis are enjoying election successes, first on a local, then on a regional level, particularly in the countryside and among the middle classes. But even so, not many people seem to take them seriously. What counts is class difference: The DNVP, the major farmers, the Reich Association of German Industry are worlds apart from the Nazi mob. You don't sit down at the same table with these people. As late as January 1932 the Ruhr industrialists refuse Hitler the financial aid that he requests. But it would at least have been worth listening to them. The Nazis have always said what they wanted.

The Nazis (NSDAP) and the Communists (KPD) gained electoral support during the Depression years, but the Nazis were far more successful than the communists in broadening their appeal. Before 1929, the Nazis' core support came from the lower-middle class, the Mittelstand. Their support among this group – white-collar workers, small shopkeepers, independent craftsmen – increased after the Wall Street Crash, but their main gains were among the broader middle class and the farmers. The Nazis were very adept at exploiting the widespread discontent among farmers by promising higher prices and protection against imports. Their success with farmers is shown by the results in some rural constituencies in 1930, where they secured 68 per cent of the vote in one district in north-west Germany. The Nazis also attracted increasing support from the middle class, who were worried by the perceived threat of a communist revolution and were disillusioned with established middle-class parties such as the DVP and the DNVP. The Nazis did well amongst young voters and women. In geographical terms, the Nazis were strongest in the Protestant north, east and centre of Germany but were less successful in the Catholic south and west.

Table 1 *Support for the NSDAP and KPD in elections from 1928 to July 1932*

Election/Year	NSDAP		KPD	
	Total of votes (in millions)	Percentage of votes	Total of votes (in millions)	Percentage of votes
1928 Reichstag	0.81	2.6	3.3	10.6
1930 Reichstag	6.40	18.3	4.6	13.1
1932 Presidential (1st ballot)	11.30	30.1	4.9	13.2
1932 Presidential (2nd ballot)	13.40	36.8	3.7	10.2
July 1932 Reichstag	13.75	37.3	5.3	14.3

Hindenburg had been elected President in 1925 and his seven-year term of office ended in 1932, by which time he was 84 years old. He was reluctant to stand for election again but was persuaded to do so. As in 1925, his main opponent on the left was Thälmann of the KPD. Hitler was reluctant to stand against such a conservative icon as Hindenburg but eventually he decided to do so. There was also another right-wing candidate, Theodor Duesterberg. In the first ballot, Hindenburg fell just short of the 50 per cent of the vote needed for outright victory. This triggered a second ballot in which Duesterberg was no longer a candidate. Hitler rented an aeroplane and flew all over Germany, presenting himself as a national saviour. Although Hindenburg won in the end, with 53 per cent of the vote, Hitler received nearly 37 per cent of the vote in the second ballot. In some rural areas, Hitler received more votes than Hindenburg. Soon after the presidential election there were state elections in many areas, the results of which confirmed the Nazis' status as the most popular party.

The working class made up nearly half of the electorate and their votes were, therefore, crucial in the electoral battle between the Nazis and the communists. Since 1919, most working-class voters in large industrial centres, especially trade union members, had supported either the SPD or the communists, and this pattern continued through the elections of the early 1930s. The communists made gains at the expense of the SPD, but their support was largely confined to large cities. The communists were strongest in the poorest areas of cities such as Berlin, especially among the unemployed. This does not mean, however, that the Nazis failed to attract any working-class voters. Indeed, in the 1930 election, about 27 per cent of Nazi voters were manual labourers.

Over the course of the three elections between September 1930 and July 1932, the Nazis more than doubled their electoral support. The communists also made gains but were unable to appeal to voters beyond their traditional core supporters. The Nazi Party became the main party of protest by winning support amongst all classes and generations, and across different regions of the country.

The appeal of Nazism

As the economic crisis in Germany deepened, society became more polarised and the political system failed to provide governments equal to the situation. The Nazis projected an image of decisiveness and energy, and offered the prospect of change. Their appeal was based on a number of factors.

Nazi ideology

Hitler and the Nazis put forward a wide-ranging but loose collection of ideas which, when assembled, might be described as an ideology. Nazi policy was first put forward in their Twenty-five Point Programme of 1920, which was still officially the statement of their aims in 1933 even though Hitler did not agree with many of its points. While he was in prison after the failed Munich Beer Hall Putsch in 1923, Hitler started writing *Mein Kampf*, his most complete statement of his ideas and aims. His ideas were not original, nor were they coherent or consistent, as he modified his policy statements according to the audience he was addressing. The book was also not widely read before 1933. It is possible, however, to identify some key themes in Nazi propaganda, as outlined below.

The power of the will

Hitler presented himself and the Nazi movement as being a force for change in Germany: 'If one has realised a truth, that truth is valueless so long as there is lacking the indomitable will to turn this realisation into action' (Hitler, 1922). Nazi propaganda claimed that power, strength and determination to succeed

The 1932 presidential election

Fig. 1 *Hitler giving a speech at a rally in the 1932 election campaign*

Table 2 *Support for the Nazis in selected German states in 1932*

Prussia	36%
Bavaria	32.5%
Hamburg	31.5%
Saxony-Anhalt	40.9%

Fig. 2 *An election poster for the Nazis, 1932*

CROSS-REFERENCE

Read more about the Twenty-five Point Programme later in this chapter, on page 76.

Fig. 3 *This 1933 poster projects the image of a 'genetically healthy' family as the racial nucleus of the nation*

CROSS-REFERENCE

A fuller explanation of Nazi racial ideology, including *Volksgemeinschaft*, Social Darwinism and *Lebensraum*, can be found in Chapter 17, pages 140–142.

KEY TERM

Aryan race: the term used by racial theorists to describe the white, European race; the Nazis used this term to distinguish themselves from Jews and other 'inferior' racial groups

KEY PROFILE

Fritz Thyssen (1873–1951) was chairman of the United Steelworks Company and one of the early financial backers of the Nazi Party. He joined the Nazi Party in 1931 and acted as a link between the party and big business interests. By the late 1930s, however, he had become highly critical of the regime's economic policies. He opposed the outbreak of war and fled the country in 1939.

were qualities personified by Hitler. The Nazi movement, with its parades of Stormtroopers (SA), presented an image of discipline and unity that would sweep all opponents aside.

Struggle and war

Struggle, violence and war were at the heart of Nazi thinking and actions. Hitler defined his outlook in terms of struggle and claimed scientific justification for his view that struggle and conflict between races was part of the natural order of things. War, he believed, would reconstruct German society and create a new German Reich through conquest and the subjugation of other races. Nazi propaganda, therefore, glorified the military virtues of courage, loyalty and self-sacrifice, and the SA was projected as an organisation that gave German males the chance to demonstrate their manliness.

A racial community

The concept of a 'people's community', or **Volksgemeinschaft**, was a key element in Nazi ideology. Although it was never defined very clearly, Hitler advocated a state based on a racial community. Only **Aryans** could be citizens of the state; all others were to be denied the rights of citizenship and its benefits, and would be treated as mere 'subjects' of the state. Within the 'real community of the people', there would be no social classes and all Germans would have equal chances to find their own level in society. All would work together for the good of the nation, thereby demonstrating their commitment to common 'German values', and in return would benefit from access to employment and welfare benefits.

Nazism thus aimed for a cultural and social revolution in Germany. The objective was to create a 'new man' and a 'new woman', individuals who would have awareness of the importance of their race, the strength of character to work unselfishly for the common good, and the willingness to follow the leadership in the pursuit of their aims. Yet this revolutionary ideology was essentially backward-looking. When the Nazis talked of a 'people's community', they wanted to return to a romanticised, mythical German past before the race had become 'polluted' with alien blood and before industrialisation had divided society along class lines. Their *Volksgemeinschaft* would be based on 'blood and soil' – that is, on the German peasants who they believed had retained their racial purity and their traditional values more than city dwellers.

A national socialism

The Nazis adopted the title National Socialist German Workers' Party (NSDAP) in an attempt to gain working-class support, but at the same time to differentiate themselves from the international socialism of the Communist Party. The points laid out in the Twenty-Five Point Programme were economically radical and were similar to many of the anti-capitalist policies of the communists and the socialists. They called, for example, for the confiscation of war profits, the nationalisation of large monopoly companies and the confiscation of land from the large estates without compensation to the landowners. Hitler, however, never fully committed to these radical aims and modified his message according to the audience he was addressing. Increasingly, after 1929, Hitler sought the support of wealthy businessmen such as Hugenberg and **Fritz Thyssen**, and was at pains to reassure them that a Nazi government would not threaten their interests.

Hitler used the word 'socialism' loosely, in a way that might appeal to working-class voters. In his view, socialism and the *Volksgemeinschaft* were one and the same thing: 'To be national means to act with a boundless, all-embracing love for the people and, if necessary, even to die for it. And similarly, to be social means to build up the state and the community of the people so that every individual acts in the interest of the community of the people.'

The Führerprinzip

Hitler set out to destroy the Weimar Republic because it was a parliamentary democracy, a system he viewed as weak, ineffective and alien to Germany's traditions of strong, authoritarian government. He also believed that parliamentary democracy encouraged the growth of communism, in his opinion an even greater evil. He argued in a speech in April 1922: 'Democracy is fundamentally not German; it is Jewish. This Jewish democracy, with its majority decisions, has always been only a means towards the destruction of any existing Aryan leadership.' Weimar democracy, established at the end of the First World War, was regarded by the Nazis as being based on a betrayal, in which the 'November Criminals' had stabbed the German army in the back. As such, it should be destroyed and replaced by a dictatorship, a one-party state run on the basis of the Führerprinzip (the principle of leadership).

The Führerprinzip was the basis on which the Nazi Party had been run since 1925. Within the party, Hitler had supreme control over policy and strategy, and party members became subordinated to Hitler's will.

CROSS-REFERENCE

For more detail on the November Criminals, see Chapter 2, page 16.

Aggressive nationalism

As a German nationalist, Hitler had three main aims:
- to reverse the humiliation of the Treaty of Versailles – which he described as an instrument of 'unlimited blackmail and shameful humiliation' – and restore to Germany those lands taken from it
- to establish a 'Greater German Reich' in which all Germans would live within the borders of the state
- to secure for Germany its '*Lebensraum*' to settle its people and provide it with the food and raw materials needed to sustain it as a great power, since 'only an adequately large space on this earth assures a nation its freedom of existence'.

This was an aggressive form of nationalism. Hitler did not merely want to restore Germany to its borders of 1914 but also to expand the territory of the Reich. This would involve a war of conquest to secure Germany's *Lebensraum* in the east, which was justified by Hitler's racial theories and his belief in the necessity of struggle.

KEY TERM

Lebensraum: 'living space', a concept by which Hitler justified his plans to take over territory to the east of Germany

CROSS-REFERENCE

See Chapter 17, page 142 for more information on the concept of *Lebensraum*.

Anti-Semitism

SOURCE 2

Hitler wrote the following about the Jews, in *Mein Kampf*, published in 1925:

The Jewish people are incapable of establishing their own state. The very existence of the Jews becomes parasitic on the lives of other peoples. The ultimate goal of the Jewish struggle for survival is therefore the enslavement of productive peoples. The weapons the Jew uses for this are cunning, cleverness, subterfuge, malice, etc., qualities that are rooted in the very essence of the Jewish ethnic character. They are tricks in his struggle for survival, like the tricks used by other peoples in combat by the sword. The end of the Jewish struggle for world domination therefore will always be bloody Bolshevism.

ACTIVITY

Working in groups, draw up a chart showing the key points in Nazi ideology. Try to identify the links between the main ideas.

CROSS-REFERENCE

More information about Albert Speer and his role in the Nazi regime can be found on page 183 of Chapter 22.

ACTIVITY

Evaluating primary sources

1. Identify three ways in which Source 3 would be valuable to an historian studying the appeal of Hitler.
2. Compare the views in Source 3 with that in Source 1. Identify any similarities and differences.

STUDY TIP

These sources come from different perspectives. Source 3 in Chapter 4 was written by a British journalist in 1923, whilst Source 3 in this chapter was written by a supporter of Hitler and referred to hearing him speak in 1930. There are points of similarity and difference between the sources regarding the authors' reactions to Hitler. Which might be more valuable is a matter of your judgement but it must be based on what the sources say and how they either clarify or obscure the reasons for Hitler's appeal.

Hitler saw the Jews as responsible for all of Germany's ills. Jews were represented in Nazi propaganda as greedy, cunning and motivated only by selfish motives. They were described as 'a parasite in the body of other nations', having no state of their own and working through a worldwide Jewish conspiracy to establish their dominance over other races. The Jews were held to be responsible for the evils of capitalism and, at the same time, for the growth of communism. On that basis, they were held responsible for Germany's defeat in the First World War, the hated Treaty of Versailles and Germany's decline as a great power, together with the political weaknesses of the democratic system in the Weimar Republic. Above all, Hitler regarded communism as a Jewish creed that had undermined the political and social cohesion of Germany and should be eradicated.

The importance of Hitler to Nazi success

SOURCE 3

Albert Speer, a key figure in the Nazi regime, recalled in his autobiography how he was drawn to Nazism through listening to Hitler speak in 1930:

Hitler entered and was tempestuously hailed by his numerous followers among the students. This enthusiasm in itself made a great impression on me. His initial shyness soon disappeared; his pitch rose, he spoke urgently, with hypnotic persuasiveness. I was carried on the wave of enthusiasm which bore the speaker along from sentence to sentence. It swept away my scepticism. Opponents were given no chance to speak. This furthered the illusion, at least momentarily, of unanimity. Finally, Hitler no longer seemed to be speaking to convince; rather, he seemed to feel that he was expressing what the audience, by now transformed into a single mass, expected of him. The peril of communism, which seemed unstoppable, could be checked, Hitler persuaded us, and instead of hopeless unemployment Germany could move towards economic recovery.

 PRACTICE QUESTION

Evaluating primary sources

With reference to Source 3 in this chapter and Source 3 in Chapter 4 (page 31) and your understanding of the historical context, which of these two sources is more valuable in explaining the appeal of Hitler?

By 1929, Hitler had established undisputed control over the Nazi Party and a leadership cult had been created around him. His political skills and qualities were therefore of crucial importance to the party. For many, although certainly not all Germans, he possessed great charisma and unparalleled oratorical skills. His speeches often went on for hours and contained a lot of repetition and outright lies, but he had a hypnotic effect. He knew how to play on people's emotions and fears, and to convince them that he had the answers. He was also an opportunist who could tailor his message to his audience. His mass appeal was therefore vital to the success of the Nazis in winning votes.

The role of anti-Semitism in Nazi electoral success

The Nazis used the Jews as scapegoats in their propaganda, portraying them as responsible for Germany's economic and political problems. During the Depression, many shopkeepers and small business owners were receptive to the idea that their problems were caused by 'Jewish capitalism'. People who had previously kept their anti-Semitic views quiet were now willing to express them more freely.

However, although many ordinary Germans were still unwilling to go along with openly anti-Semitic propaganda, they were so preoccupied with immediate economic hardships that they heard the messages they wanted to hear. Their previous disapproval of Nazi extremism faded as they focused on Nazi promises to provide work and bread. Many people who voted Nazi in 1932 did so in spite of Nazis' anti-Semitism, not because of it.

Nazi propaganda was frequently adapted according to local circumstances. In January 1932, for example, when Hitler addressed 650 businessmen at the Industry Club in Düsseldorf, he did not make even a single mention of the Jews in the whole two-and-a-half-hour speech. At the same time, there were many other meetings where Nazi speakers openly encouraged hostility against Jews by accusing them of being the cause of the audience's economic troubles. The rapid expansion of the SA also encouraged radical anti-Semitism – 'Juda verrecke' ('Down with the Jews') was a favourite chant of the SA (or Brownshirts), who often beat up Jews in the street. On the other hand, many men were attracted into the SA because it was anti-communist, or for comradeship in the pub, or because membership was a meal ticket. Anti-Semitism was rarely the main motive for joining the SA.

Fig. 4   *Nazi propaganda poster showing anti-Semitism*

Widening the support for Nazism meant winning over people the Nazis had not previously targeted. This meant emphasising issues the Nazis had previously neglected. Most Nazi propaganda in 1932 had little or nothing to do with anti-Semitism. In January 1932, for example, there was a coordinated sequence of 16 mass meetings, all on the issue of unemployment.

Reaching a judgement about the political appeal of anti-Semitism is extremely difficult. Millions of people voted for the NSDAP (Nazi Party) who had never done so before. It is likely that only a small minority of these new voters had anti-Semitism as a main motive or were influenced by it in any way at all. A statistical analysis of Nazi propaganda posters and campaign speeches in 1931–32 shows an overwhelming concentration on economic issues with very little emphasis on anti-Semitism.

The role of propaganda in Nazi electoral success

The Nazis were very skilled in **propaganda** techniques and this played an important part in their success in winning votes. Hitler understood the importance of propaganda and **Joseph Goebbels**, his Reich Propaganda Chief from 1928, was a master of the medium. We have already seen how Hitler's oratorical skills played a key role in Nazi success; with the money provided by big business leaders such as Hugenberg and Thyssen, Hitler was able to travel by air and car to make speeches in all the main cities in Germany. The Nazis had their own newspapers. They also published many posters and leaflets, put on film shows and staged rallies. Nazi marches and rallies, with their banners, songs, bands and the sheer force of numbers, made a powerful statement about Nazi strength.

KEY TERM

Propaganda: the systematic spreading of ideas and information in order to influence the thinking and actions of the people at whom it is targeted, often through the use of media such as posters, film, radio and the press

KEY PROFILE

Joseph Goebbels (1897–1945) was the chief propagandist of the Nazi movement from 1928 to 1945. He could claim to be an intellectual, having gained a PhD at Heidelberg in 1921. He became fanatically loyal to Hitler from the mid-1920s. He was Gauleiter (Nazi Party leader) of Berlin and founded his own newspaper there. He had worked as a journalist before joining the party and had written novels and plays. He was thus experienced in the use of the written word to communicate ideas. He also had a taste for violence and street-fighting, having provoked many battles with left-wing opponents. As an orator, he was not as mesmerising as Hitler; nevertheless, he was able to make effective use of his talent for sarcasm and insinuation in attacking the Jews and communists. Goebbels played a key propaganda role in the Nazi rise to power and became Minister of Propaganda in 1933. He committed suicide in 1945, shortly after Hitler's death.

Fig. 5   *Dr Joseph Goebbels*

CROSS-REFERENCE

To remind yourself about the Red-Front Fighters' League, go back to Chapter 9, page 73.

Fig. 6 *KPD poster for the 1932 elections, stating 'Against fascism, hunger, war'*

ACTIVITY

Revision

Using the evidence in this chapter and in Chapter 9, write a paragraph explaining the reasons why many ordinary Germans were more receptive to extremists' electioneering in 1930 than in previous elections in the 1920s.

KEY TERM

Social-fascists: a theory supported by the Comintern during the early 1930s, which held that **social democracy** was a variant of **fascism** because, in addition to a shared corporatist economic model, it stood in the way of a complete and final transition to communism

Nazi propaganda skilfully targeted different groups in the population and adapted the Nazi message to particular target audiences. Nazi speakers were well trained in oratorical techniques and in the party's ideology. Anti-Semitic slogans were used with some audiences but not with others, depending on how useful the Nazis judged them to be. For the most part, the Nazis concentrated on their simple message that Weimar democracy was responsible for economic depression, national humiliation and internal divisions. In its place, they offered a vague but powerful vision of a prosperous and united Germany, restored to its rightful position among the great powers of Europe.

The appeal of communism

The KPD gained two million votes in the Reichstag elections between 1928 and July 1932. Its membership also increased, from 117,000 in 1929 to 360,000 in 1932. It was, therefore, a significant and growing force in German political life, especially at street and neighbourhood level in large industrial cities. Whereas in the 1920s the KPD had concentrated on building a strong presence in factories and workshops where **trade union** membership was well established, after 1929 the party was forced by economic circumstances to focus more on the unemployed. It set up 'committees of the unemployed', staged hunger marches and agitated against benefit cuts. It also attempted, with some success, to co-opt the so-called 'wild cliques' of working-class youths into communist-led campaigns against the police, reform schools and labour exchanges. The Red-Front Fighters' League of the KPD was engaged in frequent battles with the Nazi SA, and with the police, as the communists presented themselves as the defenders of working-class districts against the Nazis. These tactics had some success. Some areas of the cities, such as the Wedding district of Berlin, effectively fell under communist control.

Policies and ideology

SOURCE 4

The KPD programme stated:

Working men and women unite – unite and rise up. We have nothing to lose except the political and economic chains that bind us. We must destroy this so-called 'democracy'. The Weimar system serves the interests of the ruling capitalist and landowning classes that rob us of the fruits of our hard labour. Until we seize the means of production – the factories and the land – we will remain slaves and our children will continue to starve.

The election platform of the KPD reflected its revolutionary communist ideology. As well as demanding an end to cuts in unemployment benefits and wages, and the legalisation of abortion, the KPD also advocated close cooperation with the USSR, the end of military spending and the establishment of a workers' state. Even though the KPD participated in elections and won seats in the Reichstag, its ultimate aim was the overthrow of the Weimar Republic. Following the lead of the Communist Party in the Soviet Union, the KPD viewed the Depression as the final nail in capitalism's coffin, which would lead inevitably to a workers' revolution. Its priority, therefore, was to replace the SPD as the leading party on the left, since it accused the SPD of being as damaging to working-class interests as the Nazi Party. Indeed, the KPD labelled the SPD as '**social-fascists**', and expended as much time and energy in fighting them as it did in fighting the Nazis.

Strengths

Communist propaganda helped attract membership, particularly through its posters but also in the speeches of Thälmann: they emphasised class struggle and the smashing of the capitalist system. There were explicit appeals to the unemployed, as for example in the slogan 'Bread and Freedom', and there were images of capitalists being smashed with hammers wielded by workers. There were also posters which emphasised the KPD's links with the USSR and its belief in internationalism. Much of the KPD's propaganda attacked the SPD as the tool of the capitalist classes. It projected an image which would appeal to its committed followers and to many of those whose situation had become desperate as a result of the depression. It must be remembered that electoral support for the KPD grew through the years 1930 to 1932, reaching a peak of 16.9 per cent of the votes cast in the November 1932 Reichstag election.

With its growing membership, success in attracting votes and organisation at street and neighbourhood level, the KPD had considerable strength. Indeed, the perceived threat of a communist revolution frightened many middle-class voters into supporting the Nazis and led business leaders such as Thyssen to give financial support to the Nazis. Hitler was very adept at playing on these fears.

Weaknesses

The reality, however, was that the KPD never came close to launching a successful revolution. Its membership turnover was very high – more than 50 per cent of its new members in 1932 left within a few months, only to be replaced by new recruits. It failed to attract support outside the main industrial areas and had very limited appeal amongst women. Because a high proportion of its members were unemployed, the KPD was forever short of money. Finally, its concentration on fighting the 'social-fascists' in the SPD blinded the KPD to the serious threat posed by the Nazi Party and divided anti-Nazi forces at a crucial time.

 PRACTICE QUESTION

'Fear of communism was the main reason why increasing numbers of Germans voted for the Nazis in the years 1930–32.' Assess the validity of this view.

Summary

Both the NSDAP and the KPD gained votes at the expense of other parties between 1929 and 1932. The KPD, however, did not succeed in breaking out of its working-class strongholds in the main industrial areas and, despite its revolutionary rhetoric and its capacity to stage large-scale protest movements, it was never in a position to mount a serious challenge to the Weimar Republic.

The Nazis, on the other hand, did succeed in becoming a broad-based political movement. By the summer of 1932, Hitler was the leader of the largest party in the Reichstag and was in a position to demand that the Nazis should form a government. It is somewhat ironic that Hitler was the main beneficiary of the rise in support for the KPD and the increasingly frequent battles between the SA and the Red-Front Fighters' League. He was able to convince millions of middle-class voters that only the Nazis could stem the tide of communist revolution. As we shall see in the next chapter, when Hitler made his bid for power, this was a strong hand for him to play in his dealings with Hindenburg and his advisers.

ACTIVITY

Extension

In pairs or in groups, conduct further research into the appeal of communism in Germany during this period to understand why it posed a threat to the Nazi Party, and present your findings to the class. You may wish to examine KPD propaganda posters or slogans and speeches, and evaluate the extent of their success.

STUDY TIP

This type of question asks you to balance the importance of the fear of communism in Nazi electoral success against a range of other factors. Fear of communism was undoubtedly one of the main factors and therefore deserves to be considered thoroughly. There was also a range of other factors, which you will need to identify, analyse and weigh against the main factor. The best answers will show a clear and consistent line of argument and also make links between the different factors.

11 The appointment of Hitler as Chancellor

KEY PROFILE

Fig. 1   Franz von Papen

Franz von Papen (1879–1969) was a former aristocratic army officer with a wide network of political influence. Although a member of the Centre Party, he was thoroughly anti-democratic. He wanted to restore the powers of the old elite and to re-establish an authoritarian state. Despite not being a member of the Reichstag (he was Minister-President of Prussia), he was appointed Chancellor in May 1932 and headed a 'cabinet of the barons' selected from the industrial and landowning elite. He was brought down by the intrigues of Schleicher in December 1932, but then conspired with Hitler and Hindenburg to remove Schleicher. He returned to power in a coalition with Hitler.

The appointment of Hitler

On 30 January 1933, Adolf Hitler was summoned to the office of the President of the Weimar Republic, Field Marshal Hindenburg. At this short but momentous meeting Hitler was invited by Hindenburg to lead a new 'government of national concentration', a coalition government in which the Nazi Party would share power with the DNVP and others, including **Franz von Papen**. When he left the meeting to return to his party headquarters, Hitler had been appointed Chancellor of the new government. Although Hitler was the leader of the largest party in the Reichstag, Hindenburg and Papen believed his inexperience meant that he could easily be manipulated by the more experienced politicians in his cabinet.

The process that brought Hitler to power in January 1933 was long and complex. Hitler and the Nazis won enough votes in the 1932 elections to become the largest party in the Reichstag, but that did not mean Hitler was carried into power on a wave of popular support. The NSDAP was the largest party in the Reichstag, but it did not have an absolute majority, and a large majority of German voters supported other parties. Nor did Hitler become Chancellor as the result of a Nazi-led political uprising, even though subsequent Nazi propaganda presented it in that way. His appointment involved negotiations and secret deals between many key German political figures, including Hindenburg and his close circle of advisers. As the historian Alan Bullock has written, Hitler came to power 'as part of a shoddy political deal with the 'Old Gang' whom he had been attacking for months past. Hitler did not seize power; he was jobbed into office by a backstairs intrigue.' To understand how this came about, we need to look in detail at the worsening political and economic crisis during 1932 and the beginning of 1933.

KEY CHRONOLOGY

Events leading to Hitler's appointment as Chancellor

1932	**April**	Hindenburg was re-elected as President
		Brüning imposed a ban on the Nazi SA
	May	Brüning was forced to resign as Chancellor and replaced by Papen
	June	Papen lifted the ban on the SA
	July	Papen declared a state of emergency in Prussia and dismissed the SPD-led government
		Reichstag election – Nazis became the largest party
	September	Reichstag passed a vote of no confidence in Papen's government
	November	Reichstag election – Nazis lost votes but still the largest party
	December	Papen was forced to resign and replaced by Schleicher
1933	**January**	Hitler and Papen agree to work together in a coalition government
		Hitler appointed Chancellor

The political and economic crisis

The fall of Brüning's government, May 1932

Brüning's coalition government was in power from March 1930 until May 1932, despite not having majority support in the Reichstag. His appointment by Hindenburg had been heavily influenced by Schleicher and he could only remain in office, or indeed pass any new laws, with Hindenburg and Schleicher's continued support. Kurt von Schleicher, who had become the key power broker in Weimar politics, was determined to establish a more authoritarian style of government in Germany and his first attempt to achieve this was during Brüning's government, which ruled largely through presidential decree.

In economic policy, Brüning's priority was to reduce state expenditure by cutting welfare benefits, reducing the number of civil servants and cutting wages, a policy for which he was dubbed the 'Hunger Chancellor'. Far from improving the economic situation, these measures contributed to the deepening of the Depression and, by February 1932, unemployment in Germany exceeded 6 million for the first time. As unemployment increased, so too did electoral support for the Nazi Party and the Communist Party, and the level of street violence rose. By the spring of 1932, there was growing alarm among the middle and upper classes that Germany was descending into chaos and that a communist revolution was a real possibility.

Although Brüning imposed a ban on the SA in April 1932 in an attempt to stop street violence, the political situation continued to deteriorate and Schleicher withdrew his support. Schleicher was concerned that the ban on the SA would provoke a Nazi uprising and he also came to the conclusion, after the presidential election, that no government could rule without the support of the Nazi Party. In talks with Schleicher, Hitler refused to join a coalition government unless he was appointed Chancellor, something that Schleicher was not willing to concede. However, Hitler did agree not to oppose a new government, on condition that there would be a new Reichstag election and that the ban on the SA was lifted.

Brüning's fate as Chancellor was sealed. When Hindenburg, acting on Schleicher's advice, refused to sign a presidential decree Brüning had submitted, Brüning had no alternative but to resign. Hindenburg replaced him with Franz von Papen, with Schleicher as Defence Minister in the new cabinet.

CROSS-REFERENCE

For more on Kurt von Schleicher, the political head of the army in this period, read his key profile on page 71 of Chapter 9.

SOURCE 1

In April 1932, General Groener, who was Minister of the Interior in Brüning's government, outlined his thinking on the Nazi Party and the SA to General von Gleich:

The Ministers of the Interior of the states are coming to a meeting about the SA. I have no doubt that we will master it — one way or the other. I think we have already drawn its poisonous fangs. One can make good tactical use of the endless declarations of legality made by the SA leaders, which they have handed to me in thick volumes. The SA is thereby undermining its credibility. But there are still difficult weeks of political manoeuvring until the various state elections are over. Then, one will have to start working towards making the Nazis acceptable as participants in a government because the movement, which will certainly grow, can no longer be suppressed by force. Of course the Nazis must not be allowed to form a government of their own anywhere, let alone in the Reich. But in the states an attempt will have to be made here and there to harness them in a coalition and to cure them of their utopias by constructive government work. I can see no better way, for the idea of trying to destroy the party through an anti-Nazi law on the lines of the old anti-Socialist law I would regard as a very unfortunate undertaking. With the SA of course it is different. They must be eliminated in any event.

ACTIVITY

Evaluating primary sources

Read Source 1 and the section on the fall of Brüning's government. Answer the following questions:

- What was General Groener's view of the SA and how they should be dealt with?
- What was his attitude towards the participation of the Nazi Party in government?
- How far did Groener's views differ from those of Schleicher?

Papen's credibility

Papen was not taken seriously by anyone apart from Hindenburg. The French ambassador wrote that his appointment was 'met with incredulity'. The ambassador went on to say that Papen 'enjoyed the peculiarity of being taken seriously by neither his friends nor his enemies'.

See Chapter 10, page 79 for more on the Chief Nazi propagandist Joseph Goebbels.

Discussion point

Discuss in pairs or as a group whether you agree or disagree with the view: 'Papen's destruction of democratic government in Prussia was a crucial turning point in the struggle between democracy and authoritarianism in Weimar Germany.'

For more information on Kurt von Schleicher, see Chapter 9, page 71.

Read about how the Nazis and the KPD both gained votes and seats in the July 1932 Reichstag election on page 74 in Chapter 10.

See Chapter 1, page 7, for more on the DDP.

Papen's government, May–December 1932
The 'cabinet of barons'

Following the orders of Hindenburg and Schleicher, Papen, in an attempt to establish a 'government of national concentration', constructed his government on a non-party political basis. The only political party that supported his coalition was the DNVP, which was rewarded with two posts in the cabinet. All other cabinet positions were filled by men who were not members of the Reichstag, most of whom came from the landowning and industrial elite, hence the nickname 'cabinet of barons'. With limited support in the Reichstag, Papen continued to rule by decree, a situation that suited his authoritarian leanings.

Papen believed that the greatest threat to Germany was a communist revolution and that Weimar democracy had allowed this threat to grow. Although, as an aristocrat, he looked down on the Nazis, he nevertheless sympathised with many of Hitler's ideas and saw the Nazis, with their mass popular support, as useful allies in his quest to establish a government of 'national concentration'. In June 1932, therefore, he lifted the ban on the SA and imposed curbs on the left-wing press. The result was a new wave of street violence, especially during the Reichstag election campaign of July 1932, which gave Papen an excuse to impose authoritarian rule in Germany's largest state, Prussia.

Papen's destruction of democratic government in Prussia

One of the most serious incidents of political violence occurred in the Altona suburb of Hamburg on 17 July. This mainly working-class district, in which the KPD had a strong following, was the scene of a large SA march, which was confronted by several hundred communists. The police panicked and opened fire on the communists, killing 18 and injuring over 100. Although the deaths were caused by police violence, Papen blamed the SPD-led state government of Prussia (of which Hamburg was a part) for the breakdown of law and order. He used this as an excuse to dismiss the government. He declared a state of emergency in Prussia, used the army to impose order in Berlin, and appointed himself Reich Commissioner in charge of Prussia. He also purged the civil service in Prussia of SPD supporters. Although Papen had the support of Hindenburg, his actions nevertheless went far beyond his constitutional powers. The SPD, however, did not try to organise resistance to this blatant assault on the democratic constitution. As Joseph Goebbels wrote in his diary, 'You only have to bare your teeth at the reds and they knuckle under. The reds have missed their chance. It's never going to come again.'

July 1932 election

One of the terms of the agreement between Hitler and Schleicher was that there should be a new Reichstag election. This was held at the end of July.

Table 1 *July 1932 election results*

Left			Centre		Right		
Party	KPD	SPD	State Party (DDP)	Centre Party	DVP	DNVP	NSDAP (Nazis)
Number of seats	89	133	4	75	7	37	230
% of vote	14.3	21.6	1.0	12.4	1.2	5.9	37.3

Most moderate parties, with the exception of the Centre, suffered losses in the July 1932 election as Germany's political life had become even more polarised compared with the previous election in September 1930. The DVP and the State Party (DDP), in particular, experienced a serious loss of support and were reduced to the ranks of fringe parties. The DNVP also suffered heavy losses as the Nazis established themselves as the main party of the right. The Nazis succeeded in attracting large numbers of middle-class voters, many of whom had never participated in elections before and many of the unemployed. They did not, however, succeed in winning voters from the SPD or KPD, nor were they able to attract Catholic voters away from the Centre Party. Despite their success, some Nazis were aware that they were reaching the limits of their appeal in an open election. As Goebbels noted in his diary, 'We have won a tiny bit. We won't get to an absolute majority this way. Something must happen. The time for opposition is over. Now deeds!'

Nevertheless, Hitler was now in an even stronger position in his dealings with Papen and Schleicher. After the election, Papen invited Hitler to join his government but Hitler still refused. Again he would only participate in a coalition government if he were the Chancellor. He also felt free to break his agreement with Schleicher and attack Papen's government. Indeed, the Nazis joined with other parties, including even the communists, to debate a vote of no confidence in Papen's government, which was passed by the massive majority of 512 votes to 42. Papen's position had weakened and he was forced to ask Hindenburg to dissolve the Reichstag and call a new election in November.

November 1932 election

Table 2 *November 1932 election results*

Party	Left		Centre		Right		
	KPD	SPD	State Party	Centre Party	DVP	DNVP	NSDAP (Nazis)
Number of seats	100	121	2	70	11	52	196
% of vote	16.9	20.4	1.0	11.9	1.9	8.8	33.1

The most striking aspect of the November 1932 election result was the loss of support for the Nazi Party. Although they remained the largest party in the Reichstag, they lost two million votes and 34 seats in the Reichstag. It appeared that Nazi support had peaked in July and was now in decline. Part of the explanation for this was that many middle-class voters had been alienated by Hitler's attacks on Papen and by his refusal to join a coalition government if he could not lead it. These middle-class voters returned to the DVP and the DNVP, both of which saw a modest revival in their electoral support. The fact that the Nazis had supported a communist-led transport strike in Berlin during the election campaign also damaged the party in the eyes of middle-class voters, who were terrified of a communist revolution. Moreover, three election campaigns in the space of eight months had exhausted Nazi funds. Hitler appeared to have lost his chance to take power by legal means. The centre parties suffered losses, whilst the communists made significant gains.

The end of Papen's government

Overall, the biggest loser in the November 1932 election was Papen, even though he was not a candidate. His government still faced a hostile Reichstag majority and he was beginning to lose credibility in the eyes of the army. Papen considered banning the Nazis and the communists, and using the army

ACTIVITY

Statistical analysis

Compare Tables 1 and 2. Answer the following questions.
- Which party/parties gained the most in the two elections of 1932?
- Which party/parties experienced the greatest losses?
- How far did the two elections alter the balance between left, centre and right wings in the Reichstag?

to enforce an authoritarian style of government, which would bypass the Reichstag altogether. However, when Schleicher informed Papen that the army would not support him, he had no alternative but to resign.

The role of 'backstairs intrigue'

Hindenburg's inner circle

Throughout the complicated twists and turns of the political situation in 1932, a small group of men who made up President Paul von Hindenburg's inner circle of advisers were involved in all of the key decisions. It was this group which advised Hindenburg on the appointment of Chancellors and the signing of presidential decrees. Chief among these was Kurt von Schleicher who, since 1926, had been the political head of the army. Indeed, since 1929, he had been the head of the Ministerial Office whose function was to represent the army in its dealings with the government. Schleicher had been instrumental in persuading Hindenburg to withdraw his support from Brüning in May 1932 and appoint Papen in his place. Then, in November 1932, Schleicher was deeply involved in the downfall of Papen, since Papen had proved to be far too independent-minded for Schleicher's liking. Schleicher was ambitious, quick-witted and addicted to behind-the-scenes intrigue. As a conservative, he worked for the restoration of authoritarian rule in Germany but, as a pragmatist, he recognised that this could not be achieved through a straightforward return to the past. The rise of the Nazi Party had transformed German politics. Schleicher aimed for an alliance between the forces of old conservatism and the Nazis who, with their popular support, would legitimise an authoritarian regime dominated by the old conservatives.

Within Hindenburg's private office, two other men occupied key positions. **Oskar von Hindenburg**, the President's son, was another army officer with close links to Schleicher. He controlled access to the President and his opinions were highly valued by his father. Also in a key position was **Dr Otto Meissner**, a civil servant who ran the President's Office and acted as a key go-between in negotiations between Hitler and Hindenburg. Hindenburg regarded Hitler with disdain and viewed the Nazis as a noisy, undisciplined rabble. He was, therefore, reluctant to concede Hitler's demand to be made Chancellor without any checks on his freedom of action. After the fall of Papen's government, however, Hindenburg was running out of options.

Schleicher's government, December 1932 to January 1933

After the fall of Papen, Schleicher persuaded President Hindenburg to appoint him as Chancellor. He was reluctant to take this step as he preferred to exercise influence from behind the scenes. Moreover, his task of constructing a stable government was fraught with difficulty since he had alienated Papen and lost some of Hindenburg's trust because of the way he had conspired against Papen. He believed that his best chance of success lay in persuading the Nazis to join a coalition government led by him.

At first, this did not seem to be an impossible dream. The Nazis had suffered a setback in the November election and, in state elections in December, their support continued to fall. They were also virtually bankrupt. Criticism of Hitler's tactics in refusing to join a coalition government after several invitations was beginning to surface within the Nazi Party itself. All of this contributed to the impression that Hitler had overplayed his hand and that his bargaining position had weakened. Schleicher, believing that he could put pressure on Hitler by playing on these divisions in the party,

Oskar von Hindenburg (1883–1960) was the son of Field Marshal/President Paul von Hindenburg. He followed his father into the army and reached the rank of major. When his father became President, Oskar became his father's aide-de-camp, which allowed him to control access to the President. He was a close friend of Schleicher. For a long time he opposed the appointment of Hitler as Chancellor but, in January 1933, he changed his mind after discussions with Papen and Hitler.

Fig. 2   *Otto Meissner*

Dr Otto Meissner (1880–1953) was the Head of the Office of the President under both Ebert and Hindenburg. He had considerable influence over Hindenburg and helped organise the talks between Papen and Hitler that led to Hitler's appointment as Chancellor. He continued to serve the Nazi regime after 1933, in a similar capacity, but with much less power or influence.

opened negotiations with the party's organisation leader, **Gregor Strasser**, about joining his government. Hitler, however, moved quickly to get rid of Strasser and reassert his control over the party. Schleicher's bid to win Nazi support for his government had failed.

CROSS-REFERENCE

More information on the Night of the Long Knives can be found in Chapter 13, page 117.

A CLOSER LOOK

Divisions in the Nazi Party

Despite its image of discipline and unity, there were some fundamental divisions within the Nazi Party over ideology and tactics. For Gregor Strasser and his brother Otto, the inclusion of the word 'socialist' in the party's name was more than just window-dressing. They advocated socialist policies such as the nationalisation of banks and industry, and they supported workers taking strike action against their employers. They saw the Nazi Party as a vehicle for a 'national revolution' that would sweep away the old elite, ideas which had a strong following among members of the SA. The Strasser brothers built up a strong power base in Berlin, but their policies caused many potential middle-class supporters to be wary of the Nazi Party and they were seen by Hitler as a threat to his authority. In 1930, Hitler purged Otto Strasser from the party and Gregor was purged in 1932.

KEY PROFILE

Fig. 3   *Gregor Strasser*

Gregor Strasser (1892–1934) was a member of the Nazi Party from 1921 and a veteran of the Beer Hall Putsch of 1924. From 1926 to 1928, he was in charge of the party's propaganda, following which he took over responsibility for the party's national organisation. He advocated a strong anti-capitalist stance to appeal to working-class voters, but was also strongly anti-communist and anti-Semitic. He was purged from party leadership in 1932 and murdered by the Nazi SS in the Night of the Long Knives in 1934.

Schleicher changed tack. He believed that a progressive social policy could win support from the trade unions and, through them, gain support in the Reichstag. With the economic situation at last beginning to improve, he cancelled the cuts in wages and benefits made by Papen in September, considered a large-scale job creation scheme to relieve unemployment, and even talked about breaking up some of the large estates in the east and distributing the land to small farmers. All of this was too much for the industrialists and landowners, who were the backbone of German conservative politics, and it also failed to attract trade union support. Schleicher's last throw of the dice was to ask Hindenburg to suspend the constitution, dissolve the Reichstag and give him virtually dictatorial powers. Hindenburg refused and Schleicher resigned.

Meanwhile, Papen had been involved in negotiations with Hitler over forming a new coalition government. Although Hitler still insisted on being Chancellor in any government he was part of, he was now prepared to consider a coalition. Alfred Hugenberg, the DNVP leader, indicated that he was prepared to support a Nazi-led coalition. Talks between Hitler, Papen and Hindenburg's inner circle (now minus Schleicher) led to a deal in which Hitler would form a coalition government with himself as Chancellor. Hindenburg's doubts about this were laid to rest by assurances from Papen and Oskar von Hindenburg that Hitler would not have a free hand to govern the country as he wished. Papen would be Vice-Chancellor and Hugenberg would run the Economics and Food Ministries. Apart from Hitler, there would be only two other Nazis in the cabinet. Both Papen and Hindenburg believed that Hitler, who was poorly educated and inexperienced in government, would be easy to control.

CROSS-REFERENCE

Further information on Alfred Hugenberg can be found in Chapter 5, page 41.

SOURCE 2

The banker Kurt von Schroeder gave an account to the Nuremberg Tribunal into Nazi war crimes in 1946 of a meeting between Hitler and Papen:

On 4 January 1933 Hitler, Papen and others arrived at my house in Cologne. Hitler, Papen and I went into my study where a two-hour discussion took place. The negotiations took place exclusively between Hitler and Papen.

Papen went on to say that he thought it best to form a government in which the conservative and nationalist elements that had supported him were represented together with the Nazis. He suggested that this new government should, if possible, be led by Hitler and himself together. Then Hitler made a long speech in which he said that, if he were to be elected Chancellor, Papen's followers could participate in his (Hitler's) Government as Ministers if they were willing to support his policy. Papen and Hitler reached agreement in principle whereby many of the disagreements between them could be removed and cooperation might be possible.

This meeting was arranged by me after Papen had asked me for it on about 10 December 1932. Before I took this step I talked to a number of businessmen and informed myself generally on how the business world viewed a collaboration between the two men. The general desire of businessmen was to see a strong man come to power in Germany who would form a government that would stay in power for a long time.

SOURCE 3

Head of the President's Office Otto Meissner's account to the Nuremberg Tribunal in 1946 of how Hitler became Chancellor:

In the middle of January, when Schleicher was first asking for emergency powers, Hindenburg was not aware of the contact between Papen and Hitler — particularly, of the meeting which had taken place in the house of the Cologne banker, Kurt von Schroeder. In the second part of January, Papen played an increasingly important role in the house of the Reich President, but despite Papen's persuasions, Hindenburg was extremely hesitant, until the end of January, to make Hitler Chancellor. He wanted to have Papen again as Chancellor. Papen finally won him over to Hitler with the argument that the representatives of the other right-wing parties which would belong to the Government would restrict Hitler's freedom of action. In addition Papen expressed his misgivings that, if the present opportunity were again missed, a revolt of the National Socialists and civil war were likely.

 PRACTICE QUESTION

Evaluating primary sources

With reference to Sources 2 and 3 and your understanding of the historical context, which of these two sources is more valuable in explaining the appointment of Hitler as Chancellor?

Summary

Hitler could not have become Chancellor without the Nazis' success in elections. As leader of that party, Hitler had the right to be included in any discussions about forming coalition governments and, indeed, to be considered for the Chancellorship. There were a number of meetings between Hitler and leading figures such as Schleicher, Papen and even Hindenburg about Hitler joining a coalition, but all these discussions broke down when it became clear that Hitler would only take power on his own terms, something that Hindenburg and his inner circle were reluctant to concede. Attempts to form governments without the Nazis, however, all failed through lack of support in the Reichstag. Moreover, there was always the implied threat from the Nazis that, if their demands were not conceded, they would push Germany over the brink into civil war. Hindenburg's advisers came to the conclusion that it would be safer to have Hitler in government rather than excluded from it and Papen, in particular, deluded himself into believing that he, with all his experience, could control and manipulate Hitler from behind the scenes. It was not long before he discovered how wrong he was.

 PRACTICE QUESTION

'Hitler became Chancellor in January 1933 mainly as the result of "backstairs intrigue".' Explain why you agree and disagree with this view.

STUDY TIP

This practice question requires you to balance one factor in Hitler's appointment ('backstairs intrigue') against a range of other factors. Clearly, 'backstairs intrigue' played a crucial role in the events of January 1933. There was also a range of long-term economic and political factors, which need to be included in the analysis before you reach a final judgement.

12 The establishment of the Nazi dictatorship, January–March 1933

ACTIVITY

Evaluating primary sources

Source 1 was written by Louise Solmitz, a conservative, middle-class German woman.

- Who did she credit for the appointment of the new cabinet?
- What was it about the appointment of the new cabinet that made her so excited?
- What note of warning does she include in her comments?

KEY TERM

Stahlhelm (Steel Helmets): a paramilitary organisation of ex-servicemen dedicated to the restoration of the monarchy and the revival of Germany as a military power, which took its name from the steel helmets issued to German soldiers in the First World War; founded in 1918 by Franz Seldte, it grew rapidly and had 500,000 members by 1930, making it the largest paramilitary organisation in Weimar Germany

SOURCE 1

Louise Solmitz, a schoolteacher from Hamburg, recorded her thoughts about the appointment of Hitler in her diary entry for 30 January 1933. Her opinion here is characteristic of the attitude of the nationalist conservative middle class at the time (more unusual, however, is that she was also married to a baptised Jew):

The news that Hitler is Chancellor of the Reich! And what a Cabinet!!! One we didn't dare dream of in July. Hitler, Hugenberg, **Seldte**, Papen!!!

On each one of them depends part of Germany's hopes. National Socialist drive, German National reason, the non-political **Stahlhelm**, not to forget Papen. It is so incredibly marvelous that I am writing it down quickly before the first discordant note comes, for when has Germany ever experienced a blessed summer after a wonderful spring? What a great thing Hindenburg has achieved!

Huge torchlight procession in the presence of Hindenburg and Hitler by National Socialists and Stahlhelm, who at long last are collaborating again. This is a memorable 30 January.

Fig. 1 *A Stahlhelm parade*

KEY PROFILE

Franz Seldte (1882–1947) was the leader of the paramilitary Stahlhelm. He was a conservative German nationalist who had been hostile to the Weimar Republic but retained his independence from the Nazis. In April 1933, however, he joined the Nazi Party and his Stahlhelm organisation was incorporated into the SA.

Fig. 2 *Franz Seldte*

The Hitler cabinet

On 30 January 1933, Hitler was appointed Chancellor by President Hindenburg. Later that day, Hitler held his first cabinet meeting. It was a cabinet in which the Nazi Party held only three posts out of a total of twelve ministers, reinforcing Papen's view that no fundamental political change would occur by including the Nazis. Franz Papen held the position of Vice-Chancellor and was also the Minister-President of Prussia, Germany's largest state. He also had won the right to be present whenever Hitler met with President Hindenburg. The real decisions in cabinet would be taken by the non-Nazi majority, many of whom belonged, like Papen himself, to the old aristocratic elite. Papen believed that Hitler would not be able to dominate his own cabinet; still less would he be able to become the dictator he aspired to be. Hitler, on the other hand, was determined to establish a Nazi dictatorship as soon as possible. By the end of March 1933, he was well on the way to achieving this.

KEY CHRONOLOGY

January—March 1933

1 February	Hitler dissolved the Reichstag and called new elections
27 February	Reichstag building was set on fire
28 February	Decree for the Protection of the People and the State
5 March	Reichstag elections – Nazis won 288 seats (43.9 per cent of the vote), still short of overall majority
6–7 March	Nazis began taking over state governments
8 March	First permanent concentration camp was established
13 March	Ministry for Public Enlightenment and Propaganda was established
24 March	Enabling Act passed

KEY PROFILES

Wilhelm Frick (1877–1946) was interior minister from 1933 to 1943. He had studied law before working for the Munich police 1904–24. He joined the Nazi Party and was elected to the Reichstag in 1924. He was tried and executed by the Allies after the war.

General Blomberg (1878–1946) had been the army commander in East Prussia before becoming Defence Minister in Hitler's first cabinet. Described as weak, Blomberg was persuaded by Hitler's promise of an aggressive foreign policy and rearmament to steer the army towards increasingly enthusiastic support for the regime. In 1938, however, Hitler removed Blomberg from the government.

Freiherr von Neurath (1873–1956) was a German aristocratic diplomat. In the 1920s, he had served as German ambassador in Rome and then London, before becoming Foreign Minister in Papen's government in 1932. He continued in this post under Hitler until 1938. He joined the Nazi Party in 1937, but was dismissed from the Foreign Ministry in 1938 after opposing Hitler's aggressive plans for German expansion.

Later, in the evening of 30 January, Hitler stood on the balcony of the Reich Chancellery to review a torchlight procession by around 100,000 Nazi members winding its way through the streets of the capital Berlin. Organised by Hitler's propaganda chief, Joseph Goebbels, this demonstration was designed to show that Hitler's appointment as Chancellor was not going to be a normal change

A CLOSER LOOK

Hitler's first cabinet

Apart from Hitler (Chancellor) and Papen (Vice-Chancellor), the cabinet contained:

- two Nazi Party ministers: Minister of the Interior **Wilhelm Frick** and **Minister without portfolio Hermann Goering** (who was also Minister of the Interior in Prussia). Since the Minister of the Interior controlled the police, Nazi ministers occupied key positions in the government
- the aristocratic army officer **General Blomberg** was Defence Minister
- Alfred Hugenberg, the media tycoon and leader of the DNVP, was Minister for Economics
- **Freiherr von Neurath**, an aristocratic, conservative, professional diplomat with wide experience of foreign affairs, was made Foreign Minister at Hindenburg's insistence
- Franz Seldte, the leader of the paramilitary Stahlhelm, as Minister of Labour.

KEY TERM

Minister without portfolio: a member of a government who has no specific responsibility over a particular government department; this means that they are free to be involved in a number of policy areas

Fig. 4   *Hermann Goering*

Hermann Goering (1893–1946) was a fighter pilot in the First World War. He joined the Nazi Party in 1922 and took part in the Munich Putsch of 1923. He was elected to the Reichstag in 1928 and became the President (speaker) of the Reichstag in 1932. In 1933, he was appointed Chancellor and Interior Minister of Prussia. He also became Reich Aviation Minister in 1933 and was responsible for the rebuilding of the Luftwaffe (air force). As Interior Minister of Prussia, he established the Gestapo and the first concentration camps. In 1936, he was placed in charge of the Four Year Plan (see Chapter 15). After the failure of the Luftwaffe to defeat the RAF in the Battle of Britain, his influence declined and he was expelled from the party in 1945. He was captured by the Allies and put on trial but committed suicide in prison.

Fig. 3   *The torchlight procession on 30 January 1933*

of government, one of the many that had been seen in the 14 years since the German Republic had been established. It was a spectacular demonstration of Hitler's personal triumph and of the victory of the Nazi movement. Hitler and his Nazi Party were making it clear that their accession to power would mark a historic break with the past and the start of their 'National Revolution'.

Nazi use of terror

Nazi violence against political opponents

SOURCE 2

The Nazi torchlight parade on 30 January was watched by a young girl, Melita Maschmann. She recalled these events in her 1963 book *Account Rendered*:

For hours the columns marched by. Again and again amongst them we saw groups of boys and girls scarcely older than ourselves. At one point somebody leaped from the ranks of the marchers and struck a man who had been standing only a few paces away from us. Perhaps he had made a hostile remark. I saw him fall to the ground with blood streaming down his face and I heard him cry out. Our parents hurriedly drew us away from the scuffle, but they had not been able to stop us seeing the man bleeding. The image of him haunted me for days.

The horror it inspired in me was almost imperceptibly spiced with an intoxicating joy. 'We want to die for the flag', the torch-bearers had sung. I was overcome with a burning desire to belong to these people for whom it was a matter of death and life. I wanted to escape from my childish, narrow life and I wanted to attach myself to something that was great and fundamental.

Evaluating primary sources

What can an historian learn from Source 2 about the propaganda value of Nazi parades?

The violence of Nazi Stormtroopers (SA) had played a key role in Hitler's rise to power. Once he was in power in January 1933, he used state resources to consolidate his position and rapidly expanded the SA, since the Stormtroopers' violence and terror were vital weapons in his struggle to eliminate opposition. From a membership of around 500,000 in January 1933, the organisation grew to around 3 million strong a year later. Another result of the Nazis being in power was that the activities of the SA gained legal authority. In late February 1933, the SA and the Stahlhelm were merged and became recognised as 'auxiliary police'; orders were issued to the regular police forces forbidding them from interfering with SA activities. Frick and Goering occupied key positions in the cabinet – Frick as Minister of the Interior for the whole Reich and Goering as Minister of the Interior in Prussia – which enabled the Nazis to control the police.

The Nazi 'legal revolution' and the 'revolution from below', in which the SA unleashed a reign of terror against socialist and communist opponents, were opposite sides of the same coin. Using their newfound powers, the SA unleashed a sustained assault on trade union and KPD offices, as well as on the homes of left-wing politicians. Gangs of Stormtroopers broke up SPD and KPD meetings. On 5 February, a young Nazi shot dead the SPD mayor of a small town in Prussia and, later in the month, a communist was killed in clashes with the SA. Not only were these crimes ignored by the police but, when the SPD newspaper condemned the killings, the paper was banned. The Centre Party also became a target after its newspapers criticised the Nazi regime. Centre Party newspapers were banned and Stormtroopers attacked the party's meetings.

Fig. 5 *Dachau concentration camp*

Thousands of communists, socialists and trade unionists were rounded up and imprisoned in makeshift concentration camps set up in old factories or army barracks. The first permanent concentration camp was established on 8 March at Dachau near Munich, with accommodation for over 5000 people. This became the model for later concentration camps. By July 1933, 26,789 political prisoners had been arrested by the SA, or taken into 'protective custody' to use the official Nazi terminology, and imprisoned in some 70 camps.

The Reichstag fire

On taking power, Hitler persuaded Hindenburg to dissolve the Reichstag and call a new election in March. He believed that the Nazis could win an outright majority in this election, thereby strengthening his position. This election campaign was the occasion for an intensification of Nazi terror against their opponents. By the time the election took place on 5 March, the SPD and KPD had virtually been driven underground by the atmosphere of terror and intimidation generated by the Nazis. A key moment in the campaign was the burning down of the Reichstag building on 27 February. A young Dutch communist, Marinus van der Lubbe, was arrested and charged with causing the fire. There have been suspicions ever since that the Nazis deliberately set up van der Lubbe to set fire to the Reichstag in order to justify introducing repressive measures, but no definitive evidence has ever emerged to show

Fig. 6 *The Reichstag building on fire, February 1933*

exactly who was responsible. Whoever that was, it was clear that the Nazi regime gained the most from the fire, as they claimed that it was part of a communist plot to start a revolution in Germany and the event was used to justify the immediate suspension of civil liberties. Terror had now become a legal means to crush opposition.

Evaluating primary sources

1. What is the value of Source 3 to an historian studying Nazi violence and the Reichstag fire?
2. Sources 1 and 3 are both taken from the diary of Louise Solmitz. In what way did her attitude towards Hitler changed between 30 January and 27 February?

SOURCE 3

Louise Solmitz wrote about the Reichstag Fire in her diary:

The communists have set the Reichstag on fire, a horrible fire, which has been deliberately started in various places in the building. The thoughts and hopes of most Germans are completely concentrating upon Hitler; his reputation soars to the stars; he is the saviour for an evil and saddened German world. When we ask people of every rank and educational background 'Who are you voting for?' the answer is always the same: 'Why we're voting for the same as everyone else, only Hitler.' And a few cases, like us, are hesitating between NSDAP and DNVP. An ordinary-looking young man walked by, seeing nothing, hearing nothing, but all by himself singing in a booming voice a Nazi song. Franz said 'It sounded like he was praying. It's becoming a religion.'

The use of legal power

The Decree for the Protection of the People and the State

Hitler was appointed Chancellor by Hindenburg in a way that was strictly legal, according to the constitution of the Weimar Republic. That constitution technically remained in force during the period of the Third Reich but, in the aftermath of the Reichstag fire, Hitler was able to persuade Hindenburg to sign a decree giving him 'emergency' powers. This was the Decree for the Protection of the People and the State, which suspended important civil and political rights that had been guaranteed under the Weimar Constitution. Thus the police were given increased powers to arrest, and detain without charge, those deemed to be a threat to state security. The police also gained increased powers to enter and search private premises, while the government had the power to censor publications. In practice, these powers were used to arrest communists and socialists, to ban their newspapers, and to disrupt their organisations. The decree also gave the central government the power to take over state governments if they refused to act against the Nazis' political opponents.

The decree was designed primarily to legalise a full-scale assault on the communists. Backed by a propaganda campaign in which the Nazis claimed that Germany was on the brink of a 'German Bolshevik Revolution', the SA launched a ferocious campaign of violence across Germany. The police arrested 10,000 communists in two weeks, including most of the leaders. Although the KPD was not yet officially banned, and the party was still able to put up candidates in the March election, party membership was treated by the courts as an act of treason and many communists were given long sentences. Civil servants, judges and the police, who were overwhelmingly conservative and nationalist in their political sympathies, were only too willing to give legal sanction to the Nazis' campaign of terror.

March 1933 election

The election campaign was conducted against this backdrop of terror and intimidation. The SA controlled the streets, many of the Nazis' opponents were locked up, the offices of the SPD and KPD had been smashed up and their funds confiscated. It was virtually impossible for the left to organise election meetings and their posters were removed as soon as they were put up. Anyone distributing leaflets for the SPD or KPD was liable to be arrested. Meanwhile, the Nazi propaganda machine flooded the country with posters, leaflets, radio broadcasts, election rallies and parades.

Even with the resources of the state at their disposal, and their opponents effectively banned from campaigning, the Nazis did not achieve the resounding success they desired in the election.

Table 1 *March 1933 election results*

	Left		Centre		Right		
Party	KPD	SPD	State Party	Centre Party	DVP	DNVP	NSDAP (Nazis)
Number of seats	81	120	5	73	2	52	288
% of vote	12.3	18.25	0.85	11.25	1.1	8.0	43.9

The Nazi vote had increased since the previous election in November 1932, but not as much as Hitler hoped and expected. Despite the violence and intimidation, SPD and communist support had held up remarkably well, as did support for the Centre. Perhaps the most significant point about the election result was that nearly 64 per cent of voters had supported non-Nazi parties. On the other hand, the Nazis, with the support of their DNVP allies, now had a Reichstag majority.

The end of democracy

Enabling Act: The Law for Removing the Distress of the People and the Reich

The first meeting of the new Reichstag was held in the Kroll Opera House on 23 March. Hitler's sole objective at this meeting was to secure the necessary two thirds majority for his Enabling Act, a law that would allow him to make laws without the approval of the Reichstag and without reference to the President, for a period of four years.

SS (Schutztaffel)

The SS was Hitler's personal bodyguard, created in 1926. Heinrich Himmler had taken charge of the SS in 1929. Under Himmler's leadership, and especially after the Nazis came to power in 1933, the SS grew rapidly and expanded its role. Once the Nazis came to power, its policing role was expanded and it became the main Nazi organisation involved in the identification, arrest and detention of political prisoners

Fig. 7   *The meeting of the new Reichstag at the Kroll Opera House on 23 March*

SOURCE 4

The non-Nazi deputies who were able to attend the session were subjected to an atmosphere of violence and intimidation, as outlined in this account by the SPD deputy, Wilhelm Hoegner:

The wide square in front was crowded with dark masses of people. We were received with wild choruses, 'We want the Enabling Act!' Youths with swastikas on their chests eyed us insolently, blocked our way, in fact made us run the gauntlet, calling us names like 'Centre pig', 'Marxist sow'. The Kroll Opera House was crawling with armed SA and **SS men**. The assembly hall was decorated with swastikas and similar ornaments. When we Social Democrats had taken our seats on the extreme left, SA and SS men lined along the walls behind us in a semi-circle. Their expression boded no good.

CROSS-REFERENCE

More information about Himmler can be found in Chapter 14, page 108.

ACTIVITY

Evaluating primary sources

From your reading of Source 4, and the other information in this section, to what extent did the Nazis' intimidation at the Opera House succeed in silencing opposition to the Enabling Act?

ACTIVITY

Discussion point

How 'legal' was Hitler's establishment of a dictatorship in Germany in 1933?

The Enabling Act was passed by the Reichstag on 24 March 1933. Further to this, Hitler was also given the power to make treaties with foreign states without the Reichstag's approval. Because this law was a change in the constitution, it required a two thirds majority of the Reichstag in order to be legally enforceable. With the communist deputies unable to take their seats and the DNVP willing to collaborate with the Nazis in passing the bill, the Centre Party held the key to getting the necessary two thirds majority. By offering the Centre Party the reassurance that he would not use his powers without first consulting Hindenburg, Hitler won its support. Only the SPD deputies voted against the bill and the Enabling Act duly became law. With full executive and legislative powers, Hitler could rule without needing a Reichstag majority and, after 1933, the Reichstag rarely met.

The Enabling Act was the final piece in the legal framework that legitimised the Nazi dictatorship. Hitler was now able to issue decrees without needing Hindenburg's approval. Although the law was presented as a temporary measure for four years, in practice it was a permanent fixture of the Nazi regime. With the new law in force, the Nazis could now begin to construct the one-party, terror state that Hitler wanted.

Summary: The state of Germany in March 1933

Within two months of being appointed Chancellor, Hitler had laid the legal foundations of the Nazi dictatorship and the process of *Gleichschaltung* had already begun. The establishment of a one-party state, the banning of free trade unions, media censorship, control over education and youth groups, and the creation of a racial state were tasks that the Nazi regime was about to embark upon. Nevertheless, there were already clear signs indicating the regime's direction of travel. The KPD was effectively banned and its press silenced. Those of its leaders who were not in custody were attempting to leave the country. The police were under Nazi control, and the SA and SS could beat up and kill their opponents with impunity. The rule of law was effectively over and individual rights were being trampled underfoot. Violent attacks on Jews were on the increase.

SOURCE 5

On 13 March 1933, Joseph Goebbels was appointed to head the new Ministry of Popular Enlightenment and Propaganda. He made clear what his intentions were:

I view the first task of the new ministry as being to establish coordination between the government and the whole people. It is not enough for people to be more or less reconciled to our regime, to be persuaded to take a neutral attitude towards us; rather we want to work on people until they no longer oppose us. The new ministry has no other aim than to unite the nation behind the ideals of the national revolution.

Uniting the nation 'behind the ideals of the national revolution', if it could be achieved at all, would require a range of measures and policies. In particular, it would require the Nazis to succeed in tackling the severe economic crisis that Germany was still experiencing. It would also require some compromises on the part of Hitler and the Nazis. There were still powerful interests and institutions in Germany – in particular, the army – which retained some independence from the Nazi Party, even while many of their members sympathised with Nazi aims. Even with his legal powers to rule by decree, Hitler fully appreciated that the army was the only force that could remove him from power. The aristocratic officers who still controlled the army were not Nazis themselves and were worried by the implications of Nazi talk of a 'national revolution'. Therefore, on 3 February, Hitler met the army's senior officers and outlined his plans for rearmament. He also took care to reassure the army leaders that, despite pressure from the SA for a Second Revolution, Hitler would not undermine the army's role as the most important institution in the state. In return, the army leaders gave Hitler a free hand in establishing a dictatorship.

Then, on 20 February, Hitler met a group of leading industrialists to ask for financial support for the Nazi election campaign and secured donations of three million Reichmarks. Big business would benefit from a government that was anti-communist but, as with the army, the anti-capitalist rhetoric of the SA and the more radical Nazi leaders worried the businessmen. Hitler, for his part, needed strong businesses to help him to achieve his aims of rearmament and reviving the economy. The price of business support for the Nazis, therefore, was that Hitler had to stop Nazi attacks on large capitalist enterprises.

The lines of the future development of the Nazi regime were laid down in the early months of 1933. On the one hand, the Nazis would not allow any open opposition to stand in their way. On the other hand, conservative

A CLOSER LOOK

Gleichschaltung

Gleichschaltung meant 'forcing into line', and was the process through which the Nazis attempted to control or 'coordinate' all aspects of German society. It was Hitler's intention that there should be no independent organisations standing between the state and the individual. Individuals would have no private space in which they could either think or act independently of the regime

CROSS-REFERENCE

More information about the SA's demand for a 'Second Revolution' can be found in Chapter 13, page 102.

This is a comparative question, focusing on the relative value of the two sources. It would be useful to remember that all sources are of value to historians, but some may be more valuable than others, or each may be valuable in different ways. Both sources are from young women, although there is obviously a difference in ages as one is a teacher and the other would appear to be a schoolgirl. Provenance is therefore relevant in your answer, but part of your main focus must be on what they actually say and the tone of the two sources.

forces in the army and big business still retained much influence and authority, and Hitler knew he could not ignore them or ride roughshod over them. The historian Kershaw has referred to the 'pact of 1933' in which Hitler, the army leaders and big business agreed to cooperate. Although there was no formal written agreement between them, it is clear that Hitler needed their support and that the price of this support was that he had to leave these institutions largely untouched by the process of *Gleichschaltung*.

 PRACTICE QUESTION

Evaluating primary sources

With reference to Sources 1 and 2 and your understanding of the historical context, which of these two sources is more valuable in explaining the reactions of young Germans to the new Nazi regime?

This view is open to challenge, but it is also possible to agree with it to some extent. In your answer to this type of question you need to identify the weaknesses in the constitution and the way in which these created problems for democratic governments. You will also need to identify and explain a range of other factors including the circumstances in which the Republic was founded. A good answer will have a range of factors, a well-directed and sustained argument, and a clear conclusion.

 PRACTICE QUESTION

'The failure of the Weimar Republic by 1933 was due to the weaknesses of its constitution.' Assess the validity of this view.

4 The Nazi Dictatorship, 1933–39

13 Hitler's consolidation of power, March 1933 to August 1934

On 30 June 1934 at the Stadelheim prison in Munich, the leader of the Nazi SA, Ernst Röhm, was executed by two SS officers. Earlier that day the SS had arrested Röhm and other SA leaders at a lakeside hotel. This was part of a wide-ranging purge of the SA that Hitler had ordered, as the organisation had outlived its usefulness and was becoming an embarrassment. Hitler ordered that a revolver be left in Röhm's cell, but Röhm refused to commit suicide. 'If I am to be killed,' he was reported to have said, 'let Adolf do it himself.' He was shot at point-blank range. This so-called 'Night of the Long Knives' was one of the final acts in Hitler's consolidation of power in 1933–34.

At the end of March 1933, Hitler's government had been granted exceptional powers by the passing of the Enabling Act. However, there were still some political and constitutional limitations on Hitler's power. Hindenburg, as President, had the final say in constitutional matters and the army was loyal to Hindenburg, not to Hitler. There were a number of political parties that were independent of the regime, some of which, such as the SPD (Social Democratic Party), were prepared to openly voice their opposition. Although the Nazis effectively controlled the state government in Prussia, the largest of Germany's federal states, elected governments in most other German states were under the control of other parties. The period between March 1933 and August 1934 saw the Nazis remove the remaining obstacles to their exercise of dictatorial power.

KEY CHRONOLOGY

Events leading to Hitler becoming Führer

1933

24 March	Enabling Act passed
31 March	1st Law for the Coordination of the Federal States
7 April	Law for Restoration of a Professional Civil Service
	2nd Law for the Coordination of the Federal States
22 June	SPD outlawed as a 'party hostile to the nation and the state'
5 July	Centre Party voluntarily disbanded
14 July	Law against Formation of New Parties: Germany was now a one-party state
12 November	Reichstag elections; Nazis won 92 per cent of the vote

1934

30 January	Law for Reconstruction of the Reich
14 February	Reichsrat abolished
30 June	Night of the Long Knives
2 August	Death of President Hindenburg; Hitler became President as well as Chancellor and the army swore an oath of allegiance to him
19 August	Hitler took the title of Führer

LEARNING OBJECTIVES

In this chapter you will learn about:

- government and administrative changes, and the establishment of a one-party state
- the Night of the Long Knives in June 1934
- the impact of Hindenburg's death in August 1934.

CROSS-REFERENCES

The SA (Stormtroopers) and Ernst Röhm are described in Chapter 4, page 33.

The SS (Schutzstaffel) was Hitler's personal bodyguard team. More detail about them is in Chapter 12, page 96.

The Enabling Act allowed Hitler to make laws without the approval of the Reichstag or reference to the President. More information on this is in Chapter 12, page 95.

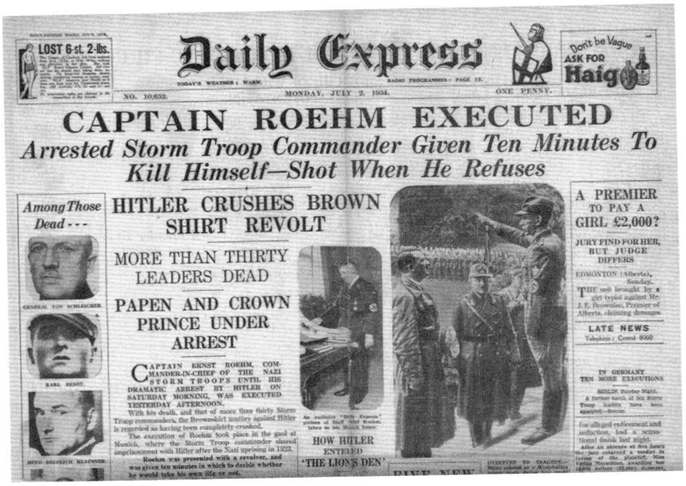
LOST 6 st. 2-lbs.

Daily Express

Don't be Vague ASK FOR Haig

NO. 10,652. MONDAY, JULY 2, 1934. ONE PENNY.

CAPTAIN ROEHM EXECUTED

Arrested Storm Troop Commander Given Ten Minutes To Kill Himself—Shot When He Refuses

Among Those Dead - - -

GENERAL VON SCHLEICHER

KARL ERNST

HERR HEINRICH KLAUSNER

HITLER CRUSHES BROWN SHIRT REVOLT

MORE THAN THIRTY LEADERS DEAD

PAPEN AND CROWN PRINCE UNDER ARREST

CAPTAIN ERNST ROEHM, COMMANDER-IN-CHIEF OF THE NAZI STORM TROOPS UNTIL HIS DRAMATIC ARREST BY HITLER ON SATURDAY MORNING, WAS EXECUTED YESTERDAY AFTERNOON.

With his death, and that of more than thirty Storm Troop commanders, the Brownshirt mutiny against Hitler is regarded as having been completely crushed.

The execution of Roehm took place in the gaol at Munich, where the Storm Troop commander shared imprisonment with Hitler after the Nazi uprising in 1923.

Roehm was presented with a revolver, and was given ten minutes in which to decide whether he would take his own life or not.

HOW HITLER ENTERED 'THE LION'S DEN'

A PREMIER TO PAY A GIRL £2,000?

JURY FIND FOR HER, BUT JUDGE DIFFERS

EDMONTON (Alberta), Sunday.

THE suit brought by a girl typist against Mr. J. E. Brownlee, Premier of Alberta, claiming damages for alleged enticement and seduction, had a sensational finish last night.

LATE NEWS

IN GERMANY TEN MORE EXECUTIONS

Fig. 1 *The front page of the English newspaper the* Daily Express *reports on the execution of Ernst Röhm*

Government and administrative changes

SOURCE 1

In a speech to Nazi officials in July 1933, Hitler outlined his thinking on changing the way Germany was governed:

The present structure of the Reich is something unnatural. It is neither conditioned by the needs of the economy nor by the necessities of life of our people. We have taken over a given state of affairs. The question is whether we want to retain it. The task lies in keeping and reshaping the given construction in so far as it is useable, so that what is good can be preserved for the future, and what cannot be used is removed.

ACTIVITY

In Source 1 Hitler was talking about the extent to which the Nazis would change the institutions of the German state. As you read this chapter, make two lists of state institutions – those the Nazis considered to be 'useable' and those they put in the category of 'cannot be used'.

For Hitler and his Nazi Party, the coming to power in January 1933 was the beginning of a national socialist revolution. For Hitler this meant the conquest of political power. Many Nazis, however, especially the SA, had a very different view of the Nazi revolution. This was to cause continuing tensions between Hitler and the SA during the early months of the Nazi regime, and will be considered in more detail later in this chapter. For Hitler, the Nazi revolution began with acquiring dictatorial power, and then continued with the elimination of non-Nazi political parties and other independent organisations, together with Nazi control over the **institutions of the state** at both central and local government level.

KEY TERM

Institutions of the state: a state is an organised political community under one government; the institutions of the state include the civil service, the armed forces, the police and the judicial system

The creation of a one-party state

Hitler viewed conventional political parties with contempt, seeing them as mere election machines, which represented narrow, sectional interests rather than the interests of the nation as a whole. He claimed that the Nazi Party was the 'racial core' of the entire German people. Although its members were a minority of the population, even after a surge in party membership in 1933, Hitler believed it was nevertheless made up of the superior Germans and was committed to fighting and sacrificing on behalf of the entire German people. In the Nazi ***Volksgemeinshaft***, therefore, there could be no parties other than the Nazi Party. By the middle of July 1933, this ambition had become a reality. This was achieved in a number of stages:

- The KPD was effectively banned after the Reichstag fire in February. Most of the communists who had not been arrested and imprisoned in concentration camps had fled into exile.

CROSS-REFERENCES

Refer back to Chapter 12, pages 93–94 to the section on the Reichstag fire.

Volksgemeinschaft was very significant to the Nazi ideology. Hitler advocated a state based on a racial community where only Aryans could be citizens. You can read more about this in Chapter 10, page 76.

- Having stood up to Hitler in the Reichstag debate on the Enabling Act in March, the SPD continued to voice its opposition to the regime until it was outlawed as a 'party hostile to the nation and the state' on 22 June 1933.
- Realizing that their days as political parties were numbered, the DNVP and the Centre Party dissolved themselves – the DNVP on 27 June and the Centre Party on 5 July.
- On 14 July 1933, the Law against the Formation of New Parties outlawed all non-Nazi political parties.

Centralisation of power and control over local government

The Weimar Republic was a **federal state** in which a large number of powers were devolved to state governments. Each state, for example, controlled its own police force. Prussia, the largest of the German states, comprised sixty per cent of the territory and fifty per cent of the population of the entire country. It was so large that its state government could operate largely independently of the central government. In July 1932, however, the Prussian state government had been dismissed by Papen and a Reich Commissioner had been appointed to run the state. In Hitler's cabinet after January 1933 this position was held by Goering. This paved the way for the centralisation of power within the whole Reich, which the Nazis began in March 1933.

Table 1 *Laws passed to centralise power in 1933–34*

Date	Laws passed
31 March 1933	First Law for the Coordination of the Federal States dissolved the existing state assemblies and replaced them with Nazi-dominated assemblies.
7 April 1933	The Second Law for the Coordination of the Federal States created the new post of Reich Governor (RG) to oversee the government of each state (Prussia was excluded as it already had a Reich Commissioner). These new RGs were accountable to the Minister of the Interior and responsible for ensuring that the state governments followed the policies laid down by central government.
30 January 1934	The Law for the Reconstruction of the Reich took the centralisation process a stage further. State assemblies were abolished and the governments of the states were formally subordinated to the government of the Reich. This meant that the posts of RGs had now become redundant but Hitler did not abolish the posts. Rivalry and tension between state governments and RGs continued in the coming years.
14 February 1934	The Reichsrat was abolished. This was the parliamentary assembly to which the state assemblies sent delegates. Since the state assemblies no longer existed, it was a logical next step to abolish the Reichsrat.

The Nazi Party had its own organisational structures at both national and local level. At state level the Nazi leaders, known as *Gauleiters*, wanted to control local government and many of them took over the roles of Reich Governors within their areas. The Nazis also instituted violent campaigns to oust political opponents from important local positions, such as town mayors, and replace them with Nazi Party nominees. However, the precise relationship between the Party and the state at local level, as at national level, was never clearly defined.

CROSS-REFERENCE

The reasons behind Papen's dismissal of the Prussian government are covered in Chapter 11, page 84.

More information about the Reichsrat can be found in Chapter 1, page 9.

KEY TERMS

Federal state: a state in which a number of small states or provinces keep control over many of their internal affairs, but decisions about national issues are the responsibility of the central government

Gauleiter: a Nazi party leader at regional or state level. The Nazi political organisation had leaders (*leiters*) at both national (Reich) and regional (Gau) levels; Gauleiters were therefore the second ranking Nazi political officials

Control over the Civil Service

Under the Kaiser, civil servants enjoyed a status almost on a par with that of soldiers. The higher ranks of the Civil Service were recruited almost exclusively from the aristocracy and civil servants closely identified with the authoritarian values of the Second Empire. These conservative-minded civil servants would not embrace the democratic values of the Weimar Republic and many welcomed Hitler's appointment in 1933. Their support for the new regime was based, however, on a misunderstanding. They believed that the conservative ministers in Hitler's cabinet would restrain the Nazis and allow the Civil Service to continue serving the state in much the same way that it had done under the Kaiser. What they had failed to understand was that the Nazis had no intention of being bound by the rules and regulations that civil servants had to follow. The Nazis regarded the Civil Service as an obstacle to their exercise of dictatorial power. Many local officials were forced to resign and were replaced by Nazi Party appointees, most of whom had no experience of government. The Nazi SA also began to place Party officials in government offices to ensure that civil servants were carrying out the orders of the regime. All of this placed the Nazis firmly in control.

The Night of the Long Knives

The SA's position before June 1934

In January 1933, the SA was the Nazis' main instrument of terror and violence. One of the immediate results of the Nazis coming to power was the rapid expansion of the SA. From a membership of around 500,000 in January 1933, the organisation grew to around 3 million-strong a year later. Another result of the Nazis being in power was that the activities of the SA gained legal authority. In late February 1933, the SA and the Stahlhelm were merged and became recognised as 'auxiliary police'. Orders were issued to the regular police forces forbidding them from interfering with SA activities.

Hitler benefited from the violence of his supporters, but he was not always in control of events. Much of the violence of the SA against the Nazis' political opponents, and against the Jews, was unplanned, uncoordinated and piecemeal. In the period from February to June 1933, when the Nazis were eliminating opposition and establishing undisputed control, Hitler was prepared to go with the flow of SA violence. He was careful to ensure, however, that the SA did not attack the State itself. Assaults on the police and the army were avoided, as Hitler was careful not to alienate those conservative forces that had shoe-horned him into power. Violence was a vital tool in the hands of the Nazi leadership but, in its uncontrolled form, its usefulness was limited and at some point Hitler was bound to want to call a halt.

CROSS-REFERENCE

The Stahlhelm, the largest paramilitary organisation in Weimar Germany, is described in Chapter 12, page 106.

ACTIVITY

Read Source 2 and use your contextual knowledge from Chapter 12 to answer the following questions:

1. Who is Hitler threatening when he warns 'we will drown such an attempt in blood'?
2. Who is Hitler trying to reassure when he states that 'Revolution is not a permanent condition'?

SOURCE 2

In July 1933 Hitler made a speech to leading Nazis containing a warning to the SA:

Revolution is not a permanent condition. The stream of revolution has been undammed, but it must be channelled into the secure bed of evolution. The slogan of the Second Revolution was justified as long as positions were still present in Germany that could serve as points of crystallisation for a counter-revolution. That is not the case any longer. We do not leave any doubt about the fact that if necessary we will drown such an attempt in blood.

Hitler was warning that, in the future, the SA could become the target for Nazi violence and terror. He did not, however, act on this warning for a further

11 months. In July 1933, after passing the Law against Formation of New Parties, Hitler was able to declare that the Nazi revolution was over. He had acquired dictatorial powers, all other parties had been banned or had voluntarily dissolved themselves and the process of *Gleichschaltung* had been completed. For **Ernst Röhm**, the leader of the SA, however, the Nazi revolution was far from complete and the SA were determined to continue with their violence until they had achieved the Second Revolution. Chief among Röhm's aims was for the SA to become the nucleus of a new national militia that would eventually absorb and replace the existing army. With a combined SA and Stahlhelm membership of 4.5 million in January 1934, Röhm's forces already vastly outnumbered the army. However, since the summer of 1933 the role and importance of the SA had declined. In August 1933, they had lost their 'auxiliary police' status and were subject to stricter regulations over their powers of arrest. In the election campaign of November 1933, there was only one party, hence there was no longer a need for SA violence and intimidation. Lacking an 'official' outlet for their violence, and feeling resentment at the way that former conservative opponents of the Nazis were allowed to join the Nazi Party and take important jobs in local and central government, SA members became disillusioned and restless. Drunken brawls, always a feature of the SA, became increasingly common and the police became targets of the SA when they tried to intervene.

CROSS-REFERENCE

Gleichschaltung is defined in Chapter 12, page 97.

SOURCE 3

In early 1934, Ernst Röhm confided his thoughts about Hitler in a letter to a friend:

Adolf is a swine. He will give us all away. He only associates with the reactionaries now. Getting matey with the generals. They're his **cronies** now. Adolf knows exactly what I want. I've told him often enough. Not a second edition of the old imperial army. Are we revolutionaries or aren't we? If we are, then something new must arise out of our fighting spirit. If we're not, then we'll go to the dogs. We've got to produce something new, don't you see that? Don't you understand that what's coming must be new, fresh and unused? The basis must be revolutionary. You only get the opportunity once to make something new and big that'll help to lift the world off its hinges. But Hitler puts me off with fair words.

KEY TERM

Cronies: close friends

KEY PROFILE

Ernst Röhm (1887–1934) had been a captain in the First World War. Afterwards, he joined the Freikorps and was employed by the army to gather information on opposition groups. He met Hitler in 1919 and recruited him to infiltrate the German Workers' Party. He later joined the renamed National Socialist German Workers' Party and helped to set up the SA. He took part in the Beer Hall Putsch and was briefly jailed after its failure. He was recalled to Germany by Hitler in 1930 to take control of the SA. He turned the SA into a formidable fighting force but his radical views and his lifestyle – he drank heavily and was homosexual – proved a source of embarrassment to Hitler after the Nazis took power in 1933.

Fig. 2   *Ernst Röhm shakes hands with Adolf Hitler, c. 1933*

The Night of the Long Knives, June 1934

The army remained the only institution with the power to remove Hitler from office. It was also loyal to Hindenburg, not to Hitler. Despite the fact that Werner von Blomberg, the Defence Minister, had brought it closer to Nazi ideology, the army was not a Nazified institution and still retained some

ACTIVITY

What were the main differences in the aims of Hitler and Röhm?

CROSS-REFERENCE

For more information on Freikorps, see Chapter 4, page 28.

CROSS-REFERENCES

For more information on Gregor Strasser, see Chapter 11, page 87.

Gustav von Kahr's involvement in Hitler's early political career is explained in Chapter 4, page 32.

ACTIVITY

How might the Night of the Long Knives have affected the future development of the Nazi regime?

CROSS-REFERENCE

General Schleicher had been significant in Hindenberg's government and in the militarisation of German politics in the early 1930s. More information on this is in Chapter 9, page 71.

independence. The ambitions of the SA and its leader Röhm were regarded as a serious threat by the army leaders, the more so when in the summer of 1934 SA units began stopping army convoys and confiscating weapons and supplies. Moreover, the pressure on Hitler increased on 17th June, when Papen made a major speech at Marburg University in which he criticised Nazi excesses. Papen called for an end to terror and for Hitler to clamp down on the SA's calls for a Second Revolution. Papen's speech had Hindenburg's approval and, despite Goebbels' efforts to censor it, it was reported in the press.

When Blomberg, again with Hindenburg's support, threatened to declare martial law and give the army power to deal with the SA, matters came to a head. Hitler had dithered since the spring of 1934, delaying taking decisive action against the SA, but in June he knew he could wait no longer. A ruthless purge of the SA, known as the 'Night of the Long Knives', was launched on 30 June 1934 when the SS, acting on Hitler 's orders, eliminated the leadership of the SA and many other political opponents of the Nazis.

A CLOSER LOOK

Victims of the Night of the Long Knives

At least 84 were executed and another 1000 or more were arrested. The victims included Röhm and other leaders of the SA, but Hitler took the opportunity to remove other opponents and settle some old scores. Among the other victims were General Schleicher, Gregor Strasser and Gustav von Kahr. Von Kahr had played a key role in crushing the Beer Hall Putsch in 1923. Members of Papen's staff were executed and, although Papen himself was spared death, he was placed under house arrest and whatever power he still had was destroyed. Many leading conservative politicians were also targeted.

When Hitler addressed the Reichstag on 13 July, he accepted full responsibility for the executions. He was acting, he said, as the 'supreme judge' of the German people and had been compelled to act in order to save the country from an SA coup. This secured the army's support. Hitler also gained public support for his apparently decisive actions. The SA declined sharply after the purge. By October 1935, its membership had declined to 1.6 million and, without Röhm as its leader, its political power was destroyed. Violence and terror remained vital weapons in the Nazi Party's efforts to retain political control but, after the Night of the Long Knives, the SS controlled the terror machine. After the events of June 1934, violence and terror were used more systematically and in a more controlled manner.

SOURCE 4

An eye-witness statement about the killing of General Kurt von Schleicher in June 1934, was given by his cook:

Today, around noon, I was looking through the window toward the street, where I spotted two gentlemen. I asked what they wanted, to which they replied that they 'had to see' General Schleicher. I replied that 'I would go and see.' I then made my way into the general's study, while being followed by the strangers. Once we had arrived, the strangers stood behind me and asked the general if he were General Schleicher. The general said yes and turned his body in order to see the men who had asked the question. At that very moment shots rang out. I do not know what happened then, because I was terrified; I screamed and ran out of the room. When I later went back to the room I found Frau Schleicher and the general, both shot and lying on the floor.

PRACTICE QUESTION

Evaluating primary sources

With reference to Sources 2, 3 and 4 and your understanding of the historical context, assess the value of these sources to an historian studying the Night of the Long Knives.

STUDY TIP

All three sources contain useful information. Sources 2 and 3 give insights into the views of Hitler and Röhm – the main protagonists in the events of June 1934 – whilst Source 4 is an eye-witness account of the killing of Schleicher. The sources need to be placed in context and your analysis should identify both their usefulness and their limitations by examining provenance, tone and emphasis, and information.

The impact of President Hindenburg's death, August 1934

Fig. 3   *The death of Field Marshal von Hindenburg, followed by the speedy appointment of Adolf Hitler as President of Germany, as reported on the front page of the Daily Mirror, 1934*

In the summer of 1934, 86-year-old President Hindenburg was bedridden, dying of lung cancer. The question of his succession became a matter of urgency for Hitler, especially as Hindenburg himself had drawn up a political will in which he expressed his preference for a restoration of the monarchy. Hitler aimed to merge the offices of Chancellor and President after Hindenburg's death, thus making himself the undisputed head of government and the State. As long as Hindenburg lived, Hitler's power was not absolute. The army owed allegiance to the President, not to Chancellor Hitler, and that President, with the support of the army, could theoretically remove Hitler from power.

Before his death, Hindenburg had become so concerned by the excesses of the SA that he considered handing power to the army and dismissing Hitler. His views were shared by the army commanders and by Papen, and Hitler was left in no doubt that, unless he brought the SA under control, he could not count on the army's support once Hindenburg had died. This was the trigger that led Hitler to launch the purge of the SA. With the threat of the SA removed, Blomberg and the army leaders had no further objection to Hitler succeeding Hindenburg as President.

Hindenburg died on 2 August 1934. The announcement that the office of President would be merged with that of Chancellor was made within an hour of his death. On the same day the officers and soldiers of the army took an oath of allegiance to Hitler. On 19 August, a **plebiscite** was held to get the German people's seal of approval on Hitler's appointment as Führer (Leader) and Reich Chancellor, the title by which he was henceforth to be known. The result was that 89.9 per cent of the voters approved of the change. More surprising perhaps was the fact that the other 10.1 per cent, or four-and-a-half million voters, had the courage to vote 'No'.

This was the final act in the Nazi consolidation of power. Hitler had asserted his authority over his own party and had become Führer.

Summary

By the summer of 1934, Hitler's dictatorship had been firmly established. Non-Nazi political parties had either been banned or had voluntarily disbanded. Opponents of the Nazis had been divided, demoralised and, in many cases, thrown into prison. The Civil Service, the justice system and local government had all been coordinated into the Nazi state. After Hindenburg's death in August 1934, Hitler became President as well as Chancellor and had taken the title of Führer. The army swore allegiance to Hitler. The consolidation of power had been achieved in little more than 18 months after Hitler became Chancellor at the end of January 1933. In this process, Hitler used a combination of terror, legal power and compromises with established conservative forces.

 PRACTICE QUESTION

'The Nazi consolidation of power between January 1933 and August 1934 was achieved through the use of terror'. Assess the validity of this view.

14 The 'Terror State'

The Nazis and the law

Hitler was determined that the Nazi regime would not be bound by the law and legal systems. The Nazi concept of authority was based on the leadership principle. As a 'man of destiny', who had been chosen to lead **Third Reich** Germany and express the will of the people, Hitler's word was law. The Nazis did not introduce a new constitution or legal system after 1933. Instead they introduced some new laws to deal with political offences and forced the existing justice system to adapt and bend to their will. At the same time, they introduced new courts and new police organisations to ensure that political opponents were dealt with. The result was that in Nazi Germany, the legal principles on which German law had been based in the Weimar period no longer applied. No longer were all citizens treated as equal before the law. The judges were not permitted to operate independently of the government. Individuals could be arrested and imprisoned without trial, without the police having to produce any evidence against them. The law was applied in an arbitrary and inconsistent fashion.

The police system in the Third Reich

In the Weimar Republic, individual state authorities controlled the police forces. The Nazis did not abolish these separate police forces but created a system of party-controlled, political police forces answerable to Hitler, which gradually gained control over the entire police system. This proliferation of police forces created confusion and competition, both between the various police forces and between the powerful men who controlled them. The following forces existed:

- the SS, controlled by **Himmler**
- the SD, an intelligence gathering offshoot of the SS
- the SA, controlled by Röhm, in 1933. The SA also acquired police powers to arrest and detain political prisoners

LEARNING OBJECTIVES

In this chapter you will learn about:

- the Nazi view of the law
- the police system in Nazi Germany, including the role of the SS and Gestapo
- the courts and the justice system
- the extent of opposition and non-conformity
- the use of propaganda
- the extent of totalitarianism in Nazi Germany.

KEY TERM

Third Reich: ('Third Empire' in English); by using this term to describe their regime from 1933 to 1945, the Nazis were asserting that it was the successor to the First Reich (Holy Roman Empire, which existed from the medieval period until 1807) and the Second Reich (1871–1918)

Gestapo: Geheime Staatspolizei
Kripo: Kriminalpolizei
Orpo: Ordnungspolizei ('order' police), including Schutzpolizei and the gendarmerie
SD: Sicherheitsdienst (Security Service)
Sipo: Sicherheitspolizei (Security Police)
SS: Schutzstaffel (defence echelon)

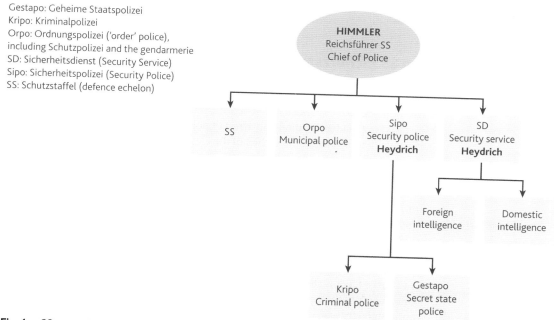

Fig. 1   *SS control over the police after 1936*

- the Gestapo, the secret State police force in Prussia, of which Goering was the Minister-President. During 1933, the remit of the Gestapo was extended to cover the whole country.

Between 1933 and 1936, there was competition and rivalry between Himmler, Röhm and Goering for control over the police. Himmler's power was strengthened by the Night of the Long Knives in 1934 in which Röhm was eliminated and the SA's powers were reduced. Himmler was also able to exploit the rivalry between Goering and the Minister of the Interior, Wilhelm Frick. The situation was partially resolved in 1936 when the SS, SD and Gestapo were placed under Himmler's command. Himmler's victory was sealed in 1939 with the creation of the Reich Security Department Headquarters (RHSA), which placed all party and State police organisations under one organisation supervised by the SS.

KEY PROFILE

Fig. 2   Heinrich Himmler

Heinrich Himmler (1900–45) was the Reichsfuhrer (leader) of the SS. He joined the Nazi Party in 1923 and took over the SS leadership in 1929. After Hitler came to power, Himmler extended his power within the Nazi state, gradually taking control over police forces and running concentration camps (see Fig. 3 for the SS membership growth during the 1930s). Under his command the SS also established military units (the Waffen SS) and its own industrial conglomerate. During the war, the SS was responsible for carrying out the rounding up and killing of Jews in occupied countries. Near the end of the war, Himmler was appointed as a military commander to organise the fight against the Red Army's advance, but his lack of military experience caused Hitler to relieve him of his command. Although Himmler had been one of Hitler's most trusted subordinates, the rift between the two led Himmler to betray Hitler by attempting to negotiate a secret peace deal with the Allies. When Hitler found out, Himmler went on the run and was captured by British forces. He committed suicide whilst in custody.

ACTIVITY

Read the information on the following pages, then answer the following questions:
1. Explain the different roles of the SS, SD and Gestapo in the police system of the Third Reich.
2. To what extent were their roles clearly separated?

CROSS-REFERENCE

More information on the Night of the Long Knives can be found in Chapter 13, page 102.

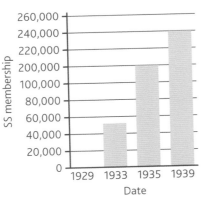

Fig. 3   Membership of the SS, 1933–39

The SS (*Schutzstaffel*)

As Hitler's bodyguard, the SS had certain police functions from the start. Once the Nazis came to power, and especially after the Night of the Long Knives, the police role of the SS was expanded and it became the main Nazi Party organisation involved in the identification and arrest of political prisoners. By 1936, after Himmler had been appointed chief of the German police, the SS controlled the entire Third Reich police system and the concentration camps. Under SS control, the police system in Germany was an instrument of the Führer and the Nazi Party.

Himmler intended the SS to be strictly disciplined, racially pure and unquestioningly obedient. The key values for an SS member were loyalty and honour, defined strictly in terms of adherence to Nazi ideology.

After 1936, there was a noticeable tightening of control and an increase in repression, as can be seen in the increase in concentration camp inmates. Whereas the SA had engaged in violence and terror through undisciplined street brawls, the SS operated in a far more systematic way. Violence and murder were instruments of State power to be employed ruthlessly and without reference to moral standards. SS concentration camp guards were deliberately brutalised to remove any feelings of humanity they might feel towards their prisoners.

Concentration camps

Concentration camps were essentially prisons in which the inmates were forced to work. They should not be confused with the extermination camps that were established in occupied countries after 1942. The first concentration camp was set up at Dachau, near Munich, in 1933, although there were also around 70 temporary camps. The vast majority of prisoners in the early months of the regime were communists, socialists and trade unionists. Many of the temporary camps were closed down and, by May 1934, there were only a quarter as many prisoners as there had been a year before. Torture and brutality had rendered the majority of prisoners unwilling to continue resistance against the Nazis and many were released.

Fig. 4 *Prisoners of the Dachau concentration camp were forced to manufacture arms in a workshop*

All concentration camps came under SS control after 1934 with the result that the treatment of prisoners became systematised. After 1936, having crushed the communists and socialists, the regime reoriented the concentration camp system to deal with 'undesirables'. Habitual criminals, **asocials** and non-Aryans made up the majority of concentration camp inmates as the regime tried to purify the race. This change also coincided with an increase in violence and brutality in the camps. Camp guards had been given immunity from prosecution by Himmler.

The SD

The SD (*Sicherheitsdienst*) was established in 1931 as the internal security service of the Nazi Party. An offshoot of the SS, it was set up to investigate claims that the party had been infiltrated by its political enemies. The SD was led by **Reinhard Heydrich**. After 1933, the SD's role was intelligence gathering. One of its important roles was to monitor public opinion, identify those who voted 'no' in plebiscites, and to report on these to Hitler. By 1939, the SD had 50,000 officers, a sign of how important its role was considered to be, and also of how successful Heydrich had been in establishing his own power base.

The SD, as a Nazi Party organisation, worked independently of the Gestapo, which was a State organisation. This could, and did, lead to overlap and confusion between the two organisations. The SD was staffed not by professional police officers but by amateurs who were committed Nazis.

KEY TERM

Asocials: those, according to the Nazis, who did not conform to the norms of the *Volksgemeinschaft*, including beggars, tramps, alcoholics, prostitutes and pacifists, but also the mentally and physically disabled

CROSS-REFERENCE

Reinhard Heydrich was the most important senior commander in the SS after Himmler. More information on him is in Chapter 19.

Fig. 5 *Member of the Gestapo searching somone on the streets in front of a cafe in Unter den Linden*

The use of torture

Many people were arrested by the Gestapo to extract information from them. One communist, Richard Krebs, later wrote that for several weeks he was beaten and whipped while being questioned. In his cell he was chained to a cot and not allowed to wash. The Gestapo were unable to break him until they arrested his wife and threatened to torture her. He then agreed to provide information, but in fact he became a double-agent, working for the communists while providing information of little value to the Gestapo.

ACTIVITY

a. How far did the Gestapo succeed in its task of keeping German society under surveillance?

b. What can we learn from this about the relationship between the regime and its citizens?

The Gestapo

The Gestapo, or *Geheime Staatspolizei* (secret state police), was originally set up in Prussia alone, but under the Nazi regime its operations were extended to cover the whole country. The Gestapo developed a reputation for being all-knowing. Ordinary Germans believed that the Gestapo had agents in every workplace, pub and neighbourhood. The reality was very different. It was actually a relatively small organisation, with only 20,000 officers in 1939 to cover the whole country. Most of its agents were office-based, not field agents, and they were generally not members of the Nazi Party. Instead, they were professional police officers who saw their role as being to serve the State.

The Gestapo depended on information supplied by informers. Nazi Party activists, who were asked to spy on neighbours and workmates, were one important source of information. Every block of flats and every residential street had its 'block leader', who would report suspicious activity. Even more information came from voluntary denunciations of workmates and neighbours by ordinary Germans. Most of these informers were motivated not by political commitment but by personal grudges. So overwhelming was the volume of information received that it was impossible to investigate all alleged crimes and the Gestapo increasingly resorted to arbitrary arrest and preventive custody.

Despite its small size, therefore, the Gestapo was very successful in instilling an atmosphere of fear and suspicion in the German population. Political debate and criticism was stifled. People believed that there were Gestapo agents and informers everywhere and adjusted their behaviour accordingly.

The courts and the justice system

Judges and lawyers were generally very conservative but few belonged to the Nazi Party in January 1933. The long tradition of freedom from political interference for lawyers and judges posed a problem for the Nazis, as the violence and intimidation carried out by the SA and SS was clearly illegal and many prosecutions against Stormtroopers were begun by lawyers who were determined to uphold the law. Hitler was also angered by the fact that the Supreme Court acquitted all but one of the defendants in the Reichstag fire trial. A few judges and state prosecutors were dismissed by the regime. Far more effective in 'coordinating' the justice system were:

- the merging of the various professional associations of judges and lawyers with the League of National Socialist Lawyers, creating the Front of German Law in April 1933. It was made clear to judges and lawyers that their career prospects depended on their doing the regime's bidding
- introducing new courts. Special Courts were set up in 1933 and the People's Court in April 1934 to run alongside the existing court system. These courts, set up to deal with political crimes, had three Nazi 'judges' alongside two professional judges. There were no juries and defendants had no rights of appeal against their sentences.

With these measures, backed by threats from the SA and SS, lawyers and judges fell into line. Although the old court system continued to exist, and many non-Nazi judges continued in their jobs, the justice system had no power to interfere with the Nazis' use of terror.

Between 1934 and 1939, around 3400 people were tried by the People's Court, most of whom were former communists and socialists. Many of those brought before the courts were given the death penalty, which was used increasingly in the Third Reich.

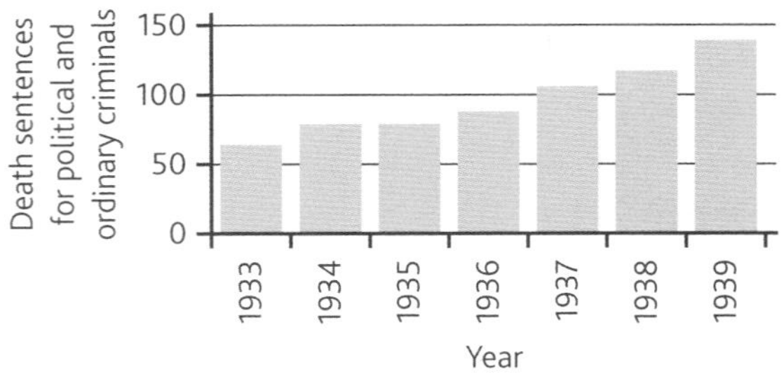

Fig. 6 *The use of the death penalty in Nazi Germany*

The extent and effectiveness of opposition and non-conformity

SOURCE 1

An article in an SS newspaper from 1939 stated how those who did not conform were to be treated:

In politics there are only two possibilities: for Germany or not. Anyone who is not basically for Germany does not belong to us and will be eliminated. If he does not emigrate on his own initiative, then he will have to be locked up. If that does not help then we will have to make him a head shorter.

When assessing the nature and extent of State terror in Nazi Germany, it is important to acknowledge that there was a strong base of support for the regime. Through the use of propaganda, and through *Gleichschaltung*, the regime was able to gain acceptance from the majority of people. The Nazi SS police system was presented as an instrument to protect the majority against the corrupting influence of minorities. The terms 'Peoples' Court' and 'popular justice' portrayed repression and persecution as something that reflected the will of the people. To a large extent this propaganda appears to have been effective. The Gestapo, with its limited resources, could not have instilled fear and suspicion to the extent that it achieved without the cooperation of many ordinary citizens.

On the whole, there was very little active opposition and there was evidence of Hitler's increasing popularity. Life in Nazi Germany became depoliticised; there was no open and free debate about the regime or its policies. Historians generally agree that there was a widespread acceptance of the regime and most Germans subscribed to the view that the Third Reich was preferable to the disorder of the final Weimar Republic years. Nevertheless, various individuals and groups did, from time to time, try to resist Nazi attempts to 'coordinate' them into the *Volksgemeinschaft*.

ACTIVITY

Group work

Divide into five groups. Each group should undertake detailed research, using this book and other sources, into one of the following: political resistance; resistance by workers; resistance by the Churches; resistance by young people; resistance by the elite.

In your group, focus on the aims and motives of those who resisted, the extent of resistance and the effectiveness of their actions. When the research is completed, report your findings to the class.

CROSS-REFERENCE

Gleichschaltung, the process through which the Nazis attempted to control or 'coordinate' all aspects of German society, is discussed in Chapter 12, page 97.

Return to Chapter 10, page 76, for an explanation of *Volksgemeinschaft*. Go ahead to Chapter 17, pages 141, for more information on its role in Nazi ideology.

A LEVEL PRACTICE QUESTION

'By 1939, German society was a society engaged in self-surveillance.' To what extent do you agree with this view?

STUDY TIP

This view can be challenged but can also be agreed with to some extent. Your answer to this type of question should therefore be a balanced assessment of the extent to which German people acted as the eyes and ears of the Gestapo, contrasting that with the extent to which the Gestapo and other police organisations were able to spy and keep records on the mass of German citizens. There needs to be a clear and consistent argument throughout the answer.

Political resistance

The parties of the left – the SPD and the KPD – were expected to mount the stiffest resistance to Hitler. Indeed, Hitler himself feared that the unions, which were linked to SPD, would stage a general strike to thwart the Nazi takeover in 1933, just as they had done in 1920 to defeat the Kapp Putsch. In the event, the left did not pose a serious threat to the Nazi regime, partly because it was bitterly divided, with the KPD attacking the SPD as 'social-fascists'.

The SPD

In January 1933, the SPD was unprepared for the Nazi takeover. As a constitutional party committed to working within the State's legal framework, the SPD was not equipped to organise resistance to a regime that did not respect the law. SPD activists continued to campaign openly for the election campaign in March 1933 and suffered SA violence as a result. SPD deputies bravely defied SA and SS intimidation to vote against the Enabling Act in the Reichstag but, once the regime had acquired legal powers to establish a

CROSS-REFERENCE

Refresh your memory on Nazi violence against political opponents and the Enabling Act in Chapter 12, pages 92–96.

There is a key profile for Ernst Thälmann in Chapter 7, page 57.

KEY TERM

Sopade: reports produced by agents of the banned Social Democratic Party (SPD) to inform the exiled Party leadership about the situation in Germany

ACTIVITY

Evaluating primary sources

Using Source 2 and your contextual knowledge, assess how valuable this source would be for an historian researching the extent of German resistance to the Nazi regime.

dictatorship, it began to crush the SPD. By the end of 1933, thousands of SPD activists had been murdered or placed into 'preventive custody' and the SPD leadership had fled into exile.

Gradually, the SPD adapted to the changed conditions in Germany. Organised in exile by Ernst Schumacher from a base in Prague, the party established small, secret cells of supporters in factories. There were also some city-based groups such as the Berlin Red Patrol. Propaganda pamphlets were smuggled across the border from Czechoslovakia. The constant fear of exposure and arrest by the Gestapo limited the scope of these illegal activities. The priority for those involved was to survive and be prepared for a future collapse of the regime rather than to mount a serious challenge.

The KPD

With its background in revolutionary politics, the KPD was much better prepared than the SPD for engaging in underground activity. The KPD was, however, devastated by the wave of repression unleashed upon communists in Germany after Hitler came to power. It was the first party to be banned and its leader, Ernst Thälmann, was arrested at an early stage. About 10 per cent of the KPD's membership was killed by the Nazis during 1933. Nevertheless, the KPD established an underground network in some German industrial centres. Revolutionary unions were set up in Berlin and Hamburg to recruit members and publish newspapers. All these networks were, however, broken up by the Gestapo.

Secret communist activity was not completely eradicated by the Gestapo in 1934–35. Factory cells were established and contact between members was confined to word of mouth to reduce discovery. As with the SPD, however, the priority of communist cells was very much on survival since the party had ceased to exist and no serious challenge to the regime was possible.

Resistance by workers

SOURCE 2

This is an extract from a **Sopade** report written in 1935:

It became clear that the effects of the economic crisis on the inward resistance of the workers were more appalling than had previously been thought. We see it time and time again: the most courageous illegal fighter, the most relentless antagonist of the regime, is usually the unemployed man who has no more to lose. Whereas if a worker gets a job after years out of work then – however bad his pay and conditions – he at once becomes apprehensive. Now he does have something to lose, however little, and the fear of the renewed misery of unemployment is worse than the misery itself. The National Socialists have not conquered the factories. But the National Socialists have destroyed the workers' self-confidence; they have crushed the forces of solidarity and crippled their will to resist.

Before 1933, the German working class was the largest and most unionised workforce in Europe. The largest unions in Germany were linked to the SPD and had been consistently opposed to the Nazi Party. After January 1933, however, union resistance crumbled surprisingly quickly. The ideology of class conflict had sustained the trade union movement before 1933. After the Nazis came to power, the trade unions were absorbed into the DAF (German Labour Front) and Nazi propaganda emphasised the importance of national as opposed to class solidarity.

Taking strike action was very risky but strikes did occur. In September 1935, 37 strikes were reported in Rhineland-Westphalia, Silesia and Württemberg. In the whole of 1937, a total of 250 strikes were recorded. Most of these strikes were reactions to poor working conditions or low wages. Significantly, there was increased strike activity in 1935–36 at a time when then was widespread discontent over food prices. From the point of view of the regime, however, any expression of dissent was regarded as a challenge. Of the 25,000 workers who participated in strikes in 1935, 4000 spent short periods in prison. After a 17-minute strike at the Opel car factory in 1936, seven ringleaders were arrested by the Gestapo and imprisoned.

There were also less overt, but nonetheless effective, means by which workers could express their dissatisfaction. Absenteeism was often a reaction against the pressure to work longer hours. The regime was so concerned about the level of absenteeism in 1938 that new labour regulations were introduced, laying down severe penalties for 'slackers'. In 1938, for example, the Gestapo arrested 114 workers at a munitions plant in Gleiwitz for absenteeism and slow working. Another tactic by some workers was to deliberately damage their machinery. Again the regime was concerned enough to make 'sabotage' a criminal offence and there were an increasing number of prosecutions in 1938–39.

Resistance by the Churches

The Christian Churches were the only organisations in Nazi Germany that retained an alternative ideology, independent of the regime. The Churches also retained some organisational autonomy. This placed the Churches in a powerful position. The influence of the pastor or the priest in many communities was at least as important as that of the Nazi Party. On the other hand, the Churches were well aware that, in a sustained conflict with the regime, they would be the losers. The Churches' leaderships needed to protect their organisations if they were to survive at all, and this led them into making compromises. There were inevitably, however, issues on which the Churches were not prepared to compromise; at times, Protestants and Catholics felt it necessary to draw a line under Nazi efforts to force them into conformity and this led them into resistance. The response of the Christian Churches to the Nazi regime, therefore, was both complex and fluid, and varied not only over time but even from one priest or pastor to another.

The Protestant Church

The efforts of the Nazi regime to coordinate the Protestant Church into the *Volksgemeinschaft* led to division within the Protestant congregation. The establishment of the Pastors' Emergency League in 1933 and its development into the Confessional Church in 1934 were, in themselves, acts of resistance. This was led by pastors who were not members of the Nazi Party and who came largely from academic backgrounds. Their refusal to accept being part of a 'coordinated' Reich Church was due to three main factors:
- They were trying to protect the independence of the Protestant Church from the Nazi regime.
- They were resisting the attempt to impose the **Aryan paragraph** on the Church. This involved purging from the Church any pastor who had converted from Judaism.
- They were trying to defend orthodox **Lutheran theology**, which was based purely on the Bible.

During 1934, there was a growing struggle between the Confessional Church and the Nazi regime. Pastors spoke out against the 'Nazified Christ' from their

CROSS-REFERENCE

Read page 135 of Chapter 16 to consider the degree of success of Nazi policies towards workers.

CROSS-REFERENCE

To find out more about the Nazi regime's efforts to coordinate the Protestant Church, see page 136 of Chapter 16.

KEY TERM

Aryan paragraph: Under the 1933 Law on the Reconstruction of the Professional Civil Service, the third paragraph stated that those who were not of Aryan birth had to be dismissed from their jobs; this applied to pastors in the protestant Evangelical Church who had converted to Christianity from Judaism.

CROSS-REFERENCE

Martin Luther and the origins of German Protestantism are discussed in Chapter 16, page 136.

pulpits. Many Churches refused to display swastika flags. When two Confessional Church bishops were arrested, there were mass demonstrations in their support. The Nazi regime responded with increased repression. Dissenting pastors had their salaries stopped, they were banned from teaching in schools and many were arrested. By the end of 1937, over 700 pastors had been imprisoned.

SOURCE 3

A statement made in 1946 by **Martin Niemöller**:

In Germany, they came first for the communists, and I didn't speak up because I wasn't a communist;
　And then they came for the trade unionists, and I didn't speak up because I wasn't a trade unionist;
　And then they came for the Jews, and I didn't speak up because I wasn't a Jew;
　And then … they came for me … And by that time there was no one left to speak up.

ACTIVITY

Evaluating primary sources

Read Source 3. What can we learn from this source about the weaknesses of the opposition to the Nazi regime?

KEY PROFILE

Fig. 7　*Martin Niemöller*

Martin Niemöller (1892–1984) was a Protestant pastor who had been a U-boat commander during the First World War and held strong nationalist views. Although he initially welcomed Hitler's appointment as Chancellor in January 1933, he was not a Nazi Party member and he began to oppose Nazi efforts to politicise the Evangelical Church. He was anti-Semitic himself, but he opposed the Church adoption of the Aryan paragraph because he believed that Jews should be welcomed into the Christian faith. He was a co-founder of the Confessional Church. He was arrested, put on trial and acquitted on all charges, but was immediately rearrested and sent to a concentration camp in 1937. In prison, he was treated as Hitler's personal prisoner and allowed certain privileges. Within the Confessional Church, he was seen as a martyr. His experience in prison led him to repudiate his anti-Semitic views.

The Nazi regime failed to silence the Confessional Church, but for its part, the Confessional Church did not form full opposition to the regime. The majority of its members professed their loyalty to Hitler and the Third Reich. Much of their energies were expended in fighting the bitter internal struggle against the official Reich Church, with the result that the Protestant Churches became rather inward-looking. Although individual pastors risked their lives and liberty in speaking out against the barbarities of the regime, the Churches as a whole remained silent. There was no sustained defence of human rights and no official condemnation of atrocities, issues on which the Churches might have been expected to give a moral lead.

The Roman Catholic Church

The Catholic Church was, in some ways, in a stronger position to retain its independence than the Protestant Church. This was because the Catholic Church was more united, more centralised and had more of a tradition of independence from the State. Nevertheless, the Catholic leadership in both Rome and Germany tried to come to terms with the Nazi regime. It was when the privileges granted to the Catholic Church in the **concordat of 1933** came under attack that the Church found itself increasingly at odds with the regime.

In 1937, the pope issued the papal encyclical 'With Burning Grief' against the background of mounting pressure on the Catholic Church in Germany. It

CROSS-REFERENCE

Turn to page 137 of Chapter 16 for details of the 1933 Concordat and Nazi-Catholic relations.

condemned Nazi hatred upon the Church. The document was smuggled into Germany, secretly printed and distributed by messengers on bicycle or on foot and read out from almost every church pulpit in March 1937. This was the only time that the Catholic Church placed itself in open conflict with the regime. The regime's response was to increase repression. Charges against priests for 'abuse of the pulpit' became regular occurrences. Again there was some resistance. The arrest of one priest led to noisy public demonstrations at his trial. Intimidation and harassment of priests, however, had the desired effect. A local government official reported in 1937 that the clergy were beginning to show 'cautious restraint'.

Many individual Catholic priests and members showed great courage in opposing aspects of the Nazi regime's religious policies. However, the Church did not move beyond a narrow defence of its independence to a wider opposition to Nazism and Catholic resistance was therefore partial, spasmodic and ineffective.

Resistance by young people

In the early years of the Nazi regime, the Hitler Youth (HJ) was able to channel youthful energy and rebelliousness into officially approved activities. By the mid-1930s, however, there were growing signs of disillusionment with the official movements among young people. This was partly because membership was made compulsory in 1936 and partly because of the growing regimentation in youth movements. Membership of the HJ and League of German Girls (BDM) made great demands on a teenager's free time, including compulsory gymnastic sessions on Wednesday evenings, all-day hikes on Sundays and endless military drilling. Indeed, this was the intention since the Nazi policy of *Gleichschaltung* was based on the premise that individuals should have no independent activity. Increasingly in the late 1930s, the response of many young people was to opt out, either by allowing their membership to lapse or simply not attending the weekly parades. Those who did attend sometimes hummed the tunes that had been banned. This nonconformist behaviour amounted to little more than normal teenage rebelliousness, but under the Nazis any assertion of independence was considered to be a threat.

Some young people formed cliques, or gangs, to show their independence. Some were little more than criminal gangs, but others were more overtly political, such as the Meuten gangs, which flourished in old communist strongholds in Leipzig in the late 1930s.

Resistance by the elites

Many members of the German conservative, traditional elites had serious misgivings about the Nazi Party in general and Hitler in particular. Some aristocratic generals in the army and senior civil servants regarded Hitler as a threat to the old Germany, even after the Night of the Long Knives. This was significant because, after the death of Hindenburg, a military coup was the only way to get rid of the regime. The conservative elites were, however, fatally compromised in their dealings with Hitler: the regime consolidated its power in 1933 by an alliance with the army, big business and conservative politicians. The conservative elites broadly shared Hitler's aims for Germany, even if they sometimes disapproved of his methods. Both the Civil Service and the army had a strong tradition of serving the State, whoever was in charge, and active opposition to the Nazi leadership, therefore, would involve a major intellectual and emotional shift on their part. The number of those within the army and Civil Service who opposed the Nazis was therefore very small.

Opposition to Hitler within the army and Civil Service came to a head in the autumn of 1938. For some time there had been growing unease within the elites about the drift of Nazi foreign policy. The opposition agreed with Hitler's long-term aims of rebuilding Germany's military strength and

A CLOSER LOOK

Catholic resistance

Clemens von Galen, the Archbishop of Münster, spoke out against the atheistic views of one of the leading Nazi ideologists, Alfred Rosenberg. In 1935, Galen issued a pamphlet and an Easter message refuting Rosenberg's views, particularly his concept of the 'racial soul'. In response, 19,000 Catholics – double the usual number – turned out for the annual July procession through Münster to show support for their bishop. Local Nazi Party officials complained to Berlin that Galen was meddling in politics, but Galen was considered to be too important to be arrested. Controversies such as this, which drew thousands of ordinary Catholics into demonstrating their support for the Church, helped to build Catholic resistance to the regime.

ACTIVITY

Thinking point

To what extent can we describe the rebelliousness of young people in Germany in the 1930s as a form of resistance to the regime? You may wish to read ahead the Nazi policies towards young people in Chapter 16 for further context before answering this question.

CROSS-REFERENCE

Information on Hitler's foreign policy can be found in Chapter 19, page 156.

General Werner von Fritsch (1880–1939) was promoted to Germany army Commander-in-Chief in 1934. As an anti-Semite and anti-democrat, he welcomed the appointment of Hitler in January 1933 and helped him to gain army support to succeed Hindenburg as President in 1934. However, he became increasingly critical of the regime as he realised that the SS was developing into a rival to the army and because he feared that Germany was not ready for the war that Hitler's foreign policy seemed likely to provoke. He was forced to resign in February 1938 after he was accused of being a homosexual. He was cleared of the charges and continued to serve in the army until he was killed in action in Poland.

ACTIVITY

On what issues did members of the old elites agree with the Nazis? On what issues did they disagree with the Nazis?

expanding to the east but felt that he was leading an unprepared Germany into war. In November 1937, Hitler outlined his secret thoughts to senior army commanders and leading Nazis such as Goering, making it clear that he envisaged a union with Austria and an invasion of Czechoslovakia within a year. At this meeting, the Defence Minister, General Blomberg, and the Commander-in-Chief of the army, **General Fritsch**, expressed their doubts to Hitler. Within three months, Hitler purged them both from the army leadership and replaced them with more compliant generals.

In late September 1938, Hitler ordered the army to prepare plans for an invasion of Czechoslovakia. Had the invasion been launched, it seemed likely that Britain and France would support Czechoslovakia and war would result. The imminent threat of war prompted Head of Army General Staff General Beck and a number of senior army figures to plot to remove Hitler from power in a military coup. Detailed plans were made for a march on Berlin if war was declared, but the whole enterprise depended on Britain and France standing by Czechoslovakia and making the threat of war credible. An envoy was sent to inform the British and French governments of the plans but, although the plotters were listened to sympathetically, those governments would not risk war. The British and French agreed to a peaceful German takeover of the Sudetenland area of Czechoslovakia, and Hitler had achieved another 'victory without bloodshed'. The conspiracy to overthrow him receded quietly into the background.

The extent and effectiveness of opposition

Dissent within Nazi Germany was expressed in a variety of ways and was motivated by different factors. Grumbling about economic hardship appears to have been widespread at times. This was essentially non-political, but in a society in which the regime demanded total subservience and conformity, even a moan about the shortage of essential foodstuffs could lead to arrest and criminal charges. Propaganda, indoctrination and repression had created an atmosphere in which the vast majority of Germans were prepared to support the regime. There was no basis for an organised and sustained resistance in Nazi Germany, certainly not one commanding mass support. Opposition to the Nazi regime was therefore fragmented and hampered by the fact that, even among those who were prepared on occasion to speak or act against the regime, there was a belief that the Nazi regime should be credited with having restored order, prosperity and national pride, and rid Germany of its internal enemies.

The use of propaganda

The aims of propaganda

Joseph Goebbels spoke at his first press conference about the aims of his new Ministry of Popular Enlightenment and Propaganda after it was established in March 1933:

I view the first task of the new ministry as being to establish coordination between the government and the whole people. It is not enough for people to be more or less reconciled to our regime, to be persuaded to take a neutral attitude towards us; rather we want to work on people until they have ceased to resist us. The new ministry has no other aim than to unite the nation behind the ideals of the national revolution. It is not enough to reconcile the people more or less to our regime, to move them to a position of neutrality towards us, we want rather to work on people until they have become addicted to us.

Through propaganda, Hitler and Goebbels were aiming for what Goebbels called the 'spiritual mobilisation' of the German people.

SOURCE 5

In March 1933 Hitler set out his view of the aims of propaganda when he stated:

The government will embark upon a systematic campaign to restore the nation's moral and material health. The whole education system, theatre, film, literature, the press and broadcasting – all these will be used as a means to an end.

ACTIVITY

Read Sources 4 and 5 and the contextual information from this chapter. Summarise the main aims of Nazi propaganda for Hitler and Goebbels.

The methods of propaganda

As the Nazi Party's propaganda chief before 1933, Goebbels had shown himself to be very adept at using all kinds of media to convey Party messages. He was able to control, direct and censor the media to ensure that Nazi ideas and values were spread effectively. Through his new ministry, he oversaw the work of organisations covering the work of the press, radio, film, literature, theatre, music and fine arts. He thus created a vast bureaucratic empire that gave him enormous power over German cultural life. Goebbels had the power to control who could and could not be employed in the cultural field. Those deemed to be 'racially impure' or 'politically unreliable' were purged. Those remaining in work quickly came to realise that any criticism would lead to the loss of their livelihoods.

Table 1 Methods of propaganda

Newspapers	• In January 1933 there were some 4700 privately owned newspapers in Germany. Nazi newspapers had limited circulation. • Socialist and communist newspapers were closed using the powers of the Decree for the Protection of the People and State. • The Nazis began to buy up more newspapers. By the end of the year they had acquired 27 daily newspapers with a combined circulation of 2.4 million a day. • News agencies that supplied the press with information were all merged into a State-controlled organisation. The result was that newspapers became bland and conformist, and the circulation figures of many declined.
Radio	• Hitler and Goebbels believed that the spoken word had much more impact than written communication and had used radio broadcasts effectively in the 1932 and 1933 election campaigns. • Radio broadcasts gave Hitler the opportunity to talk directly to German people and in 1933 alone he made over 50 such broadcasts. Loudspeakers were set up in town squares and factories so that everyone could hear important speeches. When Hitler's speeches were being broadcast, sirens would sound as a signal to stop work and gather around the radio or loudspeaker. • Goebbels promoted the mass production and sale of cheap radio sets. As a result of this policy, 70 per cent of German households possessed a radio set by 1939, the highest proportion in the world. • Goebbels initiated a purge of those working in radio. As a result 13 per cent of staff were dismissed on racial or political grounds. • In April 1934, all radio stations in Germany were brought under the control of the Reich Radio Company, controlled by the Propaganda Ministry.
Film	• Goebbels was a keen fan of cinema and recognised the potential of film as a propaganda medium. He understood that film could work on the subconscious, delivering subliminal messages and reinforcing prejudices. • Goebbels was personally responsible for approving every film made in Germany after 1933. Foreign films were not banned outright but were carefully checked for political and racial content. Most American films were banned, although the popularity of Disney cartoons meant that many of these were still approved. • Between 1933 and 1945, over 1000 feature films were produced in Germany and cinema attendances increased four-fold in the years 1933 to 1944. Of these films, only 14 per cent had an overtly political theme. The most common types of films were historical dramas, comedies and musicals. • All films, to some degree, contained political messages. Leadership was glorified; 'Blood and soil' (the close relationship of race and land) was a common theme, as was the demonising of Jews and communists. Films with a pacifist message were banned outright.

Parades and spectacles	• In 1930, a Nazi Party pamphlet, *Modern Political Propaganda*, stated that 'good discipline is the best propaganda' and this discipline was best displayed in marches and parades. • The theatricality of these marches was heightened by the wearing of uniforms and medals, the carrying of banners and the choreographed singing of party songs. The carrying of lighted torches in night-time processions was particularly effective in capturing people's attention. • Householders were expected to show support for national parades by hanging out swastika flags from their windows. Compliance was monitored by Nazi Party 'block leaders' and failure to conform was reported to the authorities. To be labelled 'politically unreliable' in this way could lead to a person being dismissed from his or her job or possibly more serious consequences. • Ritual parades and flag waving were visual 'proof' that German people were solidly behind the regime, even though this support was being manipulated by Goebbels and his Propaganda Ministry. 'All that goes on behind the backcloth' said Goebbels, 'belongs to stage management.' • The annual Party rallies at Nuremberg in September were stage-managed to achieve maximum theatrical effect. Vast numbers of Party members attended; the 1937 rally involved some 100,000 people.
Other forms of propaganda	• For Hitler, the arts were an expression of race. He believed that only the Aryan was capable of producing true art and that the 'degenerate art' of the Weimar period was evidence of racial decline. Nazi policy was to promote arts that glorified the healthy, strong and heroic, particularly heroes from Germany's past, whether real or mythical. • On 6 May 1933, a group of Nazi students and Stormtroopers made a huge bonfire in Berlin of about 20,000 books. This was followed on 10 May by similar actions in 19 university towns. The books that were burned were deemed 'un-German' because they were about family planning or written by Jews or Marxists. • A weekly poster, with a quotation expressing Nazi ideas, was displayed in offices and public buildings.

Group work

The Nazis also used the arts for propaganda purposes. In groups, research one of the following aspects of the arts in Nazi Germany: painting and sculpture; music; literature and theatre; cinema; architecture. Focus on how the Nazis used these media for propaganda purposes. Then present your findings to the class.

Evaluating primary sources

How valuable is Source 5 for an historian investigating the effectiveness of Nazi propaganda?

The effectiveness of propaganda

Liselotte Katscher, who was a young woman at the time the Nazis came to power, recalled in her 1945 memoir how she became converted to Nazism:

In the streets after January 1933 suddenly in every shop there were little swastika flags and pictures of Hitler. I heard that Hitler was at the Hotel Rosa. I was curious. I got there just at the end of Hitler's speech, so I didn't really hear him speak. There was a huge crowd singing the Deutschland anthem and the Horst Wessel song. Until then I had always laughed at the Hitler salute, but when they sang the Horst Wessel song, I suddenly realised I was raising my arm. Much later I thought that's what they call mass suggestion. In my youthful innocence I thought that if all these people were so enthralled and enthusiastic about it, then there must be something in it. So I tried to do something myself for this new movement.

The Nazi regime placed great emphasis on the effort to indoctrinate the German population. Undoubtedly Hitler and Goebbels were very skilled propagandists, but the effectiveness of their efforts is very difficult to gauge. The Nazis carried out occasional plebiscites to demonstrate the support of the people for the regime, but since these were in no way free elections they cannot be regarded as evidence of genuine support. It is possible to conclude, from the many Gestapo reports on the state of public opinion, that there was at the very least scepticism among parts of the population towards particular Nazi policies. Attitudes of Germans towards the regime depended on a range of factors – age, class, occupation, religion, to name but a few. Attitudes could also change over time. It is therefore impossible to give a definitive judgement on whether the majority of Germans supported the regime, whether they did so consistently, and whether the support they did show was due to propaganda or fear of repression. Any judgements on the success of propaganda and indoctrination, therefore, can only be tentative.

Nazi propaganda and indoctrination appears to have been most successful when it was aimed at the young, whose opinions were not yet strongly formed, or when their messages overlapped with the traditional values of particular groups. Aristocratic, old conservatives shared the Nazis' beliefs in the need for order and their anti-democratic sentiments, although many were reluctant to swallow the more radical Nazi elements. Germany's middle class shared the Nazis' hostility to communism and socialism and were susceptible to the propaganda message that the Nazis were the only credible alternative to a left-wing takeover in Germany. Anti-Semitism and nationalist resentment of the Treaty of Versailles ran through all classes and the Nazis were able to reinforce these attitudes through their propaganda. Thus Third Reich propaganda was most successful when it built upon existing beliefs and values. Where Nazi propaganda challenged deeply held beliefs, such as religion, it was less successful.

The Hitler Myth

Nazi propaganda presented Hitler as being unlike other politicians. He was presented as a 'man of the people'. In other words, he symbolised the unity of the Nazi Party and the people. He was presented as a man who:

- was hard-working, tough and uncompromising in fighting and defeating the nation's internal and external enemies
- was a political genius who had mastered the problems faced by Germany in 1933 and was responsible for Germany's 'national awakening'; order had been restored, the economy revived and Germany had thrown off the humiliating shackles of the Treaty of Versailles
- was dynamic and forceful, in contrast with the weak politicians of the Weimar years
- lived a simple life and sacrificed personal happiness to devote himself to his people. He was invariably shown as being alone and removed from the Nazi Party
- was the guardian of traditional morality and popular justice, and a statesman of true genius.

The reality was in many ways very different from these propaganda images:

- Hitler was surrounded by officials who competed with each other to gain his attention and implement his wishes. Hitler supplied the vision, his ministers and officials interpreted this and turned it into detailed policies. He was actually not very involved in decision-making.
- Far from working hard, Hitler stayed up late watching films and would usually not get up until mid-day. His days were spent eating, walking in the grounds of his mountain retreat and delivering long, rambling speeches to his subordinates. He disliked reading official documents and rarely got involved in detailed discussions on policy. His officials often had great difficulty in getting him to make decisions.

The extent of totalitarianism in Nazi Germany

Through the policy of *Gleichschaltung*, the Nazi Party set out to 'coordinate' every aspect of individual and family life under Party control. The regime exercised control over the flow of information through propaganda and censorship, and influenced the youth through education. The police, courts and prison system ensured that the population were under surveillance and liable to punishment. The Party had a large body of activists, who were able to insinuate themselves into every aspect of life. For the average German citizen, regular contact with the Party at some level was unavoidable. There were some pockets of resistance and non-conformity – in the Churches, among the young, workers and the old elites – but fear of punishment deterred any open defiance of the regime's authority.

The Hitler Myth

Fig. 8 *A poster of Hitler from 1939; the Swastika has been partly hidden in order to draw attention to his face*

In 1941, Goebbels claimed that the creation of the 'Hitler Myth' had been his greatest achievement. In 1933, the majority of the German population remained unconvinced by or hostile to Hitler. By the end of 1934, however, a powerful 'Hitler cult' had taken hold in the national consciousness. Hitler was being hailed as the 'symbol of the nation' and the 'leader for whom the nation had been waiting'. This image of Hitler became so powerful that in time Hitler himself came to believe in it. The Hitler Myth helped to sustain the regime in power, masking its failings and inconsistencies.

The Nazi State

When he came to power in 1933, Hitler did not have a clear plan for constructing a Nazi State. The Party took over the existing state and also created a number of Party organisations to run alongside central and local government institutions. The result was a system of overlapping responsibilities and rivalries between Party and state officials. For example, there was rivalry between Wilhelm Frick, the Minister of the Interior, and Himmler over police control. In economic affairs, Goering was put in charge of a Supreme Reich Authority to run the 1936 **Four Year Plan**, even though there were existing ministries of Economics, Agriculture, Labour and Transport, which were involved in aspects of the Plan. There were also serious divisions and rivalries within the Nazi Party itself, with the result that the Party was not able to fully impose its will on the State. At the centre of this chaotic system was Hitler himself, who took very little interest in the details or coordination of policy. He gave power to those he trusted and dealt with each senior official on an individual basis. Cabinet meetings became increasingly rare events. Officials who succeeded in this system did so by 'working towards the Führer'; in other words, they worked out what Hitler wanted and produced detailed policies that would get his approval.

Himmler, the leader of the SS, was one of the most successful Nazis in turning this situation to his advantage and built a powerful regime for himself and the SS. By 1936, he had taken control over the police system. Through the **Waffen SS**, Himmler was able to develop a military force in parallel with the regular army. After war broke out, he was placed in charge of the occupied territories in the east and had overall control over Nazi racial policy. It is possible to argue that, by 1941, there was an SS state at the heart of the Nazi state, and that it was this that brought some order into the chaos and anarchy of the Nazi governmental system.

CROSS-REFERENCE

More information about the Four Year Plan can be found in Chapter 15, page 123.

KEY TERMS

Waffen SS (armed SS): military wing of the SS. Although originally dependent on the regular army for its weapons and training, the Waffen SS grew and became a rival to the army

STUDY TIP

To evaluate the extent of totalitarianism, it is useful to consider the nature of Hitler's dictatorship. Read the conclusion on pages 201–203 for a detailed analysis.

ACTIVITY

Summary

Summarise your thoughts on how successful the Nazi regime was in terms of establishing a totalitarian state.

15 Economic policies

In January 1933, the German economy was in the depths of depression, with nearly 6 million people out of work. Previous regimes had failed to make any significant impact on the unemployment problem and many people had voted for the Nazis during the depression years of 1930–32 because Hitler promised decisive action to get people back to work. By 1935, the official figures showed that unemployment had fallen to 2 million, while by 1939 there were labour shortages in key industries. This, in essence, was the basis on which Nazi propagandists hailed the success of the regime's policies as an 'economic miracle'.

Nazi economic policies

When Hitler was appointed Chancellor on 30 January 1933, the Nazi Party did not have a coherent and carefully thought-out economic policy. Nevertheless, Hitler had some clear aims. In the short term, the priority was economic recovery from the Depression and the reduction of unemployment. Achieving these aims would boost the regime's popularity and help the Nazis to consolidate their power. In the longer term, the Nazis aimed to create an economy capable of sustaining a major rearmament programme and geared to the needs of a future war. Such an economy would need to be self-sufficient in the production of food and vital raw materials – something the Nazis referred to as 'economic **autarky**'.

The roles of Schacht and Goering in the implementation of Nazi policies

Recovery from the Depression

During the years 1933–36, Hjalmar Schacht, President of the Reichsbank and, from August 1934, Economics Minister, was the key figure in Nazi economic policy. Under his direction the regime stimulated economic recovery by:
- pumping money into the economy to build homes and Autobahns
- stimulating consumer demand by giving tax concessions and grants to particular groups
- giving subsidies to private firms to encourage them to take on more workers
- putting controls on wages and prices to control inflation
- introducing the 'New Plan' in 1934 to control Germany's foreign trade and improve the country's balance of payments
- taking the first steps towards rearmament, using an ingenious method for financing the expenditure – the **Mefo bill**.

LEARNING OBJECTIVES

In this chapter you will learn about:

- Nazi economic policies and the roles of Schacht and Goering
- Nazi policy towards management and the industrial elites
- the degree of economic recovery achieved by 1939.

KEY TERM

Autarky: economic independence or self-sufficiency

CROSS-REFERENCE

For more information about Schacht, see Chapter 5, page 36.

KEY TERM

Mefo bill: scheme whereby the German government paid by credit notes

ACTIVITY

What was the propaganda value of building the Autobahns?

A CLOSER LOOK

Autobahns

Richard Evans has described the Autobahns as 'one of the most durable propaganda exercises mounted by the Third Reich'. Photographs from the start of the construction of the first Autobahn showed thousands of workers employed on the project. Posters showed strikingly modern bridges and viaducts. They were a visible sign of economic revival and national renewal, achieved by Hitler's government. In reality, the construction of the Autobahns employed relatively few people. At the peak of construction only 125,000 people

Fig. 1 *Hitler walking on the new Autobahn in Dresden during the celebratory opening ceremony*

were directly employed. Construction slowed after 1938 and stopped altogether in 1942, by which time some 3870 km of road had been constructed. Since few Germans owned cars, the Autobahns were underused.

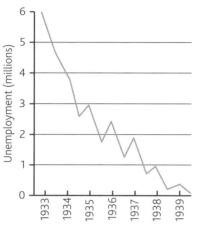

Fig. 2 *Unemployment figures between 1933 and 1939*

The battle for work

The Nazis' first priority after coming to power in 1933 was to reduce unemployment – a project which they labelled the 'battle for work'. Large sums of money were spent on the building of roads and public buildings and increased industrial production was stimulated through loans and tax relief to private companies. They were fortunate that, when they came to power, the economy was already beginning to revive but their measures undoubtedly helped to reduce unemployment faster than might otherwise have been the case. In 1935, a Reich Labour Service was introduced under which unemployed young men were compelled to do six months' labour in farming or construction. Later that same year, military conscription was reintroduced for young men.

The 'New Plan' of 1934

As the economy began to revive in 1933 and 1934, foreign trade increased and this led to imports growing faster than exports. This in turn led to a shortage of foreign currencies, which were needed to purchase imported goods. Under the New Plan, Schacht placed controls on imports and on access to foreign currency. He also initiated a series of trade agreements with foreign countries, especially states in the Balkans and South America, whereby Germany was supplied with food and raw materials, which were paid for in German Reichsmarks. The supplying countries could then only use this money to buy German goods.

Schacht and the use of Mefo bills

In order to finance rearmament, the Nazis needed to borrow money whilst at the same time avoid the dangers of runaway inflation, which were still fresh in the memories of the German people. In Schacht, they had a financial genius who devised a scheme whereby the government paid for its military equipment using credit notes, or Mefo bills. These bills could be exchanged for cash at the Reichsbank, thereby ensuring that private companies had confidence they would get their money. However, the companies were given an incentive to defer asking for payment by the offer of 4 per cent per annum (p.a.) interest on the bills if they kept them for the full five-year term. In this way, the rearmament programme could be started in 1935 without the government having the funds to finance it. It also had the advantage that the rearmament programme could be kept secret since the expenditure did not appear in the government's accounts.

Rearmament and the creation of a war economy

Schacht's measures succeeded in reviving the German economy and reducing unemployment but the revival created a new set of problems. In addition to the balance of payments problems and shortage of foreign exchange, there were also food shortages, rising prices and lower living standards for ordinary Germans in 1935–36. Reports from around Germany at this time spoke of growing disillusionment with the regime. This raised important questions about the regime's priorities. The food shortages could be resolved through imports, but this would use up valuable reserves of foreign currency also needed for the import of raw materials for the armaments industry, thus damaging the rearmament programme. This conflict of priorities, sometimes referred to as a choice between 'guns or butter', was finally resolved by the decision to strive for economic self-sufficiency. Expanding home production of both food and raw materials would, in theory, reduce the dependence on imports and the need for large reserves of foreign currency. This policy, referred to by the Nazis as economic autarky, was the basis of a new Four Year Plan, which was introduced in 1936. Schacht, who had opposed the move towards autarky, was marginalised and responsibility for the Four Year Plan was given to Hermann Goering.

The Four Year Plan

SOURCE 1

In 1936, Hitler set out his thoughts on the Four Year Plan in a memorandum given to Goering:

I consider it necessary that, from now on, with iron determination we attain 100 per cent self-sufficiency in all these areas such as steel and coal so that we will not be dependent on foreign countries for these important raw materials, and that thereby we will also be able to save the foreign currency we require during peacetime in order to import our foodstuffs. I therefore set the following tasks: 1. The German army must be operational within four years, and 2. The Germany economy must be fit for war within four years.

The aim of this plan was to make Germany ready for war within four years. Although a future war was always implicit in the Nazi quest for *Lebensraum* ('living space') in the east, the gearing of the German economy to war in the Four Year Plan was the first explicit indication that the regime was planning for war.

The priorities of this plan were rearmament and economic autarky. These were to be achieved by:

* creating a managed economy with controls on labour supply, prices, raw materials and foreign exchange
* setting production targets for private companies
* establishing new State-owned industrial plants such as the Hermann Goering Steelworks
* increasing production of key commodities such as iron, steel and chemicals
* encouraging research and investment in the production of substitute products such as artificial rubber and extracting oil from coal, thereby reducing Germany's dependence on imports.

Economic autarky

The Four Year Plan aimed to achieve autarky (self-sufficiency) in food production and vital raw materials in order to prepare the German economy for war. Autarky, with its links to national sovereignty and its embodiment of national pride and independence, fitted well with the Nazis' ideological aims. It would, according to the Nazi Party programme, 'free Germany from the chains of international capital'. The effort to increase production was presented as a battle in which the whole 'people's community' had to participate. Propaganda campaigns to persuade people to buy only German goods, eat only German food and use only German raw materials in their

ACTIVITY

Evaluating primary sources

How valuable would Source 1 be to an historian studying the Four Year Plan?

CROSS-REFERENCES

Lebensraum is explained in Chapter 10, page 77. The impact of *Lebensraum* in Nazi Germany is examined in Chapter 17, page 142.

The ways in which *Lebensraum* played a part in Nazi foreign policy and Hitler's plans for war is laid out in Chapter 19, page 156.

More information on Hermann Goering can be found in Chapter 12, page 92.

work presented these targets as the patriotic duty of all German citizens. There were also propaganda campaigns to persuade Germans to save more, since savings would help to fund investment in new production facilities. In 1937, the regime launched a campaign to collect scrap metal from people's homes and gardens and from public spaces, such as parks, to make up for serious shortages in raw materials. Garden fences, park railings and iron lampposts were removed to be melted down. Pots and pans were collected from people's homes by the Hitler Youth and local committees were set up to coordinate collections.

CROSS-REFERENCE

For more information on Sopade reports, refer back to Chapter 14, page 112.

ACTIVITY

Evaluating primary sources

How valuable would Source 2 be to an historian studying the success of Nazi economic policies?

CROSS-REFERENCES

Fritz Thyssen was chairman of the United Steelworks Company. His key profile is in Chapter 10, page 76.

Alfred Hugenberg owned newspapers and film companies as well as being a deputy in the Reichstag. His key profile is in Chapter 5, page 41.

SOURCE 2

A Sopade report in 1938 analysed the problems with the Four Year Plan:

It is true that as long as the German people are prepared to put up with their living standards being held at the lowest of crisis levels, the mechanism by which 12–13 billion Reichmarks are squeezed from the national income for rearmament will keep on functioning. But even then one cannot do everything at once with these billions. One cannot at the same time use them to increase armaments for the land and sea forces endlessly, to build up a massive fleet, to build gigantic installations for the production of synthetic substitutes, to construct megalomaniacal buildings and to tear down large parts of cities in order to build them somewhere else. On the basis of the living standards of the German people hitherto, one can either do one or the other or a bit of everything, but not everything at the same time and on an unlimited scale.

The results of the Four Year Plan did not match the propaganda claims. German industry, despite massive investment, did not meet the targets set by the regime and, in 1939, Germany still imported one third of its raw materials. In food production, there were similar failings. The reality was that the German economy did not have the resources to achieve all of the regime's aims. In order to maintain the levels of consumption and avoid the risk of alienating the people, labour and capital had to be diverted from war industries. By 1939, the German economy was under severe strain.

Nazi policy towards management and the industrial elites

Many, but not all, of Germany's business leaders welcomed the Nazi takeover of power in 1933. Fritz Thyssen and Alfred Hugenberg had helped Hitler in his bid to take power and Hitler was careful to offer reassurance to business leaders that they need not be alarmed by the more socialist elements in the Nazi Party programme. In the early months of the Nazi regime, many of their policies were of benefit to businesses: the suppression of free trade unions, the establishment of political stability and the revival of the economy all helped to create an environment favourable to business. On the other hand, as Nazi economic policies began to develop, there were many business leaders who did not welcome the greater state intervention in the economy with its controls on the supply of labour and raw materials, and price controls.

In general, the Nazi regime was able to enlist the cooperation and expertise of big business and management in the implementation of its economic policies. When the Four Year Plan was launched, there were many opportunities for businesses to make profits through involvement in the rearmament programme. One firm that benefitted enormously was the large chemicals company, I.G. Farben, which was heavily involved in the research and production of synthetic materials. One of the directors of I.G. Farben, for example, held a key post in the administration of the Four Year Plan, and between 1935 and 1939, the profits of I.G. Farben increased from 71 million to 240 million Reichsmarks. On the other hand, some companies were sceptical about the Plan. Many of the Ruhr iron and steel firms were reluctant to invest in new steelworks to produce steel from poor-quality and expensive German iron ore, rather than use cheaper and superior imported ore. The regime's response was to bypass them altogether by establishing a very large state-owned steelworks: the Hermann Goering Steelworks.

The degree of economic recovery achieved by 1939

Goebbels and the Nazi propaganda machine used all their resources and skills to project an image of the success of Nazi economic policies. Speeches and radio broadcasts by Hitler repeatedly claimed that the 'battle for work' had been won by 1936. Indeed, the 'battle for work' was not even mentioned after 1936, reflecting the success of propaganda in convincing people that unemployment was no longer a problem. Advertising campaigns for products such as the 'people's receiver', the 'people's car' and for cruise ship holidays gave the impression that Germans were experiencing an unprecedented rise in their living standards as a result of the regime's policies. Military parades showing off the latest equipment and patriotic campaigns to persuade Germans to buy only German goods were designed to show that Germany was achieving autarky and was ready for war. In each case, there was an element of truth in the claims, but propaganda exaggerated the successes and covered up the failures in Nazi economic policies.

The reduction of unemployment

Official unemployment figures show a dramatic reduction in the number of unemployed by 1934 and a continuing fall after that. This was the basis of the claim that the 'battle for work' had been won due to Nazi economic policies. There were several flaws in these claims:

- Economic recovery had actually begun before the Nazis took power in January 1933. Many of the job creation schemes used by the regime to reduce unemployment were actually based on policies introduced by Chancellor Heinrich Brüning in the early 1930s.
- Part of the reduction in the unemployment figures was achieved by persuading married women to give up their employment, through granting them marriage loans, thereby releasing jobs for unemployed male workers.
- The reintroduction of conscription in 1935, for young men aged 18–25, took a large proportion of young males out of the labour market.
- Official figures also showed a dramatic increase in the numbers of Germans in employment. This was partly achieved through various statistical devices to inflate the figures. Those who only had occasional employment, for example, were counted as permanently employed while those drafted into unpaid work in agriculture were also counted as employed.

Historian Richard Evans has estimated that 'invisible unemployment' (those who were out of work but were not counted in the official figures) was as high as 1.5 million workers. By this estimate, the official figure of 1.6 million people out of work in 1936 should in fact be increased to over 3 million, far

A CLOSER LOOK

The Hermann Goering Steelworks

This was an enormous enterprise established and owned by the State but partly financed by private companies, which were forced to invest in it. The company was given priority over private companies in the allocation of materials and labour. By 1939, it had become the largest industrial enterprise in Europe and was of obvious value for the regime's propaganda. It expanded its operations into coal mining and the manufacture of heavy machinery and synthetic fuels. As Germany began to expand its territory after 1938, so the Hermann Goering Steelworks expanded into Austria, Poland and France.

CROSS-REFERENCE

To find out more about the economic developments under Chancellor Brüning and his Central Party, see Chapter 9, pages 71–73.

Fig. 3 *An advertising campaign for the 'people's receiver'*

too many to support the claim that the 'battle for work' had been won. After 1936, however, rearmament led to a rapid expansion of employment and resulted in labour shortages appearing by 1939.

Living standards

Nazi propaganda emphasised the duty of all German citizens to make sacrifices on behalf of the 'people's community', by working harder and for longer hours and by accepting a squeeze on wages. At the same time, propaganda also stressed the benefits that the Nazi regime had bestowed on workers through improved working conditions, better social and welfare provision, and access to goods and services that had previously only been available to the privileged few.

Despite official attempts to hold down money wages, incomes for many workers did increase during the years 1933–39. Some employers were prepared to pay bonuses and other benefits to get round the freeze on wage levels and so attract more skilled workers. Pay increased due to the longer hours being worked but, on the other hand, workers' wages were subject to increased deductions because of the compulsory contributions they had to make to the German Labour Front and to welfare organisations. It is, therefore, difficult to generalise about what happened to the standard of living of the majority of German workers in these years. Workers in key industries such as armaments were undoubtedly better off than before, while those producing consumer goods were not.

Living standards depend as much on prices as they do on incomes. Prices rose during the 1930s and there were shortages of some key commodities. German consumers were able to buy enough food to feed their families but could afford few luxuries. The consumption of higher value foods such as meat, fruit and eggs declined while the consumption of cheaper foods such as potatoes and rye bread increased. There was, then, pressure on living standards and Gestapo and Sopade reports occasionally show some discontent with the regime. On the other hand, the fact that the regime succeeded in persuading the population to shoulder the burden of the rearmament programme, without triggering a wages explosion or mass opposition, indicates the success of propaganda campaigns such as the 'battle for production'.

CROSS-REFERENCE

The Gestapo is explained in Chapter 14, page 110, and the German Labour Front is explained in Chapter 16, page 133.

A CLOSER LOOK

Fig. 4 *Hitler inspects the new Volkswagen at a car factory in 1938*

The 'people's car'

The Volkswagen (the 'people's car') was a pet project of Hitler's. The car was promoted by Strength Through Joy with a huge campaign advertising 'a car for everyone'. This successfully persuaded workers to pay into a savings scheme to purchase one. The Volkswagen car was one of the great successes of Nazi propaganda, the more so since cars never went into full production during the Nazi regime and only the Nazi elite were able to acquire the few models that were actually made.

A Sopade report from April 1939 reflected on the impact of the Volkswagen propaganda campaign:

The announcement of the people's car is a great and happy surprise. For a long time the car was the main topic of conversation in all sections of the population in Germany. All other pressing problems, whether of domestic or foreign policy, were pushed into the background for a while. The grey German everyday sank beneath notice under this impression of the music of the future. Wherever the test models of the new Strength Through Joy construction are seen in Germany, crowds gather around them. The politician who promises a car for everyone is the man of the masses if the masses believe his promises. And as far as the Strength Through Joy car is concerned, the German people do believe Hitler's promises.

ACTIVITY

Use Source 3 and your contextual knowledge to answer the following:
1. In what ways did the Volkswagen project reflect Nazi ideology?
2. How far did the Volkswagen project show that Nazi propaganda was successful?

The drive for rearmament and the target of achieving economic autarky placed considerable strains on the German people, including longer working hours, higher prices and growing shortages. From time to time, there were serious shortages of eggs and meat, as well as wheat and rye for making bread. Price controls and the introduction of rationing on some key commodities in the late 1930s helped to alleviate the pressure. Despite these growing hardships, however, there were few signs of unrest. Nazi propaganda, together with the use of terror, had succeeded in persuading the majority of German people to accept these burdens.

ACTIVITY

Revision

Using the information in this chapter, complete the following table. Under each heading, list the successes and/or failures of Nazi economic policies.

Reducing unemployment	Raising living standards	Achieving economic autarky

Summary

The success of Nazi economic policy was mixed. Unemployment was reduced and, by 1939, there were labour shortages in some key sectors of the economy. The demands of the Four Year Plan placed the economy under severe strain and its targets were not achieved. In 1939, there were shortages of food and other basic necessities. Moreover, the progress that was achieved came at the cost of holding down the living standards of the majority of the German population.

 PRACTICE QUESTION

'The Nazi economic miracle between 1933 and 1939 was merely a propaganda myth.' Assess the validity of this view.

STUDY TIP

This quotation invites challenge but it is also possible to agree with it to a certain extent. This type of question requires an assessment of the success or failure of Nazi economic policies. To help make the analysis of such a large topic manageable, it would be sensible to concentrate on several key areas of policy. Try to maintain a consistent line of argument through the answer and present a balanced assessment of the evidence.

16 Social policies

LEARNING OBJECTIVES

In this chapter you will learn about:

- Nazi social policies towards young people, women, workers and Churches
- the degree of *Volksgemeinschaft*
- the benefits and drawbacks of Nazi rule.

CROSS-REFERENCE

Volksgemeinschaft is defined as the concept of a 'people's community' in Chapter 10, page 76. It was a key element in Nazi ideology. There is more information on the role of *Volksgemeinschaft* later in this chapter, and also Chapter 17, page 141.

ACTIVITY

Analysing primary sources

Read Source 1. What were the aims of Nazi education policy?

It was Hitler's intention that there should be no independent organisations standing between the State and the individual. Individuals would have no private space in which they could either think or act independently of the regime. All Germans must be made to conform to the norms of the regime in order that the Nazis could achieve their ultimate aim of creating a *Volksgemeinschaft*, or 'people's community'. The *Volksgemeinschaft* would be unified by blood, race and ideology, with a common bond of loyalty to the Führer. By coordinating German society using propaganda, indoctrination, terror and repression, the Nazis aimed to eliminate all opposition and create a community in which all *Volksgenossen* (national comrades) would be loyal, show self-discipline and a readiness to make personal sacrifices. Men would be imbued with a fighting spirit and women would be willing to place their bodies at the service of the State by producing large numbers of children. In short, the Nazis aimed at nothing less than the creation of a new German man and a new German woman. The starting point for this experiment in social engineering was Germany's youth.

Nazi policies towards young people

SOURCE 1

An extract from a speech by Hitler at the 1935 Nuremberg rally:

In our eyes the German boy of the future must be slender and supple, swift as greyhounds, tough as leather and hard as Krupp steel. We must bring up a new type of human being, men and girls who are disciplined and healthy to the core. We have undertaken to give the German people an education that begins in youth and will never come to an end. It starts with the child and will end with the 'old fighter'. Nobody will be able to say that he has a time in which he is left entirely alone to himself.

Schools

The Nazi regime established control over the school system in two main ways: control over teachers and control over the curriculum.

Control over the teachers

- Under the Law for the Re-establishment of a Professional Civil Service (1933), a number of teachers were dismissed on the grounds of political unreliability or because they were Jewish.
- Teachers were pressurised into joining the National Socialist Teachers' League (NSLB), but most teachers were willing to comply with the regime's demands. The historian Joachim Fest has claimed that 'the teaching profession was one of the most politically reliable sections of the population'.
- Vetting of textbooks was undertaken by local Nazi committees after 1933. From 1935, central directives were issued by the Ministry of Education covering what could be taught and, by 1938, these rules covered every school year and most subjects.

Control over the curriculum

Political indoctrination permeated every area of the school curriculum:

- The Nazis' aim to promote 'racial health' led to an increasing emphasis on physical education. Military-style drills became a feature of P.E. lessons.

CROSS-REFERENCE

Lebensraum was introduced as a concept in Chapter 10 of this book, page 77. The impact of *Lebensraum* on Germany is discussed in more detail in Chapter 17, page 142.

- In German lessons, the aim was to instill a 'consciousness of being German' through the study of Nordic sagas and other traditional stories.
- In Biology, there was a stress on race and heredity. There was also a strong emphasis on evolution and the survival of the fittest.
- Geography was used to develop awareness of the concepts of *Lebensraum* ('living space'), 'blood and soil' and German racial superiority. Atlases implicitly supported the concept of 'one people, one Reich'..

Universities

With their stress on physical education and political indoctrination, the Nazis downgraded the importance of academic education and the number of students attending university decreased between 1933 and 1939. Access to higher education was strictly rationed and selection was made on the basis of political reliability. Women were restricted to 10 per cent of the available university places, while Jews were restricted to 1.5 per cent, their proportion within the population as a whole.

Coordination of universities followed much the same pattern as schools:

- Under the Law for the Re-establishment of a Professional Civil Service, about 1200 university staff were dismissed on racial or political grounds. This amounted to around 15 per cent of the total.
- In November 1933, all university teachers were made to sign a 'Declaration in support of Hitler and the National Socialist State'.
- Students had to join the German Students' League (DS), although some 25 per cent managed to avoid doing this.
- Students were also forced to do four months' labour service and two months in an SA camp. Labour service would give students experience of real life, considered by the Nazis to be more important than academic learning.

The Nazis encountered very little resistance to their policies of bringing the universities under their control. Indeed, coordination was made easier by the voluntary self-coordination of many faculties. Even in the Weimar period, the universities had been dominated by nationalist and anti-democratic attitudes and traditional student 'fraternities' were a breeding ground for **reactionary** politics. The Nazis were, therefore, able to tap into a pre-existing culture of extreme nationalism and infuse it with Nazi ideology. This was helped by the students' knowledge that their prospects of employment after graduating depended on showing outward support for the regime.

The Hitler Youth

The Hitler Jugend (HJ), or Hitler Youth, was created in 1926 and in its early years was relatively unsuccessful. When the Nazis came to power in 1933, all other youth organisations, except those linked to the Catholic Church, were either banned or taken over by the Hitler Youth. Only then did the Nazis' own youth movement begin to flourish.

In 1936, a Law for the Incorporation of German Youth gave the Hitler Youth the status of an official education movement, equal in status to schools and the home. At the same time, Catholic youth organisations were banned and the Hitler Youth became the only officially permitted youth organisation. Also by 1936, the Hitler Youth had been granted a monopoly over all sports facilities and competitions for children under the age of 14. Membership of the Hitler Youth was made compulsory in 1939.

In the Hitler Youth, there was a constant diet of political indoctrination and physical activity. Boys from the age of 10 were taught the motto 'Live faithfully, fight bravely and die laughing'. The emphasis in youth activities was on competition, struggle, heroism and leadership, as boys were prepared for their

A CLOSER LOOK

New Nazi schools

New Nazi boarding schools for boys were created to train the future elite. The emphasis of their teaching was on physical fitness, political indoctrination and military drill. These included Napola schools for boys aged 10–18, Adolf Hitler Schools for boys aged 12–18 and *Ordensburgen* (Castles of Order), which were for young men in the 25–30 age group.

KEY TERM

Reactionary: holding political viewpoints that oppose social change, and support a return to a previous state in a society

Fig. 1 *Propaganda poster for the Hitler Youth, who were viewed as the future Aryan supermen*

future role as warriors. Hitler Youth members had to swear a personal oath of allegiance to the Führer. There was a set syllabus of political indoctrination which all members had to follow and a heavy emphasis on military drill. Boys were taught to sing Nazi songs and encouraged to read Nazi political pamphlets. They were taken on hikes and on camping trips. Ritual, ceremonies and the singing of songs reinforced their induction into Nazi ideology.

A former HJ leader Arno Klönne recalled his experiences in his 1982 memoir written after the war:

What I liked about the Hitler Youth was the comradeship. I was full of enthusiasm when I joined the **Jungvolk** at the age of 10. What boy isn't fired up by being presented with high ideas such as comradeship, loyalty and honour? Later, however, when I became a leader in the *Jungvolk* the negative aspects became very obvious. I found the compulsion and the requirement of absolute obedience unpleasant. I appreciated that there must be order and discipline in such a large group of boys, but it was exaggerated. It was preferred that people should not have a will of their own and should totally subordinate themselves.

KEY TERM

Jungvolk: the division of the Hitler Youth for boys in the 10–14 age group; at 14, they graduated to the Hitler Youth proper

ACTIVITY

Evaluating primary sources

How valuable would Source 2 be for an historian studying the Hitler Youth?

The opportunity to participate in sports and camping trips away from home made the organisation attractive to millions of German boys, many of whom grew up in the 1930s with no experience of any other system. For these boys, their growing up was shaped by the Hitler Youth and the Nazi emphasis on struggle, sacrifice, loyalty and discipline became accepted as the norm. Many children joined against the wishes of parents who were not Nazi sympathisers and had grown up in a different era. For these boys, the Hitler Youth offered an outlet for their teenage rebelliousness. By the late 1930s, however, as the organisation became more bureaucratic and rigid, there were signs that enthusiasm was beginning to wane. There were reports of poor attendance at weekly parades. Boys resented the harsh punishments imposed for minor infringements of the rules.

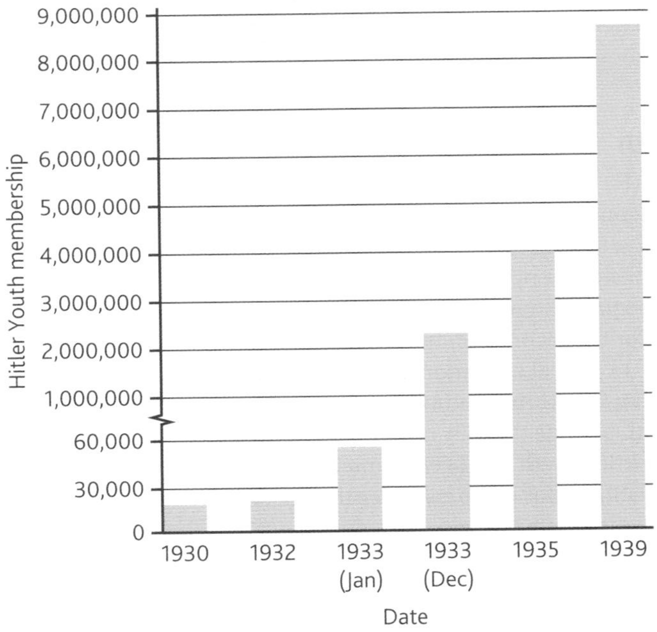

Fig. 2 *Membership of the Hitler Youth 1930–39*

The League of German Girls

The Bund Deutscher Mädel (BDM), or League of German Girls, was the female equivalent of the Hitler Youth. Its motto – 'Be faithful, be pure, be German' – was part of a process of preparing girls for their future role as housewives and mothers in the *Volksgemeinschaft*. Membership became compulsory in 1939.

In the BDM, girls were taught that they had a duty to be healthy since their bodies belonged to the nation. They needed to be fit for their future role as child bearers. They were also instructed in matters of hygiene, cleanliness and healthy eating. Formation dancing and group gymnastics served the dual purpose of raising fitness and developing comradeship. At weekly 'home evenings', girls were taught handicrafts, sewing and cooking. There were also sessions for political education and racial awareness. Annual summer camps were highly structured, every minute being taken up with sports, physical exercise and route marches, as well as indoctrination, flag-waving and saluting. In the Faith and Beauty groups, young women were instructed in baby care and social skills such as ballroom dancing.

Fig. 3 *Bund Deutscher Mädel poster*

SOURCE 3

Part of the rules of the BDM:

Your body belongs to your nation, to which you owe your existence and for which you are responsible.

Always keep yourself clean, tend and exercise your body. Light, air and water can help you in this.

Look after your teeth. Strong and healthy teeth are a source of pride.

Eat plenty of raw fruit, uncooked greens and vegetables, first washing them thoroughly in clean water.

Drink fruit juice. Leave coffee to the coffee addicts.

Shun alcohol and nicotine; they are poisons which impair your development and capacity for work.

Take physical exercise. It will make you healthy and hardy. Sleep at least nine hours every night.

Practise first aid for use in accidents. It can help you save your comrades' lives.

All your activities are governed by the slogan: 'Your duty is to be healthy'.

ACTIVITY

Evaluating primary sources

What can we learn from Source 3 about Nazi policies towards girls and women?

A LEVEL PRACTICE QUESTION

Evaluating primary sources

With reference to Sources 1, 2 and 3 and your understanding of the historical context, assess the value of these three sources to an historian studying Nazi policy towards youth.

STUDY TIP

The value of a source depends on many factors. Be sure to consider the provenance of each source and its tone and emphasis, as well as its contents. Make sure that you also place each source in its historical context before coming to a judgement about its value.

Many girls found their experiences in the BDM liberating. They were doing things that their mothers had not been allowed to do and they could escape from the constraints of the home. They also developed a sense of comradeship. Although strictly run on the leadership principle, the BDM groups were relatively classless, bringing together girls from a wide range of backgrounds. This was part of the strategy for capturing the minds of German youth and moulding them to the purposes of the Nazi regime. Racial awareness was an important element in this indoctrination. Jutta Rüdiger, the leader of the BDM, instructed girls on their future partners in marriage: 'Only the best German soldier is suitable for you, for it is your responsibility to keep the blood of the nation pure. German girl, your honour lies in being faithful to the blood of your race.'

After 1934, girls were expected to do a year's work on the land or in domestic service. The aim was to put girls in touch with their peasant roots and give them practical experience in child care. It also developed their sense of serving the community. This was very unpopular with girls from the cities and many tried to avoid it. In 1939, this scheme was made compulsory. All young women up to the age of 25 had to do a year's unpaid work with the Reich Labour Service before they could get paid employment. This was the female equivalent to compulsory military service for the boys and was part of the growing 'coordination' of all levels of German society under Nazi rule.

The degree of success of Nazi youth policies

The Nazis were successful in bringing schools and universities under their control. The HJ had, by 1939, become the only youth movement allowed in Germany, and membership of both HJ and BDM had grown. The HJ undoubtedly reinforced certain values that had long been well established in German culture, particularly the importance of duty, obedience, honour, courage and physical strength. This picture of success, however, must be balanced by the fact that attendance at HJ parades was beginning to slip by 1939 and that the Nazis themselves were concerned about the re-emergence of independent youth cliques.

Nazi policies towards women

> **SOURCE 4**
>
> **Hitler's view of the role of women, from his speech at the 1934 Nuremberg rally:**
>
> If one says that man's world is the State, that his world is his struggle, his readiness to devote himself to the community, then one might be able to say that the world of women is a smaller one. For her world is her husband, her family, her children and her house. But where would the larger world be if no one wanted to care for the smaller world? How could the larger world exist if there were no one to make the cares of the smaller world the essence of their lives? No, the larger world is built on this smaller world! What man offers in heroism on the field of battle, woman equals with unending pain and suffering. Every child she brings into the world is a battle, a battle she wages for the existence of her people.

The Nazis opposed the trend towards greater emancipation for women that had been evident in the Weimar period. They viewed the declining birth rate in the 1920s with alarm as it threatened to undermine their aim to expand Germany's territory and settle Germans in the newly acquired lands to the east. The main priority for Nazi policy towards women after 1933, therefore, was to raise the birth rate. This was closely linked to attempts to restrict the employment of married women outside the family home. These aims were pursued through a number of policies:

- Marriage loans were introduced for women who left work and married an Aryan man. For each child born, the amount of the loan that had to be repaid was reduced by a quarter.
- The Nazis awarded medals to women for 'donating a baby to the Führer'. Those with four or five children received a bronze medal, six or seven qualified for silver, and eight for gold.
- Birth control was discouraged. Abortion was severely restricted.
- Women were encouraged to adopt a healthy lifestyle, with plenty of exercise

and no smoking or drinking.

The Nazis also sought to promote their values through a number of organisations for women:

- The German Women's League (DFW) was set up in 1933 to coordinate all women's groups under Nazi control. It had a domestic science department, which gave advice to women on cooking and healthy eating. By 1939, the DFW had over 6 million members, seventy per cent of whom were not members of the Nazi Party.
- The National Socialist Women's Organisation (NS-F) was an elite organisation to promote the nation's 'lovelife, marriage, the family, blood and race'. It was primarily an organisation for propaganda and indoctrination among women to promote the Nazi ideology that women should be child-rearers and homemakers.
- The Reich Mother's Service (RMD) was a branch of the DFW for training 'physically and mentally able mothers, to make them convinced of the important duties of motherhood, experienced in the care and education of their children and competent to carry out their domestic tasks'. By March 1939, 1.7 million women had attended its motherhood training services.

The degree of success of Nazi's policies towards women

The Nazis' campaign to raise the birth rate had some success. To what extent this was due to policy, however, is debatable, since the improved economic situation would also have encouraged couples to have more children. Moreover, despite the Nazis' ideological objection to the paid employment of married women, the number of women in the workforce increased between 1933 and 1939 as ideology had to give way to economic realities. After 1936, there was a growing labour shortage in Germany as the pace of rearmament increased, so the regime began to encourage women to take up employment.

Nazi policies towards workers

The Nazi *Volksgemeinschaft* would be a society in which class differences, religious loyalties, as well as regional, age and gender differences would be put aside and replaced by national unity. Given their traditional ties to trade unions and non-Nazi political parties, industrial workers presented the greatest challenge to the process of *Gleichschaltung*. The Nazis could not ignore the working class nor could they rely solely on repression to achieve their objective of 'coordinating' this very important part of German society. Their first step was to ban the existing free trade unions, which was done on 2 May 1933. Following that, the next step was to coordinate workers into a Nazi-run organisation, the German Labour Front (DAF).

The German Labour Front (DAF)

The *Deutsches Arbeitsfront* (DAF), or German Labour Front, was established on 6 May 1933, under the leadership of **Robert Ley**, to coordinate workers into the National Socialist regime. The DAF took over the assets of the banned trade unions and became the largest organisation in the Third Reich. Although membership of the DAF was not compulsory, its membership grew rapidly since it was the only officially recognised organisation representing workers. The DAF had two main aims: to win the workers over to the *Volksgemeinschaft* and to encourage workers to increase production. Because it was a symbol of the Nazi *Volksgemeinschaft*, the DAF included employers as well as workers. The DAF replaced the trade unions but was not a trade union itself. It had no role in bargaining over wages and little influence over the regime's social and economic policies. It did, however, have its own propaganda department to spread Nazi ideology among working-class Germans. It also established a subsidiary

CROSS-REFERENCE

The economic situation between 1933 and 1939 is covered in more detail in Chapter 15.

CROSS-REFERENCE

Gleichschaltung was the term used to describe the process through which the Nazis attempted to control all aspects of German society. It is described in more detail in Chapter 12, page 97.

Fig. 4 *The German Labour Front (DAF)*

Robert Ley

A former fighter pilot in the First World War, **Robert Ley** (1890–1945) joined the Nazi Party in 1924. He was elected to the Reichstag in 1930, became Reich Organisation Leader in 1932 and leader of the DAF in 1933. He committed suicide in 1945.

ACTIVITY

Discussion point

Discuss: 'The KdF gave German workers a positive reason to support the Nazi regime.'

CROSS-REFERENCE

For more information on Sopade reports refer to Chapter 14, page 112.

ACTIVITY

Evaluating primary sources

How valuable is Source 5 for an historian studying working-class attitudes to the Nazi regime?

organisation, 'Strength Through Joy', to organise workers' leisure time. In 1936, the DAF started to provide vocational training courses to improve workers' skills. The DAF also built up a large business empire of its own. This included banks, housing associations and construction companies, the Volkswagen car plant and its own travel company. By 1939, the DAF had 44,500 paid employees.

The Nazi system of labour relations was heavily weighted in favour of the employer and the State. Workers in the Third Reich had to work harder and accept a squeeze on wages and living standards. Nazi propaganda tried to promote the message that the reward for working was not material gain but the knowledge that they were serving the community. Nevertheless, the Nazis were well aware that they could not take workers for granted. Improved leisure facilities and opportunities, provided by Strength Through Joy, were a key part of this strategy.

Strength Through Joy (KdF)

The *Kraft durch Freude* (KdF) organisation, or Strength Through Joy, was set up by Robert Ley and the DAF to organise workers' leisure time. The basic idea behind the scheme was that workers would 'gain strength for their work by experiencing joy in their leisure'. Workers who were refreshed by holidays, sports and cultural activities would be more efficient when they returned to work. The KdF also aimed:

- to submerge the individual in the mass and encourage workers to see themselves as part of a *Volksgemeinschaft*. With leisure time as well as work time regulated by the regime, there would be no time or space for workers to develop private lives. To this end, the KdF was a propagandist organisation, which used its activities to indoctrinate workers and their families into Nazi ideology
- to encourage a spirit of social equality. All KdF activities were organised on a one-class basis with no distinction between rich and poor
- to bring Germans from the different regions of the country together and to break down regional and religious differences
- to encourage participation in sport to improve the physical and mental health of the nation. Every youth in employment was obliged to undertake two hours each week of physical education at their workplace
- to encourage competition and ambition. A KdF National Trades Competition was organised for apprentices to improve skills and standards of work.

Through the KdF, workers were offered subsidised holidays in Germany and abroad, sporting activities and hikes, as well as theatre and cinema visits at reduced prices. Classical music concerts were put on in lunch breaks in factories. There were KdF wardens in every factory and workplace employing more than 20 people. Supporting these were over 7000 paid employees of the organisation by 1939. Membership of the KdF came automatically with membership of the DAF so that, by 1936, 35 million belonged to it.

Despite the gap between myth and reality in the KdF, it was one of the regime's most popular organisations. By offering opportunities that were not available to ordinary Germans before 1933, the KdF was valued by workers and thus helped to reconcile people, and even former opponents, to the regime.

SOURCE 5

A 1938 Sopade report on the popularity of the KdF:

Strength Through Joy is very popular. The events appeal to the yearning of the little man who wants an opportunity to get out and about himself and participate in the pleasures of the 'top people'. It's a clever appeal to the petty-bourgeois inclinations of the unpolitical worker. For such a man, it's really something if he goes on a Scandinavian cruise or even just travels to the Black Forest or the Harz Mountains. He imagines that this has moved him up a rung on the social ladder.

Mass tourism through the KdF

Mass tourism was one of the KdF's most successful activities and cruises to foreign destinations opened up new opportunities for many Germans. Cruises took ordinary Germans to Madeira, Libya, Finland, Norway, Bulgaria and Turkey. Rail trips took Germans to Italy and countries in south-eastern Europe. KdF ships were built on a one-class basis to emphasise the unity and classlessness of the *Volksgemeinschaft*. Facilities on board ships included gyms, theatres and swimming pools. Life on the cruise ships was regimented. Passengers were instructed to dress modestly, to avoid excessive drinking, not to have holiday affairs with other passengers and to obey the instructions of their tour leaders. In case any passengers might be tempted to voice critical opinions of the regime, Gestapo and SS agents travelled on the cruises to spy on them. The cruises were designed to demonstrate to the world how socially and technologically advanced Germans had become under the Nazi regime and to remind Germans how superior they were to the inhabitants of the countries they visited.

Yet the reality of the cruise ships actually contradicted the ideological assumptions on which the whole enterprise was based. Tickets were too expensive for ordinary workers and passengers were drawn mainly from the middle classes. Only 10 per cent of the passengers on one cruise to Norway were from the working class. The best cabins on the ships were allocated to party officials and civil servants. There was little mixing between classes on the ships and there were reports of fights between passengers from different regions of Germany. Gestapo agents reported mass drunkenness and riotous behaviour, especially from party officials. The worst offender was Robert Ley himself, who frequently went on KdF cruises where he spent his time getting drunk and womanising. A popular nickname for the KdF was the 'big-wigs' knocking shop' (i.e. the 'important persons' brothel').

The degree of success of Nazi policies towards workers

The evidence from Sopade and Gestapo reports shows that workers' reactions to Nazi schemes to win their support were mixed. Many workers, of course, had been influenced by socialist and communist ideas before 1933 and would therefore have been resistant to Nazi ideology. According to these reports, Strength through Joy (KdF) was popular not because people shared its Nazi ideological aims, but because it offered workers a means of escaping the boredom and pressure of their working lives. On the other hand, trade unions had been abolished and workers had no independent means by which they could voice their grievances.

Nazi policies towards the Churches

Coordinating the Churches into the *Volksgemeinschaft* posed serious challenges for the Nazi regime since the Germans were divided by faith. Although the majority of Germans were Protestant, a significant minority were Roman Catholic. Secondly, religious loyalties were deep-rooted in some communities and were an obstacle to the Nazi aim of making the Führer the focus of loyalty for all Germans. Hitler realised that he would have to proceed cautiously at first, with his initial objective being to gain control over the Churches before later trying to weaken their influence.

The Nazis did not have a coherent view towards religion and the Churches. Hitler himself had been raised a Catholic in Austria and he talked often of 'positive Christianity'. Yet at other times Hitler stated that he wanted to eradicate Christianity from Germany. Hitler was hostile to the Christian faith but, especially in the early months of his regime, he was careful not to alienate the Churches and so tried to reassure Church leaders that Nazism posed no threat to their faith. Other Nazis, notably Robert Ley, were atheists who wanted to replace the Christian Churches with a new Nazi faith. This lack of coherence in Nazi religious policy is evident in their dealings with the different Churches.

The Beauty of Labour (SdA)

The KdF department devoted to improving workplace conditions was *Schönheit der Arbeit*, or Beauty of Labour. Its aim was to get workers to work harder. Beauty of Labour campaigned for better washing facilities in factories, which linked with the Nazi's ideological belief in racial health. It encouraged the provision of workplace sports facilities and campaigned for employers to provide canteens serving hot, nourishing meals. The regime claimed that, by 1938, 34,000 companies had improved their working conditions and facilities, but the workers had to bear most of the cost of these improvements. Many firms expected their workers to paint the factory and clean up and build the new facilities in their own time and for no extra pay.

CROSS-REFERENCE

To help you evaluate the degree of *Volksgemeinschaft*, return to Chapter 14 to consider the effectiveness of resistance to Nazi policies.

Table 1 *Relative strengths of the two main Churches in Germany during the Weimar period*

	Protestant (German Evangelical Church)	Roman Catholic
Membership	40 million (58% of population)	22 million (32%)
Geographical spread	North and east	South (Bavaria) and west (Rhineland)
Social influence	Youth organisations (0.7 million members)	Youth organisations (1.5 million members), schools and charities
Political influence	Connected to DNVP and DVP	Close link with Centre Party

KEY PROFILE

Martin Luther (1483–1546) was a German Catholic monk who challenged the authority of the papacy in 1517 by nailing his 'theses' (criticisms) to a church door. This set in train a process which started the Reformation and the beginnings of German Protestantism.

CROSS-REFERENCE

Joseph Goebbels was the chief propagandist of the Nazi movement from 1928 to 1945. More information on his life is in Chapter 10, page 79.

KEY TERM

German Christians: a pressure group of Nazis operating within the German Evangelical Church; first established in May 1932, by the mid-1930s it had some 600,000 supporters; describing themselves as the 'SA of the Church', German Christian pastors wore SA or SS uniforms and hung swastika flags in their churches

The Protestant Church

The main Protestant Church in Germany was the German Evangelical Church, which many Nazis saw as a potential nucleus for a single national Church. Evangelicals were politically very conservative and staunch nationalists, regarding Germany as a Protestant state. Within the German Evangelical Church, there was a strong tradition of respect for, and cooperation with, the State. Many Protestants were anti-Semitic and vigorously anti-communist. There were, therefore, many points of convergence between Nazi ideology and the views of German Protestants and it was no coincidence that, before 1933, the strongest areas of Nazi support were in the Protestant north and east of Germany. In the early months of the Nazi regime, some Nazi-leaning Protestant pastors staged mass weddings of SA brownshirts and their brides. For their part the Nazis, in 1933, turned the 450th anniversary of the birth of **Martin Luther** into a major national celebration.

The Reich Church

In the spring and summer of 1933 the Nazi regime began to 'coordinate' the Evangelical Church into a single, centralised Reich Church under Nazi control. In the Church elections of July 1933, the German Christians, with the support of Goebbels' Propaganda Ministry, won a sweeping victory and were now in a position to 'Nazify' the Church. **Ludwig Müller**, a Nazi nominee, was appointed as Reich Bishop and took over the administrative headquarters of the Evangelical Church with the help of the SA. Müller abolished all elected bodies within the Church and reorganised it on the leadership principle. In November 1933, the **German Christians** celebrated their triumph in taking over the Reich Church by holding a mass rally at the Sports Palace in Berlin. Here, they demanded that those pastors who had not declared their allegiance to the new regime should be dismissed, along with all non-Aryans. As a State institution, the Reich Church was forced to adopt this so-called 'Aryan paragraph' and 18 pastors, mostly men who had converted to Christianity from Judaism, were dismissed. By the end of 1933, it appeared that the Reich Church had successfully been 'coordinated' into the *Volksgemeinschaft*.

KEY PROFILE

Ludwig Müller (1883–1945) was a Protestant pastor who had been associated with the Nazis since the 1920s. His appointment as Reich Bishop was imposed on the Church by the Nazis but he failed to establish complete mastery of the Church because of his own political ineptness and a growing resentment at his appointment. He committed suicide in 1945 after Germany's defeat.

The Confessional Church

Not all Protestant pastors, or their congregations, were willing to support these developments within the Church. In September 1933, a group of dissident pastors, led by Martin Niemöller and **Dietrich Bonhoeffer**, established a Pastors' Emergency League. This evolved into a breakaway Church known as the Confessional Church. With the support of about 5000 pastors, the new Church was established to resist State interference in the Church and to re-establish a theology that was based purely on the Bible. The Confessional Church was thus in opposition to the official Reich Church. Some rural congregations went over to the Confessional Church because, as the Gestapo reported on the Potsdam district, 'farming people seem to want to celebrate their Church festivals in the traditional form'.

The very fact that the Confessional Church was established in defiance of the Nazi policy of *Gleichschaltung* shows that the regime's attempts to 'coordinate' the Protestant Church were a failure. In 1935, a new Ministry for Church Affairs was created and Reich Bishop Müller was marginalised. The regime then switched to a policy of trying to weaken the Confessional Church through repression while at the same time trying to exploit the divisions that were beginning to appear within it. The regime also attempted to marginalise Christianity by trying to reduce the influence of the Churches over young people through the abolition of Church schools in the late 1930s and pressure on young people to join the Hitler Youth. The regime also launched a Church Secession Campaign to persuade party members to renounce their Church membership.

This campaign had some success:

- By 1939, five per cent of the population were listed as 'god-believers', or people who retained some faith but had renounced formal membership of the Christian Churches.
- Party members were not allowed to hold any office in the Protestant or Catholic Churches.
- Stormtroopers were forbidden to wear uniforms at church services.
- Priests and pastors were forbidden from playing any part in the Nazi Party.
- Pressure to renounce their faith was also put on those whose employment depended on the regime; teachers and civil servants were particular targets.

The Roman Catholic Church

The Roman Catholic Church presented a far greater obstacle than the Protestants to the Nazi policy of *Gleichschaltung*. Catholics in Germany were part of an international Church and took their lead in religious matters from the pope. The Roman Catholic Church, therefore, was less susceptible to Nazi ideology than the wholly German Evangelical Church. The Nazis regarded the fact that the Roman Catholic Church demanded obedience to the pope from German Catholics as undermining Germany's unity as a nation. In the early 1930s, Catholic voters were among the least likely people to vote for the Nazi Party. On the other hand, Catholics as a group were keen to be seen and accepted as part of the German nation and, after Hitler came to power, the Catholic Church was prepared to compromise. There were also some points of convergence between Catholics and Nazism: the Catholic Church regarded communism as a far greater evil than Nazism and there were also many within the Church who shared the Nazis' anti-Semitism.

The Concordat

After Hitler came to power in 1933, the Roman Catholic Church opted for cooperation and compromise with the new regime in the belief that this would preserve its autonomy. When the free trade unions were taken over

Dietrich Bonhoeffer (1906–45) was co-founder of the Pastors' Emergency League and joined the Confessional Church. He was an outspoken opponent of the Aryan paragraph and of Nazi attempts to take over the Church. Unlike Niemöller, he retained his freedom and became involved with other anti-Nazi elements among army officers. He was finally arrested in 1943 and murdered by the Gestapo in 1945.

CROSS-REFERENCE

For more information on Niemöller and the Confessional Church, see Chapter 14, page 114.

ACTIVITY

Class debate

'The Nazis' efforts to coordinate the Protestant church were a failure.' Discuss.

by the German Labour Front in May 1933, Catholic trade unions voluntarily disbanded. Then, in July 1933, the regime and the Vatican (the headquarters of the Catholic Church and home of the pope) reached an agreement called a concordat, under which:

- the Vatican recognised the Nazi regime and promised that the Catholic Church would not interfere in politics
- the regime promised that it would not interfere in the Catholic Church and that the Church would keep control of its schools, youth organisations and lay groups.

It was not long, however, before the Nazi regime was breaking the terms of this agreement. In the summer of 1933, the Nazis began to seize the property of Catholic organisations and forced them to close. Catholic newspapers were ordered to drop the word 'Catholic' from their names. The Gestapo and SS put Catholic priests under surveillance. In the Night of the Long Knives in June 1934, a number of leading Catholics were executed by the SS. Among them was Fritz Gerlich, the editor of a Catholic journal and a known critic of the regime. In the face of this mounting repression and blatant illegality, the Catholic hierarchy made no protest, believing instead that continued declarations of support for the regime would be the best way to protect the Catholic Church from the Nazis.

Conflict between the regime and the Catholic Church

Some Catholic priests did begin, in 1935–36, to speak out from their pulpits about the dangers of Nazi religious ideas. Leading this criticism was Clemens von Galen, the Archbishop of Münster. In response, the regime increased the pressure on the Catholic Church:

- Permission to hold public meetings was severely restricted.
- Catholic newspapers and magazines were heavily censored and many publications had Nazi editors imposed upon them.
- Goebbels launched a propaganda campaign against financial corruption in Catholic lay organisations. Many had their funds seized and their offices closed by the SA.
- Membership of the Hitler Youth was made compulsory for all young people. Although Catholic youth organisations were still tolerated, they experienced increasing difficulty in holding onto their members.

In 1937, Pope Pius XI issued an encyclical entitled 'With Burning Grief'. In response, the regime again increased the pressure:

- Gestapo and SS agents were placed inside Catholic Church organisations.
- There was a tightening of restrictions on the Catholic press. Pilgrimages and processions were restricted and Catholic youth groups were closed down.
- Many monasteries were closed down and their assets were seized. Crucifixes were removed from Catholic schools.
- Goebbels' Propaganda Ministry publicised many sex scandals involving Catholic priests, attempting to portray the Church as corrupt. Around 200 priests were arrested and tried on sex charges.
- Finally, the Nazis began a campaign to close Church schools. By the summer of 1939, all Church schools had been converted into community schools.

By the summer of 1939, the power and influence of the Roman Catholic Church in Germany had been severely weakened. The concordat had not been formally repudiated by the regime but the Nazis had ceased to honour the agreement. The regime paid particular attention to young people of Catholic parents, denying them the opportunity to attend Church schools or belong to separate Catholic youth organisations. This was part of a long-term strategy to weaken the influence of the Church. Many older Catholics,

ACTIVITY

1. a. How did the Catholic Church benefit from its compromise with the Nazi regime?
   b. Why did the compromise break down?

CROSS-REFERENCE

For more information on Archbishop Galen and Catholic resistance to the regime, see Chapter 14, page 115.

however, were torn between their faith and their wish to be seen as 'good Germans'. With the Church under attack, older Catholics, particularly in rural areas, reaffirmed their strong support for it by continuing to attend services. Although many had complaints about the treatment of their Church at the hands of the Nazis, they were careful not to place themselves in outright opposition. For Catholics, as for other Germans, the Hitler myth cast a powerful spell over them. Although individual Catholics did oppose many of the regime's policies, the Church as a whole did not mount any organised resistance to the Third Reich.

The degree of success of Nazi policy towards the Churches

The regime's religious policy was confused and inconsistent as leading Nazis differed in their attitudes towards Christianity. The Nazis had failed to establish a single, unifying Protestant Church based on the German Christian Movement. By 1939, the concordat with the Catholic Church was effectively dead, yet Hitler held back from formally renouncing the agreement. He could still see some value, from a tactical point of view, in keeping the façade of cooperation while at the same time pursuing policies designed to weaken its hold. It is clear that the Nazis had failed to 'coordinate' the Churches into the *Volksgemeinschaft* and that organised religion remained a powerful force within German society.

 PRACTICE QUESTION

'The Nazi regime achieved its objectives in its policies towards the Christian churches.' Assess the validity of this view.

Summary: the benefits and drawbacks of Nazi rule

A survey carried out in West Germany in 1951 revealed that nearly half of the population of this part of Germany viewed the years 1933–39 as a positive experience. It was a time when there was full employment, guaranteed pay packets and leisure opportunities through the KdF, together with political stability and an ordered society. In contrast with the Depression years under Weimar, the first years of the Third Reich brought many benefits to large numbers of Germans. This, of course, was not the experience of everyone, nor did it happen without considerable costs in terms of the loss of liberty and civil rights. The spectre of unemployment was banished but living standards for the majority of those in work did not improve. The Nazis had championed the cause of the farmers and the Mittelstand (the professional middle classes) during their rise to power but neither of these groups saw much benefit from Nazi policies. The Nazis had attacked big business on occasions during the Weimar years but after 1933 large corporations did very well. Nazi social policies did not fully succeed in creating the classless national community they aspired to, but they did consolidate their own rule by closing down political debate and providing the majority of the population with enough material benefits to win their acceptance.

ACTIVITY

To what degree did the Nazis succeed in creating a *Volksgemeinschaft*? Draw a summary chart to help you evaluate Nazi policies towards young people, women, workers and Churches.

ACTIVITY

Revision

Divide into groups, then conduct a detailed study of one of the following: youth, workers, women and Churches. Use information from this book and other sources. Focus your research on:

- the aims of Nazi policy
- the organisations and methods for implementing their policy
- the effectiveness of the policy.

When the research is complete, each group should present its findings to the rest of the class.

STUDY TIP

When tackling this type of question, you need to explain the objectives of Nazi policy towards the Churches as well as assess their effectiveness. Remember to differentiate between the Protestant and Catholic Churches, and identify failures as well as successes. Try to maintain a consistent line of argument throughout the answer and offer a conclusion that is balanced and based on the evidence you have presented.

Fig. 5 *A propaganda poster for the KdF travel pass*

17 The radicalisation of the State

Fig. 1 *A poster for the 1936 Olympic Games*

CROSS-REFERENCE

Look back at Chapter 10, page 76 for an explanation of the term 'Aryan', and Chapter 12, page 91 for details on Blomberg and Chapter 14, page 116 for details on Fritsch.

KEY TERMS

Slav peoples: a very diverse ethnic group including Czechs, Slovaks, Poles, Russians, Ukrainians, Croats, Serbs and Slovenes, living mainly in Central and Eastern Europe

Degenerate: a person considered to be lacking some usual or expected property or quality, such as physical, mental or moral

The radicalisation of the State

The Nazi regime could not act just as it wished in its first few years in power. Nazi ideological aims could only be implemented when it was politically possible. There were three distinct phases in the development of the Nazi regime.

1. Phase one: The legal revolution, 1933–34. When Hitler came to power in 1933, he depended on political allies. Hitler could not completely prevent the radical SA's violence, but he controlled it as much as he could. He consolidated his power by legal means.

2. Phase two: Creating the new Germany, 1934–37. By August 1934, the Nazi regime was secure, but Hitler still did not have a free hand. He worried about public opinion both at home and abroad. One example of this was the Olympic Games in Berlin in 1936. Before and during the Games, Nazi anti-Semitism was put under wraps while Nazi propaganda projected the image of Germany as a civilised society. Between 1934 and 1937, Hitler avoided confronting powerful groups like the army or the Churches. He also knew that Germany was not yet ready for a war, whatever the propaganda said.

3. Phase three: The radicalisation of the State, 1938–39. By the end of 1937, the Nazi regime was far stronger than in 1933. The economy had recovered. The SS completely controlled the police system. Hitler felt Germany was militarily ready for war. In 1938 and 1939, therefore, the Nazis took bold steps they would not have dared to take earlier. Hitler took control of the army, sacking its two most important commanders, Blomberg and Fritsch. He also let loose radical persecution of his 'racial enemies'.

Nazi racial ideology

Social Darwinism and race theory

Social Darwinism was a theory that was widely discussed in nineteenth-century Europe. Social Darwinists adapted Darwin's scientific principles of natural biological selection ('the survival of the fittest') to rather unscientific theories about human society in order to justify ideas of racial superiority and the theory of eugenics. In the late nineteenth and early twentieth centuries, many Social Darwinists put forward theories designed to justify European imperialism, by arguing that 'advanced' Europeans had the right and responsibility to rule over 'inferior' or 'backward' colonial peoples. In Sweden, there was an influential group of scientists seeking to eliminate disabilities through population planning and birth control. Many of these ideas were incorporated into Nazi ideology.

Hitler's obsession with this 'biological struggle' between different races easily fitted with his view of the Jews. He viewed humanity as consisting of a hierarchy of races: the Jews, black people and the **Slavs** were inferior races, while the *Herrenvolk* (master race) was the **Aryan** peoples of northern Europe. Another key Nazi idea was the need to 'purify' the stronger races by eliminating the 'germs' that threatened to poison them through inter-marriage with so-called '**degenerate**' races. Hitler believed that it was the destiny of Aryans to rule over the inferior races. In order to ensure their success in this racial struggle, it was vital for Aryans to maintain their racial purity.

SOURCE 1

Hitler's views on the racial struggle, from *Mein Kampf*:

The Jewish people are incapable of establishing their own state. The very existence of the Jews becomes parasitic on the lives of other peoples. The ultimate goal of the Jewish struggle for survival is therefore the enslavement of productive peoples. The weapons the Jew uses for this are cunning, cleverness, subterfuge, malice, qualities that are rooted in the very essence of the Jewish ethnic character. They are tricks in his struggle for survival, like the tricks used by other peoples in combat by the sword.

Hitler's own concept of Social Darwinism was, therefore, on an all-or-nothing basis. Biologically and culturally, the Jews were to be treated as posing a deadly threat to the German Volk. There could be no compromises and no exceptions. Conversion to Christianity could make no difference, nor could medals won in the First World War. The germ had to be eliminated. This is how Himmler later justified the killing of Jewish women and children as well as men.

SOURCE 2

Hitler speaking to a Nazi Party meeting in 1920:

Do not imagine that you can combat a sickness without killing what causes it, without annihilating the germ; and do not imagine that you can combat tuberculosis without taking care to free the people from the germ that causes racial tuberculosis. The effects of Judaism will never wane and the poisoning of the people will never end until the cause, the Jews, are removed from our midst.

In the same way, the Nazi principles of 'racial hygiene' justified the sterilisation (or eliminating altogether) of the mentally and physically disabled, the Roma and other 'racial undesirables' such as homosexuals, pacifists and Jehovah's Witnesses. This theme of removing racial enemies ran through much of the more extreme Nazi propaganda of the 1920s.

The *Volksgemeinschaft*

SOURCE 3

Alfred Rosenberg, a Nazi theorist, writing in his book written in 1924 about the *Volkisch* state:

In all of Europe, only National Socialism has really taken seriously the idea of the *Volkisch* state and fought against not only the results of Marxism and parliamentary democracy but also the causes — the weak-kneed teachings of democracy and the greedy spirit of the Jews. By recognising race as a motive force, the idea of the *Volkisch* state results in the rejection of today's concept of citizenship. One may only become a citizen in the new Germany if he is free from Asiatic-Jewish blood.

Hitler's concept of the *Volksgemeinschaft* ('people's community') was not inclusive of all people living in Germany. In a way that was typical of many other aspects of Nazi ideology: the concept of the national community was twisted by anti-Semitism and racial thinking. The key word was the 'Volk'. To qualify as a member of the Volk it was essential to be a true German, both in terms of loyalty and of racial purity. To protect the Volk, it was essential to ruthlessly eliminate all un-German elements, especially the Jews. So the best way of defining the Volk came through identifying the racial enemies to be excluded from it, rather than the people who naturally belonged to it.

Membership of the *Volksgemeinschaft* – known as *Volksgenossen* (national comrades) – was reserved for those of Aryan race, members of which were expected to be genetically healthy, socially efficient and politically reliable.

A CLOSER LOOK

Groups excluded from the *Volksgemeinschaft*

The Nazis divided those who were to be excluded from the *Volksgemeinschaft* according to three criteria:

- Political enemies
- 'Asocials', i.e. people who didn't fit the social norms imposed by the Nazis
- Racial enemies, subdivided into:
- those of a different race (e.g. Jews, Gypsies)
- those with hereditary defects, such as disabilities or disease.

STUDY TIP

Two sources are from Hitler, and the third comes from a leading Nazi. They can therefore be said to give a clear insight into Nazi thinking about Jews and how they should be treated, but they are only partial 'glimpses' into Nazi ideology. With a question like this, you need to place these sources in their wider context to be able to give a balanced assessment of their value.

CROSS-REFERENCE

The wider context of Nazi ideology is discussed in Chapter 10.

 PRACTICE QUESTION

With reference to Sources 1, 2 and 3, and your contextual knowledge, assess the value of these sources to an historian studying Nazi racial ideology.

Lebensraum

The Nazi ideal of *Lebensraum* (living space) was yet another example of an ideological concept being twisted by anti-Semitism. Like Social Darwinism, the idea of *Lebensraum* was not new, nor originated by Hitler and the Nazis. In the later nineteenth century, many European thinkers had proposed opening up space for the expanding populations of the superior white race. In Germany, there was widespread support for the idea that the country was already over-populated and that industrious German farmers needed more land. Many argued that Germany's destiny lay in the east, conquering the supposedly inferior Slav peoples of Poland and the former Russian Empire to gain access to fertile farmland and raw materials.

Nazi ideology fitted in smoothly with these ideas about Germany's destiny to expand eastwards, but Hitler's concept of *Lebensraum* had a particular focus on race. *Lebensraum* would not only allow for the 'Germanisation' of the eastern lands and bringing the 'Lost Germans' back to the Reich. More importantly it would provide the battleground for a war of racial annihilation, wiping out the inferior Slav races and smashing Bolshevism in Russia.

ACTIVITY

Copy the table below. As you read the rest of this chapter, complete the blank columns.

Outsider group	Reasons for exclusion	Treatment at hands of Nazis
Mentally ill and physically disabled		
Tramps and beggars		
Homosexuals		
Religious sects		
Roma and Sinti		

Policies towards the mentally ill and physically disabled

In Nazi racial ideology, the mentally ill and physically disabled were considered to be 'biological outsiders' from the *Volksgemeinschaft* because their hereditary 'defects' made them a threat to the future of the Aryan race. Nazi thinking on the issue of mental and physical disability borrowed much from the 'science' of **eugenics**, which had become increasingly influential in Europe and the USA from the late nineteenth century and especially in the aftermath of the First World War. Declining birthrates, the loss of millions of healthy young men in war and improvements in medicine that prolonged the lives of those suffering from hereditary conditions all combined to raise concerns about the long-term health of nations. Eugenicists proposed the improvement of a race through selective breeding, which might involve the use of birth control and sterilisation of those who had hereditary 'defects'.

Sterilisation

Even before the Nazis came to power, the State government of Prussia had drawn up a draft law to allow the voluntary sterilisation of those with hereditary defects. In July 1933, the Nazis took this further by introducing the Law for Prevention of Hereditarily Diseased Progeny (Sterilisation Law), which introduced compulsory sterilisation for certain categories of 'inferiors'. This law specified the 'hereditary diseases' that sterilisation was to be applied to: congenital feeble-mindedness; schizophrenia; manic-depressive illness; epilepsy; chronic alcoholism; hereditary blindness and deafness; severe physical malformation (if proven to be hereditary). Later amendments permitted sterilisation of children over 10 years, and the use of force to carry it out after 14 years, with no right to legal representation.

Two years later, the law was amended to permit abortions in cases where those deemed suitable for sterilisation were already pregnant. In 1936, x-ray sterilisation of women over 38 years was introduced (due to the greater risk of offspring with mental and physical disabilities). In the opposite direction, there was a ban on abortion and contraception for Aryan women and girls in an attempt to increase the birth rate.

Decisions about sterilisation were made at Hereditary Health Courts. Most of the judges were strongly in favour of the sterilisation policy. The decision process often took only 10 minutes. The operation took place, by force if necessary, within two weeks. Sixty per cent of those sterilised were 'feebleminded', categorised as suffering from idiocy (IQ of 0–19) or imbecility (IQ of 20–49). The idea of 'moral insanity' was also used as a basis for sterilisation. This was often merely an excuse to prevent births among the 'criminal underclass' or 'anti-socials'.

During the Third Reich, 400,000 people were sterilised.

Euthanasia

The Nazi desire to create their 'master race' did not stop at sterilisation and banning sexual relationships between Aryans and Jews. By October 1939, the regime had authorised euthanasia for the mentally and physically disabled, regarded by the Nazis as an 'unproductive burden' on Germany's resources and as a threat to 'racial hygiene' and the 'biological strength of the Volk'.

A recurrent theme of Nazi propaganda was the idea that something had to be done about the 'burden' of the long-term ill and disabled. The openly stated solution was to pass new legislation allowing mentally and physically disabled children to be 'mercifully' put to death and so 'relieve the burden on the

KEY TERM

Eugenics: the theory that a race or group of people could be genetically improved through selective breeding, first formulated by Sir Francis Galton (Charles Darwin's cousin) in 1883

A CLOSER LOOK

Eugenics

In the decades before and after the First World War, ideas about eugenics gained support in America, Europe and especially in Scandinavia. Eugenicists suggested that 'interventions' were necessary to deal with 'handicapped' people such as the mentally ill, those with physical deformities and even homosexuals. Family planning, sterilisation (and in extreme circumstances even euthanasia) were proposed as a means of eliminating biological and social flaws. From 1899, 35 states in the USA permitted the eugenic sterilisation of mentally handicapped people.

KEY TERM

Euthanasia: intentionally ending a life to relieve pain and suffering

Fig. 2   *Dr Philipp Bouhler*

Dr Philipp Bouhler (1899–1945) served in the First World War and worked for the Nazi Party newspaper, the *Volkischer Beobachter*, in the 1920s. He became Reich secretary of the NSDAP in 1925. In 1933, he was appointed head of Hitler's party office, handling internal correspondence. He used his control over letters to Hitler to influence the decision to introduce the euthanasia programme, later known as Aktion T4, in 1939. Together with Karl Brandt, Bouhler was one of the chief architects of the killings programme. He committed suicide in 1945 to avoid arrest by American forces.

Dr Karl Brandt (1904–48) was a senior SS doctor who was a member of Hitler's inner circle. Together with Philipp Bouhler, he founded the Nazi euthanasia programme in 1939. Brandt rose to the rank of SS Major General and was appointed Reich Commissioner for Health and Sanitation. He was guilty of supervising medical experiments during the war. He was arrested in 1945 and executed for war crimes in 1948.

national community'. This idea was closely linked to the policy of sterilisation, which was a well-developed policy by 1939 and had attracted quite a lot of public support.

The first euthanasia programme for disabled children originated from one specific case of a badly disabled child early in 1939. The child's father wrote a personal letter to Hitler asking for his child, 'this creature' as he called him, to be put to sleep. **Dr Philipp Bouhler**, chief of the Führer's party office, made sure the letter was brought to Hitler's attention. Hitler sent a senior SS doctor, **Karl Brandt**, to examine the baby. Brandt's report advised euthanasia for the child. Hitler approved the report and issued a directive announcing that he would personally protect from prosecution the doctors who carried out 'mercy killings'.

This one case was the catalyst for the whole euthanasia programme. Hitler gave Philipp Bouhler authority to deal with similar cases in the future. All petitions were to go through the 'Chancellery of the Führer'. Hitler also made it clear that any such actions were to be secret. Medical staff in hospitals and asylums had to report on children suffering from mental illness or physical 'deformities'. On the basis of these reports, children were sent to special hospitals to be starved to death or given lethal injections. Parents were assured their child had died in spite of receiving the very best treatment. The technical and administrative methods used to kill more than 5000 innocent children, deemed by the Nazis to be 'incurable' and worthless to society, would be applied later to the Jews of occupied Europe. Philipp Bouhler and Karl Brandt then used their authority to extend euthanasia to adults.

A CLOSER LOOK

The T4 programme

From October 1939, the programme was rapidly expanded and later moved to new, larger headquarters in Berlin, Tiergarten 4. It was from this address that the name by which the euthanasia programme is best known, Aktion T4, originated. The basis of T4 was bureaucracy and paperwork. Forms about patients were to be filled in at clinics and asylums, and passed on to assessors, who were paid on a piecework basis to encourage them to process as many patients as possible. Those who made judgements of life and death did so without having to look the patients in the eyes, but rather simply looked at forms. Some doctors took part because they were careerists. Several doctors and nurses complained about the programme, but their objections were ignored.

The end of the T4 programme

By 1941, rumours about the policy of euthanasia were spreading widely and aroused opposition. One public official filed a complaint with the Reich Justice Ministry and also an accusation of murder against Philipp Bouhler. These proceedings got nowhere, but they worried the regime. From July 1940, there was also a groundswell of protests from the Churches. Protestant Pastor Braune wrote a long memorandum on July 1940, protesting about the T4 programme. On 12 August, Braune was arrested by the Gestapo. The Roman Catholic hierarchy made official protests behind the scenes. This led to intervention on behalf of the pope. An official statement from Rome on 2 December 1940 pronounced that the direct killing of people with mental or physical defects was against 'the natural and positive law of God'.

On 3 August 1941, Catholic Archbishop Galen of Münster preached a sermon making an emotive attack on euthanasia, backed by specific evidence provided by local congregation members. Galen's sermon was designed to mobilise mass protest in the Rhineland-Westphalia province. Thousands of copies of Galen's sermon were printed and widely distributed. As intended, this sparked further protests and public demonstrations. The Nazi regime was alarmed by the hostile public reactions. On 24 August 1941, Hitler halted the programme.

However, this was an isolated success for public protest against Nazi race policies. Archbishop Galen never took a public stance on behalf of the persecuted Jewish victims. The halting of the T4 programme in August 1941 did not mean the end of the drive to implement Nazi racial ideology; it was only a tactical pause. In many respects, the euthanasia programme provided the techniques, the trained personnel and the administrative experience for the coming 'Final Solution'.

Nazi policies towards asocials and homosexuals

Asocials

The term 'asocial', as used by the Nazis, covered a wide range of people who were deemed to be social outcasts. These included criminals, the 'work-shy', tramps and beggars, alcoholics, prostitutes, homosexuals and juvenile delinquents. Nazi policy was to introduce tough measures against these groups and to give the police more power to enforce them. As with other aspects of Nazi racial policy, the approach towards asocials hardened and became more systematic as time went on.

- In September 1933, the regime began a mass round-up of 'tramps and beggars', many of whom were young homeless, unemployed people. Since the Nazis did not have enough space in concentration camps to house all of these people (estimates of their total vary from between 300,000 and 500,000), they began to differentiate between the 'orderly' and the 'disorderly' homeless. The 'orderly', who were fit, willing to work and had no previous convictions, were given a permit and forced to work for their accommodation. The 'disorderly' were considered to be habitual criminals and sent to concentration camps.
- In 1936, before the Olympic Games were held in Berlin, the police rounded up large numbers of 'tramps and beggars' from the streets of the capital in order to project an image of a hard-working and dynamic society to the world.
- In 1936, an 'asocial colony' was set up, known as Hashude, in northern Germany. The aim of the colony was to re-educate the asocials so that they could be integrated into society.
- In 1938, there was an even bigger round-up of 'beggars, tramps, pimps and gypsies'. Most of these were sent to Buchenwald concentration camp, where few survived the harsh treatment.

A CLOSER LOOK

Concentration Camp badges

The Nazis adopted an elaborate system of badges to identify the different categories of prisoners in concentration camps. Fig. 3 shows a series of colour-coded triangles, stars (for Jewish prisoners) and other shapes for prisoners to wear on their uniforms. The categories of prisoners (from left to right) were: political enemies; habitual criminals; foreign forced labourers; 'Bible students' (e.g. Jehovah's Witnesses); homosexuals; asocials and the work-shy. The basic colours for each category are shown along the top line. Bars were placed above these triangles to denote repeat offenders and black, concentric circles identified members of penal battalions. Markings for Jews were the Star of David made of a yellow base triangle overlaid with an inverted triangle of a different colour to identify Jewish political enemies, etc. The yellow and black stars below showed special categories of 'Jewish race defilers' (e.g. Aryans who had converted to Judaism) and 'female race defilers' (i.e. Aryan women who had had sexual relations with Jews). The triangles with the letters 'P' and 'T' at the bottom showed prisoners of Polish and Czech nationality.

CROSS-REFERENCE

More information about Archbishop Galen can be found on Chapter 16, page 148.

ACTIVITY

In pairs or in groups, consider the following statement: 'The Churches failed in their moral duty to oppose the Nazis' atrocities'. To what extent do you agree or disagree with the statement?

CROSS-REFERENCE

The Final Solution is explained in Chapter 23, page 187.

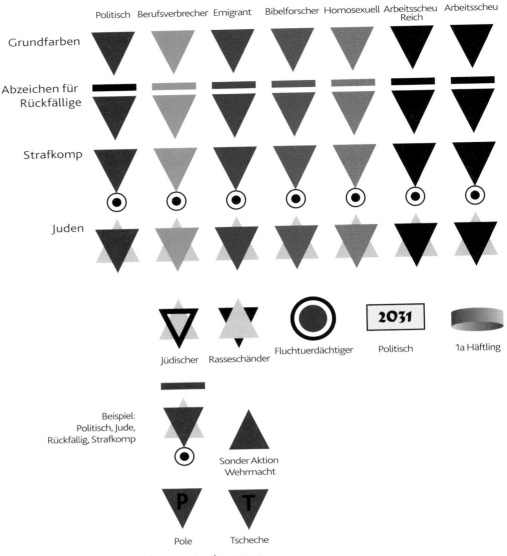

Fig. 3 *Labels for prisoners in concentration camps*

Homosexuals

In common with most other European countries at the time, homosexuality was outlawed in Germany before 1933. In the relatively liberal climate of the Weimar Republic, however, homosexuality flourished in Berlin and other large cities. Most Nazis regarded homosexuals as degenerate, perverted and a threat to the racial health of the German people.

In 1933, the Nazis began a purge of homosexual organisations and literature. Clubs were closed down, organisations for gay people were banned and gay publications were outlawed. In May 1933, Nazi students attacked the Institute of Sex Research, a gay organisation, and burned its library. They also seized the Institute's list of names and addresses of gay people. This was the beginning of a long and sustained persecution of gay people in Nazi Germany.

- In 1934, the Gestapo began to compile lists of gay people. In that same year, the SS eliminated Röhm and other leaders of the Nazi SA who were homosexuals.
- The law on homosexuality was amended in 1935 to widen the definition of homosexuality and to impose harsher penalties for those convicted. After the law was changed, over 22,000 men were arrested and imprisoned between 1936 and 1938.

- In 1936, Himmler created the Reich Office for the Combatting of Homosexuality and Abortion.
- Overall, some 100,000 men were arrested for homosexuality, of whom about 50,000 were convicted. Even when the men arrested had served their sentences, they were immediately rearrested by the Gestapo or SS and held in concentration camps under 'preventive custody'.
- In the camps, they had to wear a pink triangle to distinguish them from other prisoners and they were subjected to particularly brutal treatment by the guards.
- Many of those imprisoned were subjected to 'voluntary castration' to 'cure' them of their 'perversion'.
- Gay men who would not agree to abandon their sexual orientation were sent to concentration camps where they were subjected to unusually harsh treatment. Many were beaten to death. It has been estimated that about 60 per cent of gay prisoners died in the camps.
- Lesbians did not suffer the same degree of persecution as they were considered to be 'asocial' rather than degenerate.

Policies towards religious sects

There were a number of Christian sects that had become established in Germany by the time the Nazis came to power – the Jehovah's Witnesses, Christian Scientists, Mormons, Seventh-Day Adventists and members of the New Apostolic Church. All had international links, which aroused Nazi suspicions about their loyalties, and most were banned by the regime in November 1933. The ban on some sects, however, was lifted when they demonstrated their willingness to cooperate with the regime. Where sects were allowed to continue, however, Gestapo agents attended and reported on their services.

The Jehovah's Witnesses were the only religious group to show uncompromising hostility to the Nazi State. With around 30,000 adherents in Germany in 1933, the Jehovah's Witnesses were a small but closely knit sect. Their belief that they could only obey Jehovah (God) led them into conflict with the Nazi regime because they refused to take a loyalty oath to Hitler. They refused to give the Hitler salute, participate in Nazi parades or accept army conscription. They regarded persecution as a test of their faith and became more resistant under pressure from the regime. Many were arrested. In prison, they refused to obey orders, to attend parades or remove their caps. By 1945, around 10,000 Jehovah's Witnesses had been imprisoned and many had died. However, the regime had failed to break their resistance and the Witnesses had made some converts to their beliefs in the camps.

Unlike the Jehovah's Witnesses, the Seventh-Day Adventists gave a positive welcome to the Nazi regime, describing it as the beginning of Germany's rebirth. The ban on the sect was removed within two weeks as it agreed to display the swastika flag in its churches, conclude its services with the 'Heil Hitler' greeting and remove the so-called 'Jewish' language of the Old Testament from its services. Its well-developed welfare organisation, which provided food and shelter, agreed to exclude asocials, Jews and other 'race enemies' from receiving help.

Other sects also strove to make the necessary compromises with the regime in order to ensure their survival. The Mormons' welfare organisation, like that of the Seventh-Day Adventists, selected its recipients according to Nazi criteria. The New Apostolic Church incorporated SS and SA flags into its church parades.

Policies towards the Roma and the Sinti

Jews were not the only victims of the intensification of Nazi race policies after 1935. There was also growing persecution of Germany's 30,000 gypsies (Roma and Sinti people), known in Germany as *Zigeuner*. Gypsies had been subjected to

ACTIVITY

Discussion point

'The compromises made by religious sects to ensure their survival was the only sensible course of action for them to follow.'

A CLOSER LOOK

The Roma and Sinti are two gypsy tribes. Gypsies are believed to have arrived in Europe from northern India in the fifteenth century and were called Gypsies because Europeans thought they came from Egypt. Gypsies are made up of distinct 'tribes' or 'nations'. The Sinti generally predominated in Germany and Western Europe, and the Roma in Austria, Eastern Europe and the Balkans.

legal discrimination well before 1933. Local authorities frequently harassed them into moving away. The Nazis made the persecution much more systematic.

A directive from Himmler on the treatment of gypsies, issued in December 1938:

Experience gained in combating the Gypsy nuisance, and knowledge derived from race-biological research, have shown that the proper method of attacking the Gypsy problem seems to be to treat it as a matter of race. Experience shows that part-Gypsies play the greatest role in Gypsy criminality. On the other hand, it has been shown that efforts to make the Gypsies settle have been unsuccessful, especially in the case of pure Gypsies, on account of their strong compulsion to wander. It has therefore become necessary to distinguish between pure and part-Gypsies in the final solution to the Gypsy question.

The aim of the measures taken by the State to defend the homogeneity of the German nation must be the physical separation of Gypsydom from the German people and the regulation of the Gypsy way of life. The necessary legal foundation can only be created through a Gypsy Law which prevents further intermingling of blood.

ACTIVITY

Evaluating primary sources

In what ways does Source 4 reflect Nazi racial ideology?

CROSS-REFERENCE

The Nuremberg Laws of 1935, which further extended the Nazi's anti-Semitic legislation, are dealt with in Chapter 18, pages 152–154.

In 1935, Nazi legal experts ruled that the Nuremberg Laws applied to Gypsies, even though they were not specifically mentioned in the laws. In 1936, the SS set up a new Reich Central Office for the Fight Against the Gypsy Nuisance. A university psychologist, Dr Robert Ritter, became the expert 'scientific adviser' to the SS and the Ministry of Health. Using Ritter's criteria, the SS began the process of locating and classifying Gypsies. The centralised files they collected were essential to facilitate police action against them. Ritter was particularly concerned to identify and isolate those whose heritage was part-Gypsy (the 'so-called *Mischlinge*, or 'mongrels') and who had become fully integrated into German society, since they represented a threat to the Aryan racial purity.

In December 1938, Himmler issued a Decree for the Struggle against the Gypsy Plague, which led to a more systematic classification of Gypsies. After war broke out in September 1939, Gypsies were deported from Germany to Poland.

Summary

The treatment of various groups excluded from the Nazi concept of *Volsksgemeinschaft* was a stark illustration of the Nazi belief that the individual counted for nothing when the interests of the community were at stake. In the Third Reich, the all-powerful State could, and did, take action to exclude those it considered to be political, social or racial enemies of the People's Community. These groups were subjected to increasing levels of discrimination and persecution as the Nazis began to feel more secure and confident in their hold on power. After 1938, Nazi racial policy became more radical and the use of euthanasia against the mentally and physically disabled prefigured the policy of extermination applied to Jews after 1942.

STUDY TIP

It is important to give a clear definition of the concept of *Volksgemeinschaft* when answering a question like this. There are various ways to approach this, but you could for example, focus on the extent to which *Volksgemeinschaft* was more about exclusion than inclusion. Try to cover a broad range of Nazi social policies, using the information in Chapter 14 as well as this chapter.

 PRACTICE QUESTION

'The Nazi concept of *Volksgemeinschaft* was primarily a means of justifying the systematic persecution of minority groups in German society.' Assess the validity of this view.

18 Nazi policies towards the Jews, 1933–37

SOURCE 1

Bea Green, a German Jewish schoolgirl in 1933, later recounted the experience of her father at the hands of the SA (Brownshirts) in *The Holocaust*, an account of the Jewish experience during World War II:

One day in March 1933, my father, who was a lawyer, went to the police headquarters in order to lay a complaint on behalf of one of his Jewish clients who owned one of the big stores in Munich and who had been arrested. When he got there, somebody directed him to a room in the basement. It was full of Brownshirt thugs who proceeded to beat him up. They knocked his teeth in and burst his eardrums. The one thing my father was worried about was that they would damage his kidneys. So he held his arms against his back and of course that meant his head was unprotected. They then cut off his trouser legs and took off his shoes and socks and hung a placard around his neck with the notice, 'I'm a Jew and I will never complain to the Nazis again.' They led him around Munich like that.

Between 1933 and 1939, the Nazi regime began an intensive campaign of persecution and legal discrimination against Jews in Germany. To carry out Nazi policies towards the Jews, Hitler needed to steer a careful course, emphasising legality. During this period, Hitler and the Nazi leadership set about a scheme of anti-Semitic legislation. At the same time, a relentless propaganda campaign was launched to 'educate' the German people about the need to purge Jewish influences from German society.

Fig. 1   *SA man imposes the boycott of Jewish shops, with a sign reading 'Germans! Defend yourselves! Do not buy from Jews!'*

The boycott of Jewish shops

On 1 April 1933, the Nazi regime imposed a boycott of Jewish shops and businesses. Hitler claimed that this action was justified retaliation against Jews in Germany and abroad who had called for a boycott of German goods. Goebbels organised an intensive propaganda campaign to maximise the impact of the boycott, which was carried out by gangs of brown-shirted SA

LEARNING OBJECTIVES

In this chapter you will learn about:

- the boycott of Jewish shops and businesses in 1933
- further anti-Semitic policies and legislation
- the Nuremberg Laws of 1935
- growing action against the Jews.

ACTIVITY

Evaluating primary sources

What can an historian learn from Source 1 about the Nazis' attitude towards the law?

CROSS-REFERENCE

For an explanation of the reasons for anti-Semitism refer back to Chapter 17.

KEY CHRONOLOGY

Anti-Semitic legislation, 1933–35

1933
April   Boycott of Jewish shops and businesses

Law for the Restoration of the Professional Civil Service

Law against Overcrowding of German Schools and Universities

October   Exclusion of German Jews from the press

1935
September The Nuremberg Laws
November   Supplementary Decree on the Reich Citizenship Law

CROSS-REFERENCE

For further information on Goebbels, refer back to Chapter 10, page 79.

men. The SA marked out which places of business were to be targeted and stood menacingly outside to intimidate would-be customers.

Shops were the main target of the boycott, but it also applied to Jewish professionals such as doctors and lawyers. Court proceedings involving Jewish lawyers and judges were disrupted in Berlin, Breslau and elsewhere. Many Jewish lawyers were attacked in the street and had their legal robes stripped from them. Jewish doctors, school teachers and university lecturers were also subject to similar rough treatment by the SA.

John Silberman was a German Jewish schoolboy in Berlin. In 2005, he gave an account of his experiences for a book of oral histories:

My father's business simply died. Nobody would trade with Jews: you couldn't get supplies, customers, and you couldn't get staff to work for you. If you did you were at their mercy; they could do as they liked – they could steal, they could rob and there was no remedy. A Jew had no rights. I remember that my parents' Gentile friends did not stand by them.

The boycott made a big public impact and featured prominently in news coverage both in Germany and in foreign countries, but it was not an unqualified success. It was unclear in many cases what was a 'Jewish' business and what wasn't. Many businesses were half-Jewish or half-German in ownership; many others were controlled by foreign creditors or German banks. A number of German citizens defiantly used Jewish shops to show their disapproval of Nazi policies. The boycott was abandoned after only one day, even though the SA had hoped it would last indefinitely.

At the time, the boycott seemed to show the unleashing of Nazi violence by an aggressive new dictatorship flaunting its power just a week after the passing of the Enabling Act. The real situation was rather different. Hitler was not at all enthusiastic about a 'revolution from below' bringing chaos in Germany. He was anxious to keep the SA under control and he was genuinely concerned about adverse reactions from his conservative allies in Germany or from foreign public opinion.

It is possible that Hitler only ever intended the boycott to be a brief affair. From this perspective, Hitler allowed the boycott to go ahead only as a limited, grudging concession to the radical activists. His main aim was to avoid instability while he carried through his 'legal revolution'. However, Hitler was willing to allow a considerable degree of Nazi intimidation. It was useful to him as an expression of 'spontaneous public anger' that only his new government could satisfy. For Hitler, anti-Semitic violence was a two-edged sword. Just enough and the Nazis could claim that only they could maintain order in an unstable Germany; too much and Hitler's position might be threatened by the conservative elites on whom he still depended.

The Civil Service Laws in 1933

In April 1933, the Nazi regime introduced the Law for the Restoration of the Professional Civil Service, requiring Jews to be dismissed from the Civil Service. This was not as straightforward as the Nazis hoped. There was no objective, scientific definition of who was racially Jewish according to physical characteristics or blood group. Under the 1933 law, people were considered 'non-Aryan' if either of their parents or either of their grandparents were Jewish. Another difficulty was that President Hindenburg insisted on exemptions for German Jews who had served in the First World War and for

ACTIVITY

Using the evidence of Source 2 and your own knowledge, make a list of three reasons why Jews like John Silberman's father experienced the difficulties they did.

CROSS-REFERENCE

The Enabling Act was a law that allowed Hitler to make laws without the approval of the Reichstag and without reference to the President. It is discussed in more detail in Chapter 12, page 95.

ACTIVITY

Group work

Working in two groups, assemble a range of evidence to support the views that:
- organised violence against Jews strengthened the Nazi regime in 1933
- uncontrolled violence against Jews in 1933 showed that Hitler was not in full control of the Nazi movement.

those whose fathers had been killed in the war. Hitler reluctantly accepted this as a political necessity and the exemption was kept in place until after Hindenburg's death in 1934. The exemptions amendment lessened the law's impact because it applied to up to two thirds of Jews in the Civil Service.

The Civil Service Law had a devastating economic and psychological impact on middle-class Jews in Germany and contributed to the increasing levels of Jewish emigration. In 1933, 37,000 Jews left Germany. Most Jews, however, stayed behind. At that time, they could not know how much worse the persecution would become.

Further anti-Semitic legislation in 1933

Similar laws were passed after the Law for the Restoration of the Professional Civil Service, aimed at excluding Jews from the professions. These measures were not as effective as the Nazis would have hoped, partly because there were exemptions for those who had fought in the First World War and partly because Jews in medicine, the law and education were numerous and well-established, so it was not feasible to remove them all at once.

The legal profession

Jewish lawyers made up about 16 per cent of Germany's legal profession, often working in family firms. Of the non-Aryan lawyers practising in 1933, 60 per cent were able to continue working in spite of the new regulations. In the years that followed, the regime introduced stricter regulations to try to close these 'loopholes'. The exclusion of lawyers was a gradual process over several years.

Doctors

More than ten per cent of German doctors were Jews. They were attacked by Nazi propaganda as 'a danger to German society'. Nazi officials at local government level and in private associations initiated their own anti-Semitic measures. Some local authorities started removing Jewish doctors from their posts. Anti-Semitic propaganda against Jewish doctors treating Aryans was laced with lurid stories about inappropriate and malicious actions supposedly carried out by Jewish doctors. The Nazi regime was pushed along by these local initiatives. The regime announced a ban on Jewish doctors in April 1933. In theory, Jewish doctors could now treat only Jewish patients, but many Jewish doctors carried on their normal practice for several years after 1933.

Education

Also in April 1933, the Law against Overcrowding of German Schools and Universities restricted the number of Jewish children who could attend state schools and universities. It was promoted on the basis that Aryan students would receive more resources and attention, instead of wasting time and money on pupils who would 'grow up to be enemies of Germany'. Nazi propaganda stressed the danger that a well-educated Jew would be a greater threat to Germany than an uneducated one. German children were being told that their former friends and classmates were unworthy of being in the same schools as them and that they were a burden and threat to Germany.

Not all Jewish children were forced out of state schools at this point. The process was not completed until 1938. Jewish children could also still attend private education and Jewish schools (which were one of the few places Jewish teachers could find work). These schools had many problems in gaining funding and in maintaining academic standards, but Jewish children were not yet completely denied an education. The key aim of the Nazis, of course, was the segregation of Jewish children from Aryan children.

Fig. 2 *A cartoon of Jewish children being expelled from a German school; why do you think the Jewish boy on the right has been shown pulling the Aryan girl's hair?*

In the universities, many Jewish professors came under pressure from students and local government officials. Many lost their jobs. German academics willingly seized the opportunity to replace them.

The press

In October 1933, the Reich Press Law enabled the regime to apply strict censorship and to close down publications they disliked. Jews had had a prominent role in journalism and publishing in Weimar Germany, and the Press Law effectively silenced the large number of Jewish journalists and editors, many of whom were forced to leave the country. The closing down of the free press was not only a matter of laws and regulations; there were also many instances of violence and intimidation.

The Nuremberg Laws, 1935

In 1935, the Nazi regime extended the anti-Semitic legislation through the Nuremberg Laws, so called because they were announced at the annual party rally at Nuremberg. By 1935, many fanatical anti-Semites in the Nazi movement were restless because they believed Nazi persecution of the Jews had not gone far enough. They urged Hitler to move further and faster. These radicals became the driving force behind the demands for anti-Jewish legislation. At the Nuremberg Party Rally in 1935, Hitler announced that the Communist International had declared war on Nazism and that it was time to 'deal once and for all with Jewish-Bolshevism'.

On 15 September, the Nuremberg Laws were introduced:

- The Reich Citizenship Law meant that someone could be a German citizen only if they had purely German blood. Jews and other non-Aryans were now classified as subjects and had fewer rights than citizens.
- The Law for the Protection of German Blood and Honour outlawed marriage between Aryans and non-Aryans. It was made illegal for German citizens to marry Jews. It was also illegal for Jews to have any sexual relations with a German citizen.

The laws made the enforcing of anti-Semitism the major concern of civil servants, judges and the Gestapo.

The law was later extended to cover almost any physical contact between Jews and Aryans. The mere fact of an allegation was enough to secure a conviction. Aryan women were pressured to leave their Jewish husbands, on the grounds that men who lost their jobs through anti-Semitic legislation would be a burden on their partners. Although some relationships continued, there was a high risk of being denounced to the Gestapo. Punishments were harsh and Jewish men convicted under the terms of the Law for the Protection of German Blood and Honour were often re-arrested by the Gestapo after being released and then sent to concentration camps.

In November 1935, the First Supplementary Decree on the Reich Citizenship Law defined what constituted a 'full Jew' – someone who had three Jewish grandparents, or who had two Jewish grandparents and was married to a Jew. 'Half Jews' were labelled ***Mischlinge***. The law was difficult to interpret as the definition of a Jew was based on the number of Jewish grandparents. In many cases, Jews or their Jewish parents had converted to Christianity. This confused situation meant that legal classifications were often arbitrary and inconsistent.

The position of Jews without the rights of citizenship left them with obligations to the state, but with no political rights and powerless against the Nazi bureaucracy. Possessing documentary proof of a person's ancestry became a high priority for many people. Many non-practising Jews attempted to prove their Aryan ancestry; some acquired falsified documents on the black market. There was further discrimination by local authorities and private companies that would not employ Jews, although *Mischlinge* were able to continue relatively 'normal' lives and could even serve in the lower ranks of the military.

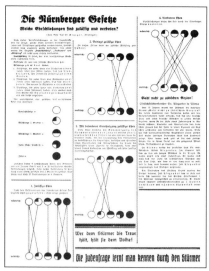

Fig. 3 *A poster explaining the Nuremberg Law for the Protection of German Blood and German Honour*

Mischlinge: meaning 'crossbreed' in German, Nazis used this term to denote persons with both Aryan and Jewish ancestry

 PRACTICE QUESTION

'By 1935, the Nazis had effectively excluded the Jews from German society.' Assess the validity of this view.

This question is about the extent of Nazi anti-Jewish legislation in the years 1933–35, and its impact on Germany's Jewish population. There is scope for a balanced assessment, but be sure to offer a clear view and argue for it consistently through the answer.

Discrimination

SOURCE 3

An extract from a Bavarian police report, 1935:

On the same day (14 July 1935), there were anti-Jewish demonstrations in the swimming pool in Heigenbruken, Bezirksamt Aschaffenburg. Approximately 15–20 young bathers had demanded the removal of the Jews from the swimming bath by chanting in the park which adjoins the baths. The chant went: 'These are German baths, Jews are not allowed in, out with them' and such like. A considerable number of other bathers joined in the chanting so that probably the majority of visitors were demanding the removal of the Jews.

Discrimination against Jews occurred all over Germany as a result of local interventions like the one described in Source 3. In this instance, local agitation resulted in the Mayor issuing a ban on Jews using the swimming pool. It was a similar picture elsewhere. Pubs and other businesses put up signs saying that Jews were not welcome. Pro-Nazi activists took the lead in pushing for anti-Jewish measures in local schools, village committees and almost all areas of public life.

Evidence suggests that these signs were often displayed to keep Nazi officials happy rather than to stop Jews from using the establishments. One Jewish customer was assured that a sign in his local pub was just there for show and he should ignore it. In other places, however, the discrimination against Jews was very real. Albert Herzfeld, a middle-class Jew who had served in the German army, was barred from his artists' club in 1935. Later, Herzfeld was barred from his favourite restaurants and the spa in Wiesbaden.

Many Germans were embarrassed by overt discrimination. Such people were reluctant, for example, to break off from family doctors they had relied on for years, or were appalled to see literary classics seen as Jewish purged from the local library. When Nazi activists in Leipzig demanded the removal of a statue to the great composer Felix Mendelssohn, even the local party boss drew the line and blocked the proposal. Open opposition to discrimination was rare. Most people who were unhappy about the discrimination kept their heads down and retreated into '**internal exile**'.

SOURCE 4

A Sopade report from Saxony in September 1935:

The Jewish laws are not taken very seriously because the population has other problems on its mind and is mostly of the opinion that the whole fuss about the Jews is only being made to divert people's attention from other things. But one must not imagine that the anti-Jewish agitation does not have the desired effect on many people. On the contrary, there are many people who are influenced by the defamation of the Jews and regard the Jews as the originators of many bad things. But the vast majority of the people ignore this defamation of the Jews; they even openly buy in Jewish department stores.

 PRACTICE QUESTION

Evaluating primary sources

With reference to Sources 1, 3 and 4 assess the value of these sources to an historian studying discrimination towards the Jews in the years 1933 to 1937.

Summary

The boycott of Jewish shops, the Civil Service Laws and the Nuremberg Laws deepened the influence of anti-Semitism in German society. Nazi radicals were delighted whilst many, otherwise moderate, Germans did not see the measures as being too extreme. On the one hand, some claimed that discrimination in public areas through signs such as 'Jews not wanted here' was little different from segregation in the southern states of the USA. On the other hand, many Germans were troubled by the anti-Semitic legislation. Evidence from both Gestapo records and the Sopade reports suggest that German public opinion was not fully in support of the Nuremberg Laws. There was no public outcry, but this probably owed more to passivity, fear and propaganda than any great enthusiasm for the laws.

19 The development of anti-Semitic policies, 1938–40

Anti-Semitic policies

1938	April	Registration of Jewish assets over 5000 marks
	October	Jewish passports stamped with a large 'J'
	November	Jews forbidden to visit theatres, etc.
		Reichkristallnacht
		Expulsion of all Jewish pupils from schools
	December	Compulsory sale of all Jewish businesses
1939	September	German invasion of Poland
		Ghettoisation of Jews in Poland
	October	Euthanasia programme authorised by Hitler
	November	Jews in occupied Poland made to wear Star of David
1940	April	German invasion of Western Europe

LEARNING OBJECTIVES

In this chapter you will learn about:

the growth of anti-Semitism in relation to

- the effect of the *Anschluss* with Austria
- Reichkristallnacht
- attempts to encourage Jewish emigration
- the impact of the war against Poland
- The Madagascar Plan.

The effect of the *Anschluss* with Austria, March 1938

Although the *Anschluss* (union) with Austria was banned under the Treaty of Versailles, it was a long-term ambition of German nationalists and was achieved in March 1938. The German takeover of Austria was achieved without a shot being fired and German troops were welcomed enthusiastically by the Austrian people. This 'bloodless victory' further emboldened Hitler and the Nazi leadership to pursue their ambitions in foreign policy and to adopt more radical racial policies in the Greater Germany they had created.

A CLOSER LOOK

The *Anschluss* with Austria

A union between Germany and Austria (Hitler's birthplace and formerly a part of Germany) into a greater Germany was one of Hitler's key aims, although it had been prohibited by the Treaty of Versailles. In the years after 1933, Hitler encouraged Nazi groups in Austria to agitate for union but the Austrian government banned Nazi demonstrations and called a plebiscite in March 1938 to show that the majority of Austrians were opposed to union. When it became clear that Britain, France and Italy would not intervene to support Austrian independence, the government resigned and Hitler ordered the German army to invade.

Hitler's foreign policy aims to create a 'Racial State'

Hitler had long made clear his ambitions for Germany. These included:

- an end to the restrictions of the Treaty of Versailles on Germany's armed forces and its territorial expansion
- the creation of a Greater Germany which would 're-unite' Germans living in Austria, Czechoslovakia and Poland with the Reich
- the acquisition of land in the east to give *Lebensraum* to the Aryans, as a superior race.

Fig. 1 *Soldiers receive gifts from Austrian women after the* Anschluss, *1938*

CROSS-REFERENCE

The aim of the Four Year Plan in 1936 was to make Germany ready for war within four years. It is explained in Chapter 15, page 123.

Further information on Blomberg can be found in Chapter 12, page 91. More on Fritsch can be found in Chapter 14, page 116.

KEY TERM

Aryanisation: Nazi policy of removing all Jews and other non-Aryans from key aspects of Germany's cultural and economic life; the policy was designed to lead ultimately to the complete expulsion of non-Aryans from Germany

By 1938, therefore, Hitler was growing in confidence that Germany was ready for war if necessary and that the Allied powers lacked the resolve to act against him. After his 'bloodless victory' in Austria, his next target was Czechoslovakia, which included a large German minority living in the area known as the Sudetenland. In September 1938, Hitler risked war with Britain and France over his demand for the Sudetenland to be handed over to Germany. Once again, he achieved a 'bloodless victory' after Britain and France agreed to the German takeover. In March 1939, he achieved another success with the occupation of the rest of Czechoslovakia. In August 1939, Nazi Germany and Soviet Russia signed a non-aggression pact (known as the Nazi-Soviet Pact) under which the USSR agreed not to oppose the German invasion of Poland. This invasion followed on 1 September 1939, which led to war between Germany and Britain and France two days later.

The more radical phase of Nazi anti-Semitism was part of the more general radicalising of the regime's policies, which began in the winter of 1937–38. By late 1937, the Four Year Plan was beginning to improve both the economic and the military situation in Germany. Those who had been urging caution – Schacht in economic policy and Blomberg and Fritsch in the military – were swept aside and the balance of power in the regime shifted towards the more radical elements in the Nazi Party. Schacht had argued strongly against radical anti-Semitism in the economic field because he did not want to alienate foreign investors. Goering, in charge of the Four Year Plan, did not care about foreign opinion and was determined to remove Jews from businesses as soon as possible. The occupation of Austria in March 1938 led to a rapid acceleration of the economic campaign against Jews as the Nazis in Austria were allowed to act against Jews without constraint. This prompted Goering to take more radical action in Germany itself.

Anti-Semitic decrees, April to November 1938

In April 1938, the Decree of Registration of Jewish Property provided for the confiscation of all Jewish-owned property worth more than 5000 marks. This was the starting point for the **Aryanisation** of Jewish property and businesses. In April 1938, there were roughly 40,000 Jewish-owned businesses in Germany; a year later only around 8000 had avoided being closed down or 'Aryanised'.

Fig. 2 *Jews are made to clean the streets of Vienna after the* Anschluss, *1938*

A CLOSER LOOK

Nazi persecution of Jews in Austria

There were 183,000 Jews living in Austria at the time of the Nazi takeover. Overnight, they were subjected to the loss of their rights, property and employment, and to physical assaults. Within a month, over 500 Jews had committed suicide in Austria. Thousands more decided to emigrate to escape Nazi persecution. More than 1500 were sent to Dachau and Buchenwald concentration camps in Germany during 1938.

Further legislation banned Jews from work as travelling salesmen, security guards, travel agents and estate agents – 30,000 Jewish travelling salesmen lost their jobs. In 1938, Jews also lost their entitlement to public welfare. The increasing number of unemployed and poor Jews depended completely on the charities set up by the Jewish community, such as the Central Institution for Jewish Economic Aid.

From October 1938, the passports of German Jews had to be stamped with a large 'J'. The drive to make Jews easily identifiable and, at the same time, strip them of their individuality led to a new law in 1939 – Jews that were deemed to have non-Jewish names had to change them. Jewish women had to take the name 'Sarah' and Jewish men had to take the name 'Israel'. At this stage, Hitler turned down the suggestion of making all Jews wear a yellow star in public – this did not come into practice within the Reich until 1941.

Reichkristallnacht, 9–10 November 1938

Between 1933 and 1938, Jews in Germany were subjected to increasing pressure of persecution, through anti-Semitic legislation, propaganda and the growing power of the police state. For many Jews, however, it was still possible to carry on some kind of normal existence. However, all this was changed on Reichkristallnacht (the Night of the Broken Glass) on 9–10 November. Jewish homes and businesses were looted and vandalised, synagogues were set ablaze and thousands of Jews were arrested, beaten up and killed.

Pogrom: an organised massacre of an ethnic group; the Reichkristallnacht pogrom was not the first massacre against Jews in Europe – there had been a number of pogroms against Jews living in the Russian Empire during the nineteenth century

CROSS-REFERENCE

The boycott of the SA is covered in Chapter 12.

ACTIVITY

Evaluating primary sources

Assess the value of Source 1 for an historian studying Reichkristallnacht.

The Reichkristallnacht **pogrom** can be viewed as an uncontrolled outpouring of anti-Semitic feeling amongst radical elements of the Nazi movement, partly supported by German public opinion. Certainly this was the view put out by Nazi propaganda, which announced that 'the National Soul has boiled over'. It is also true that some people in the Nazi hierarchy were concerned about the violence running out of control. In the days after the pogrom, Hitler gave Hermann Goering a coordinating role to 'sort things out'. From this point of view, it might appear that the situation in November 1938 was similar to that of April 1933, when the regime had to rein in the SA boycott.

In reality, Reichkristallnacht was orchestrated by the Nazi leadership and the majority of those involved in the violence and vandalism were SA and SS men who had been instructed not to wear uniforms. The Nazis seized the opportunity presented by the murder of Ernst vom Rath on 9 November. Rath was a minor German official in Paris who was killed by Herschel Grynszpan, a young Polish Jew angry at the treatment of his parents by the Nazi regime. The killing of vom Rath was more an excuse for unleashing anti-Jewish terror than the real cause.

The chief instigator of the pogrom was Joseph Goebbels. He gave instructions to the Nazi officials in the regions to organise the violence and vandalism, but to be careful to make it appear that it was not orchestrated by the Nazi Party. The fifteenth anniversary of the 1923 Munich Putsch was on 9 November and Goebbels hoped to please Hitler by marking the occasion with a spectacular event.

In the violence, 91 Jews were killed and thousands injured. There was looting of cash, silver, jewellery and works of art. Damage to shops and businesses amounted to millions of marks. Much of the vandalism was purely destructive, not for gain. Orders from the SS directed the police not to intervene against the demonstrators; they were ordered to place 20,000–30,000 Jews in 'preventive' detention. The fire brigades watched and did nothing as synagogues burned to the ground; their only concern was to stop the fires spreading to other buildings.

SOURCE 1

An extract from the Nazi Party Supreme Court report into Reichkristallnacht, issued in February 1939:

The first known case of the killing of a Jew, a Polish citizen, was reported to Dr Goebbels on 10 November at about 2 o'clock and in this connection the opinion was expressed that something would have to be done in order to prevent the whole thing from taking a dangerous turn. Dr Goebbels replied that the informant should not get excited about one dead Jew, and that in the next few days thousands of Jews would see the point. At that time most of the killings could still have been prevented by an official order. Since this did not happen, it must be deduced from that fact as well as from the remark itself that the final result was intended or at least considered possible and desirable.

The anti-Jewish violence of November 1938 was not received with universal approval in Germany. Some ordinary citizens joined in the violence, looting alongside SA thugs who were equipped with crowbars, hammers, axes and petrol bombs, but many German people were horrified by the destruction. In Leipzig, the American consul reported that silent crowds of local people were 'benumbed and aghast' at the sight of the burned-out synagogue and the looted shops the next morning. In Hamburg, a young mother, Christabel Bielenberg, witnessed similar crowds of pedestrians appalled by what they saw, murmuring quietly to each other: '*Schlimm. Schlimm.*' (It's terrible). A British official in Berlin claimed 'he had not met a single German from any walk of

Fig. 3 *Attacks on Jewish property on Reichkristallnacht*

life who does not disapprove to some degree of what has occurred.' All over Germany, the great majority of people understood that the violence was not spontaneous but organised by the State.

The events of the night of 9–10 November 1938 were a watershed for Jews in Nazi Germany. Hermann Goering pronounced, 'Now the gloves are off.' In the aftermath of Reichkristallnacht, Goering moved quickly to prevent insurance companies from paying out compensation to Jewish victims. The 'Decree for the Restoration of the Street Scene' in relation to Jewish business premises meant that the Jews had to pick up the costs of repairs. The Jewish community was also made to make a 1 billion Reichsmark contribution in compensation for the disruption to the economy. The Decree Excluding Jews from German Economic Life was issued on 12 November and the Aryanisation of Jewish businesses was accelerated.

Emigration

From the early days of the Nazi movement, Hitler had spoken of making Germany *Judenfrei*, or 'Jew free'. The culmination of this ideology was the mass killings of the Holocaust, but the first method of achieving it was through voluntary emigration. As war approached and the Nazi regime moved to more radical policies, the focus moved to forced emigration. From late 1938 until the autumn of 1941, emigration was seen as the 'solution to the Jewish problem' by the Nazi leadership.

Voluntary emigration

The Nazi regime allowed for Jewish emigration, but strictly controlled it. In 1933, 37,000 Jews left Germany, including many leading scientists and cultural figures. Perhaps the most prominent was Albert Einstein, world-famous for his work on the theory of relativity. Einstein described the German people as having a 'psychic illness of the masses'. Overall, 150,000 Jews voluntarily left Germany between March 1933 and November 1938. The question of whether to leave or stay was agonising and Jews frequently disagreed among themselves about the issue of emigration.

The situation was made even more confusing by the fact that the Nazis were both encouraging the Jews to emigrate and threatening to confiscate some of their assets. For those with skills that were easily transferable to other countries, the decision was easier; the same was true of those who had family members living in another country. The Nazis were also willing to encourage **Zionists** to emigrate to Palestine, then under British rule. The majority of German Jews were not Zionists and did not choose this option.

Most German Jews, especially the older generation, felt thoroughly German and wanted to stay. Many Jews believed that the Nazi persecution was just one more example of the surges of anti-Semitism that had come and gone in the past.

Making the Reich 'Jew free' through emigration was not straightforward. It was difficult to find foreign countries willing to accept large numbers of Jews, as many countries had begun to raise barriers to limit Jewish immigration. Even Palestine could only receive a limited number, partly because the British, who controlled it, were worried about Arab hostility to mass Jewish immigration. Nazi policies were also contradictory, pressuring people to emigrate but, at the same time, making it harder for them to do so by stripping them of their wealth.

The situation became more urgent after Reichkristallnacht. Many Jews now desperately sought safe refuge from the obvious dangers they faced in Germany. Jewish parents were particularly keen to get their children out of Germany and to safe countries. For example, 9000 Jewish children were sent to Britain in 1938–39.

Fig. 4   *German-occupied Poland*

Controlled emigration

Controlling emigration was a key policy aim of the Nazi regime, not least because it enabled massive economic exploitation. After the *Anschluss* in March 1938, **Reinhard Heydrich** used Austria as a laboratory for developing SS policy. The Central Office for Jewish Emigration was set up; 45,000 of Austria's 180,000 Jews had been forced to emigrate. The illegal seizure of Jewish property was used to fund the emigration of poorer Jews.

In January 1939, Heydrich took charge of the Reich Office for Jewish Emigration, with the task of promoting the emigration of Jews 'by every possible means'. Goering's claims to have jurisdiction over Jewish affairs were bypassed. The SD set about amalgamating all Jewish organisations into a single 'Reich Association of the Jews in Germany'. The organisation was modelled on methods used in Austria by the SS emigration expert **Adolf Eichmann** in 1938. This system suited the Nazis because organisational difficulties had to be dealt with by the Jews themselves.

The impact of the war against Poland

The situation changed with the outbreak of war in September 1939. The German conquest of western Poland provided the regime with new territories in which Jews could be settled. It also brought many more Jews under Nazi rule. The emphasis moved away from forced emigration to deportations and the 'resettlement' of Jews. From September 1939, Nazi race policies were shaped by war. Nazi anti-Semitism had already become more blatant and extreme by 1938, but it was war that brought about the final radicalisation of race policies. War provided the regime with:

- a national emergency that enabled them to act with more dictatorial power and in greater secrecy
- a propaganda machine to whip up patriotism and hatred of Germany's enemies
- new territories to the Reich under the expanding bureaucratic power of the SS
- a way for the Germanisation of the occupied territories in Poland and a 'Jew-free' Nazi empire.

The conquest of Poland carved the country up into three separate areas. Eastern Poland was occupied by the USSR, in accordance with the Nazi-Soviet Pact of August 1939. The western parts of Poland, Upper Silesia, West Prussia and the Warthegau were incorporated into the German Reich and placed under the rule of Nazi *Gauleiters*. The area in between was designated the '**General Government**' of Poland, under a Nazi Governor, Hans Frank. The Nazi master plan was to create *Lebensraum* for ethnic Germans by driving Poles and Jews out of West Prussia and the Warthegau so that the 'empty' lands could be completely 'Germanised'.

However, the conquest of Poland also enormously increased the number of Jews under Nazi control. According to the official census in Poland in 1931, there were 3,115,000 Jews in Poland, of whom 1,901,000 (61 per cent) were in the territory occupied by Germany at the end of 1939. These Polish Jews were different from the assimilated Jews in Germany. They were in the main poor and more Orthodox. In appearance they fitted the Nazi stereotype of racially inferior *Untermenschen*. Their sheer numbers posed difficult strategic problems for the Nazi regime.

CROSS-REFERENCE

The 'Final Solution' is outlined in Chapter 23, page 187.

KEY PROFILE

Reinhard Heydrich (1904–42) was the most important senior commander in the SS after Himmler. He played a vital role in organising the Reich Security Head Office. In 1941, he was responsible for coordinating the 'Final Solution' and the plans launched at the Wannsee Conference in January 1942 were code-named 'Operation Reinhard'. Heydrich was also Reich Protector of Bohemia and Moravia, governing the Czech territories incorporated into the Reich. In July 1942, Heydrich was assassinated by Jewish partisans trained in Britain.

KEY PROFILE

Adolf Eichmann (1899–1961) rose to prominence in the Race and Resettlement Unit of the SS. He was involved in planning for Jewish emigration to Palestine in the 1930s, but later became one of the architects of the 'Final Solution'. Eichmann had a key role in arranging the 1942 Wannsee Conference and was the main driving force behind the deportation and mass murder of Hungarian Jews in 1944. After the war, he escaped to South America. In 1961, Israeli secret agents kidnapped him. He was brought back to face trial as a war criminal and was sentenced to death.

KEY TERM

General Government: the area of Poland occupied by the Nazis in 1939 that was not incorporated into the German Reich but controlled as a semi-autonomous area under Governor Hans Frank; it became a dumping ground for Jews deported from the Reich; most of the death camps that were built in 1941–42 were located within the General Government

SOURCE 2

An extract from a report written by the SS chief of the Kracow district (also known as Cracow) of Poland in January 1940:

Attention must be drawn to the large number of evacuees from Posen and the Warthegau who are incapable of work. Further difficulties have been created by the uncoordinated direction of the trains. Thus, trainloads of Jews and townspeople were directed to rural districts, whereas transports with peasants arrived in the towns. Thus, transports of women and children were placed in overcrowded and unheated cattle trucks without even the minimum provisions necessary. As a result there were many deaths during the journeys and a large number of physical injuries and cases of frostbite.

The Nazis intended to use the General Government district as a dumping ground for Poles and Jews displaced from the areas that were to be colonised by ethnic Germans. At the end of September, Hitler informed Alfred Rosenberg, his minister for the eastern occupied territories, that all Jews, including those from the Reich, were to be moved to the area between the river Vistula and the river Bug. On the same day, Heydrich reported that 'in the area between Warsaw and Lublin' a reservation, or 'Reich ghetto', was established to contain the deported Poles and Jews. The Nazis deliberately intended conditions in the reservation to be so bad that most of the people deported there would die.

SOURCE 3

A Decree of November 1939 concerning the identification marks to be worn by Jews living in the General Government area:

1   All Jews and Jewesses resident in the General Government and more than ten years old must wear on the right sleeve of their clothes and outer garments a white strip at least 10cm wide with a Star of David upon it.
2   Jews and Jewesses must obtain this armlet themselves and provide it with the appropriate sign.
3   Infractions will be punished with imprisonment, or a fine up to an unlimited amount, or both.

SOURCE 4

An account of the punishment of a Jewish woman who did not display the yellow star by eyewitness Maja Zarch, recounted in Martin Gilbert's *The Holocaust* (a historical record of the oral testimonies of Jews during World War II):

One Sunday, when no one was going to work, an order was issued. Panic broke out once more. What now? We were all out in the yard when an announcement was made. We were terrified. The announcement was: 'You are about to witness what happens to a woman who wants to hide her Jewishness.' A beautiful blond woman was brought in with a noose attached to her neck and publicly hanged. Her crime? She was found walking in the street with her shawl covering her yellow star.

STUDY TIP

All three sources, although only giving a partial insight into Nazi policy, nevertheless have value in themselves and as part of a wider picture. Try to identify the particular strengths of each source by referring to the information it provides, but also assess its limitations. It is also important that you place each source in the wider context of Nazi policy at that time.

 PRACTICE QUESTION

Evaluating primary sources

With reference to Sources 2, 3 and 4, and to your contextual knowledge, assess the value of these sources to an historian studying Nazi policy towards the Jews in Poland in the period 1939 to 1940.

In October 1939, the Gestapo chief Heinrich Müller instructed Adolf Eichmann, the head of the Central Agency for Jewish Emigration, to arrange the deportation of 70,000–80,000 Jews from the district of Katowice in Germanised Poland. Eichmann quickly expanded this to include Czech Jews from the Reich Protectorate of Bohemia-Moravia. On top of this, Hitler demanded the deportation of 300,000 Jews from Germany and the removal of all Jews from Vienna. Although these orders were given, it would prove to be impossible to implement them because the problems of dealing with Jews already in Poland were so pressing.

Between November 1939 and February 1940, the SS attempted to deport one million people eastwards – 550,000 were Jews. They were transported to the General Government where they faced terrible conditions. The fact that so many people were entering this area meant that the authorities there could not possibly cope with mass deportations of western Jews from Germany and Austria at the same time. Governor Hans Frank complained vigorously to his superiors in Berlin that the General Government could not take any more Jews.

 A LEVEL PRACTICE QUESTION

'The Nazis followed a clear and consistent plan for removing the Jews from the mainstream of German society in the years 1933–39.' Assess the validity of this view.

The Madagascar Plan

The idea of removing Europe's Jews to the island of Madagascar was first promoted by French anti-Semites in the late 1930s. At that time, it was merely a wild idea with little or no prospect of becoming a reality. The rapid conquest of France by German armies during May to June 1940 changed the situation. The foreign ministry's department for Internal German Affairs proposed that the island of Madagascar should be taken away from France to become a German mandate. **Vichy France** would be responsible for resettling the French population there of approximately 25,000 so as to make Madagascar available for a 'solution' to the 'Jewish question'.

The Nazis planned to send 4 million Jews to Madagascar. In the first phase, farmers, construction workers and artisans up to the age of 45 would be sent out to get the island ready to receive the mass influx of Jews. The sale of remaining Jewish property in Europe would finance the initial costs. As with the ghettos being established in Poland at this time, the living conditions on Madagascar were intended to be harsh, leading in the long term to the elimination of the Jews by 'natural wastage'.

Since 1936, SS experts at the RSHA (Reich Security Head Office) led by Adolf Eichmann had been working on schemes for mass emigration of Jews to Palestine. (This actually involved a remarkable cooperation between SS racists and the leaders of the Zionist community in Germany.) However, there were huge practical problems about Palestine, which was a small territory under British rule and not so far from Europe. Madagascar was far away, offered infinitely more space and there were no serious political problems to get around.

There was only a short period of time, however, in the late summer and early autumn of 1940, when the Madagascar Plan seemed viable. Germany's failure to end the war with Britain, either by military victory or a peace agreement, meant that the British Royal Navy would be able to disrupt the mass transportation of Jews by sea to Madagascar. Attention turned back to the east. By October 1940, Hitler was already planning for Operation Barbarossa. The Madagascar Plan was shelved in favour of the plan to send Europe's Jews deep into Siberia, 'East of the Urals', once the forthcoming conquest of the USSR was complete.

STUDY TIP

You should consider the information from Chapter 18 and this chapter. The focus here is on the consistency of Nazi policy towards the Jews in these years and whether they were following any clear plan. It is possible to argue for a consistent policy based on clear underlying aims, but it is also possible to make a case that the Nazi policy was a series of improvisations without any clear and consistent plan.

A CLOSER LOOK

Vichy France

After France was defeated by Germany in June 1940, the northern part of the country became an occupied territory ruled over by the Germans. The southern part of the country, with a capital city at Vichy, was under the rule of Marshal Petain. Although in theory independent, Vichy France was closely allied to Nazi Germany.

What can we learn from the Madagascar Plan about Nazi policy towards the Jews in 1940?

What the Madagascar Plan reveals about Nazi intentions towards the 'Jewish question' in 1940 is open to debate. On the one hand, it is plausible that it proves the decision to exterminate all Jews had not been made at this point, that all kinds of different plans were under consideration and that the 'Final Solution' was still not inevitable. On the other hand, the driving force behind the Madagascar Plan was the determination to remove the Jews from Europe to some reservation where they would slowly die off through harsh conditions. The Plan could be regarded as proof that the long-term goal of sending the Jews to die somewhere far away was fixed, even if the exact location was not.

Summary

During 1938–39, the Nazi regime became radicalised. The constraints that had persuaded Hitler to proceed cautiously between 1933 and 1938 were pushed aside and the regime began to adopt more radical policies in economics, foreign affairs and racial policy. By the time war broke out in September 1939, the Jews in Germany, Austria and Czechoslovakia had been subjected to humiliation, discrimination and violence, leading many to conclude that they should emigrate. The outbreak of war, and the beginnings of German expansion into Eastern Europe, brought many more Jews under German control and exposed them to the full force of Nazi anti-Semitism.

20 Policies towards the Jews, 1940–41

The spreading war and the development of anti-Semitic policy

Invading Poland caused Britain and France to go to war, but this did not save Poland. In October 1940, Hitler won a series of *Blitzkrieg* victories in the west, defeating France and leaving Britain isolated. France came under a Nazi puppet regime ruled from the town of Vichy. Hitler seemed to have a free hand to fulfil his aim of *Lebensraum* in the east. In August 1939, Hitler and Stalin, the leader of the communist USSR, had concluded the Nazi-Soviet Pact, which guaranteed that the USSR would not intervene when Germany invaded Poland. The Pact was only ever intended to be a temporary truce. In October 1940, Hitler started detailed planning for the conquest of the USSR and, in June 1941, he launched **Operation Barbarossa**. German armies swept across the USSR, occupying vast territories in eastern Poland, the Baltic States (Lithuania, Latvia and Estonia), western Russia and Ukraine. Complete victory seemed almost certain. The way was open for the fulfilment of the dream of *Lebensraum*. All of these events had an impact on the development of Nazi anti-Semitic policy, since the war in the east was to be a war of racial annihilation, fought with a savagery and ideological intensity on a completely different scale than the relatively civilised struggle against the western Allies.

The German invasion deep into the western parts of the USSR in 1941 immediately brought more than 3 million Soviet Jews under German rule. The war was especially brutal. Before the invasion had even been launched, Hitler issued the instruction to 'eliminate' the 'Bolshevik-Jewish intelligentsia'. The Nazis made it clear in numerous directives that the war was to be one of 'extermination' of Germany's racial enemies. There was no explicit Hitler order in June 1941 to kill all the Jews of the Soviet Union. There was, however, an atmosphere in which troops saw killing as part of the overall mission. This was made clear in July 1941 when Goering issued a general order to kill communist commissars (party officials assigned to the Red Army) and Jewish sympathisers.

The war with Soviet Russia intensified the pressure on Hitler to deal with the 'Jewish question' in Germany as well as in the occupied territories. A series of measures had further isolated Jews from German society by late 1941:

- Radio sets were confiscated from Jews. In November 1939 Jews were banned from buying radios. A month later, they were banned from buying chocolate.
- In 1940, Jews were excluded from the wartime rationing allowances for clothing and shoes. In July, an order limited them to entering shops at restricted times only – in Berlin it was from 4 pm to 5 pm.
- In 1941, regulations were tightened up to require Jews to have a police permit to travel. An order in December 1941 compelled Jews in Germany to wear the yellow Star of David, as was already the case with Jews in the occupied territories.

Deportations and ghettoisation

The Nazi regime urgently needed a clear plan to deal with the huge Jewish populations that were displaced by military conquest and Germanisation. One solution they turned to was the creation of Jewish **ghettos**. In February 1940, the first ghetto was set up in Lodz, the second biggest city in Poland. About 320,000 Jews were living in the city. The Nazis considered their 'immediate evacuation' to be impossible. The majority of Jews were accommodated

LEARNING OBJECTIVES

In this chapter you will learn about:

- the spreading war and the development of anti-Semitic policy
- the policy of deportation and ghettoisation
- the *Einsatzgruppen*.

KEY TERMS

Blitzkrieg: literally 'lightning war'; used to describe the German strategy of attacking an enemy with maximum force, combining air attacks with fast-moving motorised army units on the ground in order to achieve a quick victory

Operation Barbarossa: the German codename for the invasion of the USSR; the operation was named after Frederick Barbarossa (Redbeard), a medieval German king who invaded Russia

KEY CHRONOLOGY

Development of anti-Semitic policies, 1940–1

1940

February First ghetto set up in Lodz, Poland

Summer Further exploration of Madagascar Plan

October The largest ghetto was established in Warsaw, Poland
Jews excluded from wartime rationing

1941

July *Einsatzgruppen* ordered to kill Jewish sympathisers and communist commissars

1941

December Jews in Germany were compelled to wear the Star of David

Ghetto: a controlled area of a town or city reserved for a particular race, and a feature of life in Europe since medieval times; in the early stages of the conquest of the east, Nazi authorities herded Jews into overcrowded ghettos in cities such as Warsaw and Lodz

in a closed ghetto, set up in a single day by barricades – later the Jews had to build a surrounding wall. The remaining Jews were formed into labour gangs, accommodated in barrack blocks and kept under guard. The Jewish Council of Elders was given responsibility for food, health, finance, security, accommodation and registration.

Fig. 1 *The partition of Poland after September 1939*

Jews sent to the ghettos had their homes confiscated. Most Jews had to sell their valuables to survive. There was further economic exploitation in the form of forced labour. The Nazis massively restricted the amount of food, medical supplies and other goods that entered the overcrowded ghettos. Conditions in the ghetto were terrible. Six people shared an average room; 15 people lived in an average apartment. Few homes had running water. With no economic links to the outside world, basic necessities such as food and fuel were scarce. There were terrible lice infestations and diseases spread rapidly, including spotted fever, typhus, typhoid and tuberculosis.

The Jewish authorities worked within the regulations laid down by the Nazis, but also tried to get around them where possible. There was a black market for food smuggled in from outside. Jewish leaders organised prayers and religious festivals, despite the fact that they were strictly forbidden by the Nazis. The ghettos had illegal schools and even illegal printing presses. Most Jewish elders in positions of authority in the ghettos acted responsibly and did their best to relieve suffering, although some were accused of corruption or collaboration with the Nazis.

The Warsaw ghetto

The largest ghetto established in Poland was in the capital city, Warsaw. Governor Hans Frank ordered the Jews to build a high wall around the Jewish Quarter in October 1940, forming the Warsaw ghetto. Jews also had to pay for its construction costs. In November, the ghetto was sealed off completely from the rest of the city. More than 400,000 Jews were concentrated there and over the following months, many more Jews and Gypsies were forced out of the countryside into the ghetto. Richer Jews were housed in the 'small ghetto'; the mass of ordinary people were squeezed into the so-called 'large ghetto', which was not large at all and became desperately overcrowded. Food rations in the large ghetto were at starvation levels. Germans in occupied Poland were consuming an average of 2310 calories per day, close to the 2500 calories a day for an adult man recommended by present-day nutritionists. In Warsaw in 1940, Poles received 634 calories a day. The figure for Jews was 300.

Malnutrition and overcrowding inevitably led to outbreaks of killer diseases, above all typhus. More than 100,000 people died in the ghetto in 1940–41. Later, almost all the remainder died in the death camps after mass deportations to Auschwitz during Operation Reinhard, which began in 1942. The Nazis never saw the ghettos as a long-term solution to the 'Jewish problem'. The conditions in the ghettos and work gangs did however give some insight into the fate that was intended for the Jews. The ghettos were designed to ensure that Jews died in large numbers of starvation, cold and disease. Many were worked to death carrying out forced labour for the Nazis. In total, around 500,000 Jews died in the ghettos.

Fig. 2 *Jews in the Warsaw ghetto*

Toshia Baler, a Polish Jew, described in a personal testimony given in 1943 the scene on the day the Warsaw ghetto was established:

Try to picture one third of a large city's population moving through the streets in an endless stream, dragging all their belongings from one part of the city to one small section, crowding one another more and more as they converged. Pushcarts were about the only method of conveyance we had, and these were piled high with household goods, furnishing much amusement to the German onlookers who delighted in overturning the carts and seeing us scrambling for our effects. In the ghetto there was appalling chaos. Thousands of people were rushing around at the last minute trying to find a place to stay. Everything was already filled up but still they kept coming and somehow more room was found.

SOURCE 2

Zivia Lubetkin, another Polish Jew, described conditions in the Warsaw ghetto in 1941 in testimony she gave at the trial of Nazi Adolf Eichmann in 1961:

When I came to look for this family, I found them on the floor, one on top of the other. They were in a corner of a room. In this house, there was no lavatory. They had a lavatory in the yard and they were on the fourth floor. There was no water in the house. And people lived this way. They degenerated because there was no possibility of getting work, no employment. There was hunger. Sanitary conditions were below description and, of course, the typhoid epidemic began in those houses.

ACTIVITY

Evaluating primary sources

Assess the value of Sources 1 and 2 to an historian studying the Warsaw ghetto.

The *Einsatzgruppen* ('Special Groups')

As German forces overran the western territories of the USSR in June and July 1941, 'Special Groups', the **Einsatzgruppen**, were sent in to eliminate communist officials, Red Army commissars, partisans and the 'Jewish-Bolshevist intelligentsia'. The activities of the *Einsatzgruppen* went far beyond their original remit. They carried out numerous mass killings of Soviet Jews in the second half of 1941. Possibly half a million Soviet Jews were killed by the *Einsatzgruppen* in June and July 1941.

The *Einsatzgruppen* were temporary units made up of police and regular troops commanded by men from the Gestapo, the SD and the Criminal Police under the overall direction of the SS. *Einsatzgruppen* had been in operation before 1941. Reinhard Heydrich and the RSHA had organised Special Groups in 1938 and 1939 to secure government buildings and to seize official files at the time of the *Anschluss* (union) with Austria and when Germany occupied Prague. Special Groups were used extensively in support of military operations in the invasion of Poland in 1939, when they were involved in 'special actions' against Jews and many Poles, especially communists and the 'intelligentsia'. Local volunteers were often recruited to assist them.

CROSS-REFERENCE

Look back to Chapter 19, page 155 for information on the effect of the *Anschluss* with Austria

SOURCE 3

On one occasion, in Belarus in 1941, Himmler asked to see an execution. One hundred prisoners were selected. One of Himmler's aides, General Karl Wolff, described the scene in a British television documentary made in 1974:

An open grave had been dug and they had to jump into this and lie face downwards. Himmler had never seen dead people before and, in his curiosity, he stood right up at the edge of this open grave and was looking in. While he was looking in, Himmler had the deserved bad luck that from one or other of the people who had been shot in the head he got a splash of brains on his coat, and I think it also splashed into his face, and he turned very green and pale; he wasn't actually sick, but he was heaving and swayed and I had to jump forward and hold him steady.

After the shooting was over, Himmler gathered the shooting squad around him and made a speech. He had seen for himself how hard the task which they had to fulfil for Germany in the occupied areas was, but however terrible it all might be, he could not see a way round it. In the interests of the Third Reich, they must do their duty however hard it may seem.

ACTIVITY

Evaluating primary sources

What can an historian learn from Source 3 about Himmler?

The *Einsatzgruppen* played an important role in the 'ethnic cleansing' of the territories in western Poland that were incorporated into Greater Germany. Key responsibilities of the *Einsatzgruppen* included the mass shooting of Jews and forcing Jews into ghettos in the cities. It is estimated that 7000 Jews were killed in Poland in 1939 and, in total, it is believed that the *Einsatzgruppen* in Poland killed 15,000 people including Jews and members of the 'intelligentsia'.

Fig. 3 *An Einsatzgruppen soldier about to shoot a Jew kneeling at a partially filled mass grave in Vinnitsa in Ukraine in 1942*

SOURCE 4

An SS sergeant, Felix Landau, kept a diary of his time with the *Einsatzgruppen*. In this extract he recounts the execution of Jews near Vilna in Lithuania in July 1941:

We drive a few kilometres along the main road until we reach a wood. We go into the wood and look for a spot suitable for mass executions. We order the prisoners to dig their graves. Only two of them are crying, the others show courage. Slowly the grave gets bigger and deeper. Money, watches and valuables are collected. The two women go first to be shot; placed at the edge of the grave, they face the soldiers. They get shot. When it's the men's turn, the soldiers aim at the shoulder. Nearly all fall into the grave unconscious, only to suffer a long while. The last group have to throw the corpses into the grave; they have to stand ready for their own execution. They all tumble into the grave.

ACTIVITY

Evaluating primary sources

What can we learn from Sources 3 and 4 about the development of Nazi policy towards the Jews during 1941?

Four *Einsatzgruppen*, of between 600 and 1000 men, followed behind the first wave of the German army as it swept into the Soviet Union. 'Special Group A' led the way, followed by a 'second sweep' by Special Groups B, C and D as more areas deeper into the USSR were overrun. The *Einsatzgruppen* were supported by police reserve units. Police Battalion 309 carried out a massacre in Bialystok in eastern Poland on 27 June 1941. The police battalions included many 'ordinary men' conscripted into the police instead of the regular army. The total number of men involved in the mass killing of Jews and communist party officials now rose to 40,000 men. Jewish men were routinely being shot; with the extra manpower, Jewish women and children were now also to be shot. The *Einsatzgruppen* were also supported by auxiliary groups that they recruited from the local populations in areas such as Ukraine and Latvia. There were many eager volunteers.

Some groups restricted their killing of Jews to the 'intelligentsia' and partisans. In other areas, the *Einsatzgruppen* and local volunteers set about killing as many Jews as possible. In the Baltic States, Special Group A shot 250,000 Jews in 1941. In the same period, Special Group B shot 45,000.

STUDY TIP

This view is open to challenge but it is also possible to agree with it to some extent. The question calls for an analysis of the reasons why Nazi policy was radicalised and when this began. You will need to identify a range of factors leading to radicalisation and assess the relative importance of each.

 PRACTICE QUESTION

'The radicalisation of Nazi policy towards the Jews in the years 1939 to 1941 was the result of the successes achieved by German forces in the war'. Assess the validity of this view.

Summary

The war in the east brought ever-increasing numbers of Jews under Nazi rule. This posed severe challenges to a regime committed to dealing with the so-called 'Jewish problem', but it also provided that regime with opportunities to experiment with new methods of dealing with that problem. The invasion of the USSR in June 1941 marked a further stage in the radicalisation of Nazi policy as the cherished ideal of *Lebensraum* was now within touching distance and the Nazis' racial ambitions could now be given free rein. Moreover, the outbreak of war between Germany and the USA in December 1941 meant that there was no longer any incentive for Hitler to exercise any restraint in the west.

6 The impact of war, 1939–45

21 The impact of war on German society

When war started in September 1939, there were no cheering crowds in Berlin or other German cities. Although loyalty to the Führer was very strong, and his foreign policy triumphs between 1933 and 1939 had been very popular, the mood of the German public at the news of the start of hostilities with Poland was one of reluctant loyalty. In terms of public opinion, therefore, the start of the Second World War in Germany did not match Hitler's expectations. It was a principal aim of Nazi domestic policy in the early years of the war to sustain the morale of the home front and eliminate any elements of weakness in public mood.

LEARNING OBJECTIVES

In this chapter you will learn about:

- the impact of rationing
- the impact of indoctrination, propaganda and German morale
- the changing impact of war on different sections of German society.

SOURCE 1

William Shirer, an American journalist based in Berlin, recorded his observations of the mood in Berlin at the outbreak of war in September 1939 in his book *Berlin Diary* published in 1941:

It has been a lovely September day, the sun shining, the air balmy, the sort of day the Berliner loves to spend in the woods or on the lakes nearby. I walked in the streets. On the faces of the people astonishment, depression. Until today they had been going about their business pretty much as usual. There were food cards and soap cards and you couldn't get any petrol and at night it was difficult stumbling around in the blackout. But the war in the east has seemed a bit far away to them. Few believed that Britain and France would move against Germany.

In 1914, I believe, the excitement in Berlin on the first day of the world war was tremendous. Today, no excitement, no hurrahs, no cheering, no throwing of flowers, no war fever, no war hysteria.

ACTIVITY

Evaluating primary sources

Assess the value of Source 1 to an historian studying the attitude of German civilians to the outbreak of war.

The impact of rationing

One of the critical factors in maintaining civilian morale was the availability of vital foodstuffs and other commodities. Shortages and the inadequacies of the rationing system during the First World War were one of the main causes of growing war-weariness in 1917 and 1918, and the Nazi regime was determined not to make the same mistakes as the Kaiser's government. Decrees establishing a food rationing system were issued in August 1939, even before the war began. Clothing was not initially included in the rationing scheme but permits were needed to purchase clothes. This caused panic buying before the regulations took effect and led to the inclusion of clothing in the rationing scheme in November 1939.

The allocation of food rations was based on age, occupation and race. Those who were employed in manual labour received more than those who had more sedentary occupations. Jews received smaller rations. There were special allocations for groups such as pregnant women, nursing mothers and the sick. The allocations established at the beginning of the war remained largely unchanged during the first two years of the war.

The Nazi regime was reluctant to ask the civilian population to make significant reductions in their consumption at the beginning of the war for fear

 Meat	500g per person per week
Butter	125g per person per week
 Margarine	100g per person per week
Sugar	250g per person per week
 Cheese	62.5g per person per week
 Eggs	1 per person per week

Fig. 1 *Ration allowances in August 1939*

A CLOSER LOOK

In 1940, a popular joke in Berlin reflected the growing irritations over shortages.

Question: What is the difference between Germany and India?

Answer: In India, one man (Gandhi) starves for everybody; in Germany, everybody starves for one man!

ACTIVITY

For what reasons was rationing essential?

CROSS-REFERENCE

The SD and Gestapo were introduced in Chapter 14, pages 109–110

that this might provoke anti-war feelings. Nevertheless, civilian consumption was cut more in Germany than in Britain at the start of the war. The regime was able to exploit the newly occupied countries for food supplies for the German people and, while the Nazi-Soviet Pact was in force, there were also imports of grain from the Soviet Union. On the whole, therefore, the rationing system worked efficiently and there were no serious food shortages between 1939 and 1941. Shortages of coal, shoes, soap and washing powder, however, did cause discontent from time to time.

After the invasion of the Soviet Union in June 1941, some rations were reduced. The meat ration, for example, was cut from 500g per person per week to 400g, then cut again. In the later years of the war, meat could not be eaten every day and other goods were in very short supply. By the end of the war, especially in the industrial cities, food supplies had become very precarious and unpredictable and many Germans were experiencing malnutrition. In the countryside, farmers had access to food they could grow themselves but they also experienced shortages of animal feed, fuel and replacement tools, which limited their ability to produce food.

The impact of propaganda and indoctrination on morale

Maintaining the morale of Germans was a high priority for the regime. Goebbels had developed a highly sophisticated propaganda system, which controlled the flow of information to the German people. The regime also used its secret police system, the SD and Gestapo, to monitor the public mood and the effectiveness of propaganda. The SD reports provide a valuable source of information for historians about German morale at different stages of the war.

The war can be divided into a number of phases:

Phase 1: *Blitzkrieg*, September 1939–June 1941

Events in the war
- After defeating Poland in the east, German forces achieved a series of quick victories against various European countries.

Public mood
The public mood in Germany in the first 21 months of the war was volatile and propaganda was not always effective in lifting morale, even though Goebbels understood that maintaining morale was vital to the success of the Nazi war effort. Quick and relatively easy victories in the early stages of the war were a cause for celebration: edited newsreels showed German forces sweeping aside inferior opposition as they achieved stunning victories. Hitler was presented as the military genius who was responsible for these victories and his speeches, broadcast on the radio, were vital in bolstering morale. Between January 1940 and June 1941, Hitler made nine major speeches. At this stage of the war, propaganda led people to be optimistic and believe that the war would be over soon.

When the defeat of France in June 1940 did not bring immediate peace, Britain was blamed for prolonging the war.

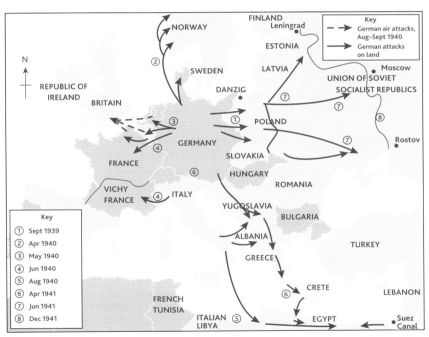

Fig. 2 *Phases 1 and 2 of the war, Sept 1939–Dec 1941*

Phase 2: The spreading war, June–December 1941

Events in the war
- Germany invaded the USSR in June 1941 and occupied vast areas of territory, but in December 1941, the Red Army launched a counter-attack against the Germans, which halted the German advance.
- Germany declared war on the USA in December 1941. The hope of another short victorious war was over. Nazi Germany now faced a world war against the Grand Alliance of the USSR, USA and Britain.

Public mood
The invasion of the USSR was presented as a crusade against 'Jewish-Bolshevism' and the success of German forces in forcing the Red Army

CROSS-REFERENCE

Jewish-Bolshevism was introduced in Chapter 6, page 49 and Chapter 18, page 152.

to retreat engendered a feeling of optimism. However, the SD reported people's fears that the war would go on for years. Although Nazi propaganda downplayed the extent of the Soviet success, letters home from soldiers at the front undermined the propaganda. Soldiers talked of the harsh winter conditions and the seemingly limitless Soviet supply of manpower and military equipment. The hopes of a quick and easy victory were dissipated. Other scapegoats were needed to explain the spreading of the war in 1941, as Germany declared war on the USA. Behind the British, the Soviet and the American enemies, according to the propaganda, lay a Jewish international conspiracy to destroy the Third Reich and the Aryan race. There was a marked increase in anti-Semitic propaganda during the war.

CROSS-REFERENCE

The Hitler myth was covered in Chapter 14, page 119

Phase 3: The turning of the tide, January 1942–January 1943

Events in the war
- German losses in the USSR started to mount in the harsh winter conditions.

Public mood
Rising casualty figures and letters home from soldiers serving on the Eastern Front gradually awakened the civilian population to the realities of the war they were engaged in. When Goebbels broadcast an appeal for people to collect winter clothing for soldiers on the Eastern Front, the mood of disillusionment deepened. Although an SD report in January 1942 stated that 'Faith in the Führer is unshakeable', the scepticism about propaganda, which was remarked upon in this report, was an early sign that confidence in the regime was beginning to erode. The defeat at Stalingrad was a major turning point in the war, both militarily and on the home front. It signalled a defeat for Nazi propaganda as much as a defeat for its armed forces. News of the defeat was such a shock to public morale because Goebbels had built up unrealistic expectations of Nazi victory and concealed the truth about the desperate situation of German forces there. War-weariness now became much more evident. Criticism of the propaganda emanating from the regime increased and the Hitler myth began to lose some its potency. On the other hand, there was undoubtedly a deep well of patriotism and willingness to endure hardship on which the regime could draw as it belatedly attempted to gear the nation up for total war.

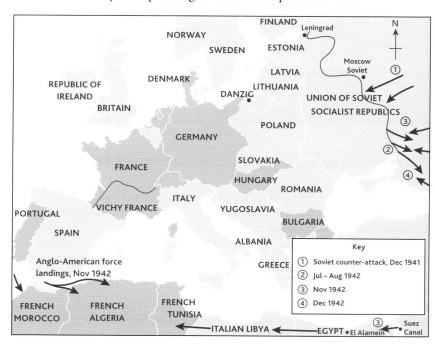

Fig. 3 *Phase 3 of the war, June 1942–Jan 1943*

A Nazi police report from January 1942 on the public mood. Reports like this were used by the regime to monitor public opinion and check the effectiveness of propaganda:

The announcement of the collection of winter things has produced a great response among all sections of the population and is still at the forefront of people's concern. It is unanimously reported that the announcement aroused great astonishment in view of the fact that recently the good and adequate provision of winter clothing for our soldiers has been repeatedly reported in the press and in various newsreels. The announcement was clear confirmation of the fact that the accounts of men on leave from the front about the lack of equipment capable of coping with the Russian cold were accurate and were not, as one would have assumed from the propaganda to the contrary, long out of date.

Phase 4: February 1943–May 1945: 'Total War' and the defeat of Germany

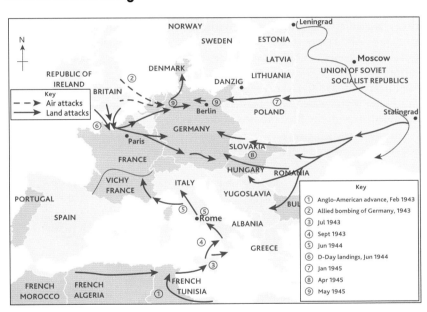

Fig. 4   *Phase 4 of the war, Feb 1943–May 1945, the defeat of Germany*

Events in the war
- In February 1943, Goebbels declared that Germany was engaged in a '**Total War**'.
- The British and Americans attempted to cripple Germany's war effort through unrelenting bombings against German cities.
- The D-Day landings in Normandy in June 1944 opened up a second front in western Europe and by early 1945 Allied forces had entered Germany itself.
- Berlin was captured by Soviet forces in April 1945 and Germany conceded unconditional surrender to the Allies on 8 May 1945.

Public mood
By the early months of 1943 it had become clear that Germany was involved in a struggle for survival. Goebbels made an important speech at the Sports Palace in Berlin in February 1943 in which he called for the nation to engage in total war. Goebbels' 'Total War' speech appears to have struck a chord with many people. His call for radical measures to mobilise the population and the economy

KEY TERM

Total War: a conflict in which a combatant state mobilises its entire population and all of its material resources to participate in the war effort

were generally welcomed and the main criticism was that these measures were being introduced too late. The aftermath of the defeat at Stalingrad, therefore, was a crucial time for the Nazi regime. However, no longer could Hitler be convincingly portrayed as a military genius, although attempts were made to shift the blame onto incompetent military commanders. With Hitler appearing less frequently in public, the Hitler myth also began to decline. By the spring of 1944, morale had declined even further. News of almost continuous retreat by German forces on the Eastern Front, the failure of the U-boat campaign to bring Britain to its knees and heavy Allied bombing raids on German cities had led to a 'a downbeat mood among the population'. The Allied landings in Normandy on D-Day in June 1944 were a further serious blow to Germany. Paradoxically, events in June 1944 brought a temporary lifting of morale. This was partly due to the feeling that the final settling of accounts with the British and Americans was now at hand, and partly to Goebbels trying to counter defeatism with talk of plans for retaliation with secret weapons. The use of VI and V2 missiles in 1944–5 did temporarily raise spirits but, neither militarily nor in terms of public opinion, could these weapons alter the course of events.

By the end of August 1944, after Paris had been liberated and German forces had suffered further reverses in the east, defeat began to be accepted as inevitable. An SD report in August 1944 stated that 'most compatriots, even those whose belief has hitherto been unshakeable, have lost all faith in the Führer.'

The final months of the war saw growing cynicism about Nazi propaganda. The 'Hitler Myth', which Goebbels claimed as his greatest achievement, crumbled away in the final months of the war.

Fig. 5 *A V1 flying bomb*

SOURCE 3

An SD report from March 1944:

At the moment large sections of the population are intimidated by the military situation. People do not know 'what they should believe'. The 'unrelenting advance' of the Bolsheviks, the lack of any prospect of a foreseeable end to the air war, the noticeable increase in tension because of the numerous air raid warnings by day and night, and the thought that, almost like in the First World War, we are being forced to fight against a group of powerful enemies, together with the destruction caused by the air terror, and the deaths in many families reduce the belief that a change for the better can occur, which will bring about final victory, and instead concentrates people's thoughts on the question — what is the point of it all? The majority of compatriots hold to the belief that whatever happens they have to keep going and 'grit their teeth'.

 A **LEVEL** **PRACTICE QUESTION**

Evaluating primary sources

Assess the value of Sources 1, 2 and 3 to an historian studying civilian morale in Germany during the war.

The impact of bombing on morale

A new phase in the air war began at the end of March 1942 when the British Royal Air Force (RAF) carried out a major bombing raid on the city of Lübeck. This was the start of the Allied mass bombing campaign in which the RAF attacked German cities by night and the United States Army Air Forces (USAAF) attacked by day, often with 1000 aircraft at a time. In 1943, the bombing campaign reached an even greater intensity, with 43 German cities being attacked between March and July. Hamburg was bombed seven times between 25 July and 3 August. All of Germany's main industrial and port cities were attacked but there was a high concentration of raids on cities in the Rhineland and Ruhr areas.

Official reports on the impact of the bombing on morale, while detailing the horrific scenes of death and destruction, spoke of the resilience of the civilian population and their continuing support for the regime. The police report from Hamburg, after the raid of 27–28 July 1943, stated that 'The behaviour of the population at no time and nowhere displayed signs of panic and was worthy of the greatness of this sacrifice.' An SD report on the impact of the raid on Lübeck in March 1942 noted that 'The population of Lübeck showed a really remarkable composure, despite the extreme destruction and loss of life.' This report went on to say that 'It was a sign of the calm, determined attitude and the unbroken spirit of the people of Lübeck that on the very next day numerous tradespeople demonstrated their unbroken spirit by opening their shops.' Personal reminiscences of people who experienced at first hand the horrors of the bombing raids paint a rather different picture.

SOURCE 4

A German woman describes the aftermath of a bombing raid on Cologne in 1943 as recorded from a Holocaust oral history archive:

At first I looked in the bunker where the children went during an alarm, but I didn't find them. I saw other children, but I could not find my own two. Later I heard that a whole group of people had been buried in a house in Nibelung St., including children from the kindergarten. My two children were pulled out dead. You could hardly see any injuries on them. They had only a small drop of blood on their noses and large bloody scrapes on the backs of their heads. I was in a state of total shock. I wanted to scream, right then and there I wanted to scream, 'You Nazis, you murderers!' A neighbour, who had only been released from a concentration camp a few days before, grabbed my arm and pulled me aside. He said, 'Do you want to get yourself arrested too?'

As morale fell, the regime took an increasingly repressive line with those who expressed 'defeatist' remarks. The definition of 'defeatist' included any remark

ACTIVITY

Revision exercise

- Identify four or five events you consider to be turning points for the Germans in the war.
- Explain your reasons for selecting these events.
- Explain how each of these events had an impact on civilian morale.

ACTIVITY

Evaluating primary sources

To what extent do Source 4 and the SD reports in the previous paragraph give different views of civilian reactions to bombing raids?

that was critical of the leadership or showed a loss of faith in Germany's ability to win the war.

Goebbels attempted to keep up morale in the face of the air raids with talk of retaliation using secret weapons that were being developed. Germany's civilian population did display resilience in defiance of the bombing but, as the raids continued, there was a serious erosion of civilian morale. The experience of sheer terror as many of Germany's cities were consumed by firestorms, the growing shortages and lengthening queues, the loss of sleep as nights were disrupted by air-raid warnings – all contributed to a growing sense of exhaustion.

The mass bombing of German cities was designed by the Allies to break the will of the civilian population to carry on supporting the war. Despite the growing war-weariness, workers continued to turn up for work and, at least until the end of 1944, production was maintained. There was undoubtedly pressure from a repressive regime to keep their heads down and not openly oppose the war. There was also, however, a need for people whose lives were being disrupted on a daily basis to try to find some stability in whatever way they could. Maintaining a daily routine of work was one way of achieving this. Bombing wore down the civilian population but it did not break their will completely.

The end of the war

For the civilian German population, the last months of the war brought unrelenting misery. Millions of Germans living in Poland, East Prussia and Czechoslovakia were driven out by hostile local people and forced to trek westwards in advance of the Soviet forces. As Soviet forces entered Germany itself in January 1945, 3.5 million Germans fled their homes to escape the fighting. They could expect no help from the army as it was also retreating nor could many find berths on trains or ships, since priority was given to the transport of military supplies. Responsibility for the evacuations rested with local *Gauleiters*, many of whom delayed the order to leave until the very last minute. The result was that people were forced to walk hundreds of miles facing cold, hunger, disease and attacks by Allied forces. Estimates of the numbers who died on these marches vary from around 500,000 to over one million.

When the survivors finally reached the western part of Germany, they found cities devastated by bombing and a civilian population facing severe hardships. Heavy bombing of cities and the added pressure of the evacuees from the east left at least a quarter of the civilian population homeless. Transport systems had ceased to function, electricity and gas supplies had been cut, water and sewage systems were seriously damaged and epidemic diseases were beginning to appear. Food supplies were running low and there was a serious risk of starvation in some areas.

Unsurprisingly, civilian morale collapsed. The civilian population was exhausted and suffering severe hardship but there were few signs of outward resistance, still less of rebellion. On the whole, the German population reacted passively and with resignation to the final collapse of the regime and Germany's occupation by foreign forces, bound together in a 'community of fate'. Once Germany was defeated and occupied, however, the Nazi regime collapsed quickly. As the historian Richard Bessel has written, 'When it came, the collapse of the Nazi dictatorship was remarkable in its speed and thoroughness. Seemingly overnight the hold of the regime evaporated'.

The changing impact of the war on German society

Elites

Among the **elites** there were diverse views regarding the Nazi regime and various reasons for opposing it. Some felt a moral conviction that the Nazi regime was evil. Others were patriotic about their country but believed that

CROSS-REFERENCE

The *Gauleiters* are explained in more detail in Chapter 13, page 101.

ACTIVITY

In pairs or in groups, write a short newspaper article reporting the end of war in 1944 from either the point of view of the Nazi Party or from the British/Allied forces. Consider how they may differ in terms of explaining Germany's civilian morale.

KEY TERM

Elites: upper classes

Hitler was leading Germany to destruction. Some were democrats, while others were traditional, aristocratic conservatives who wanted a return to an authoritarian, non-Nazi style of government.

Many of those who opposed Nazism did so because they believed in personal freedom and individual responsibility. For some, like the aristocrat Helmut von Moltke, the dismal treatment of others when they were still living quite comfortable lives was deeply disturbing.

Workers

In his 'Decree on the Conversion of the Whole German Economy onto a War Footing' of 3 September 1939, Hitler imposed wage reductions and a ban on the payment of bonuses for overtime, Sunday work and night-shift working. This caused widespread discontent among the labour force, which was reflected in an increased level of absenteeism. Consequently, in October 1939, the regime relented. Wage levels were restored to their pre-war levels and the payment of bonuses was reintroduced, but wage rates were not allowed to increase.

Total war measures began to impact on workers during 1943 and 1944. In August 1944, a total ban on holidays was imposed, the working week was increased to 60 hours and extra payments for working overtime were abolished. This increased pressure did result in some rise in absenteeism but employers had a number of disciplinary measures at their disposal. Workers could have their reserved status removed, which would result in conscription into the armed forces and, possibly, a posting to the Eastern Front. Employers could also allocate extra food rations to those employees who had good attendance records and impose fines for absenteeism and bad timekeeping. The regime also had at its disposal the DAF factory cell system, in which workers were divided into groups under a loyal Nazi Party member who was responsible for the attendance of workers in his cell. The regime also used incentives to encourage workers to raise productivity. Many plants switched from an hourly paid system to a system of piecework under which workers could earn more if they produced more.

The increase in working hours and the pressure to produce more had an impact on workers' health and welfare. Accidents at work increased and workers' health deteriorated.

Women

Women bore the brunt of the hardships endured on the home front. As housewives, married women were obliged to spend time queuing for supplies of vital foodstuffs when shortages occurred. As mothers, women had to shoulder even more of the task of childcare when their husbands were away in the armed forces. As workers, women played an increasingly vital role in the German war economy.

Table 1 *International comparison of women in employment, 1939–44*

Germany		Great Britain	
Date	Women as % of total workforce	Date	Women as % of total workforce
May 1939	37.4	June 1939	26.4
May 1941	42.6	June 1941	33.2
May 1942	46.0	June 1942	36.1
May 1943	48.8	June 1943	37.7
May 1944	51.0	June 1944	37.9

By May 1939, as a result of the Four Year Plan, the number of women in paid employment had increased; there were 6.4 million married women in

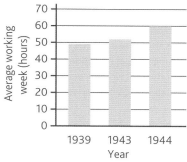

Fig. 6 *Average working week (hours) in Germany, 1939–44*

CROSS-REFERENCE

The Four Year Plan was introduced in Chapter 15, page 123.

A CLOSER LOOK

Nazi efforts to educate women

The National Socialist Women organisation, the NS-F, organised classes to teach women how to cope with wartime conditions. Cookery classes taught housewives how to make the most economical use of available food supplies and sewing classes to learn how to repair worn clothing. Women were also mobilised by the NS-F to help with the harvest, prepare parcels of food and clothing for soldiers at the front and help with evacuated children from the cities. Community evenings were organised to sustain morale and for indoctrination.

employment and women as a whole made up 37.4 per cent of the industrial labour force. The need to increase armaments production at a time when many male workers had been conscripted into the armed forces led to pressure for more women to be employed in industry. There was, however, tension between Nazi ideology and the needs of the war economy. When Hitler was advised, in the summer of 1940, that industry needed more women workers, he refused to sanction this on the grounds that women should primarily be devoted to child bearing and rearing. Although the regime had taken powers to conscript workers into essential war work, these powers were used very sparingly in relation to women. By June 1940, only 250,000 women had been conscripted and those who were conscripted were merely transferred from the production of consumer goods to war work. The regime also provided generous benefits for the families of conscripted soldiers, thus removing one of the incentives for married women to seek work. With working hours in factories increasing due to the pressures of wartime production, there was even more pressure for married women with children to give up employment. The result was that the number of women workers in industry actually declined between 1939 and 1941. A growing number of women, however, worked in agriculture.

In June 1941, Goering issued a decree that all female workers who were in receipt of **family allowance** and had given up paid employment but had not produced children should be forced to register for work or lose their allowance. This was the first tentative step towards the conscription of female labour but in practice had only limited effect since it only applied to those women who had been employed previously. It did not apply to married women who had never worked outside the home. Since this group of women was overwhelmingly middle class, whereas those who had been previously employed were mainly from the working class, Goering's decree stoked up class resentments. As a result of this decree, only 130,000 extra women were sent to the armaments factories.

The defeat at Stalingrad (USSR) in January 1943 meant that the total mobilisation of labour had become essential. The decree that same month, which forced all women aged 17–45 to register for work, appeared to show that Hitler had abandoned his ideological objection to the employment of married women. In fact, Hitler had merely been persuaded to modify his views. It was at his insistence that older women were exempted from labour registration and there were many other exemptions. Pregnant women, mothers with two or more children and farmers' wives were not obliged to register. Once again, working-class women resented the number of exemptions and the lack of consistency in implementing the decree. By June 1943, fewer than half a million extra women had joined the industrial labour force.

In November 1943, Hitler was asked to approve the raising of the upper age limit for women to register for work to 50 years of age. He refused, but, by the summer of 1944, the situation had become so grave that he was eventually persuaded to agree to this measure. More and more women were recruited and, by 1945, women comprised 60 per cent of the labour force.

Women were also increasingly assigned to auxiliary roles within the armed forces, despite Hitler's misgivings. In 1943, women began to replace men in servicing anti-aircraft guns and, in 1944, women began to operate searchlights. By the end of the war, some 50,000 women were involved in anti-aircraft operations and another 30,000 worked on searchlights. In the summer of 1944, the army established an **Auxiliary Corps** for women serving with the armed forces and, by January 1945, there were 470,000 female auxiliaries. Many of them had been conscripted. Their duties were mainly secretarial and working on radio and telephone communications but, in many cases, this involved serving at the front line. The militarisation of women was taken further in the final stages of the war when women's battalions of the army were established and women were trained for combat roles.

Youth

Membership of the Hitler Youth and BDM had become compulsory for all young people in 1939. The Nazis treated the welfare and indoctrination of youth as a high priority and believed that young people could contribute to the war effort. The regime did not, however, consider it necessary in the early stages of the war to conscript the young. Hitler Youth activities continued much as in peace time with a greater emphasis on preparing boys for their future role as soldiers, through training in fieldcraft and shooting practice. Hitler Youth members were also sent to help with the harvest and all young people were expected to participate in collecting money for the Winter Aid programme.

The transition towards total war had an impact on young people. Even before 1942, the age at which young men became subject to military conscription had been reduced. In 1940, a youth was liable to be called into the armed forces at the age of 19. In 1941, the age was reduced to 18 and in 1943 to 17. There was also an increase in the demands placed upon younger teenagers. In 1942, 600,000 boys and 1.4 million girls had been organised through their youth organisations to help with gathering the harvest. The Hitler Youth placed more emphasis on military training at camps where 17-year-old youths would attend three-week courses under army and Waffen SS instructors. By November 1942, 120 of these camps had been established.

In January 1943, as part of the implementation of total war policies, 16- and 17-year-old schoolboys were conscripted as Luftwaffe and naval auxiliaries and deployed on air defence duties. Whole school classes were conscripted *en bloc* and the boys continued their education under visiting teachers.

Young people were increasingly militarised in the final stages of the war. The age at which youths could be conscripted into the armed forces was further reduced to 16 in 1945. Conscription into the **Volkssturm** (home guard) was also introduced, in September 1944, for 16–60-year-olds who were not fit for active service. The young men dug anti-tank ditches and were trained to use anti-tank weapons. By the end of the war, boys as young as 12 were being conscripted into the *Volkssturm*. In 1943, a special Hitler Youth division of the Waffen SS was set up for 16–18-year-old boys selected by Hitler Youth group leaders. This division was sent to France in 1944 and saw action in the Battle of Normandy.

A CLOSER LOOK

Volkssturm

Founded on Hitler's orders, the *Volkssturm* was intended to be a force of six million members, although this was never achieved. Local units were under the control of *Gauleiters* to ensure that they showed the necessary ideological commitment to the struggle to defend Germany. Many units were sent to the front line, especially in the Battle of Berlin. It was referred to as the National Militia for those aged 13 to 60 who were not directly engaged in the war. It was organised by the Nazi Party.

CROSS-REFERENCE

For more information on the actions of the elites during the Nazi regime, go to Chapter 24, page 198.

PRACTICE QUESTION

The Nazi regime succeeded in maintaining the morale of the German people throughout the war.' Assess the validity of this view.

Summary

There was a clear and growing gap between the propaganda images of a German population united behind the Führer in support of the war effort and the reality of the growing war-weariness reported by the SD. Declining living standards, increasing pressure of work and the hardships people had to endure under the Allied bombing offensive eroded belief in victory and tarnished Hitler's image. Nevertheless, there was no groundswell of opposition to the regime and the majority of Germans retained their patriotism, if not their faith in Hitler, to the end of the war.

STUDY TIP

This view is intended to provoke debate. Try to present both sides of the argument in a balanced way. You will need to show how morale changed over the course of the war and how the image projected by propaganda was often very different from the reality, as revealed by SD reports. Try to avoid a chronological approach as this might become rather descriptive.

22 The wartime economy and the work of Speer

LEARNING OBJECTIVES

In this chapter you will learn about:

- mobilisation of the German economy for war
- the work of Speer
- the impact of Allied bombing
- mobilisation of the labour force
- the use of 'slave' labour and prisoners of war.

CROSS-REFERENCE

Blitzkrieg was introduced in Chapter 21, page 173

Operation Barbarossa is introduced in Chapter 20, page 165

A food rationing system was established in August 1939 to help Germany prepare for wartime. For further details, see Chapter 21, page 171.

ACTIVITY

In groups or in pairs, consider this statement: 'The poor performance of the German armaments industry in the early years of the war was due to political weaknesses in the Nazi regime.'

The mobilisation of the German economy for war

Germany had been preparing for war since the launch of the Four Year Plan in 1936. On 3 September 1939, Hitler issued a Decree for the Conversion of the Whole German Economy onto a War Footing. Despite this, the German economy did not reach a state of full mobilisation until 1942. The result was that in the years 1939–41, Germany's armed forces suffered from shortages of weapons and equipment. These supply problems did not hamper Germany in the early stages of war since the campaigns against Poland, Norway, Holland, Belgium and France all achieved quick successes through the highly effective use of *Blitzkrieg* tactics. By 1941, however, as German forces became stretched with the war in the Mediterranean and the start of Operation Barbarossa, the supply problems began to hinder the German war effort.

There were a number of reasons for these problems. Although the German economy had effectively been placed on a war footing from 1936, Hitler had not anticipated that war would begin in 1939. He fully expected Britain and France to accept the German invasion of Poland – just as they had conceded his demands over Austria and Czechoslovakia – and that the war would not begin until he launched Operation Barbarossa in 1941. Economic and military planning had been based on these assumptions, with the Luftwaffe expansion due to be completed in 1942 and the build-up of the navy to be completed in 1944–45. Moreover, the Four Year Plan concentrated in the early stages on building up Germany's productive potential through increasing iron and steel production, investing in machine tools and developing artificial alternatives to oil and rubber. Once this productive potential had been expanded, the full-scale production of armaments could begin. The outbreak of war in September 1939 came as a surprise and disrupted these plans.

German armaments production also suffered from structural weaknesses. Different branches of the armed forces demanded highly specialised equipment of very high quality. The production of many different types of weapons was expensive and required highly skilled labour. Even though the proportion of the labour force in armaments production increased from 21 per cent to 55 per cent between September 1939 and January 1941, the supply of weapons grew very slowly. Mass production of more standardised weapons would have been cheaper and capable of producing the quantities of equipment required, but many German firms were not set up in this way. Moreover, the military designed and ordered many different versions of the same weapons, making standardisation almost impossible to achieve.

At the heart of these production problems was a political problem. Goering, who was in charge of the Four Year Plan, lacked the technical and economic knowledge needed to do his job effectively. He had very poor relations with the military leaders and the leaders of large companies and banks, and he was busy building up his own economic empire. The war economy needed greater centralised coordination but Goering was incapable of providing this. In 1939 and 1940, his failings were masked by the successes of the German armed forces in battle but, by 1941, the weaknesses of the Four Year Plan and Goering's management of it became increasingly apparent. Albert Speer, who was appointed as Armaments Minister in 1942, described Goering's years in charge as an 'era of incompetence, arrogance and egotism'.

The work of Albert Speer

Hitler had recognised the need for more rationalisation of industrial production in the summer of 1941 but his order to do this was not accompanied by any action to resolve the underlying problems of the lack of central control and the interference of the military in civilian production. Indeed, when in 1941 Fritz Todt, the then Armaments Minister complained to Hitler about the shortage of vital equipment and supplies in the Russian campaign, Hitler chose to ignore him. Only after Todt was killed in a plane crash in February 1942 and was replaced by Albert Speer, was effective action taken to achieve the necessary changes. Speer was given full executive powers to establish a Central Planning Agency and was able, with Hitler's support, to coordinate and control the whole production process without interference from the military and with the full cooperation of private companies.

Rationalisation of production

Under Speer's direction, rationalisation of the production of armaments involved:

- central coordination of the allocation of labour, equipment and materials to armaments factories
- the concentration of production in fewer factories and on a narrower range of standardised products
- greater use of mass production techniques
- more shift working to keep factories operating 24 hours a day.

The 'production miracle'

Speer's innovations resulted in what many have described as a 'production miracle'. Between 1941 and 1943, German aircraft production increased by 200 per cent, whilst tank production increased by 250 per cent. The production of the Messerschmitt Bf 109, one of Germany's main fighter aircraft, was concentrated in three factories rather than the seven used previously. Despite the reduction in factory space, rationalised production methods meant that the production of this aircraft increased from 180 per month to 1000 per month.

Fig. 1 *Tank production in a German factory*

KEY PROFILE

Albert Speer (1905–81) was an architect who joined the Nazi Party in 1931. He helped design the settings for the Nuremberg rallies and was responsible for designing many iconic Nazi buildings, including Hitler's Reich Chancellery in Berlin. In 1942 he was appointed Minister of Armaments. After Germany's defeat he was tried at Nuremberg and sentenced to 20 years in prison.

The economic impact of Allied bombing

SOURCE 1

In his autobiography published in 1970, Speer gave his observations on the impact of Allied bombing:

The first thousand bomber raid in May 1942 gave us a taste of what was to come. But, in spite of the devastation, we were producing more, not less. Any loss of production was balanced out by increased effort. From my visits to armaments plants and contacts with ordinary Germans, I had the impression of growing toughness amongst the population. Neither did the bombings and the hardships weaken morale or increase opposition. Hitler's concern to avoid discontent was shown by the money spent on supplies of consumer goods, military pensions and compensation for losses. However, what saved us from defeat within months was the enemy's decision to continue its indiscriminate attacks upon our cities instead of concentrating on a few key industries.

Between 1942 and May 1945, the British and Americans carried out a sustained bombing offensive against Germany's industrial capacity and civilian morale. The gains in production achieved by Speer in 1943 and 1944 occurred

Fig. 2 *Impact of allied bombing in Dresden; the historic city centre was almost completely demolished*

despite the damage inflicted by the air raids. Undoubtedly, the bombing had an impact on production since supply lines were damaged, factories had to be dispersed and worker morale was affected. In January 1945, officials at the Ministry of Armaments calculated that the bombing had resulted in 35 per cent fewer tanks, 31 per cent fewer aircraft and 42 per cent fewer lorries being produced than would have otherwise been the case. Moreover, the intense bombing campaign of January to May 1945 caused an actual reduction in the amount of armaments that were produced.

STUDY TIP

There is scope here for a balanced assessment, especially if you consider how the impact of the bombing changed over time. Make sure you offer a clear view and sustain your argument throughout the answer.

ACTIVITY

In pairs or in groups, discuss whether you agree or disagree with this statement: 'The German invasion of the USSR revealed the weaknesses at the heart of the Nazi regime'.

 PRACTICE QUESTION

'The Allied bombing offensive against German cities had a limited impact on the ability of the German economy to produce the armaments required by Germany to continue fighting the war'. Assess the validity of this view.

Mobilisation of the labour force

The outbreak of war led to an increase in the number of men conscripted into the armed forces. At the same time, there was a need to increase the production of armaments. With a limited supply of male labour in Germany, these two demands could only be achieved by using the available labour force in the most efficient way possible and by using foreign labour. Large numbers of non-essential workers were released for military service. There was also a reduction of workers employed in consumer goods industries with a consequent rise in the numbers employed in munitions. The full-scale conscription of labour into essential war work, however, was not implemented in the first two years of the war.

The German reverse outside Moscow in December 1941 brought the labour supply issue to a head. Efforts to take labour away from civilian work to concentrate on armaments production had been frustrated by opposition from local *Gauleiters*, anxious to keep employment within their own areas. Since Hitler was opposed to the increased use of women in industry, the shortage of labour posed a serious threat to the plans to increase production of vital war materials. Part of the answer to this problem was found in the increased use of foreign labour.

The defeat at Stalingrad in January 1943 led to even more drastic measures to increase the labour supply. Even before the surrender of German forces, on 13 January 1943 Hitler issued a Decree for the Comprehensive Deployment of Men and Women for Reich Defence Tasks. This established a small committee to oversee the mobilisation of labour for the war effort. Under this decree, all men aged 16–65 and women aged 17–45 had to register for work with their local labour office. It was also decreed that small businesses that were not essential for the war effort should be closed and their employees transferred to more essential work. In terms of labour, this was the point at which the demands of total war began to have a significant impact. A rigorous 'comb-through' exercise was conducted to identify men who could be released from employment for military service and conscription of labour began to become a reality. Ideological considerations, however, still prevented the Nazi regime from treating women workers the same as males.

The use of foreign labour

From June 1940 until the spring of 1942, foreign workers in German industry were mainly recruited from occupied countries in western Europe. After the invasion of the USSR, however, there was a dramatic increase in the number of prisoners of war and, in October 1941, Hitler agreed that Russian prisoners of war could be used as slave labour. By December 1941, there were some 4 million foreign workers employed in Germany. In March 1942, Hitler established the Plenipotentiary General for Labour Allocation to organise centralised control over the procurement and allocation of foreign labour. This department was headed by Fritz Sauckel, a *Gauleiter* who used ruthless force to increase the number of foreign workers. From 1942 to 1945, Sauckel succeeded in rounding up and transporting to Germany 2.8 million workers from eastern Europe. Millions of prisoners of war were also forced to work in Germany. It has been calculated that, by 1944, there were 7 million foreign workers in Germany and another 7 million people in the occupied countries doing work for the Germans.

ACTIVITY

Why was the use of foreign labour vital to the German war effort?

SOURCE 2

In April 1942, Sauckel issued a memorandum setting out his instructions on the use of foreign labour to those in charge of the conscription of foreign labour in the East:

All prisoners of war, from the territories of the West as well as of the East, who are already situated in Germany, must be completely incorporated into the German armament and nutrition industries. Their production must be brought to the highest possible level. It must be emphasised, however, that an additional tremendous quantity of foreign labour has to be found for the Reich. The greatest pool for that purpose are the occupied territories of the East.

Consequently, it is an immediate necessity to use the human resources of the conquered Soviet territory to the fullest extent. Should we not succeed in obtaining the necessary amount of labour on a voluntary basis, we must immediately institute conscription or forced labour.

All the men must be fed, sheltered and treated in such a way as to exploit them to the highest possible extent at the lowest conceivable degree of expenditure.

ACTIVITY

Evaluating primary sources

What can we learn from Source 2 about the Nazi attitude towards prisoners of war?

Fig. 3 *Prisoners of war working at a canning factory in Wismar*

Conditions for foreign workers were harsh. Wages were low, living conditions were harsh and discipline was severe. Whereas volunteer 'guest workers' from western Europe were given the same wages and conditions as German workers, the forced labourers from the east were paid about half this amount. Prisoners of war and concentration camp inmates were also used as slave labour, without any payment and on starvation rations.

SOURCE 3

In her book, *My Father's Country,* Wibke Bruhns described the working conditions witnessed by her father at an underground factory where the V2 rockets were made:

The decision was made to transfer production below ground. With the arrival of the first 107 prisoners from Buchenwald, on 28 August 1943, a project began which, under the name of 'Mittelbau Dora', was to become synonymous with hell.

By night and day, the first production sites for the V2 were built by prisoners and forced labourers in the dark, airless tunnels. Survivors reported after liberation: 'The tunnels were extended by means of heavy compressed air drills, and the removal of even massive chunks of stone had to be accomplished with hands and shovels'. The sleeping tunnels were cramped, crowded dungeons full of excrement, vermin and decaying corpses. Some prisoners spent as long as 9 months in that underworld, if they survived.

Many of the prisoners had no shoes and had to walk barefoot in the debris; they worked in water at sub-zero temperatures, starving and suffering from exhaustion. Anyone who collapsed was ruthlessly beaten back to work.

STUDY TIP

The three sources give different perspectives on the production of armaments but all have value in their own ways. Two are about the use of foreign labour and give an insight into how important this was to the Nazi war machine and how the labourers were treated. Source 1 talks about the effect of bombing raids on production. As with all questions of this type, you need to refer to the provenance of the sources and identify the specific information each provides. You will also need to consider their limitations.

All the large German corporations, such as Thyssen, Krupp and I.G. Farben, used foreign forced labour during the war years and most German factories had some foreign labourers. It has been estimated that, by 1944, foreign labour made up a quarter of the German labour force.

 PRACTICE QUESTION

Evaluating primary sources

With reference to Sources 1, 2 and 3 and your understanding of the historical context, assess the value of Sources 1, 2 and 3 for an historian studying the German armaments industry during the Second World War.

Summary

There were undoubtedly problems for German industry in supplying the armed forces fast enough and in sufficient quantities in the early years of the war. This occurred despite the economy having been placed on a war footing from 1936 and despite the mobilisation of labour and capital for the armaments industries at the start of the war. As the historian Richard Overy has written, the 'supply of weapons grew much more slowly than the supply of resources to produce them'. Serious structural problems in the German economy, together with political chaos at the heart of the regime, led to an inefficient and uncoordinated use of the resources allocated to armaments production. After Speer was appointed Minister of Armaments in 1942, these production problems were largely solved and German industry began to produce weapons in the necessary quantities. This happened despite the Allied bombing campaign that subjected most German cities and the industries based in them to severe destruction.

STUDY TIP

Your answer to this type of question needs to compare the economic situations in Germany before and after Speer's appointment. Speer's work needs to be placed in context and evaluated against a range of other factors. As always, a balanced answer is required, with a clear and consistent argument.

 PRACTICE QUESTION

'Without the appointment of Speer as Armaments Minister in February 1942, Germany would have collapsed economically'. Assess the validity of this view.

23 The 'Final Solution'

From 1942 to early 1945, the Nazi regime implemented its so-called 'Final Solution' to the '**Jewish question**'. What had been rather confused and uncontrolled actions in 1940 and 1941, mixing mass killings with ghettoisation and deportations, were coordinated into a bureaucratic killing machine. Between 5 and 6 million people were systematically murdered. Most were Jews: from the Soviet Union after it was overrun by German forces; from the countries that were under Nazi occupation, such as Poland, France and Hungary; and from Germany itself. Countless other victims died in the same way: Soviet prisoners of war, Gypsies, the disabled and the dissidents regarded by the Nazis as 'asocial elements', or 'social undesirables'. Even when the Third Reich faced defeat in 1944, the killings were accelerated, coming to an end only when invading Allied armies liberated the camps in 1945.

The origins of the 'Final Solution'

The origins of the 'Final Solution' were complex and deep rooted. Hitler's ideological goals were fixed before 1933; if the Nazis ever came to power, it was certain that the Jewish people faced harmful consequences. Reichkristallnacht in November 1938 opened the way for increasingly violent persecution. For the Holocaust to take place, however, the Second World War was an essential precondition. Hitler himself explicitly linked the war in Europe with the fate of the Jews. When the decision was taken, late in 1940, to turn the war eastwards against the Soviet Union, it was clear that this would be a war of racial annihilation.

By the end of 1941, the Nazi regime had to face the fact that the complete conquest of the Soviet Union had not been achieved and that final victory would have to wait until the summer of 1942 at the earliest. Some of the previous plans to send millions of deported Jews to be resettled on the island of Madagascar or in Siberia had to be abandoned. It was also clear by then that the vast numbers of Jews already deported to the General Government area of Poland were too many for the authorities there to cope with. It was the urgency of the problems facing the Nazi regime late in 1941 that led to radical new policies.

The Wannsee Conference, January 1942

The key moment in the implementation of systematic murder was the **Wannsee Conference** on 20 January 1942. The meeting was originally scheduled to take place in December 1941; invitations went out in November. The timetable had to be pushed back due to the military crisis caused by the Soviet counter-offensive at Moscow in the first week of December, followed by Pearl Harbour and the entry into the war of Japan and the USA. New invitations went out on 6 January for the meeting to be held two weeks later.

The importance of the Wannsee Conference is frequently misrepresented as the occasion when the final decision was taken to exterminate Europe's Jews. In reality, Wannsee was a meeting to inform senior bureaucrats of their roles in implementing a decision that had already been taken. Most historians now agree that the decision came fairly soon after the invasion of the Soviet Union on 22 June. Exactly what that decision was, however, is still a matter of controversy and debate. Was it the signal for a new policy of all-out genocide? Or a decision to widen the existing programme of deportations to 'reservations' somewhere in the east? Or was it a sudden emergency decision, forced by the fact that the German conquest of the Soviet Union has unexpectedly stalled?

LEARNING OBJECTIVES
In this chapter you will learn about:

- policies towards Jews and the *Untermenschen* and the origins of the 'Final Solution'
- the Wannsee Conference
- the 'Final Solution'
- responsibility for the Holocaust
- Nazi state in 1945.

KEY CHRONOLOGY

The 'Final Solution', 1942–45

1942	January	Wannsee Conference
	July	Round up of Jews from Vichy France
1943	May	Concentration of all killings at Auschwitz
	June	Start of deportations of Reich Jews from Germany
1944	June	Mass deportation of Hungarian Jews to Auschwitz
	November	Destruction and evacuation of Auschwitz
1945	January	Liberation of Auschwitz
	April	Liberation of Belsen and KZ Mauthausen
		Hitler's suicide
	May	Germany's surrender

CROSS-REFERENCE

For further information on Reichkristallnacht, look back to Chapter 19, page 157.

KEY TERMS

'**Jewish question**': the term used by the Nazis when considering how to remove the Jews from German society

Wannsee Conference: conference held in a villa on the shores of lake Wannsee at Potsdam, just outside Berlin

Fig. 1 *This was the villa on Lake Wannsee in Berlin where the Nazi leaders met to decide on the final solution*

CROSS-REFERENCE

Reinhard Heydrich and his role in the Nazi Terror State are detailed in Chapter 14, page 109.

Heinrich Himmler, the leader of the SS, is also profiled in Chapter 14, page 108.

Hermann Goering was a formidable character in Nazi politics. His key profile is in Chapter 12, page 92.

ACTIVITY

Using your knowledge from this chapter and the historical context, explain the importance of the Wannsee Conference in the development of Nazi policy towards the Jews.

CROSS-REFERENCE

Joseph Goebbels was the chief propagandist of the Nazi movement from 1928 to 1945. More details of his work are in Chapter 10, page 79. His declaration of Total War is covered in Chapter 21, page 175.

SOURCE 1

Part of Reinhard Heydrich's speech to the Wannsee Conference on 20 January 1942, taken from the official record of the event:

In the course of the Final Solution, and under appropriate leadership, the Jews should be put to work in the East. Doubtless, the large majority will die of natural causes. Any final remnant that survives will doubtless consist of the most recalcitrant elements. They will have to be dealt with appropriately because otherwise, by natural selection, they would form the germ cell of a new Jewish revival. Europe will be combed through from west to east. Germany proper, including Bohemia and Moravia, will have to be dealt with first, due to the housing problem and other social necessities.

The top secret meeting at Wannsee comprised 15 high-ranking Nazi officials. Hitler and Himmler were not in attendance. The chairman was Reinhard Heydrich, the most powerful man in the SS after Heinrich Himmler. Heydrich had received orders from Hermann Goering, empowering him to organise the preparations for the 'Final Solution' to the 'Jewish question'. Some historians believe that the driving force was an unwritten order from Hitler. Others have speculated that Heydrich was involved in 'empire building', acting on his own initiative to enhance his power and authority.

What happened after Wannsee seemed to prove that the purpose of the meeting was to clarify the previously confused situation concerning deportations to the east. Heydrich considered the meeting a great success. The civilian authorities had all been willing to follow the lead of the RSHA (Reich Security Head Office) and not make objections. The deportation of Jews was no longer to vague destinations somewhere in Poland, but specific areas where there was an organised camp system. The way was open to coordinate and accelerate mass killings. More than half of all Jews to die in the Holocaust were exterminated between February 1942 and February 1943.

The 'Final Solution'

When the war turned against Germany in 1942–43, it might have been expected that the Nazi regime would slacken its attempts to exterminate the Jews and focus their efforts on fighting the Allies. In fact, the mass killings were accelerated and given higher priority than military needs. Nazi propaganda became even more hate-filled than before.

The intensification of the Nazi propaganda war against the Jews ran in parallel with the periods of crisis in Germany's war effort.

- Spring 1943: After the German surrender at Stalingrad in February 1943, Joseph Goebbels delivered the epic 'Total War' speech in Berlin in mid-February, followed by a massive propaganda drive in the Nazi press.
- Autumn 1943: When Germany suffered from mass bombing raids and the Red Army was beginning to push back German forces in the east, another similar surge of anti-Jewish propaganda occurred.
- Summer 1944: At the time of the Allied landings in France, there was another surge.

Numerous articles and speeches by Goebbels and other Nazi leaders emphasised the idea that the war would result in the destruction of the Jews. The Nazi regime did not spell out what was actually taking place in the 'Final Solution', but the general threat of destruction was hammered out repeatedly. The radical propaganda was reflected in the urgency of Nazi actions. Mass killings were accelerated. The Jewish populations of states such as France, Italy, Greece and Slovakia were rounded up for deportation. The Jewish ghettos at Minsk and

Vilnius were destroyed. In February 1944, the remaining Jews of Amsterdam were deported to Auschwitz.

By summer 1944, it was clear that Germany faced inevitable defeat in the war, but this realisation did not cause the 'Final Solution' to be abandoned – it had the reverse effect. Only in November 1944, when the Soviet armies had advanced deep into Poland, did the Nazis move to close down the killing machine and try to conceal what they had been up to. The crematoria at Auschwitz were blown up and hastily covered over. The surviving prisoners were pressed into forced marches westwards, away from the Red Army. These efforts at concealment were half-hearted and futile. The sheer size of the complex at Auschwitz-Birkenau made total destruction impossible.

The implementation of the 'Final Solution' was never completed. In January 1945, Soviet forces advancing westwards through Poland liberated Auschwitz. In the months that followed, Allied armies drove deeper into the Reich. In the west, American

Fig. 2 *Children being led by soldiers of the 3rd US Army to a hospital sick bay after the liberation of the Buchenwald concentration camp, 13 April 1945*

forces liberated Dachau and Mauthausen. In the north, British forces liberated Bergen-Belsen and Buchenwald. By May 1945, Hitler was dead, Germany had surrendered and the full horror of the camps was finally becoming apparent.

The camp system

It is important not to confuse the death camps in operation from 1942 to 1945 with the wider system of concentration camps for political prisoners that had existed from the early Third Reich, commencing with Dachau, near Munich, in 1933. There were 'ordinary' concentration camps near almost every main population centre in Germany: Dachau, Sachsenhausen near Berlin, Bergen-Belsen near Hannover, Buchenwald near Weimar, and so on. After the *Anschluss*, Mauthausen was built near Linz in Upper Austria.

Concentration camps were brutal places, but they were not designed as centres of extermination. They housed political prisoners of all kinds, from Catholics to homosexuals, from socialists to petty criminals. Most Germans knew at least a little about the concentration camps. Some approved of their existence, satisfied with the punishment of 'social deviants'. Most people feared the camps.

The system of camps in the eastern occupied territories that came into operation from the end of 1941 was on an enormous scale and fulfilled many different functions. Extermination was at the heart of the system: these were death camps built for the specific purpose of killing *Untermenschen* such as Jews and other 'racial undesirables'. The railway entrance to Auschwitz-Birkenau has become the ultimate emotive symbol of this process, the place where new arrivals were unloaded from trains and those deemed 'unproductive' were selected for immediate transfer to the gas chambers. But Auschwitz took time to build up its factory of death. Only about one-fifth of the victims of the Holocaust died there. Other death camps also had a key role in the system:

- Chelmno (Kulmhof), about 40 miles from Lodz, was the first killing centre to be established, in December 1941. Killings were first carried out by mobile gas vans using carbon monoxide. The use of **Zyklon B** was developed later in early 1942. About 145,000 died there. Chelmno was situated in a part of Poland designated for 'Germanisation' but other death camps were built further east, outside the German Reich.
- Majdanek, near Lublin, was built late in 1940 as an ordinary concentration camp. From late 1941, it became a death camp. About 200,000 people died there, 60 per cent of them Jews, the others Soviet prisoners of war or Polish political prisoners.

CROSS-REFERENCE

The *Anschluss* (union between Austria and Germany) in 1938 is detailed in Chapter 19, page 155.

KEY TERMS

***Untermenschen*:** literally 'sub-humans', used by the Nazis to describe those whom they considered to be racially inferior, including Jews, Gypsies and peoples of the Slav race

Zyklon B: a form of poisonous cyanide gas, originally developed by a Jewish scientist as a weapon for use in the First World War and later used in the gas chambers for mass killings in the death camps

The 'Final Solution' would not have been possible without the development of poisonous gas for the purpose of mass killings. The role of the chief manufacturer, I.G. Farben, led to controversy after the war.

- Belzec, near Lvov, was originally a labour camp but was used as a death camp from March 1942 until the spring of 1943, when the camp was closed down. More than half a million Jews were killed there, together with several thousand Gypsies.
- Sobibor was built near Lublin as part of the construction programme agreed upon at the Wannsee Conference. About 250,000 victims died there, mostly Jews and Soviet prisoners of war. In October 1943, a Jewish revolt led to the escape of 800 prisoners. The camp was closed down on Himmler's orders soon afterwards.
- Treblinka, about 75 miles from Warsaw, was constructed for the purpose of mass killing. From July 1942 until operations ceased in September 1943, almost 1 million people were murdered there, first about 300,000 Jews from Warsaw and later Jews from all over central Europe.

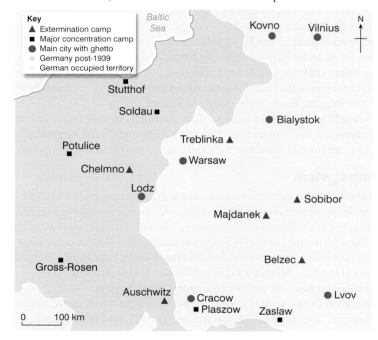

Fig. 3 *The location of Nazi death camps in eastern Europe*

SOURCE 2

Rudolf Reder, one of only two people to survive imprisonment at Belzec, recounted what happened when trains loaded with Jews arrived at the camp in his personal testimony which was published in 1946:

After the victims had been unloaded from the trains, they were gathered in the yard and surrounded by armed SS men and then the commandant delivered a speech. 'Now you're going to the bath house, afterwards you will be sent to work.' That's all.

Everyone was happy, glad that they were going to work. They even clapped. That was the one moment of hope and illusion. For a moment the people felt happy. There was complete calm. In that silence the crowd moved on, men straight into a building on which there was a sign in big letters: 'Bath and inhalation room'.

The women went about twenty metres further on – to a large barrack hut. There they had their heads shaved, both women and girls. They entered, not knowing what for. At the moment when the women were pushed naked, shorn and beaten, like cattle to the slaughter, the men were already dying in the gas chambers. The shaving of the women lasted about two hours, the same time as the murder process in the chambers.

Evaluating primary sources

Assess the value of Source 2 for an historian researching the implementation of the 'Final Solution'.

Auschwitz

In 1943 and 1944, Auschwitz (Oswiecim in Poland), a few miles west of Crakow, became the hub of the vast killing machine established by the Nazis. The development of Auschwitz took a considerable time. Until mid-1943, the main killing centres were at camps such as Sobibor, Belzec and Treblinka. Most of these camps were closed down after the Jewish populations in their vicinity had been killed.

Auschwitz was more than a death camp. It was a huge sprawling complex of buildings with many different functions. Auschwitz I, in the old Habsburg army barracks, remained active, but was overshadowed by Auschwitz II, the huge camp at Birkenau, the arrival centre for transports from the west and the place where the main gas chambers and crematoria were situated. Auschwitz III, on the other side of the railway tracks at Monowitz, was a huge industrial complex, producing munitions and other essential goods for the war effort. In outlying districts, a chain of smaller satellite camps contained industrial enterprises run by the SS and were dependent upon forced labour provided from Auschwitz.

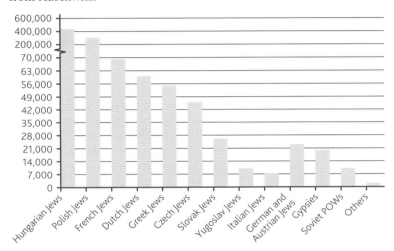

Note: Estimates of the total deaths at Auschwitz vary between 1.1m and 1.8m.

Fig. 5 *Murders at Auschwitz*

Jewish resistance

One of the persistent myths about the Holocaust is the theme of victimhood and Jewish passivity – the idea that the victims of the Nazis invariably accepted their fate with docility and resignation. In reality, there was extensive Jewish resistance. The Nazi authorities went to great lengths to prevent this, both by intimidation and by concealing what was actually happening until the last possible moment. This had only partial success and there were many instances of protest. The fact that resistance could only ever be small in scale and had no chance at all of lasting success should not obscure the fact that it was there.

Across Eastern Europe, groups of partisan fighters established base camps deep in the forests and carried out acts of sabotage against the German occupiers. Many of these groups were nationalist or communist, but there were also numerous Jewish groups. About 10,000 Jewish partisans were active in Lithuania in early 1942. In the General Government of Poland, the Nazi governor, Hans Frank, had to commit large security forces to try to deal with more than 20 different Jewish partisan groups. In Belarus, from autumn 1941 onwards, a Jewish resistance group led by the **Bielski brothers** eventually

Fig. 4 *Entrance gate to Auschwitz concentration camp*

KEY PROFILE

The Bielski brothers

The Bielski family, from Stankiewicze in Poland, were millers and grocers. After the Nazis took over this part of Poland in 1941, the parents were killed in the ghetto in Nowogrodek and the four sons, Tuvia, Alexander, Asael and Aron, fled to the nearby Naloboki forest. They set up a camp, which attracted other Jewish escapees and, at its height, housed over 1200 people. For three years, they carried out sabotage missions against Nazi forces and managed to evade capture. When the Soviet Red Army occupied the area in 1944, the partisans emerged from the forest but were treated with hostility and suspicion by the Soviet commanders.

became a permanent community of 1200 partisans. In addition to acts of sabotage, the Bielski group also provided a refuge for Jews escaping from the ghettos.

Fig. 6   *The writer Ilya Ehrenburg in Vilna (Vilnius) with Jewish partisans who entered the city with the Red Army*

ACTIVITY

Extension

1. Conduct further research into the efforts of Jewish resistors and/ or helpers of the resistance to help you understand the extent of resistance.

2. Watch the film *Schindler's List* or read the novel *Schindler's Ark* by Thomas Keneally to gain insight into the real story of a Nazi Party member who saved many Jews from concentration camps.

There were also sporadic revolts in the ghettos and camps. One violent rising against the Nazis took place in the ghetto of Bialystok. A larger rising broke out in the Warsaw ghetto in January 1943, which took the SS by surprise as 80 per cent of the Jews in Warsaw had already been sent to the death camp at Treblinka. The first attempts to crush the rising failed. It was only in May 1943 that the last resistance in the Warsaw ghetto was finally crushed by 2000 German troops, using heavy weapons and supported by air strikes.

There were organised revolts in the Sobibor and Treblinka death camps in 1943. At Auschwitz-Birkenau in 1944, Jewish prisoners blew up Crematorium 4. A network of Jewish organisations smuggled detailed evidence to inform the western Allies about the Nazi extermination programme. Messages were passed successfully to western embassies, but had little impact, partly because western governments found it difficult to take in the full horror of what was happening, partly because it was so difficult to take any practical action to stop it.

The death marches

The military defeat of the Third Reich did not bring a tidy end to the suffering of the victims of the Holocaust. From autumn 1944, as German forces pulled back, the Nazi regime carried out a frantic programme of evacuations and forced marches. Camps were hurriedly closed down and the inmates sent on long marches westwards, away from the advancing Red Army. These death marches caused terrible suffering and loss of life. Often in freezing winter weather, people who were already malnourished and had inadequate shoes and clothing were forced to march. Many died of illness and exhaustion. Hundreds were shot by their guards for failing to keep up the required pace. Even if they survived their first forced march from one camp to a new one, many prisoners had to repeat the awful experience all over again as that new camp was evacuated when enemy forces approached. It is difficult to know exactly how many victims died on the death marches; estimates range from 250,000 to 400,000. Many of them were women. The death marches continued right up to the end of the war.

Responsibility for the Holocaust

Hitler's responsibility for the Holocaust is often thought of in simplistic terms:

- He was motivated from the start by fanatical anti-Semitism.
- He dominated all aspects of power and propaganda in Germany.
- All Germans either supported his ideas or were incapable of opposing him because of terror and intimidation by Hitler's regime.

Therefore, the Holocaust was 'Hitler's war against the Jews'; without Hitler it could never have happened. There is a lot of truth in this, but the 'Final Solution' involved much more than one man. Industrialised murder on such a huge scale required actions and decisions by many Nazi leaders and by thousands of lesser officials. Millions of ordinary people were involved in acts of persecution, deportations or mass killings.

Apportioning the responsibility for the Holocaust therefore raises difficult questions. How far did Hitler and leading Nazis carry though the 'Final Solution' by force, terror and secrecy? Did Hitler provide the German people with a convenient alibi for a dreadful crime that they were actually responsible for, but could be excused as the action of a minority of 'evil Nazis', as opposed to the majority of 'good Germans'?

At one extreme, it can be argued that the Holocaust was entirely the responsibility of Adolf Hitler. The trouble with this argument is that it is based on simplistic assumptions about the Nazi dictatorship – that Hitler was an all-powerful dictator and that any kind of opposition to Nazi policies could be crushed with ease. Historians are agreed that the Nazi regime was not like that at all. In many ways, the Nazi regime depended on a mixture of 'chaos and consent'. However central Hitler's role had been, the responsibility could not have been Hitler's alone.

ACTIVITY

'Adolf Hitler bore the sole responsibility for the Holocaust.' Assess the validity of this view.

SOURCE 3

On 30 January 1942, on the ninth anniversary of his becoming Chancellor, Hitler made a speech in Berlin:

The Jews are our old enemy, they have experienced at our hands an upsetting of their ideas, and they rightfully hate us, just as much as we hate them. The war will not end as the Jews imagine it will, namely with the uprooting of the Aryans, but the result of this war will be the complete annihilation of the Jews.

Now for the first time they will not bleed other people to death, but for the first time the old Jewish law of an eye for an eye, a tooth for a tooth, will be applied. And – world Jewry may as well know this – the further these battles spread, the more anti-Semitism will spread. It will find nourishment in every prison camp and in every family when it discovers the ultimate reason for the sacrifices it has to make. And the hour will come when the most evil universal enemy of all time will be finished, at least for a thousand years.

KEY PROFILE

Martin Bormann (1900–45) was the Head of the Nazi Party Chancellery and Hitler's private secretary. In this role he exercised enormous influence since he controlled access to the Führer. He also had a key role in Party and Civil Service appointments. He died while trying to escape the Soviet advance in Berlin in May 1945.

The Nazi regime had many overlapping centres of power and many rival Nazi leaders competing for Hitler's approval. Men like Himmler, Heydrich and Eichmann, at the head of the enormous bureaucratic machinery of the SS, were key architects of mass murder. Other leading Nazis were responsible too, including Hermann Goering, **Martin Bormann**, the propaganda minister Joseph Goebbels and Albert Speer as the overlord of Germany's war industries and the use of forced labour. In the middle and lower levels of the Nazi regime, thousands of lesser officials carried out the orders that meant persecution, deportation and death for the Holocaust victims. All shared at least some of the responsibility.

CROSS-REFERENCE

For key profiles refer back to: Hermann Goering, Chapter 12, page 92; Joseph Goebbels, Chapter 10, page 79; Albert Speer, Chapter 22, page 183.

SOURCE 4

Joseph Goebbels made this speech on the radio in May 1943:

We are moving ahead. The fulfilment of the Führer's prophecy about which world Jewry laughed when he made it in 1939 stands at the end of our course of action. Even in Germany the Jews laughed when we stood up for the first time against them. Among them laughter is now a thing of the past. They chose to make war against us. But Jewry now understands that the war has become a war against them. When Jewry conceived of the plan for the total extermination of the German people, it wrote its own death sentence.

At the opposite extreme, it can be argued that the German people as a whole were responsible for genocide. This view suggests that there was some kind of national defect in the Germans that made them vote for Hitler and then become his 'willing executioners'. It can be argued that the 'German people' was not one indoctrinated mass, but consisted of countless diverse elements, many of them opponents of everything the Nazis stood for, and that many well-intentioned Germans found themselves compelled against their will to compromise or to keep silent. Even so, large numbers of ordinary Germans shared in the responsibility for Nazi crimes.

STUDY TIP

All three sources are statements or speeches by leading Nazis, made at different times. With this type of question, you need to identify the key points in each source and place them in their historical context. You should also attempt to assess the limitations of each source. Remember to look at provenance, tone, emphasis, as well as context.

 PRACTICE QUESTION

Evaluating primary sources

With reference to Sources 1, 3 and 4, assess the value of these sources to an historian studying the origins of the 'Final Solution'.

Summary

The conquest of large swathes of territory in the east in pursuit of *Lebensraum* brought millions more Jews under German rule and created the conditions under which the SS could begin to implement the 'Final Solution'. Nazi ideology had consistently made clear that the ultimate aim of their anti-Semitic policies was the annihilation of the Jewish race. The Wannsee Conference in early 1942 was concerned with the implementation of a policy that had already been decided and led directly to the creation of extermination camps and the rounding up and transportation of millions of Jews and others to the camps. Estimates of the total number of victims of the Holocaust vary but, according to the historian Martin Gilbert, there were nearly 6 million Jewish victims, which represented about 78 per cent of the total number of Jews living in Germany and the occupied territories at that time. The Nazis also eliminated between 90,000 and 220,000 Romany Gypsies, 270,000 physically and mentally disabled people in the so-called 'euthanasia programme', many millions of Russians and Poles, between 5000 and 15,000 homosexuals, and between 2500 and 5000 Jehovah's Witnesses.

24 Opposition and resistance in wartime

The growing hardships experienced by the German people during the war, together with the fact that after the defeat at Stalingrad the possibility of a German defeat loomed ever larger, induced a mood of growing scepticism. Propaganda became less effective and SD reports commented on the denting of the Hitler myth. There are indications that the Nazi Party lost support during the war. Fewer people attended Party meetings or participated in Party activities. Party membership fell. However, any individuals or groups that were opposed to the regime faced enormous obstacles. Despite their growing scepticism, the majority of Germans remained loyal to the regime. The groups that might have become the focus of opposition had either been banned (trade unions and non-Nazi political parties) or had compromised themselves by cooperating with the Nazis (the Churches, the army, the elites). Moreover, the Nazi police and surveillance system was highly effective in uncovering opposition groups and silencing them before they could become a serious threat. A small number of brave people did engage in active opposition and paid a heavy price for their courage. Many more took risks by hiding Jews, listening to BBC radio broadcasts or reading banned books. Whilst these actions show an undercurrent of resistance, they posed no real threat to the regime.

LEARNING OBJECTIVES

In this chapter you will learn about:

- opposition from young people, including students
- opposition from the Churches and individual churchmen
- communist opposition
- army and civilian critics among the elites
- attempts to assassinate Hitler.

CROSS-REFERENCE

Further information on the Hitler Myth can be found in Chapter 14, page 119.

Opposition from young people

Working-class youth

During the 1930s, the Nazis had banned all independent youth groups and made membership of the Hitler Youth (HJ) compulsory. However, there was a long-standing tradition among working-class youths to form independent youth groups. Some, such as the 'wild cliques', were criminal or semi-criminal in nature, whilst others, such as the *Wandervogel* were law-abiding but unconventional. Despite the efforts of the regime, the 'wild cliques' were never completely suppressed and began to re-emerge during the war. One such group was the Edelweiss Pirates.

Fig. 1 *The Edelweiss Pirates*

ACTIVITY

Evaluating primary sources

With reference to Source 1, how far does this report show that the Nazi regime had a serious and growing problem with disaffected youth?

The Edelweiss Pirates

SOURCE 1

An extract from a 1944 Reich Justice Ministry report:

The problem of the threat to youth and juvenile criminality manifests itself in particular in the formation of youth gangs. For, since the beginning of the war, and above all since the start of the terror air raids, there has been an increasing number of reports about combinations of young people who are pursuing partly criminal, but also to some extent political and ideological goals.

In Gelsenkirchen a gang of approximately fifty young people were involved in thefts and robberies. They called themselves 'Edelweiss Pirates', met together every evening and were opposed to the HJ. Similar observations have been made at Essen, Bochum and Wattenscheid. In Cologne the Edelweiss Pirates have also made an appearance. They carried out propaganda for the bundisch youth movement (*Wandervogel*), and printed leaflets.

The Edelweiss Pirates were groups of mostly working-class young people aged 14–18 who were mainly active in the Rhineland and Ruhr areas. Their name derived from their badge, which showed an edelweiss flower. According to the Justice Ministry report, the main 'uniform' of the group consisted of 'short trousers, white socks, a check shirt, a white pullover and scarf and a windcheater. In addition they have very long hair.' Although not overtly political, the Edelweiss Pirates were anti-Hitler Youth and tried to avoid conscription. The report also stated that 'They hate all discipline and thereby place themselves in opposition to the community. However, they are not only politically hostile but, as a result of their composition, they are also criminal and antisocial.'

The Edelweiss Pirates consciously rejected the official, disciplined and militaristic culture of the Hitler Youth by organising independent expeditions into the countryside, where they sang songs banned in the Hitler Youth. In the war years, there were an increasing number of clashes between Edelweiss Pirates and Hitler Youth groups. In 1944, the Cologne group became linked to an underground group that helped army deserters, escaped prisoners of war, forced labourers and prisoners from concentration camps. They obtained supplies by attacking military depots. The chaos and destruction caused by bombing provided the conditions for developing underground activity.

The Gestapo and Hitler Youth used their powers to crush the Edelweiss Pirates. When arrests, shaving of heads and banishment to labour camps did not work, the Gestapo turned to more severe measures. On 7 December 1942, the Gestapo broke up 28 groups in Düsseldorf, Duisburg, Essen and Wuppertal. The leaders of the Cologne Edelweiss Pirates were publicly hanged in November 1944.

Middle-class youth
Swing Youth

A different style of youth rebellion developed among young people from the prosperous middle class. The Swing Youth were motivated, according to the Ministry of Justice report, by 'the desire to have a good time'. In a conscious rejection of Nazi values, the Swing Youth groups listened to American and British swing and jazz music and wore English-style clothes. Swing clubs sprang up in Hamburg, Kiel, Berlin, Stuttgart, Frankfurt, Dresden, Halle and Karlsruhe. By adopting jazz music – which the Nazis referred to as 'negro music' – as the emblem of an alternative youth culture, they were placing themselves in opposition to the regime, but they were not overtly political or attempting to overthrow the regime. Nevertheless their 'sleaziness' and unashamed pleasure-seeking offended the moral precepts of the Nazi regime and Himmler wanted to send the leaders of the movement to concentration camps for two to three years.

ACTIVITY

With reference to Source 2, identify the main motivations for Hans Scholl's opposition to the regime.

Opposition from students: the White Rose group

SOURCE 2

An extract from a leaflet issued to members of Munich University by one of its students, Hans Scholl, in January 1943:

The war is approaching its inevitable end. With mathematical certainty Hitler is leading the German nation to disaster. Now it is time for those Germans to act who want to avoid being lumped with the Nazi barbarians by the outside world. Only in broadminded cooperation between the people of Europe can the basis be established for a new society. Freedom of speech, freedom of belief, protection of the individual citizen against criminal power – these are the foundations of a new Europe.

Fig. 2   *The White Rose group*

Based in Munich, the White Rose group was a more consciously political movement. Led by **Hans and Sophie Scholl**, and supported by Professor Kurt Huber, the group was based at Munich University and its main target audience was the educated middle class. A religiously mixed body, the White Rose group was influenced by Catholic theologians such as Bishop Galen and emphasised the importance of individual freedom and personal responsibility in questions of morality. This led the group to attack the Nazi treatment of the Jews and Slav peoples of Eastern Europe. During 1942–43, the White Rose group issued six pamphlets that were distributed mainly in Munich but also taken further afield by sympathisers. In February 1943, the group became more daring when they painted anti-Nazi slogans, such as 'Hitler Mass Murderer' on buildings. They were eventually caught by the Gestapo and executed.

Opposition from the Churches

The Roman Catholic Church

As in the 1930s, the Christian Churches were influenced in their response to the regime firstly by their desire to protect their organisations and secondly by their support for many of the regime's policies. The Roman Catholic Church, for example, supported Germany's war aims in 1939 and gave wholehearted support to the invasion of the USSR in 1941. It was again left to individual churchmen to raise their voices in protest at some aspects of Nazi policies. Bishop Galen spoke out in a sermon in 1940 to condemn the euthanasia programme that killed 270,000 mentally and physically disabled people. His protest struck a chord with other Christians and led to the temporary halting of the programme by the regime. Galen himself was not persecuted by the regime for his outspoken opposition but other priests who distributed his sermon were. Three Catholic priests were executed. Apart from Galen, the other leading Catholic who spoke out against the regime was **Archbishop Frings** of Cologne, who condemned the killing of prisoners of war.

The Protestant Church

The Protestant Confessional Church of Prussia was the only Christian body in Germany to protest publicly about the treatment of the Jews. In 1943, a statement was read from the pulpits in Prussian churches. Dietrich Bonhoeffer, who had been an outspoken critic of the regime since 1933, also called for wider Christian resistance to the treatment of Jews. Since 1940, however, Bonhoeffer had been banned from speaking in public and his criticisms could not reach a wide audience in Germany. Bonhoeffer had become involved in the late 1930s with critics of the Nazi regime from among the elites and he had extensive contacts

KEY PROFILE

Hans Scholl (1918–43) and **Sophie Scholl** (1921–43) were founder members and leading activists in the White Rose group. Hans had joined the Hitler Youth in his teens but had become disillusioned with the Nazi regime. They advocated passive resistance against the regime. They were arrested, tried and executed in February 1943. At her trial, Sophie Scholl said, 'What we have written and said is in the minds of all of you, but you lack the courage to say it aloud.'

CROSS-REFERENCE

There is more detail on Archbishop Galen in Chapter 14, page 115.

There is more detail on Dietrich Bonhoeffer in Chapter 16, page 137.

KEY PROFILE

Archbishop Frings (1887–1978) was archbishop of Cologne from 1942 to 1969. He denounced the Nazi persecution of the Jews as a 'crime that calls out to heaven'. Because of his criticism he was placed under surveillance by the Gestapo.

ACTIVITY

Discuss in pairs whether you agree with this statement: 'Neither the Catholic nor the Protestant Churches were able to uphold their religious values in opposition to the Nazi regime.'

ACTIVITY

Group work

Divide into four groups. Each group should research wartime opposition to the Nazis from one of the following – young people, the Churches, political opposition (e.g. communists) and the elites. Focus the research on the main individuals or groups involved, their motivation, actions and effectiveness. Each group should make a presentation of their findings to the whole class.

CROSS-REFERENCE

Information about General Beck and the plot to remove Hitler can be found in Chapter 14, page 116.

KEY PROFILE

Fig. 3   *Count Helmut von Moltke*

Count Helmut von Moltke (1907–45) was a Prussian aristocratic landowner and a descendant of a Prussian military leader of the nineteenth century. A lawyer by training and a Christian by conviction, Moltke was critical of the atrocities committed by German forces in occupied countries and became an opponent of the regime. He did not believe that Hitler should be assassinated or overthrown by force, advocating only non-violent resistance. Nevertheless he was arrested by the Gestapo in January 1944 and tried and executed in January 1945.

abroad. He was arrested by the Gestapo in 1943 and held in prison until his execution (just before liberation) in 1945.

Communist opposition

The underground communist resistance had been severely weakened by the Gestapo in the 1930s but had managed to survive in some areas. The 1939 Nazi-Soviet Pact had undermined communist resistance to the regime as the KPD struggled to explain and justify this arrangement. The invasion of the USSR in June 1941, however, had galvanised communist resistance to the regime. At the time of the invasion, the KPD had 89 underground cells operating in Berlin, with other cells in Hamburg, Mannheim and central Germany. Their main means of spreading ideas and attempting to recruit was through issuing leaflets attacking the regime. Infiltration by the Gestapo was always a problem for these cells and, in 1942–43, the Gestapo had considerable success in destroying the communist underground network. By the end of 1943, 22 of the communist cells in Berlin had been destroyed. The communist underground did cling to life in some areas but, under pressure from the Gestapo and linked to the USSR, the power most Germans considered to be their main enemy, the movement had no prospect of attracting widespread support.

Army and civilian critics among the elites

The plot to overthrow Hitler in 1938 by members of the army high command and senior civil servants was never activated and therefore remained undiscovered by the Gestapo. Those involved continued to oppose the regime. There was, however, no unity of purpose among those who opposed Hitler's policies. Some acted from a deeply felt moral conviction that the Nazi regime was evil, while others acted out of patriotism and the belief that Hitler was leading Germany to destruction. Some were democrats, while others were traditional, aristocratic conservatives who wanted a return to an authoritarian, non-Nazi style of government.

The Kreisau Circle

Many of the diverse views of the elite who opposed Nazism could be found within the Kreisau Circle. Kreisau was the home of **Count Helmut von Moltke**, one of the leading figures within the group, which also included other aristocrats, lawyers, SPD politicians and churchmen such as Bonhoeffer. The common denominator linking this diverse group was a belief in personal freedom and individual responsibility. Described as the 'intellectual power-house of the non-communist opposition' in Nazi Germany, the Kreisau Circle held three meetings in 1942–43 before the group was broken up by the Gestapo.

SOURCE 3

An extract from a letter written by Helmut von Moltke to a friend in October 1941:

The day is so full of gruesome news that I cannot write in peace, although I retired at 5 and have just had some tea. What affects me most is the inadequacy of the reactions of the military; dreadful new orders are being issued and nobody seems to see anything wrong in it all. How is one to bear the burden of complicity? In one area in Serbia two villages have been reduced to ashes, 1700 men and 240 women from among the inhabitants have been executed. May I know this and yet still sit at my table in my heated flat and have tea? Don't I therefore become guilty too? What shall I say when I am asked: And what did you do during that time? Since Saturday the Jews are being rounded up. A woman Kiep knows saw a Jew collapse on the street; when she went to help him, a policeman stepped in, stopped her, and kicked the body on the ground so that it rolled in the gutter; then he turned to the lady with some shame and said', 'Those are our orders'.

Assassination attempts and the July 1944 plot

Among those who had been involved in the 1938 plot, General Beck, Karl Goerdeler and Ulrich von Hassell continued to discuss acting against the regime. They had links to Dietrich Bonhoeffer and General Hans Oster. At first, Beck and Goerdeler concentrated on trying to persuade senior army generals to arrest Hitler. They also made contact, through a meeting between Bonhoeffer and Bishop Bell of Chichester, with the British government, hoping for a commitment to a negotiated peace if Hitler was removed. None of these moves was effective and, in 1943, the conspirators decided that their only option was to assassinate Hitler. The loss of the German army at Stalingrad, due largely to Hitler's refusal to allow a retreat, confirmed that Hitler was leading Germany to disaster.

A first assassination attempt was made in March 1943 when a bomb was placed on Hitler's plane. This failed to explode. Although the plot was not discovered, the arrest of Bonhoeffer and other members of the Kreisau Circle in April 1943 was a warning that the Gestapo was getting close to uncovering the full extent of the conspiracy. In 1943, the conspiracy was joined by Colonel **Claus von Stauffenberg**, who actually succeeded in planting a bomb at Hitler's headquarters in East Prussia in July 1944.

Plans were made for a military coup – codenamed Operation Valkyrie – to take over Berlin after Hitler was assassinated. If the assassination attempt had been successful, the conspirators would have established a provisional government consisting of Conservatives, Centre Party, SPD and non-Party representatives, which would then have tried to open immediate peace negotiations with the western Allies. The bomb exploded, but Hitler escaped with minor injuries. The planned coup did not materialise because of confusion among the conspirators, who failed to seize control of the radio stations. A broadcast by Hitler to prove that he was still alive was confirmation that the plot had failed. In the wake of this failed assassination, Himmler was placed in charge of rounding up the conspirators. The SS cast their net wide, arresting 7000 people and executing 5746. Beck committed suicide and Stauffenberg was shot. The failure of the plot led to the army losing the last vestiges of its independence from the regime as it was effectively placed under SS control.

SOURCE 4

In Wibke Bruhns' 2004 memoir based on her father's diaries, she writes about her father, Hans Georg Klamroth, who was one of the army officers from an elite background executed for being implicated in the bomb plot:

In the summer of 1943, Hans Georg writes about the 'violent battle of ideologies, even within', and about 'the intellectual movements that will influence our time'. He gives away his SS uniforms. I think he's finding new bearings at around this time and revolution – high treason in other words – had crossed his mind. During interrogation by the Gestapo he mentions Stalingrad as the root cause. It must have been a cumulative development.

Hans Georg knows what the regime has turned Germans into. Even if he has seen nothing of the mass murders in Poland because his regiment withdrew so quickly, his eyes must have been opened in Russia.

KEY PROFILE

Claus von Stauffenberg (1907–44) was a professional soldier from an aristocratic background who had served in North Africa before being injured and sent back to Germany. Appalled by SS atrocities in the USSR and convinced that Germany was being led into a catastrophic defeat, he recruited supporters for an assassination plot against Hitler. He carried the bomb into Hitler's headquarters in July 1944, but it failed to kill Hitler. He was arrested and executed for his part in the plot.

ACTIVITY

Extension

There have been various attempts by the German elites to challenge Hitler from 1938 to 1944. Conduct research to gain more details about the different attempts. Why were these attempts generally seen as treachery by the majority of Germans?

PRACTICE QUESTION

Evaluating primary sources

With reference to Sources 2, 3 and 4 and your understanding of the historical context, assess the value of the sources for an historian researching on resistance to the Nazi regime.

The bomb plot gained very little sympathy among the majority of ordinary Germans. The plotters came from the old elite and made no attempt to arouse popular support. SD reports spoke of a widespread feeling of relief that the plotters had failed to kill Hitler, and there is no reason to doubt the general accuracy of these reports. The plotters were vilified as traitors, a judgement with which most Germans appear to have concurred.

PRACTICE QUESTION

'The defeat of the German army at Stalingrad in January 1943 led to a complete collapse of confidence in the Nazi regime at home.' Assess the validity of this view.

Summary

Despite the dangers of discovery and severe punishment, there were groups and individuals who resisted the Nazi regime in a variety of ways. Some were motivated by their political beliefs, others by moral outrage at the atrocities the regime was committing in the name of the German people. Others, especially among young people, were not prepared to conform to the strict social norms demanded by the regime. The course of the war, and the growing awareness that Germany was heading for defeat, was a major factor in undermining faith in the regime and in the Führer. The courage of those who opposed the Nazis, however, should not obscure the fact that none of the regime's critics had broad-based support.

ACTIVITY

Revision

Complete the following table after reading this chapter:

Source of opposition	Activities	Extent of support	Effectiveness
Youth			
Churches			
Communists			
Elites			

Conclusion: An overview of the Nazi state by 1945

There are many ways to describe and characterise the Nazi state. It was a one-party dictatorship that closed down all political debate and used terror and repression against those considered to be its enemies. The suspension of the rule of law and the pervasive violence of the state were justified by the claim that the Nazi Party was acting in the name of the German people to remove the pernicious influence of Jews, Bolsheviks and other political and racial enemies from German society. Since violence and terror were central to the achievement of Nazi Party aims, the SS grew in power and importance and became, in many ways, a state within a state, charged with maintaining an iron discipline within Germany itself and implementing the regime's plans for the annihilation of Germany's racial enemies in the Reich and the occupied territories.

The Nazi state aimed to create a racial community, or *Volksgemeinschaft,* which would separate, in the words of Gregor Strasser, 'those who believe in the German future, the Germans' from 'those who, for whatever reason, are against, the non-Germans'. This aim was pursued through terror but also through the creation of party organisations to 'coordinate' various groups in German society into the racial community. Once this process had been set in motion in 1933, the ordinary German citizen could not avoid the all-pervading presence of the Nazi Party. Through organisations such as the Hitler Youth, the DAF, the BDM and Nazi welfare organisations, individuals and families were brought into contact with the Party at some level. Moreover, the Party's propaganda operation did not allow individuals any space for independent thought. Party symbols and slogans, conveyed by radio broadcasts and the printed media, were everywhere. No alternative sources of information were available. Whilst not every German citizen became a Nazi, the distortion of reality by propaganda and the absence of any alternative views created a situation in which people became predisposed to accept the Nazi version of the truth.

Fig. 1 *A German soldier sits among the ruins of Berlin during the final stages of the war in 1945*

CROSS-REFERENCE

Gregor Strasser's role in the Nazi Party is detailed in Chapter 11, page 87.

Presiding over this Nazi state was Adolf Hitler, a cult figure presented in Nazi propaganda as the very embodiment of the heroic, self-sacrificing and visionary leader Germany so desperately needed. In reality, Hitler was lazy and self-indulgent. He rarely issued written orders. Even when he did, such 'Führer Orders' were often merely his signed approval for a ready-made policy presented to him by a subordinate. Hitler's lifestyle was not suited to efficiency or attention to bureaucratic details. He was frequently absent from Berlin, either because he preferred to relax at his mountain hideaway at Berchtesgaden in the Bavarian mountains or because he was fully occupied with matters at military headquarters during the war.

Hitler's very personal approach to government often led to confusion and delay as various leaders and officials competed to gain his attention. Decision-making often seemed unpredictable and inefficient, but many historians

ACTIVITY

Group work

Discuss in pairs or in groups:
'Outwardly, the Nazi regime promoted an image of itself as ordered and efficient. In reality, it was chaotic and ineffectual.'

believe that this outwardly chaotic system actually made Hitler even more powerful. He was almost never bogged down in the time-consuming business of reading reports, attending meetings and spelling out orders in detail. He remained 'institutionally unattached', keeping his hands free to intervene as and when he chose. By standing 'alone and above', Hitler also benefited from the eagerness with which subordinates tried to compete for his approval – what was known as 'working towards the Führer'. Leading Nazis were constantly trying to work out what Hitler would most want to happen and then present proposals or take actions to bring it about.

At the heart of the Nazi state, therefore, was a chaotic duplication and overlapping of roles and responsibilities and competition for the attention and approval of the Führer. In this ruthless struggle, there were a number of key individuals who succeeded in creating their own power bases. Himmler, as leader of the SS, had control over the police and security system, the concentration camps and their associated labour camps, and became a key driving force behind the implementation of the regime's racial policies. Goebbels, through his control over propaganda, was able to extend his influence into political, economic, social and cultural fields. Goering, with responsibility for the Four Year Plan, had enormous influence over the military and industry.

By 1941, the population of the Third Reich was 65 million, with ever-expanding occupied territories gained by military conquest. Ruling over this huge state depended on several huge bureaucracies: various government ministries, Nazi organisations, the armed forces and the rival 'private empires' of powerful Nazi leaders. Political power constantly shifted from one place to another according to circumstances and personal rivalries. This complex, multi-centred political system has been described as a 'polycratic regime' or, in other words, a regime in which there are many different centres of authority, with competition between rival power bases. In the Nazi regime, there was constant infighting between the various Nazi 'leaders', such as Hermann Goering, Joseph Goebbels, Ernst Röhm, Heinrich Himmler, Reinhard Heydrich, Albert Speer and Martin Bormann.

Hitler was never a good mediator in the competition between his subordinates. This undoubtedly suited him since it prevented any serious rival to his own authority emerging. Although detached from the everyday business of government, however, Hitler was central to the overall direction of the regime's policies. It was Hitler who, more than anyone, shaped Nazi ideology and gave it a special direction towards anti-Semitism. It was Hitler who, more than anyone, built the Nazi Party into a national mass movement. Hitler, more than anyone, created the cult of personality that enabled him to dominate Germany in the 1930s. Hitler, more than anyone, pushed Nazi Germany towards the pursuit of *Lebensraum* and a war of racial annihilation in the east. It was Hitler who chose all the subordinate Nazi leaders and they all depended on him for their power. Even the most senior Nazi leaders were overawed by Hitler and almost slavishly loyal to him. Goebbels' diaries are full of expressions of admiration for the Führer and belief in his special powers.

The Nazis aimed to transform German society. Their social policies aimed to persuade the German people to put aside their sectional interests in favour of an overarching loyalty to a greater national cause. The Nazi *Volksgemeinschaft* would be a society in which social harmony was based on a shared racial purity. No independent organisations or alternative ideologies would be allowed to divide German society. In the Third Reich, every individual of Aryan ancestry who was sound in mind and body would totally identify with the regime and its aims.

The Germany of 1945 was a very different place from that of 1933, but this does not mean that the Nazis succeeded in remoulding German society in their own image. Nor does it mean that there was no continuity with the past during the Third Reich period. The Nazi organisations created under the policy of *Gleichschaltung* ('forcing into line') to unite German society did not survive Germany's military defeat. Trade unions, which had been replaced in 1933 by the DAF, were quickly re-established in industrial areas during the Allied occupation. Despite Nazi efforts to break down religious allegiances, the hold of the clergy over the population, especially in country areas, was strengthened rather than weakened by Nazi efforts to coordinate the Churches. The Nazis aimed to create a society in which traditional ties of 'blood and soil' were strengthened and to this end they attempted to protect the position of the peasant farmers. However, the over-riding need to maximise industrial war production and the insatiable demands of the armed forces for male conscripts, took men away from agriculture. Women were supposed to accept their place as housewives and mothers within the Nazi scheme of things, but here again the demands of rearmament and the war effort meant that more women worked in industry in 1945 than in 1933.

Finally, the Nazis placed great stress on social mobility and equal opportunities within their *Volksgemeinschaft*. Every German would have an equal status, that of a 'national comrade'. In reality, the social position of the elite was largely unchanged, at least until the final stages of the war. There was social mobility in Nazi Germany, not least for the many senior Nazis who came from humble backgrounds. But this new political elite existed side by side with the old social elite and these two groups compromised and worked together. The higher ranks of big business, the Civil Service and the army were still, in the Nazi period, largely recruited from the same elite social classes as before. The old elite were, however, fatally compromised by their role in bringing the Nazis to power and sustaining them thereafter.

The Nazis did not create social institutions that survived the impact of defeat in war and the collapse of the Third Reich. In this sense, their impact was essentially destructive. The authoritarian structures and political dominance of the old elite, hangovers from the pre-1914 German Empire, which had survived the 1918 revolution and the Weimar period, were finally swept away in the chaos and destruction of military defeat. Far from ensuring that a traditional way of life based on 'blood and soil' would endure, the Nazis unleashed forces that destroyed the traditional structures of German society and paved the way for a fresh start after 1945. What emerged from the ruins of defeat, in both liberal-democratic West Germany and communist East Germany, were the very antithesis of what the Nazis were attempting to build.

There was very little real substance to Nazi social policy, certainly in terms of building lasting social structure. Great emphasis was placed on propaganda and indoctrination, and in this respect the Nazis' impact on most Germans was little more than temporary. For the millions who lost their lives as a result of Nazis' experiments in social and racial engineering, however, the impact was rather more final.

ACTIVITY

Consider this view: 'The social revolution that the Nazis actually achieved was not the one that they had intended.' Do you agree or disagree with the statement? Why or why not?

Glossary

A

Anschluss: (the union) the takeover of Austria by Germany in March 1938.

anti-Semite: hatred and fear of Jews (Semites)

Aryan race: the term used by racial theorists, including the Nazis, to describe the race to which non-Jewish Germans belonged

asocials: those who did not conform to the norms of the Nazis including beggars, tramps, alcoholics, prostitutes and pacifists, but also the mentally and physically disabled

autarky: economic independence or self-sufficiency

autocracy: a system of government in which power is concentrated in the hands of one person

B

Blitzkrieg: literally 'lightning war'; used to describe the German strategy of attacking an enemy with maximum force, combining air attacks with fast-moving motorised army units on the ground

Bund Deutscher Mädel (BDM)/ **League of German Girls**: the female equivalent of Hitler Youth; membership became compulsory in 1939

C

Chancellor: the German title for a Prime Minister

Comintern: the Communist International, set up in 1919 to oversee the actions of Marxist parties across the world; Socialist groups from other countries were invited to join and receive support, but leadership was in the hands of the Russian Communist Party

Communist: a believer in a system based on public ownership of land and industry, where all are equal and people work for the common good

conservative: a person who resists change and tries to preserve social and political institutions in their current state

constitutional: any established set of principles governing a state

D

diktat: an order or decree imposed by someone in power without popular consent

E

economic armistice: a temporary agreement to suspend action; a truce.

Einsatsgruppen ('Special Groups'): temporary units made up of police and regular troops commanded by the Gestapo, the SD and the Criminal Police

eugenics: the theory that a race or group of people could be genetically improved through selective breeding

F

federal state: a state in which a number of small states or provinces keep control over many of their internal affairs, but decisions about national issues are the responsibility of the central government

foreclosure: taking possession of mortgaged property when someone fails to keep up their repayments

Freikorps: a volunteer force setup at the end of 1918 consisting of demobilised junior army officers and NCOs as well as students, adventurers and drifters

G

Gauleiter: a Nazi party leader at regional or state level

General Government: the area of Poland occupied by the Nazis in 1939 that was not incorporated into the German Reich but controlled as a semi-autonomous area

German Labour Front/DAF: (*Deutches Arbeitsfront*) a Nazi-run organisation established in 1933 to coordinate workers into the National Socialist Regime

Gestapo: Secret State Police established by Herman Goering; depended on information supplied by informers

Ghetto: a controlled area of a town or city reserved for a particular race

Gleichschaltung: 'forcing into line', the process through which the Nazis attempted to control or 'coordinate' all aspects of German society

H

Hitler Youth/*Hitler Jugend* (HJ): created in 1926 for boys aged 14–18 years; membership became compulsory in 1939

I

Inter-Allied Control Commission: commission established under the Treaty of Versailles to ensure that Germany complied with the disarmament clauses; it was staffed largely by French and British army officers

J

Jewish question: the term used by the Nazis when considering how to remove the Jews from German society

Jungvolk: the section of the Hitler Youth that was for boys aged 10–14 years

K

Kaiser: German Emperor

Kdf (*Kraft durch Freude*): (strength through joy) a movement set up by Robert Ley and the DAF to organise workers' leisure times

L

Länder: the 17 local states of Germany

League of Nations: a permanent forum of states established after the First World War to meet and resolve disputes without resorting to war

Lebensraum: 'living space', a concept by which Hitler justified his plans to take over territory to the east of Germany

lock out: an action by an employer to stop workers doing their jobs until they agree to the employer's terms and conditions

M

Mittelstand: 'middle rank'; a large but diverse social group including small farmers, small shopkeepers and artisans

P

paramilitary: a group of civilians organised into a military style group with uniform and ranks; such groups take on military functions

plebiscite: a direct vote on an important political or constitutional issue, similar to a referendum

pogrom: an organised massacre of an ethnic group

propaganda: the systematic spreading of ideas and information in order to influence the thinking and actions of the people at whom it is targeted, often through the use of media such as posters, film, radio and the press

proportional representation: a system of elections in which parties are allocated seats in parliament according to the proportion of votes they receive

putsch: a coup or violent attempt to overthrow a government

R

Red-Front Fighters' League: the paramilitary arm of the KPD Party; established in 1924, under the leadership of Ernst Thälmann, and engaged in street battles with the SA, the police and other right-wing paramilitary groups

Reichkristallnacht: 'Night of the Broken Glass', occurred on 9–10 November 1938, when Jewish homes and businesses were looted and vandalised, synagogues set ablaze and thousands of Jews were arrested, beaten and killed

Reichstag: elected lower house of the German parliament

Reichswehr: German Army

Republic: a system of government in which the Head of State, or President, is elected into office

S

Slav peoples: a very diverse ethnic group including Czechs, Slovaks, Poles, Russians, Ukrainians, Croats, Serbs and Slovenes, living mainly in Central and Eastern Europe

Sopade: reports produced by agents of the banned Social Democratic Party (SPD) to inform the exiled party leadership about the situation in Germany

SPD (Social Democratic Party): a political party which campaigned for greater democracy and social change; It was the largest party in 1912

SS (Schutztaffel): Hitler's personal bodyguard, created in 1926

Stahlhelm: (Steel Helmets) a paramilitary organisation of ex-servicemen dedicated to the restoration of the monarchy and the revival of Germany as a military power, which took its name from the steel helmets issued to German soldiers in the First World War

Stormtroopers (SA): the paramilitary wing of the Nazi Party, led by Ernst Röhm

T

Third Reich: (Third Empire) by using this term to describe their regime from 1933 to 1945, the Nazis were asserting that it was the successor to the First Reich

Total War: a conflict in which a combatant state mobilises its entire population and all of its material resources to participate in the war effort

U

Untermenschen: literally 'sub-humans', used by the Nazis to describe those whom they considered to be racially inferior, including Jews, Gypsies and peoples of the Slav race

V

Vichy France: The southern part of France, with a capital city at Vichy; although in theory independent

Volksgemeinschaft: the concept of a 'people's community'; it was a key element in Nazi ideology

Volkssturm: founded on Hitler's orders, the Volkssturm was intended to be a force of six million members, although this was never achieved

W

Waffen SS: military wing of the SS

Wall Street Crash: the sudden collapse of the stock market in New York in October 1929 after a long period of rising prosperity and overconfidence by investors

Bibliography

Books for students

Bessel, Richard, *Life in the Third Reich*, Oxford University Press, 1987

Engel, David, *The Holocaust: Hitler and the Jews*, Pearson, 2000

Farmer, Alan, *Anti-Semitism and the Holocaust*, Hodder & Stoughton, 2000

Hite, John and Hinton, Chris, *Weimar and Nazi Germany*, Hodder Murray, 2000

Kershaw, Ian, *Hitler*, Longman, 1991

Kirk, Tim, *Longman Companion to Nazi Germany*, Longman, 1995

Kitson, Alison, *Germany 1815–1990*, OUP , 2001

Layton, Geoff, *Germany, The Third Reich 1933–45*, Hodder & Stoughton, 1992

Lee, Stephen, *Hitler and Germany*, Routledge, 1998

Neville, Peter, *The Holocaust*, Cambridge University Press, 1999

Rees, Laurence, *Auschwitz: The Nazis & The Final Solution*, BBC Books, 2005

Books for teachers and extension

Bessel, Richard, *Germany 1945*, Simon & Schuster, 2009

Bullock, Alan, *Hitler, A Study in Tyranny*, Penguin, 1962

Evans, Richard J., *The Coming of the Third Reich*, Penguin, 2003

Evans, Richard J., *The Third Reich in Power*, Penguin, 2005

Evans, Richard J., *The Third Reich at War*, Penguin, 2008

Friedländer, Saul, *Nazi Germany & The Jews: Years of Extermination 1939–1945*, Harper, 2000

Grunberger, Richard, *A Social History of the Third Reich*, Penguin, 1971

Haste, Cate, *Nazi Women*, Macmillan, 2001

Kershaw, Ian, *The Hitler Myth*, Oxford, 1991

Kershaw, Ian, *The Nazi Dictatorship*, Arnold, 1993

Kershaw, Ian, *Hitler, The Germans and the Final Solution*, Yale University Press, 2008

Kershaw, Ian, *Hitler: I, Hubris*, Allen Lane, 1998

Kershaw, Ian, *Hitler: III, Nemesis*, Allen Lane, 1998

Housden, Martyn. *Resistance and Conformity in the Third Reich*, Routledge, 1996

Noakes, Jeremy and Pridham, Geoffrey, *Nazism 1919–45, Vol. 1 and 2*, Exeter, 1984

Noakes, Jeremy, *Nazism 1919–45, Vol 4*, Exeter, 1998

Overy, Richard, *The Dictators*, Penguin, 2004

Overy, Richard, *War and Economy in the Third Reich*, Clarendon Press, 1995

Overy, Richard, *The Nazi Economic Recovery, 1932–1938*, Cambridge University Press, 1996

Peukert, Detlev, *Inside Nazi Germany; Conformity, Opposition and Resistance in Everyday Life*, Penguin, 1982

Online resources

Hitler's *Mein Kampf* can be found at
www.hitler.org/writings/Mein_Kampf

Hitler's speeches can be found at
www.adolfhitlerspeeches.com

The Nazi propaganda archive can be found at
www.calvin.edu/academic/cas/gpa

Also useful are:
www.spartacus.schoolnet.co.uk
www.wienerlibrary.co.uk

In-depth source material is presented by the Wannsee House Memorial Centre:
www.ghwk.de/engl/kopfengl.htm

Index

Topics available from *Oxford AQA History for A Level*

  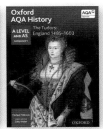    
   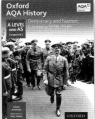   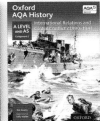

  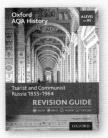